Recycling Treated Municipal Wastewater and Sludge
through Forest and Cropland

Proceedings of a Symposium conducted by the
College of Agriculture and the Institute for Research
    on Land and Water Resources
The Pennsylvania State University

in cooperation with

The Pinchot Institute for Environmental Forestry Research,
Forest Service, United States Department of Agriculture

Office of Research and Monitoring,
Environmental Protection Agency

Recycling Treated Municipal Wastewater and Sludge through Forest and Cropland

Edited by William E. Sopper
and Louis T. Kardos

The Pennsylvania State University Press

University Park and London

© 1973 The Pennsylvania State University
All rights reserved
Library of Congress Catalog Card Number 73-2382
International Standard Book Number 0-271-01159-9

Library of Congress Cataloging in Publication Data

Main entry under title:

Recycling treated municipal wastewater and sludge
through forest and cropland.

Proceedings of a symposium conducted by the College
of Agriculture, Pennsylvania State University and
others.
1. Sewage irrigation—Congresses. I. Sopper,
William E., ed. II. Kardos, Louis T., ed.
III. Pennsylvania. State University. College of
Agriculture.
TD760.R43   628'.36   73-2382
ISBN 0-271-01159-9

Contents

Preface   ix

Introduction: Needed Directions in Land Disposal   1
           Maurice K. Goddard

I   Treated Municipal Wastewater—What Is It?

   1 Chemical and Biological Quality of Treated Sewage
     Effluents   6
        Joseph V. Hunter and Theresa A. Kotalik

   2 Chemical and Biological Quality of Municipal Sludge   26
        J. R. Peterson, Cecil Lue-Hing, and D. R. Zenz

II   Fundamental Functions of the Soil and Its Associated Biosphere

   3 The Soil as a Physical Filter   38
        Richard E. Thomas

   4 The Soil as a Chemical Filter   46
        Boyd G. Ellis

   5 The Soil as a Biological Filter   71
        Robert H. Miller

   6 Site Selection Criteria for Wastewater Disposal
     —Soils and Hydrogeologic Considerations   95
        Richard R. Parizek

III   Wastewater Quality Changes during Recycling

   7 Renovation of Municipal Wastewater through Land Disposal
     by Spray Irrigation   148
        Louis T. Kardos and William E. Sopper

   8 Renovating Secondary Effluent by Groundwater Recharge with
     Infiltration Basins   164
        Herman Bouwer

   9 Phosphorus and Nitrate Levels in Groundwater as Related to
     Irrigation of Jack Pine with Sewage Effluent   176
        Dean H. Urie

  10 Restoration of Acid Spoil Banks with Treated Sewage
     Sludge   184
        Terrence R. Lejcher and Samuel H. Kunkle

IV Soil Responses

11 Effect of Land Disposal of Wastewaters on Soil Phosphorous
    Relations   200
        J. E. Hook, L. T. Kardos, and W. E. Sopper

12 Effects of Land Disposal of Wastewater on Exchangeable
    Cations and Other Chemical Elements in the Soil   220
        Louis T. Kardos and William E. Sopper

13 Factors Affecting Nitrification-Dentrification in Soils   232
        F. E. Broadbent

14 Biotoxic Elements in Soils   245
        T. D. Hinesly and R. L. Jones

15 Microbial Hazards of Disposing of Wastewater on Soil   247
        D. H. Foster and R. S. Engelbrecht

V   Vegetation Responses

16 Vegetation Responses to Irrigation with Treated Municipal
    Wastewater   271
        William E. Sopper and Louis T. Kardos

17 Anatomical and Physical Properties of Red Oak and Red Pine
    Irrigated with Municipal Wastewater   295
        W. K. Murphey, R. L. Brisbin, W. J. Young, and B. E.
        Cutter

VI Other Ecosystem Responses

18 Effects of Spray Irrigation of Forests with Chlorinated Sewage
    Effluent on Deer and Rabbits   311
        Gene W. Wood, D. W. Simpson, and R. L. Dressler

VII Systems Design, Operation, and Economics

19 Sprinkler Irrigation Systems: Design and
    Operation Criteria   324
        Earl A. Myers

20 Cost of Spray Irrigation for Wastewater Renovation   334
        John B. Nesbitt

21 Financing Municipal Wastewater Treatment Facilities,
    Including Land Utilization Systems   339
        Belford L. Seabrook

VIII   Examples of Operating and Proposed Systems

22 Large Wastewater Irrigation Systems: Muskegon County, Michigan, and Chicago Metropolitan Region   345
    W. J. Bauer and D. E. Matsche

23 Implementing the Chicago Prarie Plan   364
    Frank L. Kudrna and George T. Kelly

24 Spray Irrigation Project, Mt. Sunapee State Park, New Hampshire   371
    Terrence P. Frost, R. E. Towne, and H. J. Turner

25 Utilization of Spray Irrigation for Wastewater Disposal in Small Residential Developments   385
    T. C. Williams

26 Ecological and Physiological Implications of Greenbelt Irrigation with Reclaimed Wastewater   396
    V. B. Youngner, W. D. Kesner, A. R. Berg, and L. R. Green

27 Municipal Wastewater Disposal on the Land as an Alternate to Ocean Outfall   408
    W. A. Cowlishaw and F. J. Roland

28 The Role of Land Treatment of Wastewater in the Corps of Engineers Wastewater Management Program   422
    James F. Johnson

IX   Present Status of Guidelines for Land Disposal of Wastewater

29 Michigan's Experience with the Ten States Guidelines for Land Disposal of Wastewater   431
    Donald M. Pierce

30 Forest Service Policy Related to the Use of National Forestlands for Disposal of Wastewater and Sludge   435
    Olaf C. Olson and Edward A. Johnson

31 Spray Irrigation — The Regulatory Agency View   440
    Richard C. Rhindress

X   Research Needs

32 Research Needs — Land Disposal of Municipal Sewage Wastes   455
    James O. Evans

List of Symposium Participants   463

Preface

The Wastewater Renovation and Conservation Project was initiated at The Pennsylvania State University in 1962 under the direction of Dr. Michael A. Farrell, former Director of the Agricultural Experiment Station. An interdisciplinary team consisting of agricultural, civil, and sanitary engineers, agronomists, foresters, geologists, ecologists, microbiologists, biochemists and zoologists was assembled to investigate the feasibility and environmental impacts of disposal of treated municipal wastewater on the land through spray irrigation. From these investigations the "Living Filter" concept was evolved. The term "Living Filter" was first suggested by Mr. Gilbert Aberg, Science Information Officer, Department of Public Information, for the title of a film produced in 1965 depicting some of the early results of the project. Since then, the term "Living Filter Concept" has become more or less synonymous with the idea of spray irrigation of municipal wastewater on the land.

During the past five years there has been a tremendous increase in interest in spray irrigation of municipal wastewater and sludge throughout the United States. At the same time there appeared to be a lack of definitive information on the parameters and constraints which must be considered in the design and operation of land disposal systems under varying environmental conditions.

To partially meet this demand for information, this symposium on Recycling Treated Municipal Wastewater and Sludge through Forest and Cropland was organized and held on August 21-24, 1972 at The Pennsylvania State University. The specific purpose was to review and discuss current knowledge related to the potential of using land areas for the disposal of wastewaters and to determine technological gaps and research needs. The sessions were attended by over 400 participants from 45 States, Canada, Puerto Rico, Virgin Islands, and New Zealand.

The Program Planning Committee consisted of Louis T. Kardos, Earl A. Myers, John B. Nesbitt, Richard R. Parizek, and William E. Sopper, from The Pennsylvania State University and James O. Evans and Elwood L. Shafer, Jr. from the U.S. Forest Service.

Financial support was provided by The Pinchot Institute for Environmental Forestry Research, Northeastern Forest Experiment Station, Forest Service, U.S. Department of Agriculture, and the Office of Research and Monitoring, Environmental Protection Agency, Washington, D.C.

The program was conducted by the College of Agriculture and the Institute for Research on Land and Water Resources as a continuing education service of The Pennsylvania State University.

William E. Sopper
Louis T. Kardos

Symposium Co-Directors

Introduction

Needed Directions in Land Disposal

Maurice K. Goddard*

The "state of the art" symposium on land disposal of municipal wastewater and sludge is an excellent place to make a pitch for increased research and development on this fascinating area with its potential for dramatically improving the quality of our nation's waterways.

Land disposal is far from a new idea in this country and around the world but it is only recently that it has received the interest and the beginnings of support which are so vital to its success. The interest in land irrigation with wastewaters comes from the recognition of severe damage done to the aquatic ecosystems due to discharge of various liquid wastes directly into streams, rivers or other bodies of water. Land disposal can serve not only to recharge the ground water supplies but also to return nutrients to the soil. The concept is not new and has been practiced for thousands of years in many European and Asian countries.

The listing of papers for the symposium on Recycling Treated Municipal Wastewater and Sludge through Forest and Cropland makes clear much of the recent definitive research work on land disposal was done at Penn State by the men who organized the conference. Our concern now should be to build upon this research and push for new studies and demonstration projects to determine the parameters in which land disposal can be a useful tool in wastewater management.

One impetus for increased examination of systems for land disposal came from the recent work in Washington on the water pollution control bills. Had the Senate version of the legislation prevailed, it appeared that the land disposal of effluents would almost have been mandated, or at least made the subject of an evaluation as an alternative in every case. This might not have been that bad a result since it would have required us to face the issue squarely with time, talent and money rather than limping along on a piecemeal basis. Although this requirement was not in the final bill, the debate over it and the legislative interest in it may still lead to expansion of the work now underway in this field.

*Secretary, Department of Environmental Resources, Harrisburg, Pennsylvania.

I do not propose to engage in a technical discussion on the question of land disposal. There are many others far more capable than I of providing the latest scientific insights. Rather, speaking as an administrator of an environmental agency, I would like to emphasize the need for serious consideration of this and other alternatives to our waste problem. I have often been critical of some environmentalists who want to have things their own way without examining all the issues and alternatives involved in a particular problem. But this is one instance where the environmentalists have come closer to being on the right side.

One of the goals of the science of ecology is to maintain a balance as much as possible in the whole life-support system of the earth. Treating waste products so they are somewhat improved and then discharging them into our waterways does not really meet this goal. Taking water from underground supplies, using it and then dumping it into the streams continually depletes groundwater. Groundwater loss can be even more serious when wastewater is not treated and recycled locally but piped to large distant treatment plants for waste removal. Hence the interest of many ecologists in using wastewater to reclaim and fertilize land and using land as a filter . . . a living filter if you will . . . to purify the water. In the process, the water returns to the underground stores from which it came.

But while ecologists have been calling for this circular approach, engineers have been designing bigger and better treatment plants and they are the ones who have been getting all the attention. Unfortunately, they have been aided in their quest for more and better hardware by environmental regulatory agencies which have been more interested in specifying higher degrees of treatment necessary than they have been in forcing an investigation of the alternatives to the entire treatment and discharge method of disposing of wastes. I believe a Department such as mine must become much more involved in the question of land disposal as a plausible alternative not only from a regulatory standpoint but also from an advocacy and supportive point of view.

We have at the present time about 75 land disposal operations in the Commonwealth. Some of these land disposal facilities have been in operation for various periods of time. Most are relatively small projects and in their early stages were installed without a great deal of surveillance from the Department. No permit was necessary because there was no discharge. All this has changed now. We require permits for spray irrigation systems, just as we do for discharges, because experience has shown that some of the effluent finally ends up in the water courses anyway. So you have to consider them as an alternative in a total waste management system.

The Department now has in the final stages of preparation a manual which we call our Spray Irrigation Manual. It will establish the primary factors for consideration in the review of the design and the submission of necessary reports and data for State approval. The manual will provide a set of guidelines for use by the consulting engineers, geologists and soil scientists in locating and evaluating the area needed for spray irrigation and in designing the system for distribution of the wastewater to the land surface.

While we and other government environmental agencies are getting more into the business of regulation of land disposal operations, and this is good, we should also be getting more into the business of promoting the examination of this technique in wider applications. Despite the apparent success of the Penn State project, started several years ago, a more sophisticated and ambitious plan for Muskegon County, Michigan, was greeted with yawns and a notable lack of interest among politicians and, even worse, among pollution control officials. The elements of the Muskegon plan—lagoons and spray irrigation—are not new. What is new and exciting, however, is the application of these concepts to an entire county of some 13 communities with a combined population of 170,000 and five industries—paper, chemical, engine manufacturing and metal casting and plating.

Some of the project officials have been quoted as saying the liquid effluent after just intermediate stages of treatment will be superior to that taken from a conventional secondary treatment plant. There are also claims that the final stage of the Muskegon County project—the so-called living filter of the earth—will outperform any technology now in existence. Experiments reportedly have shown that virtually all the phosphates in domestic sewage are removed by the time the water has moved only 12 inches downward through the soil. The "living filter" also intercepts what are probably the most persistent and dangerous pollutants in domestic wastes, viruses. While conventional secondary treatment does little if anything to remove viruses and chlorination and municipal drinking water treatment also do not touch them, there are indications that using the earth as a "living filter" may provide 100 percent removal of viruses.

As attractive as the plan sounds, it met with stiff opposition from the Michigan Water Resources Commission. Much of their opposition reportedly was based on economic grounds although the project's backers believe long-term cost will actually be lower than conventional treatment and also expect increased tourism due to the cleaner waters as well as profits from crops grown on the irrigated lands. The state agency's objections spread to the Federal Water Quality Administration which was needed to help with financing.

What finally broke the deadlock was the intervention by Michigan Congressman Guy Vander Jagt who took on the Muskegon County proposal as a special project. The Federal agency, after a lot of prodding from sources all the way up to the White House, awarded Muskegon County a research and development grant and a construction grant. Vander Jagt and other congressmen led the fight recently to have the House water pollution control bill amended to equal the Senate version which was based on the Muskegon project. As summed up by the Muskegon County Planning Director, Roderick T. Dittmer, the whole thing sounds deceptively simple. "Pollutants, like phosphates, are simply natural resources out of place," Dittmer has said. "We're putting them back in place." The time when governmental agencies concerned with the environment can ignore something which seems to be so environmentally sound has long since passed.

Few agencies are proving this more today than the U.S. Army Corps of Engineers. While environmentalists have had many targets over the past few years in which the citizen ecological movement has grown, none has been more in the line of fire than the Corps of Engineers. And, to be fair about it, the Corps has deserved some of the criticism it has received as have many other agencies. To its credit now, however, the Corps is working to be more in tune with the times and to be more aware of environmental concerns in its actions. And one of the moves it is making is to become involved in the entire question of land disposal systems. Having enticed into a Corps job one of the men who had a great deal to do with developing the Muskegon County plan, the Corps has embarked on an effort to use its planning ability to design regional land disposal systems like Muskegon's. The Corps will do the planning in various areas around the country, calculate costs and benefits of alternative strategies for waste disposal both on land and in water and then let the communities make the final decisions and proceed with what they want to do. The Corps has begun its work with studies in five major cities—Cleveland, San Francisco, Chicago, Detroit and Boston—as well as the Codorus Creek Watershed near Harrisburg. The Corps investigation of alternative sites will be useful as part of the massive research effort needed on this question.

It cannot be said now whether a natural waste recycling system is as attractive an alternative for all areas of the country, for all sizes of population and for all types of waste as it seems to be for Muskegon County. The answers to questions concerning locale, soils and other variables involved in the successful operation of land disposal systems must be sought and found in the months and years ahead. If land disposal is found to be a feasible solution in many instances, one of the problems will be availability of land for this purpose. At present there is little evidence of overwhelming public acceptance of the idea, much less demand for it. Farmers have been rather skeptical about committing themselves to continued use of the treated effluents. You can't go ahead with such a project if people will only say they might be willing to try it for a month or two. There must be a long-term commitment to stick with it, if it is to succeed. Except for self-contained, on-site agribusiness industries which can irrigate their own lands, the concept is not being widely applied. For spray irrigation of municipal wastes it appears it will be necessary for municipalities to purchase and maintain their own lands. It seems to me, therefore, that a tremendous amount of public information and public relations work will have to be done to convince the farmers that the effluent is valuable and can be accepted.

Another problem we have seen thus far with spray irrigation is management — or better, the lack of management. Many sites have been operated with reasonable care but on others reasonable care is generally not given. I think it is fair to say that management has been uniformly quite poor. Maintenance personnel rarely visit the works, piping gets broken, sprinklers clog or stop up, field areas get flooded, the mosquito population builds up and soil gets completely water-logged and then the field goes anaerobic. This is one problem which may be amenable to a solution as regulatory agencies become more involved with the permitting and supervising of land disposal projects.

The other problem — that of obtaining public acceptance and willingness to put it into practice — is not so easily solvable. If we can convince politicians, environmental agencies, ecologically minded citizens and everyone else that land disposal is worthy of their interest and support for future projects on even larger scales until we find out just how helpful this ultimate recycling idea may be, the problem may be solvable.

If we all do this, the time may come in the not-too-distant future when not only is water cleaner but crops are better and economies are growing, all because we followed nature and its desire for balance.

I / TREATED MUNICIPAL WASTEWATER — WHAT IS IT?

1

Chemical and Biological Quality of Treated Sewage Effluents

Joseph V. Hunter and Theresa A. Kotalik*

Once the water carriage system for human wastes disposal became established, the unfortunate consequences of the discharge of such wastewaters to the environment became unpleasantly evident. These problems were due to constituents of the wastewaters, and the classical ones may be briefly outlined as follows:

Constituent	Problem
Microorganisms	Disease
Particulates	Sludge Banks in Streams
Organics	Odors, Color, Toxicity
	Low Stream Dissolved Oxygen

Wastewater treatment processes such as primary treatment as outlined in Figure 1-1 were designed to remove easily settleable particulates and part of the organics by primary sedimentation, and the pathogenic microorganisms by disinfection. Secondary treatment represents the addition of biological oxidation and adsorption to primary treatment for the purpose of further reducing the organic matter in effluents.

It is interesting to note from Figure 1-1 that those processes that are employed to reduce the quantities of particulates and organics in turn give rise to problems of primary sludge and waste biomass disposal. These are problems of the utmost importance, as the disposal methodologies available represent one of the major stresses on secondary wastewater treatment.

Even after secondary treatment, wastewater effluents can have significant effects on the environment. Such effluents still contain organics, salts, nutrients, particulates and varying amounts of micro-

*Department of Environmental Sciences, Rutgers University.

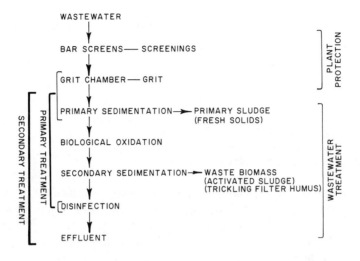

Figure 1-1. Flow diagram for a wastewater treatment plant

organisms depending on the degree of disinfection. It is the purpose of this paper to delineate the physical, chemical and biological composition of effluents so that the implications involved by their disposal on, or recycling through, agricultural and forested lands can be better understood.

Chemical Composition

Organic

In 1963, it was estimated that the BOD contributed by the sewered population of this country was 7.3 billion pounds. Assuming a removal efficiency of 90 percent for secondary treatment, 730 million pounds of BOD entered the environment that year which had its origins in domestic wastewater treatment plant effluents. Another way of expressing this is that each use of water, even after secondary treatment, added 25 mg/l BOD (equivalent to 52 mg/l organic matter (American Chemical Society, 1969)).

As water supplies rarely contain large quantities of organic matter, almost all the organics in effluents either entered during the use of the water or were formed during secondary treatment. As is true for wastewater itself, effluent organic matter is both soluble and particu-

Table 1-1. Volatile solids distributions in an activated sludge effluent

Effluent Fractions	Winter, 1965–66[a]		Spring, 1967 [b]	
	mg/l	%	mg/l	%
Soluble	71[c]	79	62	67
Colloidal	2	2	6	7
Supracolloidal	16	18	24	26
Settleable	1	1	0	0
Total	90	–	92	–

a. From Rickert and Hunter (1967).
b. From Rickert and Hunter (1971).
c. All values are averages from triplicate sets.

late in nature. Usual sanitary analyses find it sufficient to divide wastewater organics into suspended matter and soluble matter on the basis of filtration (Standard Methods for the Analysis of Water and Waste Water, 1971) through an asbestos mat, glass fiber mat or membrane filter or centrifugation (Rebhan and Manka, 1971).

Other investigators (Rickert and Hunter, 1967; Painter *et al.,* 1961) have divided these organics into a settleable portion (obtained by sedimentation), a colloidal fraction (obtained by centrifugation), a colloidal fraction (obtained by candle filtration or high speed centrifugation) and a soluble fraction (what remains when the three particulate fractions are removed). Rarely are the particulate and soluble organics analyzed together as their natures are sufficiently different to warrant different analytical schemes.

The general distribution of organic matter in effluents is shown in Tables 1-1 and 1-2. Although better than half of the effluent organics are soluble, considerable amounts of the organics are particulate. Nevertheless, most of the analyses have ignored particulate composition. There have been three extensive investigations of the nature of the organic constituents in effluents. The first, shown in Table 1-3, identified about 35 percent of the "soluble" organic constituents. The

Table 1-2. Comparison of organic carbon distributions in effluents expressed as a percentage of the total

Type	Activated Sludge[a] (American)	Trickling Filter [b] (British)
	%	%
Soluble	69	52
Fine suspended[c]	6	9
Coarse suspended[d]	25	39

a. From Rickert and Hunter (1971).
b. From Painter *et al.* (1961).
c. Equivalent to colloidal in Table 1-1.
d. Equivalent to the sum of settleable and supracolloidal in Table 1-1.

Table 1-3. Composition of an American activated sludge effluent [a]

Constituent	Percent of Total COD
Ether extractables	< 10
Proteins	< 10
Carbohydrates and polysaccharides	< 5
Tannins and lignins	< 5
MBAS [b]	~ 10
Unidentified	~65

a. For a filtered sample from Bunch *et al.* (1961).
b. Equivalent to anionic detergents.

next study, shown in Table 1-4, identified only about 25 percent of the soluble organics and 40 percent of the particulate organics. The analytical scheme used by these investigators was one that would have identified (and have been used to identify) at least two thirds to three quarters of the organics found in the original wastewaters. Part of this mystery (for the soluble constituents) was solved by the investigators whose data is shown in Table 1-5. Much of the organic matter not detected by previous investigators was found to be Fulvic, Humic and Hymathomelanic Acids. These results were obtained for a strong highly colored Israeli effluent, and how widely applicable they are is unknown at present. It is obvious, however, that at least part of the organics not determined by the first two investigations was such materials.

There have been few analyses of effluent particulates more detailed than those shown in Table 1-4. Analyses of the amino acid constituents of effluent particulates are shown in Table 1-6 and those of the fatty acid contents in Table 1-7.

Table 1-4. Composition of a British trickling filter effluent[a] (as mg/l organic carbon)

Constituent	Concentration Particulate	Soluble
	mg/l	mg/l
Fatty acids	0.12	0.0
Fatty acid esters	0.12	0.0
Proteins	2.74	0.25
Amino acids	0.00	0.00
Carbohydrates	1.39	0.24
Soluble acids	0.13	1.65
MBAS[b]	0.05	1.40
Amino sugars	0.38	0.00
Muramic acid	0.05	0.00
Total	5.0	2.6
Total carbon	12.90	14.00
Recovery (%)	38.80	25.70

a. From Painter *et al.* (1961).
b. Equivalent to anionic detergents.

Table 1-5. Composition of an Israeli trickling filter effluent with a COD of 185 mg/l [a]

Constituent	Percent of Total COD		
	Sample 1	Sample 2	Sample 3
	%	%	%
Ether extractables	10.6	6.6	7.8
Anionic detergents	12.8	13.3	15.6
Carbohydrates	10.9	12.7	11.0
Tannins	1.5	1.4	2.2
Proteins	21.0	22.0	24.1
Fulvic acid	22.5	18.8	28.8
Humic acid	10.4	11.0	11.9
Hymathomelanic acid	7.4	9.5	7.5
Total	97.1	95.3	105.9

a. For a centrifuged sample from Rebhan and Manka (1971).

A number of the miscellaneous soluble organics found in effluents are shown in Table 1-8. In addition to these, organic acids such as gallic, citric, and lactic have been detected. It is evident from the results presented in this chapter that the general distribution of effluent organics and the major groups of effluent organics have been fairly well delineated. The molecular nature of many of the organics still remains to be delineated.

Inorganic

The inorganic constituents of wastewater effluents are largely soluble, as can be observed from Table 1-9. Little has been done on the nature of the particulate inorganics, but the soluble inorganics (especially nutrients) have been of considerable interest and considerable research has been involved in their detection and estimation.

Table 1-6. Amino acid contents of an Indian effluent's particulates[a]

Amino Acid	Dry Weight Content
	mg/g
Cystine	14.8
Lysine, histidine	26.9
Arginine	18.1
Serine, glycine, aspartic acid	36.4
Threonine, glutamic acid	34.3
Alanine	22.1
Proline	Trace
Tyrosine	12.8
Methionine, valine	31.7
Phenyl alanine	27.5
Leucine, isoleucine	29.9

a. From Subrahanyam et al. (1969).

Table 1-7. Fatty acid contents of an Indian effluent[a]

Fatty Acid	Concentration
	mg/l
Lauric	0.11
Myristic	0.13
Palmitic	1.3
Stearic	0.93
Oleic	1.1
Linoleic	2.1
Linolenic	0.06

a. From Viswanathan *et al.* (1962).

Table 1-8. Miscellaneous soluble effluent organics

Constituent	Concentration	Reference
Formic acid	91.0 μg/l	Murtaugh and Bunch (1967)
Acetic acid	130.0 μg/l	Murtaugh and Bunch (1967)
Propionic acid	13.7 μg/l	Murtaugh and Bunch (1967)
Isobutyric acid	26.5 μg/l	Murtaugh and Bunch (1967)
Butyric acid	30.7 μg/l	Murtaugh and Bunch (1967)
Isovaleric acid	73.4 μg/l	Murtaugh and Bunch (1967)
Valeric acid	8.1 μg/l	Murtaugh and Bunch (1967)
Caproic acid	47.9 μg/l	Murtaugh and Bunch (1967)
Pyrene	0.4-1.0 μg/l	Wedgewood (1952)
Nonionic surfactants	0.5-1.0 mg/l	Ministry of Technology (1966)
Cholesterol	15-57 μg/l	Murtaugh and Bunch (1967)
Coprostanol	8-102 μg/l	Murtaugh and Bunch (1967)
Uric acid	5-12 μg/l	O'Shea and Bunch (1965)
Anionic surfactants	5.6 mg/l[a]	Hunter (1971)
	1.6 mg/l[b]	Hunter (1971)
Leucine	5 mg/l	Kahn and Wayman (1964)
Valine	5 mg/l	Kahn and Wayman (1964)

a. 1963 value (before conversion to biodegradable ABS).
b. 1967 value (after conversion to biodegradable ABS).

Table 1-9. Fixed solids distributions for an activated sludge plant effluent

Effluent Fraction	Winter, 1965–66[a]		Spring, 1967[b]	
	mg/l	%	mg/l	%
Soluble	223[c]	99	250	97
Colloidal	1	0	2	1
Supracolloidal	3	1	4	2
Settleable	0	0	0	0
Total	227	—	256	—

a. From Rickert and Hunter (1967).
b. From Rickert and Hunter (1971).
c. All values are averages from triplicate sets.

Table 1-10. Inorganic constituents added to effluents through domestic use

Constituent	Average Increment Added[a]
	mg/l
Group I	
Sodium	70
Potassium	10
Calcium	15
Magnesium	7
Chloride	75
Bicarbonate	100
Sulfate	30
Silica	15
Hardness (as $CaCO_3$)	70
Alkalinity (as $CaCO_3$)	85
Group II	
Phosphate	25
Ammonium	20
Nitrate	10
Nitrite	1

a. From American Chemical Society (1969).

Unlike organic constituents, which are almost wholly added to the initial water during use, the inorganic composition of a wastewater reflects the inorganic composition of the water supply. As the inorganic composition of water supplies is highly variable, it is difficult to generalize on the soluble inorganic constituents of wastewaters.

The most successful approach to this problem has been to indicate the quantity of inorganics added to the initial supply during domestic use. An example of this approach is presented in Table 1-10. Although these are generalizations only, it is apparent that one use of water adds to the water a considerable amount of dissolved inorganic salts. Most of these represent the initial amounts added to the water during use, as little or none of the salts in Group I are removed during treatment. The inorganics listed in Group II of Table 1-10 have been subjected to considerable alteration. The phosphates found in effluents are largely orthophosphate, and a significant amount of this is formed by the hydrolysis of the wastewater condensed (poly) phosphates during treatment (Bunch *et al.,* 1961). In addition, varying amounts of this nutrient are removed during secondary treatment.

Ammonia is formed by the hydrolysis of urea and the biological decomposition of compounds containing organic nitrogen. Its concentration is reduced by assimilation, volatilization, and conversion to nitrite and nitrate. Like ammonia and phosphate, nitrite and nitrate are either absent from the original water supply or present in only small amounts. Unlike ammonia and phosphate, nitrite and nitrate are not added in substantial amounts to water during its use (*i.e.,* conversion to wastewater), but are formed by the microbial oxidation of ammonia.

Although it is not completely a function of the inorganic constituents, the pH of effluents should also be noted here. In general, the pH of domestic wastewater will be close to seven, somewhat higher when fresh, lower when stale, and does not change too radically during secondary treatment. For example, the pH of raw Bernardsville sewage has a median figure of about 7.4, while the effluent from the activated sludge plant has a median figure of 7.2. Thus, even though much organic matter is converted to carbon dioxide, most of this is lost to the atmosphere or enters the bicarbonate buffer and therefore does not have a substantial effect on pH.

Biological Composition

The organisms present in the effluents from secondary wastewater treatment plants originate in the sewage entering the plant, the atmosphere, and the population growth in response to the chemical constituents utilized.

Effluents, therefore, would be expected to contain representatives from almost all the major biological groups. Although a considerable number have been identified, the major stress here has been on pathogens or organisms indicative of the possible presence of pathogens. Considering the potential population, those organisms presently identified probably represent only a small part of the total, and it is difficult to state with any assurance of accuracy what the dominant organisms are. Those which have been studied fall into the following categories:

Viruses

Although infectious hepatitis is the only viral disease proven to have been transmitted by water contaminated with sewage (Clarke and Kabler, 1964), there is little or no information as to its presence in secondary treatment plant effluents. On the other hand, Coxsackie, Polio and ECHO virus have all been detected in effluents (Clarke et al., 1961; Lamb et al., 1964; Primavesi and Weistenberg, 1965). In addition Coliphage has also been detected in effluents (Gilcreas and Kelly, 1954), not too surprising when the number of coliform organisms is considered. Due to the fact that the present methods are essentially only semi-quantitative, the exact numbers of virus units in effluents are unknown. However, it has been estimated that there are about 500 virus units/100 ml of summer sewage (Kollins, 1966). If up to 98 percent of those can be removed by activated sludge treatment

(Clarke and Kabler, 1964) (found for Coxsackie virus), then there could be as low as 10 virus units/100 ml of effluent.

Bacteria

As with the viruses, the major attention to the bacterial populations of effluents has been directed towards those of sanitary significance. *Salmonella* have been detected in effluents in numbers up to 1/100 ml (Keil, 1964). Among the various species found were:

Salmonella typhi	Kapsenberg (1958)
	Coetzie and Pretorius (1965)
Salmonella paratyphi	Kapsenberg (1958)
Salmonella typhimurium	Kapsenberg (1958)
Salmonella bareilly	Kapsenberg (1958)
Salmonella sarcon	Kapsenberg (1958)
Salmonella schottmuelleri	Buss and Inal (1957)

In addition to the *Salmonella, Clostridia* can be detected in effluents (Nussbaumer, 1963), and *Mycobacteria* have been detected in treated Tuberculosis sanitaria effluents (Coin *et al.,* 1965; Bhaskaran *et al.,* 1960).

A considerable amount of research has been directed toward the removals achieved during secondary treatment, and some of this is shown in Table 1-11. A detailed review of the removal of pathogens during treatment has been made by Kabler (1959). In addition to the pathogens and indicator organisms noted above, other studies have indicated the presence of *Proteus sp.* (City of Johannesburg, 1963) in biologically treated effluents, and 9×10^3 nitrite reducing organisms and 17×10^3 nitrate reducing organisms (van Gylswyk, 1961). It should be remembered that the microbial populations of wastewater (Dias, 1963; Farquhar and Boyle, 1971) and activated sludge (Farquhar and Boyle, 1971; Unz, 1965) have also been studied, and unquestionably most of these bacteria might also be expected to be present in effluents.

Fungi

Three main fungi groups were found in both influents to and effluents from biological treatment plants (Sladka and Otlova, 1968). These were as follows:

Phycomycetes
Ascomycetes
Rhodotorula species
Saccharomycetes

Table 1-11. Bacterial removals obtained by secondary treatment

Bacteria	Sewage Population No./ml	Reference	Biological Treatment Reduction %	Reference
Coliform	$0.5-1 \times 10^6$	Tomlinson (1962) Burm and Vaughn (1966) Benzie and Courchaine (1966)	90-99	Allen et al. (1949)
Fecal streptococci	$5-20 \times 10^3$	Benzie and Courchaine (1966) Allen et al. (1949)	84-94	Allen and Brooks (1949)
Shigella	present	Holt (1960)	90-99	Kabler (1962)
Salmonella	4-12	Coetzie and Pretorius (1965) McCoy (1957)	70	Kabler (1962)
Total count	$3-18 \times 10^6$	Tomlinson et al. (1962)	90-99	Tomlinson et al. (1962)
Pseudomonas Aeroginosa	102	Coetzie and Fourie (1965)	none, pop. incr.	Coetzie and Fourie (1965)
	7×10^3	Hoadley (1967)	99	Hoadley (1967)
Clostridium Perfringens	507	Coetzie and Fourie (1965)	90-99	Coetzie and Fourie (1965)
Mycobacterium Tuberculosis	present	Kapsenberg (1958) Coetzie and Pretorius (1965) Buss and Inal (1957)	66-88	Kabler (1962)
			95	Bhaskaran et al. (1960)

Deuteromycetes
Fusarium aquaeductum
Fusarium roseum
Fusarium oxysporum

Yeasts were also found in effluents by another investigator, ranging from 10-80 cells/ml, and included the following (Cooke, 1965):

Cryptococcus	*Saccharomyces*
Rhodotorula	*Alternaria*
Trichosporons	*Aspergillus*
Candida	*Aureobasidium*
Torulopsis	*Fusarium*
Kloeckera	*Geotrichum*
Trichoderma	*Mucor*
Hansenula	*Penicillium*

In addition, effluents may also contain many of the filamentous organisms found in activated sludge (Farquhar and Boyle, 1971).

Protozoa

A significant amount of attention has been paid to the *pathogenic Endamoeba histolytica*. It has been detected in the same effluent from which two other intestinal parasites were isolated, *Trichomonas* and *Chilomastix mesnili* (Metzler *et al.,* 1958). Eudamoeba cysts have also been detected (Dunlop and Wang, 1961), and the following relationships were found for an Israeli effluent (Kott and Kott, 1967):

Endamoeba	*histolytica*	: 7/10 liters
Eudamoeba	*coli*	: 22/10 liters

In addition to these, the amoeba *Centropyxes aculeata* has also been detected, as well as the ciliates *Stylonychia, Stentor, Paramecium,* and *Carchesium* (Murad and Bazer, 1970).

Effluents may also contain those protozoa known to be present in the wastewater treatment plants (Barker, 1943; Curds and Cockburn, 1970) in numbers of about 100/ml. Effluents could also contain the following protozoan inhabitants of tertiary lagoons (Evans and Beuscher, 1970):

PROTOZOA	FORM
Amoeba sp.	Rhizopod
Euplotes patella	Ciliate
Loxophyllum helus	Ciliate
Oikomonas sp.	Flagellate
Pelodinium reniforme	Ciliate
Phyllomitus anylophagus	Flagellate
Trigonomonas compressar	Flagellate

PROTOZOA	FORM
Vorticella campanula	Ciliate
Epistylis pliciatils	Ciliate

Nematodes
Nematodes in effluents have been reasonably well investigated since they have been shown to be able to ingest pathogens (Chang, 1961). The major groups detected in effluents have been:

FAMILY	REFERENCE
Rhabditidae and	Murad and Bazer (1970)
Diplogasteridae	Chang (1961)
	Chang and Kabler (1962)
	Calaway (1963)
	Chaudhuri *et al.,* (1964)
Diplogasteroides	Chang and Kabler (1962)
	Chaudhuri *et al.,* (1964)
Dorylaimidae	Chang (1961)
	Chang and Kabler (1962)
	Calaway (1963)
Monochidae	Chang and Kabler (1962)
	Calaway (1963)

A more detailed description of the nematodes from trickling filter effluents and their intestinal bacteria is shown in Table 1-12. Their numbers have been estimated as 200-2000/g (Chang, 1961) and 2,000-2,500/g (Chang and Kabler, 1962) and that trickling filter effluents contribute a major portion of the free living nematode population in receiving waters.

Miscellaneous
A number of investigators have concerned themselves with organisms causing schistosomiasis. It has been estimated that either activated sludge or trickling filters can remove 99.7 percent of the eggs of *Shistosoma mansoni* (Rowan, 1964a) but both the eggs and miracidea have been detected in effluents (Rowan, 1964b). In addition, algae such as *Oscillatoria* (Evans and Beuscher, 1970), *Euglena* and *Ankistrodesmus* have been detected, as well as the larva of the trickling filter fly, *Psychoda*.

Disinfection

In the United States, disinfection is practically synonymous with chlorination. This is not true in other areas, however, since ozone is

Table 1-12. Nematodes found in trickling filter effluents and their intestinal bacteria[a]

| Trickling Filter | Nematode | | Bacteria | | |
	Common	Uncommon	Count/nematode	Coli/nematode	Genera or Species
1.	Diplogasteroides Rhabditis	Rhabiditolaimus Diplogaster Tilobus Ironus	105	9.3	Pseudomonas Proteus A. aerogenes E. coli
2.	Diplogasteroides Diplogaster	Myolaimus Mononchus Plectus Rhabditis Dorylaimus	92	4.5	Pseudomonas Proteus A. aerogenes E. coli Streptococcus

a. From Chang and Kabler (1962).

widely used for disinfection in Europe and chemical disinfection of wastewater treatment plant effluents is not a general practice in Britain.

For these reasons, and as chlorination would affect the effluent characteristics previously mentioned, physical, chemical and biological characteristics of effluents are frequently studied prior to chlorination, so that the information produced would have the widest applicability. The major exception to this generality is for biological effluent constituents with public health implications.

As chlorination of effluents is widely practiced in the United States, it is necessary to indicate what effects it should have on the effluent characteristics previously described. The exact role this process has on colloidal and fine particulates is not too clear, but slight accumulation of sludges in chlorination tanks could indicate some improvements in settling characteristics.

In addition to the fact that chlorination always adds chlorides, the effect of chlorination on the inorganic constituents of effluents falls into two categories.

The first category involves the form in which the chlorine is added. Chlorine gas is rarely added directly to effluents. Instead, a concentrated "solution" of the gas in water (or effluent) is prepared, and is added. When this addition occurs, the following reaction takes place,

$$Cl_2 + H_2O = HOCl + HCl$$

forming hydrochloric acid. Thus this practice could only tend to lower the pH, decrease the alkalinity, and increase the acidity. Another chlorination procedure involves the use of sodium hypochlorite solutions, which have the opposite effect since it is highly alkaline. Wastewater effluents, however, are usually reasonably well buffered, and large changes in these values are not to be expected unless exceptionally large concentrations of disinfectants are employed.

The second category involves the reactions that chlorine or rather hypochlorite has with ammonia. These are:

$$NH_3 + HOCl = NH_2Cl + H_2O$$

$$NH_2Cl + HOCl = NHCl_2 + H_2O$$

$$NHCl_2 + HOCl = NCl_3 + H_2O$$

and result in the formation of monochloramine, dichloramine, and nitrogen trichloride. With sufficient chlorination, (a molar ratio of chlorine/ammonia of 2/1), ammonia can be almost completely removed from solution (Fair *et al.*, 1968).

In reactions with organic compounds in dilute aqueous solutions such as effluents, chlorine (*i.e.*, hypochlorite) can act in either of two ways. It can oxidize functional groups or even molecules in a manner analogous to any other oxidant. Thus, hypochlorite can oxidize aldehydes to organic acids, but will not in general, oxidize aliphatic alcohols (Manufacturing Chemists Association, 1972).

$$OCl^- + RCHO = RCOOH + Cl^-$$

In addition, hydroquinones can be oxidized readily to quinones

$$OCl^- + HOC_6H_4OH = OC_6H_4O + H_2O + Cl^-$$

Of even greater interest is the fact that in addition to simple oxidation, the reaction of hypochlorites and organic materials can actually introduce chlorine groups into the molecule. For example, reactions can occur with nitrogenous materials as follows:

$$(CH_3)_2NH + OCl^- = (CH_3)_2NCl + OH^-$$

Of even greater significance are the reaction products with aromatic compounds. Here, the usual course of events is to substitute chlorine for hydrogen on the benzene ring. In general, alkyl benzenes, aromatic carboxylic acids and aromatic nitro compounds do not react. On the other hand, aromatic amines, phenols, and poly hydroxy phenols do form substitution products with hypochlorite. The paths of these reactions are complex, in general with one or two chlorine groups being added. With increasing chlorination, up to three chlorine groups can be added. Chlorination past this point acts like simple oxidation, resulting in rupture of the benzene ring and the production of oxidized fragments (Manufacturing Chemists Association, 1972). The general approximation for sewage is that about 2 mg/l BOD reduction is achieved per mg/l chlorine added (Imhoff et al., 1971). In all probability, as effluents are already partially oxidized, the oxidation efficiency would not be as good.

As interesting as the reactions of chlorine with organic and nitrogenous materials happens to be, the goal of chlorination is disinfection. That is, the reduction of the pathogens to a degree sufficient to render water acceptable according to the prevailing standards (which may attempt to achieve complete pathogen elimination). This seems relatively simple, and the general law of disinfection was evaluated in 1908 by Harriet Chick, which stated:

$$C^n t = K$$

where C is the concentration of disinfectant, t is the time required to achieve a stated percentage kill, K is a constant for a given disinfectant-organism system, and n is a coefficient of dilution or reaction order (Fair et al., 1968).

Using this equation, comparisons of the degree of sensitivity of organisms to be disinfected can be made, and an example of this is

Table 1-13. Chick's Law constants for chlorination to 99 percent kill or inactivation

Organism	n^a	K^a	Reference
Adenovirus 3	0.86	0.098	Clarke et al. (1956)
E. coli	0.86	0.24	Butterfield and Wattie (1946)
Poliovirus Type 1	0.86	1.2	Weidenkopf (1958)
Coxsackie A2 Virus	0.86	6.3	Chang et al. (1960)

a. Constants according to Fair et al. (1968) with time in minutes and concentration of HOCl in mg/l.

shown in Table 1-13. Not all results are so neatly defined, however, and there seems to be considerable variation in the literature on the question of the chlorine dosage and/or residual required to yield a stated effect. This is not too surprising, as the effectiveness of disinfection by chlorine will not only be influenced by time and chlorine concentration, but also whether or not the chlorine residual is free or combined (hypochlorite or chloramine), how well it is distributed, whether or not there are particulates present, temperature, pH, the concentration, condition, and nature of the organism, etc. In addition, the results reported will also be a function of the sensitivity, precision and accuracy of the test procedures. Keeping these limitations in mind, Table 1-14 gives some idea of the relative resistances of organisms to disinfection by chlorine. There is little question but that virus inactivation is one of the more difficult tasks of chlorination, but as in any disinfection process, required kills can be achieved by lengthening the time or increasing the concentration. Within its limits, and despite all of the problems involved, it has been a successful disinfectant, and for domestic sewage and effluents it will probably remain the disinfectant of choice for the near future.

Summary

The chemical and biological composition of effluents reflects the quality of the wastewater entering the plant and the changes that occur during the physical, chemical, and biological processes in the plant. The chemical changes which occur during treatment reflect the biological removal of 80-90 percent of the organic matter and the production of more oxidized organics. Thus, effluents will contain such materials as proteins, carbohydrates and soluble organic acids which either persist through the plant or are formed in it, such organics as Alkyl Benzene Sulfanates which have persisted through it, or such organics as Fulvic, Humic and Hyathomelanic Acids which are probably formed during treatment.

Table 1-14. Effect of chlorination on various organisms

Group	Organism	Chlorine Residual (mg/l)	Time (min.)	Efficiency	Reference
Virus	Infectious Hepatitis	1	30	Survived	Kabler (1959)
		15	30	Inactivated	Kabler (1959)
	Coxsackie	5	2.5	Survived	Kabler (1959)
	Coxsackie	1.0	3	99.6% Kill	Kollins (1966)
	Echo	1.95	6.5	Survived	Kabler (1959)
	Poliovirus I	0.53	14	Survived	Kabler (1959)
	Coliphage B	0.03	10	20% Survival	Gilcreas and Kelly (1954)
	Theiler Phage	0.03	10	Killed	Gilcreas and Kelly (1954)
Bacteria	M. tuberculosis	1-5	120	99% Kill	Kabler (1959)
		2	30	99% Kill	Kabler (1959)
		1	30	Destroyed	Bhaskaran et al. (1961)
	E. coli	0.14	3	99.9% Kill	Kollins (1966)
	Coliforms	0.03	10	48% Survival	Gilcreas and Kelly (1954)
		1-1.2	15	99% Kill	Kabler (1959)
	Total count	some	15	98-99% Kill	Kabler (1959)
Nematodes	Diplogaster	2.5-3	120	Survived and	Chang et al. (1960)
	Cheilobus	15-45	1	Mobile	Chang et al. (1960)
Others	S. mansoni (ova and Miracidia)	0.2-0.6	30	Killed	Kabler (1959)
	S. Japonicum (ova and Miracidia)	0.2-0.6	30	Killed	Kabler (1959)

Interest in the removals of microorganisms during treatment lies mainly in the area involving the efficiency of pathogen removal. Sedimentation and biological oxidation do markedly reduce pathogens, but as removals will depend (among other things) on the concentration of the pathogen in the wastewater, their presence in the effluent from biological treatment units can be expected and demonstrated. In addition to wastewater bacteria, viruses, etc. that have persisted through the plant, large numbers of protozoa and nematodes can be developed during biological treatment. Interest here has centered on the nematodes, which can ingest pathogens and thus have public health significance.

Effluent chlorination is largely for disinfection. There is little question but that the correct combinations of time and concentration (residual) can be achieved to obtain effective disinfection. However, actual practice may not always achieve this end, and excessive chlorination without dechlorination may lead to toxicity problems in receiving waters. Although chlorine can remove nitrogen (as ammonia) from solution, it also reacts with, as well as oxidizes organic materials. The significance of these chlorine containing organics in effluents has not yet been definitely established.

Literature Cited

Allen, L., E. Brooks, and I. Williams. 1949. *Jour. Hyg., 47.*

Allen, L. and F. Brooks. 1949. *Jour. Hyg., 47*, 320.

American Chemical Society. 1969. Cleaning Our Environment, The Chemical Basis for Action, Report of the Committee on Chemistry and Public Affairs, Washington, D.C.

Barker, A. 1943. *The Naturalist,* July-Sept., 65.

Benzie, W. and R. Courchaine. 1966. *Jour. Water Poll. Control Fed., 38*, 410.

Bhaskaran, T., M. Lahiri and B. Roy. 1960. *India Jour. Med. Res., 48*, 790, *Water Poll. Abstr., 34*, 2097 (1961).

Bunch, R., E. Barth, and M. Ettinger. 1961. *Jour. Water Poll. Control Fed., 33*, 122.

Burm, R. and R. Vaughn. 1966. *Jour. Water Poll. Control Fed., 38*, 400.

Buss, W. and T. Inal. 1957. *Berl. Munch tierargt Nschr., 70*, 311, *Water Poll. Abstr., 31*, 1609 (1958).

Butterfield, C. and E. Wattie. 1946. *Pub. Health Report, 61*, 157.

Calaway, W. 1963. *Jour. Water Poll. Control Fed., 35*, 1006.

Chang, S. 1961. *Jour. Amer. Works Assn., 53*, 288.

Chang, S., G. Berg, and N. Clarke. 1960. *Amer. Jour. Trop. Med. Hyg., 9*, 136.

Chang, S. and P. Kabler. 1962. *Jour. Water Poll. Control Fed., 34*, 1256.

Chaudhuri, N., R. Siddiqi, and R. Engelbrecht. 1964. *Jour. Amer. Water Works Assn., 56*, 73 (1964).

Chick, H. 1908. *Jour. Hyg., 8*, 92.

City of Johannesburg. 1963. City Eng. Dept. Tech. Rept., Johannesburg, So. Africa, *Water Poll. Abstr., 39*, 249 (1966).

Clarke, N. and P. Kabler. 1954. *Amer. Jour. Hyg., 59*, 119.

Clarke, N. and P. Kabler. 1964. *Health Lab. Sci., 1*, 44.

Clarke, N., R. Stevenson, and P. Kabler. 1956. *Amer. Jour. Hyg., 64*, 314.

Clarke, N., R. Stevenson, S. Chang, and P. Kabler. 1961. *Amer. Jour. Pub. Health, 81*, 1118.

Coetzie, O. and N. Fourie. 1965. *Proc. Resolutions and Papers, Conf. on Problems Assoc. with the Purif., Discharge and Reuse of Municipal and Ind. Effluents*, Nat. Inst. for Water Res., C.S.I.R., Conf. No. 55, Pretoria, So. Africa, 93.

Coetzie, O. and T. Pretorius. 1965. *Pub. Health*, 415, *Water Poll. Abstr. 40*, 19 (1967).

Coin, L., M. Menetrier, J. Labonde, and M. Hannoun. 1965. *Proc. 2nd Internat. Conf. Water Poll. Res., Tokyo, 1*, 1.

Cooke, W. 1965. *Mycologia, 57*, 696.

Curds, C. and A. Cockburn. 1970. *Water Research, 4*, 237.

Dias, F. 1963. *Jour. Ind. Inst. Sci., 45*, 36.

Dunlop, S. and W. Wang. 1961. *Jour. Milk, Tech., 24*, 44, *Water Poll. Abstr., 35*, 137 (1962).

Evans, R. and D. Beuscher. 1970. *Water and Sew. Works, 117*, 35.

Fair, G., J. Geyer, and D. Okun. 1968. *Water and Wastewater Engineering*, Vol. 2, John Wiley and Sons, Inc. N.Y.

Farquhar, G., and W. Boyle. 1971. *Jour. Water Poll. Control Fed., 43*, 779.

Finstein, M. and J. Hunter. 1967. *Water Research, 1*, 274.

Gilcreas, F. and S. Kelly. 1954. *New England Water Works Assn. Jour., 68*, 268.

Gylswyk, N. van. 1961. *Jour. Biochem. Microbiol. Tech. and Engr. 3*, 115.

Hoadley, A. 1967. Thesis, Univ. Wisconsin, 1965, *Dis. Abstr. 28*, B, 459.

Holt, H. 1960. *Monthly Bull. Min. Health Lab. Service, 19*, 29.

Hunter, J. V. 1971. *Origin of Organics from Artificial Contamination in Organic Compounds in Aquatic Environments*, S. D. Faust and J. V. Hunter, Eds. Marcel Dekker, Inc., N.Y.

Imhoff, K., W. Muller, and D. Thistlethwayte. 1971. *Disposal of Sewage and Other Water-Borne Wastes*, Ann Arbor Science Publ., Inc., Ann Arbor.

Kabler, P. 1959. *Sew. and Indust. Wastes, 31*, 1373.

Kabler, P. 1962. *Environ. Health; India, 4*, 258.

Kahn, L. and C. Wayman. 1964. *Jour. Water Poll. Control Fed. 36*, 1368.

Kapsenberg, J. 1958. *Ned. Tijdschr. Geneesk, 102*, 836, *Water Poll. Abstr. 32*, 498 (1959).

Keil, R. 1964. *Arch. Hyg. Bakt., 148*, 74, *Water Poll. Abstr., 38*, 40 (1965).

Kollins, S. A. 1966. *Adv. Appl. Microbiol., 8*, 145.

Kott, H. and Y. Kott. 1967. *Water and Sew. Works, 114*, 177.

Lamb, G., J. Chen, and L. Scarce. 1964. *Amer. Jour. Hyg., 80*, 320.

Manufacturing Chemists Association. 1972. The Effect of Chlorination on Selected Organic Chemicals, Office of Research and Monitoring, Environmental Protection Agency Project No. 12020 EXg.

McCoy, J. 1957. *Proc. Soc. Water Treatment Exam., 6*, 81.

Metzler, D., R. Culp, H. Stoltenberg, R. Woodward, G. Walton, S. Chang, N. Clarke, C. Palmer, and F. Middleton. 1958. *Jour. Amer. Water Works Assn., 50*, 1021.

Ministry of Technology (Brit.). 1966. Notes on Water Pollution, No. 34.

Murad, J. and G. Bazer. 1970. *Jour. Water Poll. Control Fed., 42*, 106.

Murtaugh, J. and R. Bunch. 1967. *Jour. Water Poll. Control Fed., 39*, 404.

Nussbaumer, N. 1963. *Water Works Engr., 116*, 722, *Water Poll. Abstr., 38*, 18 (1965).

O'Shea, J. and R. Bunch. 1965. *Jour. Water Poll. Control Fed., 37*, 1444.

Painter, H., M. Viney, and A. Bywaters. 1961. *Jour. Inst. Sew. Purif. 302*.

Primavesi, C. and J. Weistenberg. 1965. *Arch. Hyg. Bact., 149*, 336, *Water Poll. Abstr., 39*, 1038 (1966).

Rebhan, M. and J. Manka. 1971. *Environ. Sci. Tech. 5*, 606.

Rickert, D. and J. Hunter. 1967. *Jour. Water Poll. Control Fed. 37*, 1475.

Rickert, D. and J. Hunter. 1971. *Water Research 5*, 421.

Rowan, W. 1964a.*Amer. Jour. Trop. Med. Hyg., 13*, 572.

Rowan, W. 1964b.*Amer. Jour. Trop. Med. Hyg., 13*, 577.

Russel, E., E. Munro, and J. Peacol. 1962. *Water Waste Treat. Jour., 8*, 575.

Sladka, A. and V. Otlova. 1968. *Hydrobiologica, 31*, 350.

Standard Methods for the Analysis of Water and Waste Water. 1971. Amer. Pub. Health Assn., N.Y., N.Y., 13th Ed.

Subrahanyam, P., C. Sastry, A. Rao, and S. Pillai. 1969. *Jour. Water Poll. Control Fed., 32*, 344.

Tomlinson, T., J. Loveless and L. Sear. 1962. *Jour. Hyg. 60,* 365.

Unz, R. 1965. Doctoral Thesis, Rutgers University, New Brunswick, N.J.

Viswanathan, C., B. Bai, and S. Pillai. 1962. *Jour. Water Poll. Control Fed., 34*, 189.

Wedgewood, P. 1952. *Jour. Proc. Inst. Sew. Purif., 20.*

Weidenkopf, S. 1958. *Virology, 5*, 56.

2
Chemical and Biological Quality
of Municipal Sludge

J. R. Peterson, Cecil Lue-Hing and D. R. Zenz*

Sewage sludge is derived from the organic and inorganic matter removed from wastewater at sewage treatment plants. The nature of
sludge depends on the wastewater sources and the method of wastewater treatment. If waste solids are to be evaluated as a soil amendment or as a fertilizer, it is important to understand their chemical and
biological properties. A comparison of sludge analyses from various
treatment plants would be confounded by the individual treatment
processes; therefore, some of the more common wastewater treatment methods will be described.

Chemical Qualities

The first treatment process is usually gravity separation of solids from
wastewater. This process is commonly known as primary settling or
primary treatment. Secondary sewage treatment may be accomplished by physical-chemical or biological processes. The physical-chemical processes include chemical precipitation using lime,
alum, or ferric chloride. Biological secondary treatment includes
trickling filters or some modification of the activated sludge process in
an aerobic suspended growth system which consists of contacting
primary treated with previously treated sludge. These processes result in nutrient consumption by microorganisms and the formation of
biological flocs which are later settled out and subsequently pumped
to concentration chambers for reuse (as activated sludge) or ultimate
disposal.

The wastewater solids separated by these primary and secondary
water treatment processes may then be dried for marketing as a low
analysis dry fertilizer, or subjected to various stabilization treatments.
Some current sludge stabilization processes include: the Zimpro process, a high temperature and high pressure, wet oxidation treatment
which produces an aqueous suspension having a granular ash; extended aeration in tanks or lagoons; and anaerobic meso- or thermophilic
digestion.

*The Metropolitan Sanitary District of Greater Chicago.

Following any of these latter processes the stabilized sludge may be further concentrated by drying beds, vacuum filtration, pressing, centrifuging, or lagooning with supernatant drawoff. The liquid fraction is high in soluble constituents. Malina and DiFilippo (1971) reported that 57 percent of the nitrogen in the waste-activated sludge digester feed was removed in the digester supernatant. The advantages of this further concentration are to save lagoon storage space, reduce handling costs, or to remove soluble chemical constituents which are usually returned to the treatment plant. The reduction in soluble chemical constituents has an advantage if the sludge is to be disposed of on land at high sludge application rates.

Land application of liquid sewage sludge requires high capital investment and is best done on a large scale. Therefore, to have a competitive disposal system on land, the area should be capable of safely accepting high application rates and provide some marketable crop which will remove nutrients and protect the soil from rapid weathering. Nitrate accumulations in ground water have been reported with high application rates of dairy manure (Adriano, Pratt, and Bishop, 1971) and digested sewage sludge (Hinesly, Braids, and Molina, 1971). Therefore, any reduction in the nitrogen content of the sludge will permit a higher application rate of sludge without endangering ground water quality.

The chemical properties of sludge at various steps in the waste-activated sludge treatment process at the Metropolitan Sanitary District of Greater Chicago (MSDGC) West-Southwest Sewage Treatment Plant are presented in Table 2-1. The sewage at this plant includes domestic and industrial wastewater at an approximate ratio of 3:2 plus stormwater from the Chicago area. Primary sludge properties are not included with these data (Table 2-1) except for lagoon sludge (column 6) with supernatant removal. Part of the waste-activated sludge is treated with $FeCl_3$ and vacuum filtered. This is blended at a ratio of 1:3 with waste-activated sludge for thickening and fed to the digesters which are completely mixed. The digester drawoff (column 4) at this plant does not have supernatant separation which may partly explain the very high total- and NH_4-nitrogen concentration compared to what Anderson (1956) reported. The lower nitrogen concentration from anaerobically digested sludge reported by Anderson (1.3-3.1 percent) was due to the use of primary sludge only while Table 2-1 represents waste-activated anaerobically digested sludge. Anaerobic digestion at MSDGC averages ca. 30 percent reduction in volatile solids. This solids reduction continues, to a much lesser degree, in the lagooned sludge because of further anaerobic degradation of the organic materials present.

Analyses of the lagooned sludge which had no supernatant drawoff

Table 2-1. Chemical properties of various sludges formed in the waste-activated sludge treatment processes at MSDGC West-Southwest Treatment Plant, Chicago, Illinois

	State of Sludge Treatment					
	Activated (1)	Vacuum Filtered & Heat Dried (2)	Digested Feed [a] (3)	Digester Drawoff [b] (4)	Lagooned Without Supernatant Drawoff [c] (5)	Lagooned With Supernatant Drawoff [d] (6)
Number of analysis	7	7	7	230	15	30
Total solids (%)	1.43	99.5	5.41	3.99	3.99	—
Volatile solids (% of total solids)	66.2	67.3	65.2	57	55.6	35.5
pH	6.7	—	6.2	7.4	7.5	7.2
Total nitrogen [e] (% oven dry basis)	6.65	6.4	5.63	7.27	7.20	2.60
NH_4-N (% oven dry basis)	0.47	trace	1.15	3.26	3.60	1.20

a. The digester feed consists of a blend of activated sludge and vacuum filtered activated sludge (3:1). The latter contains 10% $FeCl_3$ by dry weight.
b. Digested 14 days at 29-32°C without digester supernatant withdrawal.
c. Analyses estimated after 8 months of filling a lagoon with digester drawoff.
d. Earlier sludge produced at the same treatment plant which may be up to 20 years in age and has had supernatant removed from the lagoon (Peterson et al., 1971).
e. Total N analysis by Kjeldahl and NH_4-N by distillation with sludge buffered to pH 10.5.

was done by sampling three points in a 20 ha (50 acres) lagoon eight months after the start of the filling operation. The filling was done on a daily basis during these eight months after which time the total sludge volume was 1.5×10^6 m^3 when sampled. At each point five samples from the surface to the lagoon bottom were taken; these samples were from the surface, 2.7, 5.5, and 9.1 m below surface, and a bottom sample (ca. 15 m). A Kemmerer sampler was used in the cover water (0-4.6 m depth) while in the thickened underlying slurry an Ekman dredge sampler was used. The total solids for the whole lagoon were estimated to be equal to what was added (3.99 percent). The cover water-slurry partition was estimated as 1:1 (v/v basis). Laboratory columns confirmed this partition ratio. The lagooned sludge concentration was calculated for the whole lagoon by averaging the concentration of the cover water and the slurry with the assumption of a 1:1 volume ratio and a total solids of 3.99 percent in the lagoon if it were remixed. The estimated analysis of this sludge is presented in column 5 of Table 2-1. Only volatile solids showed any reduction, although NH$_3$ gas was sometimes detectable in the area.

A comparison of the two lagooned sludges in Table 2-1 (columns 5 and 6) shows the great reduction in volatile solids and nitrogen compounds that can be expected with up to twenty years of lagooning and periodic supernatant drawoff. The inputs to this lagoon included Zimpro wet ash, waste-activated sludge, primary sludge, and digested waste-activated sludge.

A comparison of sewage sludge from various parts of the United States is presented in Table 2-2. The sludge types include: primary only at Georgia and primary plus waste-activated at Minnesota, Colorado, and Illinois. Sludge treatments included are: none at St. Paul, Minn.; addition of FeCl$_3$ vacuum filtration, and heat-drying of waste-activated sludge MSDGC West-Southwest Plant; and anaerobic digestion of primary plus waste-activated sludges without supernatant drawoff at MSDGC, Hanover and Calumet Plants. The Hanover sewage is primarily from domestic sources and the Calumet and West-Southwest sewage is a blend of domestic and industrial at an approximate ratio of 3:2.

A comparison of Hasting and Hanover Park, two sewage treatment plants with the least industrial waste and the same sewage treatment processes, indicates that Hanover Park (column 3) has more Ca, Mg, and Fe in its wastewater, whereas Hastings (column 1) has more Cr and Cu, in fact, the most of any reported in Table 2-2. An industrial source at Hastings is discharging Cr into the sewage treatment plant.

A comparison of the three undigested sludges from St. Paul (column 2), MSDGC, West-Southwest (column 5), and Denver (column 6) would be valid except for changes relating to the chemical addi-

Table 2-2. Chemical analyses of sewage sludges from various wastewater treatment plants

Source:	Hastings, Minn.[a]	St. Paul, Minn.[a]	MSDGC, Chicago, Ill.[b]			Denver, Colo.[c]	Athens Ga.[d]
			Hanover	Calumet	West-Southwest		
Treatment Process:	Primary and waste activated: anaerobic digestion without supernatant drawoff	Primary and waste activated (1:2): undigested	Primary and waste activated: anaerobic digestion without supernatant digester drawoff	Primary and waste activated: anaerobic digestion without supernatant digester drawoff	Waste activated: FeCl₃ addition: vac. filtered: heat-dried	Primary and waste activated: FeCl₃ and lime: vac. filtered: undigested	Primary: anaerobic digestion
Analyses	(1)	(2)	(3)	(4)	(5)	(6)	(7)

			Percent Dry Weight Basis				
N-Total	5.84	4.69	5.57	5.20	6.37	4.57	3.5
NH₄-N	2.34	1.33	3.63	2.40	trace	–	–
P	2.61	2.20	2.59	3.90	2.49	1.75	0.75
K	0.27	0.24	0.68	0.55	0.41	–	0.22

Table 2-2. (Continued)

Analyses	(1)	(2)	(3)	(4)	(5)	(6)	(7)
				Percent Dry Weight Basis			
Ca	2.97	2.52	5.05	4.20	1.4	7.38	1.21
Mg	0.26	0.40	1.64	0.60	0.75	0.45	0.09
Zn	0.075	0.14	0.069	0.35	–	0.172	0.252
B	0.0013	0.002	–	–	0.002-0.04	0.00022	0.00199
Fe	0.45	0.76	2.22	3.68	5.32	1.48	–
Mn	0.015	0.039	0.07	0.14	0.012	0.0253	0.0199
Al	0.65	0.74	–	1.21	–	–	–
Cd	0.00079	0.036	0.0089	0.0125	0.028	–	–
Cl	–	–	0.12	0.74		–	–
Cr	0.390	0.067	0.019	0.112	0.362	–	–
Cu	0.12	0.065	0.062	0.088	0.11	0.0324	0.046
Ni	<0.001	0.015	0.032	0.020	0.034	–	–
Pb	0.039	0.070	0.083	0.18	0.141	–	0.0026

a. Unpublished data from C. E. Clapp, R. H. Dowdy, and W. E. Larson, ARS, USDA, St. Paul, Minn.
b. Unpublished data, MSDGC.
c. Parza (1969).
d. King (1970).

tions in the latter two plants. From these three plants, Chicago heat-dried sludge had the highest concentration of total N, P, Zn, and Cu, and Denver had the least total N, P, B, and Cu.

At the MSDGC, West-Southwest Sewage Treatment Plant a daily composite of waste-activated anaerobically digested sewage sludge was collected for 281 days between Aug. 19, 1971 and May 31, 1972 for chemical analyses. Other properties of this material were determined on a less frequent basis. The analytical methods used were: total N by Kjeldahl; NH_4-N by distillation at pH 10.5; total P by Technicon Auto-Analyzer method of Stanley and Richardson (1970); S by Leco induction furnace; metals were done by digestion of 10 ml of the liquid sludge in 10 ml of a mixture of concentrated H_2SO_4 and HNO_3 at a ratio of 1:1, dilution to 200 ml and determination by atomic absorption except for Hg which was by the absorption technique; Cl, pH, electrical conductivity (E.C.), total and volatile solids, COD, BOD_5, volatile acids and the hexane soluble constituents were done by standard methods (USPHS, 1971); inorganic carbon by the Bundy and Bremner (1972) method; neutralizing power was done by repeated heating of the liquid sludge for 1 hour on a steam bath and repeated acid titrations to a pH 6.5 end point (Martens, 1971); alkalinity by the USPHS (1971) method of titration to pH 4.5 end point; particle size was done by using a Coulter Counter with three and nine μ orifices; and cation exchange capacity (CEC) by the H. D. Chapman (1965) method as used for soils. The same analytical methods were used for MSDGC sludge analyses presented in Table 2-1 and 2-2.

A detailed analytical description of anaerobically digested waste-activated sewage sludge from the MSDGC West-Southwest Sewage Treatment Plant is presented in Table 2-3. The total N concentration is very high (7.27 percent) compared to other sludge sources. The soluble nitrogen (NH_4-N) content is 3.26 percent. This nitrogen is available to a growing crop or may be adsorbed by the colloidal fraction of the soil. The rate of organic nitrogen mineralization for digested sludge is less than for fresh organic wastes, e.g., animal manures or waste-activated sludges. In addition to nitrogen, this sludge is a source of P, Ca, Zn, Fe, and S for plants. Many other essential and nonessential elements exist in sewage sludge. The solubility of compounds of these elements varies with the nature of the sewage and the chemistry of the soil following sludge application. Jenkins and Cooper (1964) found that the dominant metal forms in industrial sludge were hydroxides. Parsa (1970) postulated chelation as an important mechanism of Zn release from sludge in soil. In a reduced environment, such as a digester, metal-sulfides, -sulfites, -phosphates, -carbonates, -bicarbonates, -oxides, and -hydroxides are

Table 2-3. Properties of anaerobically digested waste-activated sewage sludge from MSDGC West-Southwest Sewage Treatment Plant between August 19, 1971 and May 31, 1972

Property[a]		Avg. Concentration[b]	Property[a]		Avg. Concentration[b]
		% dry basis			% dry basis
Total N	(221)	7.27	Cd	(43)	0.034
NH$_4$-N	(221)	3.26	Cl	(78)	1.17
Total P	(238)	2.46	Cr	(42)	0.341
K	(40)	0.44	Cu	(43)	0.136
Ca	(43)	2.02	Hg	(46)	0.000038
Mg	(43)	0.99	Na	(43)	0.38
S	(6)	0.65	Ni	(43)	0.08
Zn	(43)	0.39	Pb	(39)	0.106
Fe	(43)	4.56	Al	(40)	1.04
Mn	(43)	0.02			

Property[a]	Avg. Concentration[b]
pH (136)	7.4
Electrical conductivity (221)	5 mmho/cm
Total solids (281)	3.99%
Volatile solids (281)	57% of TS
Volatile acids as HAc (136)	247 mg/l
Hexane soluble (7)	12% dry basis
COD	5400 mg/l
BOD$_5$	1140 mg/l
Particle size (14)	99%<9 μ
Particle size (14)	60%<3 μ
Neutralizing power (3)	27 meq H$^+$/100g solids
Neutralizing power as CaCO$_3$ (3)	2.76% dry basis
Alkalinity as CaCO$_3$ (75)	10.69% dry basis
Carbon, inorganic (6)	19.3% dry basis
Cation exchange capacity (6)	74 meq/100g solids

a. Number of analysis in parenthesis. Methods of analyses presented in text.
b. Percent dry basis × 10 = kg/metric ton.

all possible in organic compounds that might be present. Following sludge application to soil the solubilities of these compounds are a function of soil pH. The 4.56 percent Fe content of MSDGC sludge may be advantageous according to Lagerwerff's (1967) data. He reported that metals are competitive with Fe in biological systems. The general order of decreasing competition seems to be: $Cu > Co > Ni > Cr > Zn > Mn > Pb$.

The continued application of sewage sludge on noncalcareous soil has been reported to cause a soil pH reduction (Hinesly, Braids, and Molina, 1971; and Lunt, 1959), although digested sludge has some neutralizing power (Table 2-3). The alkalinity determination in Table 2-3 was done by a cold acid titration in which protein and NH$_4$OH added to the true value for alkalinity. The determination of neutralizing power after heating the sludge suggests that only about one fourth of the reported alkalinity was due to carbonates, bicarbonates and hydroxides. However, the inorganic carbon (19.3 percent) as released by $2N$ HCl indicate the very slight solubility of the inorganic carbon compounds which exist in this sludge. Even with heat, titration with $0.01N$ HCl over a 24-hour period released only a small fraction of the inorganic carbon present. The colloidal nature of sludge solids is reflected in a cation exchange capacity of 74 meq/100 g solids in a matrix which has 60 percent of the particles with less than three-micron diameter. These exchangeable cations may be considered as available to plants.

The chemical complexity of liquid sewage sludge continues in the soil because of the high volatile-acids and -solids which exist in the fresh sludge. These biodegradable constituents, when applied on soil, are subject to a vigorous change in their rate of degradation. Thin applications of liquid sludge on the soil surface have not resulted in reductions in water infiltration if the sludge dried between applications (Hinesly *et al.*, 1971). Organic carbon does accumulate in sludge treated soils (Peterson *et al.*, 1971).

Biological Qualities

Well stabilized sewage sludges are generally free of odors and pathogens. This stabilization may be accomplished by anaerobic digestion, by extended aeration, or extended lagooning of the sludge. Poorly digested (less than 30 percent reduction in volatile solids) or acidic sludge may produce odors. Well stabilized sludge may safely be left on the soil surface without worry of odor or vermin. This is advantageous in that sludge can be used on a growing crop for its nutrient and water benefits. Braids *et al.* (1970) reported a 99 percent decrease of fecal coliform in 30 days of dessication on the soil surface. Burd (1966) reported 99.8 percent bacterial reduction after 30 days of mesophilic anaerobic digestion and further that pathogenic organisms die within seven to ten days of digestion. Krone (1968) reported the density of non-spore forming bacteria outside their hosts decreased exponentially with time. Deliberate contamination of tomato plants with feces, *Salmonella cerro,* and *Shigella alkalescens* indicated that these pathogens did not survive the dessication and the sun for more than 35 days (Rudolfs *et al.*, 1951). Rudolfs also reported that *Endamoeba histolytica* and *Ascaris* eggs died upon dessication.

The aerobic bacteria population was reduced by two to three logs when wet sludge (4.9 percent total solids) was dewatered on a vacuum filter with Fe_2SO_4 and lime (1:6) addition to yield a product with

65.3 percent total solids (Kampelmacher and Van Noorle Jensen, 1972). They reported a two to four log reduction in enterobacteriacae with the drying of this same sludge.

Molina *et al.* (1972) observed bactericidal properties in the liquid phase of anaerobically digested sludge. Heat sterilization did not eliminate bactericidal properties, therefore, parasitic relationships, protein, antibiotics, or nutrient competition were ruled out as the toxic agent. *Escherichici coli* isolated from the sludge had a lower mortality rate than did *E. coli* from stock culture.

Soil nitrification was found to be stimulated by moderate additions of sewage sludge (≤ 114 kg NH_4-N/ha equivalent in sludge) while higher dosing rates (≥ 228 kg NH_4-N/ha equivalent in sludge) resulted in a lag in nitrification and an increase in denitrification of up to 13 percent of the sludge N (Premi and Cornfield, 1969). King (1971) reported that 22 to 36 percent of the applied nitrogen in liquid sludge was lost with surface application. This was by NH_3 volatilization and apparent denitrification.

Acknowledgment
The authors wish to thank all the personnel of the Research and Development Department of the Metropolitan Sanitary District of Greater Chicago for their assistance in collecting data for this manuscript, and the Metropolitan Sanitary District of Greater Chicago for permission to use unpublished data.

Literature Cited

Adriano, D. C., P. F. Pratt and S. E. Bishop. 1971. Nitrate and salt in soil and ground waters from land disposal of dairy manure. *Soil Sci. Soc. Amer. Proc.* 35:759-762.

Amer. Public Health Assoc. 1971. Standard methods for the examination of water and waste water. 13th Edition, APHA, New York.

Anderson, M. S. 1956. Comparative analyses of sewage sludge. *Sew. and Industrial Wastes*, 28:132-135.

Bundy, L. G. and J. M. Bremner. 1972. A simple titrimetric method for determination of inorganic carbon in soils. *Soil Sci. Soc. Amer. Proc.* 36:273-275.

Hinesly, T. D., O. C. Braids, and J. E. Molina. 1971. Agricultural benefits and environmental changes resulting from the use of digested sewage sludge on field crops, U.S. Environmental Protection Agency Reports SW-30d.

Jenkins, S. H., and J. S. Cooper. 1964. The solubility of heavy metals present in digested sewage sludge. *International Jour. Air Water Poll.* 8:695-703.

Kampelmacher, E. H., and L. M. Van Noorle Jensen. 1972. Reduction of bacteria in sludge treatment, *Jour. Water Poll. Control Fed.* 44:309-313.

King, L. D. 1971. The effect of land disposal of liquid sewage sludge on growth and chemical composition of coastal bermudagrass and rye and on soil properties, ammonia volatilization and nitrate leaching. Ph. D. thesis, Univ. of Georgia, Univ. Microfilm, Ann Arbor, Mich. (*Dissertation Abstr.* 72-10, 989).

Lagerwerff, J. V. 1967. Heavy metal contamination of soil, pp. 343-359. In *Agriculture and The Quality of Our Environment*, Plimpton Press, Norwood, Mass.

Lunt, H. A. 1959. Digested sewage sludge for soil improvement, Conn. Agric. Expt. Sta. Bull., 622.

Malina, J. F. and J. DiFilippo. 1971. Treatment of supernatant and liquids associated with sludge treatment, *Water and Sew. Works*, 118:R30-R38.

Martens, D. C. 1971. Availability of plant nutrients in fly ash, *Compost Science*, Nov.-Dec., pp. 15-18.

Molina, A. J. E., O. C. Braids, and T. D. Hinesly. 1972. Observations on bactericidal properties of digested sewage sludge, *Environ. Sci. & Tech.* 6:448-450.

Peterson, J. R., T. M. McCalla and G. E. Smith. 1971. Human and animal wastes as fertilizer. In *Fertilizer Technology and Use*, R. A. Olsen *et al.* (ed.). Soil Sci. Soc. Amer., Madison, Wisconsin.

Premi, P. R., and A. H. Cornfield. 1969. Incubation study of nitrification of digested sewage sludge added to soil, *Soil Bio. and Biochem.* 1:1-4.

Rudolfs, W., L. L. Falk, and R. A. Ragotzkie. 1951. Contamination of vegetables grown in polluted soil, *Sew. and Industrial Wastes*, 23:253-268.

Stanley, G. H. and G. R. Richardson. 1970. The automation of a single reagent method for total phosphorus, pp. 305-311, in *Advances in Automated Analysis*, Vol. II, *Industrial Analysis*, Technician Instrument Corporation, Tarrytown, New York.

Discussion

Miller: I was interested in volatile acid content, isn't this unusually high for digested sewage sludge, 247 mg/l?

Peterson: This is what we've been getting at the Chicago West-Southwest treatment plant.

Miller: It seemed a little high.

Peterson: It's a high rate digestion process.

Stevenson: Have you monitored the effect of this sludge application to the soil on the groundwater?

Peterson: Yes, we have and there'll be other speakers who will cover this topic.

Ludington: Both speakers have used terms like soluble and suspended, I was wondering if they could define what those terms are and how they were analyzed. Were conventional standard methods of procedure used or some other method?

Peterson: Standard methods of wastewater and water tailings were used.

Hunter: It depends on what results I've had with the method I'm dealing with, but in general the sizing I was dealing with there is sedimentation for an hour for settleable solids; supracolloidal being that which will not settle out but which can be removed, say, by centrifugation at about

50,000 rpm, in a Sharples supercentrifuge or the equivalent of this. A couple of different authors have done this.
Oil being the most variable one and here people have
defined it by chemical traces, to name one, by extremely
high speed centrifugation or by cellulose membrane
filtration. The soluble is what goes through all of these.

II / FUNDAMENTAL FUNCTIONS OF THE SOIL AND ITS ASSOCIATED BIOSPHERE

3
The Soil as a Physical Filter

Richard E. Thomas*

The word "soil" has many definitions, but it is generally accepted that the soil is the upper portion of the loose material covering the surface of the earth. As such the soil is a mixture of mineral particles, organic material, air, and water. The pore space occupied by air or water may be as much as 50 percent of the total volume, and the pathway of movement through these pores is a maze of varying sized channels. It is the size distribution and the nature of this maze which control the capability of the soil to filter out suspended solids that are found in treatment plant effluents or industrial wastewaters. In most soils, the pore size distribution and the nature of the water movement channels are such that suspended solids are completely removed after short travel distances in the soil. Man has devised several approaches to utilize this filtering capability of the soil for disposal or renovation of municipal effluents and industrial wastewaters. These approaches include septic tank-soil absorption systems, cropland irrigation systems, surface disposal systems, and groundwater recharge systems.

Each of these approaches that man has devised for utilizing the soil to receive wastewaters is dependent on maintaining a balance between the filtering capability of the soil and the rate of water movement through the soil--the objective being to filter out the suspended solids while maintaining the water movement at a relatively high rate. The following discussion will cover some of the research study results and practical operating experiences that have helped to identify factors which influence the balance between filtering capability and the rate of water movement.

Septic tank-soil absorption systems are the most widely used of the approaches devised by man for wastewater disposal to the soil, and there are about 15 million homes in the United States utilizing this approach. The basic concept of the approach is to provide sufficient

*Robert S. Kerr Water Research Center, Environmental Protection Agency.

subsurface filtering areas to achieve long-term service without maintenance. Failure to achieve the desired longevity and other problems
with the millions of septic tank systems installed in the late 1940's
and early 1950's stimulated a surge of research interest to determine
what caused the failure of these soil systems.

Water movement through the soil is essential to successful use of
septic tank systems, and much of the research effort has been directed
to studies on soil clogging. These research efforts have not identified
the specific causal agents of soil clogging, but they have elucidated
several factors which influence the rate and degree of clogging. The
results of several research studies have shown that clogging occurs at
or near the surface of the soil (Jones and Taylor, 1965; Thomas et al.,
1966; and Winneberger et al., 1960). The depth of the zone of
clogging may be somewhat greater for coarse textured soils, but for
most practical applications the predominant zone of clogging is confined to a depth of less than one inch. The most troublesome clogging
usually occurs when the soil surface becomes inundated and remains
submerged for an extended period of time. This clogging occurs as an
impervious mat which forms at the surface of the soil and from a
practical point of view plugs the ends of the channels through which
water moves. The actual clogging is a physical blocking of the soil
pores, but it is apparent that formation of the surface mat is the
combined effects of physical, chemical, and biochemical interactions
in the soil (McGauhey and Krone, 1967). This surface clogging mat
has two characteristics which are very important from the practical
point of view. One is the fact that the mat is formed in conjunction
with the development of anaerobic conditions during extended periods of submergence. The other is the fact that restoration of aerobic
conditions and drying of the mat removes most of the soil clogging
directly associated with the formation of the mat.

In summary, the research efforts directed to identifying the causes
of soil clogging elucidated three important factors to consider in
selecting management practices for applying wastewater to the land.
These three factors are (1) the zone of clogging which reduces the
water intake rate is at or near the soil surface; (2) the most severe
clogging develops in an anaerobic environment; and (3) the severe
clogging developed under anaerobic conditions can be removed by
drying the clogged surface layer of soil. Further studies of these three
factors under practical operating conditions have verified the results
of the small scale research studies.

Looking at crop irrigation systems, we find that good operating
practices preclude the development of anaerobic conditions leading to
formation of the troublesome clogging mat. Physical clogging of the
filter for the irrigation approach should be limited to deposition of

small amounts of suspended mineral particles and slowly degradable organic particles. The effects of these additions appear to go unnoticed at locations where wastewater irrigation has been practiced for up to 80 years (Hutchins, 1939; Hyde, 1950; and Segel, 1950). Quantitative information on differences in soil properties after 14 years of wastewater irrigation versus a fresh water irrigation source led to the conclusion that wastewater irrigation did not result in adverse effects that could not be corrected with minor changes in cultural practices (Day *et al.*, 1972). The adverse differences in soil properties observed in this study were associated with chemical interactions rather than physical clogging by deposition.

The situation is entirely different when one considers spray disposal and groundwater recharge approaches where the desire for high rates of hydraulic loading frequently lead to moisture conditions which promote development of anaerobic conditions and the consequent severe clogging of the soil filter. This situation has been counteracted by developing a routine management practice of alternating wetting periods and drying periods to take advantage of the fact that drying of the clogged surface results in recovery of the capacity to move water. The periodicity of the wetting and drying cycle can vary from a few days to a few weeks (Amramy, 1965; Bouwer, 1970) depending on local conditions and the overall objectives of a given project. Much remains to be learned in this area for improvement of techniques but we can make practical use of current knowledge, and some recharge operations have been in operation for several decades.

This brief discussion of the soil as a physical filter has been directed to factors which lead to clogging of the filter and management practices which can be used to extend the life of the filter. These aspects of the behavior of the filter are closely related to the chemical, biological, and hydrogeological interactions which are covered in companion papers presented during the symposium. Reference to these companion papers will strengthen and broaden one's understanding of the function of the soil as a filter for receiving municipal effluents or industrial wastewaters.

Literature Cited

Amramy, A. 1965. Waste treatment for ground water recharge, *Jour. Air Water Poll.* 9:605-619.
Bouwer, H. 1970. Water quality aspects of intermittent systems using secondary sewage effluent, Artificial Groundwater Recharge Conference, University of Reading, England, Paper 8.

Day, A. D., J. L. Stroehlein, and T. C. Tucker. 1972. Effects of treatment plant effluent on soil properties, *Jour. Water Poll. Control Fed.* 44(3):372-375.

Hutchins, W. A. 1939. Sewage irrigation as practiced in the western United States, U.S. Dept. of Agriculture, Washington, Technical Bull. No. 675, 60 p.

Hyde, C. G. 1950. Sewage reclamation at Melbourne, Australia, *Sew. and Industrial Wastes* 22(8):1013-1015.

Jones, J. H., and G. S. Taylor. 1965. Septic tank effluent percolation through sands under laboratory conditions, *Soil Sci.* 99:301-309.

McGauhey, P. H., and R. B. Krone. 1967. Soil mantle as a wastewater treatment system—Final Report, School of Public Health, University of California, Berkeley, SERL Rept. No. 67-11.

Segel, A. 1950. Sewage reclamation at Fresno, California, *Sew. and Industrial Wastes* 22(8):1011-1012.

Thomas, R. E., W. A. Schwartz, and T. W. Bendixen. 1966. Soil chemical changes and infiltration rate reduction under sewage spreading, *Soil Sci. Soc. of Amer. Proc.* 30(5):641-646.

Winneberger, J. H., L. Francis, S. A. Klein, and P. H. McGauhey. 1960. Biological aspects of failure of septic-tank percolation systems—Final Report, School of Public Health, University of California, Berkeley.

Discussion

Solomon: I'd like to know what is going to happen to many of the streams in the area if we implement this type of a wastewater procedure. For many streams in industrial areas and municipal areas, the flow consists of between 50 to 75 percent wastewater. If we channel this wastewater into the soil, undoubtedly we will raise the soil water table, but what will happen to the dependable flows in the streams in the area?

Kardos: Well, actually you're just delaying the return flow to the streams. It's going to go back into the stream eventually as base flow, in other words, all you're doing is delaying slightly the return to the stream. You can't pile up water indefinitely in the soil, it's got to go somewhere and eventually it ends up in the streams.

Anderson: I have a comment or two and then a question. It seems to me that part of the clogging might be due to case hardening that you get because of the coagulation of some of the larger molecular weight fragments, proteins, etc. Do you find that you have any kinds of tests that would anticipate this so you could alter your schedule of treatment accordingly?

Thomas: Not that I am aware of, this is a pretty uncertain art, and so far the management technique has been developed on pretty gross values. It depends basically on the hydraulic acceptance as measured by some device on the site.

Burge: Have you looked at the nature of that mat? Is it particulate material or is it composed mainly of micro-organisms?

Thomas: Both. There isn't a whole lot of work being done on the mat itself. There are microbiological cells present and it also looks like there are materials that were in the wastewater to start with so that I'd say, really it is both.

Rhindress: Assuming a field has developed an impermeable layer at the surface by clogging, how long or what treatment would you take to regenerate that field? Can you just plow that mat under and resume spraying or must you let it restructure in the soil?

Thomas: Where you're working with fairly coarse textured soils, if you have a mat like I was showing here you can recover a lot of the original conductivity by just stopping applications for a period of time. The resting period depends on the weather conditions but usually in the order of magnitude of a week up to three weeks. In the long run you may get clogging that you would have to go in and do physical manipulation, plowing or some kind of disturbance of the surface to restore the hydraulic conductivity.

Parizek: I think you were showing mats developed in a flooding or infiltration lagoon type of experiment. Are you likely to get such mats with a spray irrigation system?

Thomas: Yes, the mats that I showed were obtained under flooding conditions. However, you could get the first mats in an irrigation type approach, if you had restricted water movement. With the irrigation approach, if you have good site selection and you're working with a very well treated effluent, the clogging would be a very minimal problem.

Parizek: Because we need to maintain infiltration and good drain characteristics, it seems like this plugging problem can be alleviated by just not going to this flooding condition.

Schulze: You mentioned that anaerobic mats, the mat that is produced under anaerobic conditions can be a very fine layer and it usually has a black color and I assume that it consists of fine suspended solids. Now I recall that probably these conditions are always very conducive to the forming of ferrous sulphide. Usually there is some iron available under anaerobic conditions and you can have hydrogen sulphide formation and so ferrous sulphide could also very well be formed and be the plugging agent. Are there any analytical data supporting this kind of idea?

Thomas: Ferrous sulphide is there. This is the agent that causes most of the black color. My colleagues and I had heated arguments many times as to whether ferrous sulphide contributed to the clogging or whether it was just there because of the anaerobic conditions and is not one of the primary causes of clogging. We do have some data published on this. I have a publication in the Soil Science Society Proceedings.

Schulze: And what is the result now?

Thomas: The ferrous sulphide is there because of the anaerobic conditions but it is not one of the primary causes of the clogging.

Schulze: If ferrous sulphide is not. Well, what is it then?

Thomas: It's an organic matter mat of suspended material and biological cells. That's about as close as we came to really identifying it.

Hart: Have you any feeling for what the effect on the soil would be if this is actually mixed within the soil rather than placed on the surface and allowed to form there as far as the transmissibility characteristics that would result?

Thomas: I'm not sure I understand what you mean.

Hart: Well, you're talking about putting the material directly on the soil surface, now what if we mix it with the soil?

Thomas: You're talking about mixing a liquid or a solid like a sludge or something like this with the soil? I haven't any experience in this area at all. The area I've worked in is where we were working with the liquid waste and applying them at the surface.

Walker, John: Following up a comment that was made earlier, can you only irrigate pretty clean effluent and do you have to go to a flooding system to put down more dirty effluent? Is there a criterion on that or is this a point of argument?

Thomas: I would say it's a point of argument, but from the standpoint of the soil as a physical filter the dirtier the effluent or the more solids that it carries will limit the hydraulic load that you can put on and keep the system going for a long period of time. You can use a high quality effluent and go to the infiltration approach if it's advantageous for your area. In certain climatic regions you can manage to go as high as 300 feet per year, using the soil as a treatment media. This is opposed to the irrigation approach where you may go in the range of a few feet up to as much as six or seven feet a year.

Kotyk: I'm wondering if you were able to determine the distribution of water? Such as infiltration into the soil and evaporation and evapotransporation. Were you able to determine this at all?

Thomas: We did it on one type of system, which we haven't even talked about and I guess we won't during this meeting, that's the spray run off system on a heavy soil. The particular system that we studied was located in northeast Texas, with an annual rainfall of about 45 inches, and a potential evaporation something slightly more than that. In this particular case, the distribution was about 20 percent percolating down through the soil, about 20 percent loss by evaporation and about 60 percent coming as a direct runoff to the surface stream. Now this balance will be directly dependent on the geographical location and the type of system that you are designing or using.

Kotyk: Are there many systems where evaporation is the prime mode of disposal of water?

Thomas: I would say in general that with the irrigation systems in the south-western United States the amount of the water that is lost through evaporation is pretty substantial.

Vhora: What depth of water did you put on the surface and what was the depth of the filter? I mean physical soil filter.

Thomas: These details will be covered in a later paper by Dr. Bouwer.

Tarquin: Given that you need a drying period if you want to dispose of one inch of water, do you have any idea whether it would be better to put it on in one minute and dry it for 24 hours or put it on in three hours and dry for 21 or put it on for 12 and dry for 12?

Thomas: There's no general set rule on this. It depends on the strength of the waste and the soil and the site. Generally we would recommend at least several hours for application time. At the state of the art where we are now you'd have to do a feasibility study concerning the best management.

4
The Soil as a Chemical Filter

Boyd G. Ellis*

The soil has many times been referred to as "the living filter." But it serves as a chemical filter as well through the many organic and inorganic chemical reactions which occur when wastewater passes through the soil profile. In addition, the soil may chemically alter many of the materials which have been introduced into the profile by the addition of either wastewater or sludge. These alterations may lessen the environmental impact (for example, through conversion of organic materials to carbon dioxide thereby reducing the biological oxygen demand carried in the water) or may increase the environmental hazard (for example, through the conversion of organic nitrogen to nitrate, a much more hazardous material). Therefore, it is imperative that the soil chemistry be thoroughly understood and the various reactions used to optimize the "system" when applying waste to land so that environmental hazards will be at an absolute minimum.

In addition to purification of the wastewater passing through the soil profile, the accumulation of ions or compounds in the soil must not leave a residue which is harmful to either plant growth or to the animal or human consuming the crop. Our soil is a very precious resource. It must not be sacrificed in an effort to clean up our water resources.

The areas of soil chemistry which are of most importance for the soil to act as a chemical filter are: (1) ion exchange, (2) adsorption and precipitation, and (3) chemical alteration. The following discussion will include the theory of each process and the importance of each process to waste disposal systems.

Ion Exchange

The process that we now refer to as "ion exchange" was discovered in England in 1852 by a Yorkshire farmer, Thomas Way, when he found that the addition of soil to manure reduced the loss of ammonia (Tisdale and Nelson, 1956). Thus, the science of using the ion exchange properties of the soil for improving the environment had an

*Department of Crop and Soil Sciences, Michigan State University.

early beginning. We now define *ion exchange* as the reversible process by which cations and anions are exchanged between solid and liquid phases and between solid phases if in close contact with each other (Wiklander, 1964). It is more common to differentiate between cation and anion exchange since cation exchange is the dominant process in soils.

Several forms of chemical bonding may occur between ions and the solid phase of the soil during the process of ion exchange. They range from electrostatic to covalent in nature. When the bonding between ions and the solid phase is largely covalent in nature, the binding is generally more specific for the ion involved and not reversible to other ions of similar charge. Consequently, this type of binding is not truly exchangeable and will be covered as an adsorption reaction. Generally, the ion exchange reactions that we will consider here will be electrostatic and influenced by the valence and hydration of the ion involved and the location and density of the charge on the solid component of the soil.

The charge on the solid phase of the soil system may arise from several sources. First, isomorphous substitution occurs in many of the layer silicate minerals. Substitutions of aluminum for silicon or one of several divalent ions (Fe^{++} and Mg^{++}, for example) for aluminum will give rise to a negative charge site in the mineral. The strength of charge will also depend upon the location; *i.e.,* if isomorphous substitution occurs in the tetrahedral layer, the attraction to exchangeable ions will be stronger than if the substitution occurs in the octahedral layer. For a more complete discussion of clay mineral structure, the reader is referred to *Clay Mineralogy* by Grim (1953) or *The X-ray Identification and Crystal Structures of Clay Minerals* edited by Brown (1961). Secondly, SiOH and AlOH groups from exposed surfaces (generally edges) of clay minerals and hydroxides of iron, aluminum and magnesium either as coatings or gels are capable of yielding exchange sites upon dissociation. Thirdly, soil organic matter constituents were very early recognized as having a high cation exchange capacity (McGeorge, 1930; Mitchell, 1932). Organic exchange sites develop from dissociation of acidic functional groups, of which carboxyl is quantitatively most important. In addition, a broad spectrum of acidic hydroxyls (phenolic, enolic) and tautomeric pseudo-acids involving nitrogen in appropriate structural configurations is likely involved (Broadbent and Bradford, 1952; Stevenson and Butler, 1969).

A portion of the cation exchange sites is known to vary with pH. Normally the SiOH groups will give rise to negative sites; but AlOH and FeOH can yield positive sites at low pH values (Fried and

Broeshart, 1967). Thus, the decrease in net negative charge below pH 6.0 may not be an actual decrease of the negative charge but an increase in the positive charge (Wiklander, 1964). All sites originating from organic materials are expected to be pH dependent. The pK value of carboxyl groups is such that complete dissociation is expected by pH 7.0. Most other organic acidic groups would require higher pH values for complete dissociation. Soil clays containing pedogenically chloritized 2:1 layer silicates were shown to develop a proportionately large increment of cation exchange capacity after brief contact with 2 percent sodium carbonate (pH 11) according to de Villiers and Jackson (1967a, 1967b). They suggested that the mechanism accounting for the pH dependent, hysteretic cation exchange charge of the mineral portion of many soils was deprotonation of the positive hydroxy alumina in aluminated soils, clays and allophane.

The ions adsorbed by exchange sites may form a diffuse double layer where the concentration of the ions will decrease exponentially with the distance from the clay surface. Fried and Broeshart (1967) state that it is unlikely that the adsorption of anions to soil constituents will have the nature of a double layer. Although solutions for cation distribution with distance from the clay surface may be obtained by combination of Boltzmann's law with Poisson's equation, the complex nature of the cation exchange system in natural soils makes this solution little more than a rough approximation. The thickness of the double layer for a given soil will be a function of valence of the exchangeable cation and total ionic strength of the solution. In addition, Shainberg and Kemper (1966) have shown that the hydration status of the exchangeable cation also affects the double layer.

Gieseking and Jenny (1936) showed experimentally that soil clays attract individual cations with different binding strengths. In general, the greater the valence the more strongly the cation was bound. But, in addition, rather large differences were found within cations of the same valence. For example, potassium was bound much more strongly than sodium. They also found considerable hysteresis (reported earlier by Vanselow, 1932) particularly in reactions involving monovalent-divalent exchange. Several methods of accounting for unequal bonding energies have evolved and are adequately summarized by Marshall (1964).

By far the most studied exchange reaction has been that of sodium for calcium. This reaction has been particularly important in irrigation of soils because of the unfavorable soil structure which will develop if the cation exchange complex becomes sufficiently saturated with sodium so that dispersion of the soil occurs. Sodium-adsorption ratios

$$\left[SAR = Na^+ \bigg/ \sqrt{(Ca^{++} + Mg^{++})/2} \right]$$

have been used for a long time to evaluate the possible hazards of irrigation water (Richards, 1954). Anions which may precipitate either calcium or magnesium will also influence the sodium-adsorption ratios. Eaton (1950) introduced terms to correct the soluble-sodium percentage in soils for the precipitation of calcium and magnesium by carbonate and bicarbonate. Longenecker (1960) reported that sulfate reacted differently than either nitrate or chloride in soil systems. Thus, sodium sulfate salts replaced appreciably more magnesium than did the sodium salt of either nitrate or chloride. These observations have been confirmed by later work (Pratt, Branson and Chapman, 1960; Babcock and Schulz, 1963; Bower and Wilcox, 1965; Bower et al., 1965; Arshad and Carson, 1967; Rao, Page and Coleman, 1968; Bower, Ogata and Tucker, 1968; and Pratt and Bair, 1969). It is, therefore, necessary to consider both the anions and cations involved in cation exchange reactions for accurate evaluations.

Ideally, equations could be developed which would predict accurately the exchange which would occur when a given set of parameters is involved through the addition of wastewater. The first attempt was made by Kerr (1928) who introduced equations based on the law of mass action. A summary of this and other equations which have been developed since then is given in Table 4-1 (adapted from Fried and Broeshart, 1967). Generally speaking, no one equation has been successful if applied to widely varying conditions. All have been found to vary with soil series and most vary appreciably with the particular ion pair involved in the exchange. Nevertheless, they do serve an important function since the particular K may be experimentally determined in the laboratory for a given region and set of parameters. This concept has been very successfully applied to predicting the effects of applying irrigation waters to soils.

Effect of Wastewater Applications on Exchangeable Cations in Soils

For the purposes of illustration, an example will be considered for two effluents with the following composition: (1) Na = 152 ppm, Ca = 36 ppm, and Mg = 16 ppm; (2) Na = 47 ppm, Ca = 33 ppm, and Mg = 19 ppm. It will also be assumed that they will be applied to a Conover loam soil. Initially, a Michigan Conover loam contained 15.8 me Ca/100 g, 2.1 me Mg/100 g and 0.14 me Na/100 g. The SAR for

Table 4-1. Summary of ion exchange equations used in soil science laboratories (from Fried and Broeshart, 1967)

Common Name	Equation	Reference
Donnan	$\dfrac{A^+\ \text{Soil}}{\sqrt{C^{++}\ \text{Soil}}} \cdot \dfrac{\sqrt{C^{++}}}{A^+} = 1$	Vageler and Woltersdorf (1930)
Mass action	$\dfrac{A^+\ \text{Soil}}{\sqrt{C^{++}\ \text{Soil}}} \cdot \dfrac{\sqrt{C^{++}}}{A^+} = K$	Kerr (1928)
Gapon-Schofield-Eriksson-Bolt	$\dfrac{A^+\ \text{Soil}}{C^{++}\ \text{Soil}} \cdot \dfrac{\sqrt{C^{++}}}{A^+} = K_1$	Gapon (1933); Eriksson (1952); Schofield (1947); Bolt and Peech (1953)
Langmuir	$\dfrac{\sqrt{A^+\ \text{Soil}}}{\sqrt{2C^{++}\ \text{Soil}}} \cdot \dfrac{\sqrt{C^{++}}}{A^+} = b_1/b_2 = K_4$	Boyd et al. (1947)
Vanselow	$\dfrac{A^+\ \text{Soil}}{\sqrt{C^{++}\text{Soil}\,(C^{++}\text{soil} + A^+\text{soil})}} \cdot \dfrac{\sqrt{C^{++}}}{A^+} = K_2$	Vanselow (1932); Krishnamoorthy and Overstreet (1950)
Statistical	$\dfrac{A^+\ \text{Soil}}{\sqrt{C^{++}\text{Soil}\,(1\frac{1}{2}\,C^{++}\text{soil} + A^+\ \text{soil})}}$ $\dfrac{\sqrt{C^{++}}}{A^+} = K_2$	Krishnamoorthy et al. (1948); Krishnamoorthy and Overstreet (1950)

effluent number 1 is 5.3 and for effluent number 2 it is 1.62. Using the USDA salinity handbook, the estimated equilibrium exchangeable-sodium percentage would be 6.0 and 1.0, respectively. Thus, after prolonged irrigation with effluent number 1, this Conover soil would be expected to increase in exchangeable sodium percentage from 0.8 to 6 percent or from 0.14 me Na/100 g to 1.08. With effluent number 2 it would increase from 0.8 to 1 percent or from 0.14 to 0.18 me Na/100 g. As previously pointed out, the exact exchange constants would have to be determined for the soil and effluent under consideration to yield precise values. But it would appear that normal effluents would not lead to excessive levels of exchangeable sodium in most soils.

Generally, exchangeable sodium percentages greater than 15 percent would be considered very serious. Even lower values may seriously impede infiltration rates and percolation rates of water particularly in fine textured soils. It is calculated that effluent number 1 above could not tolerate more than 430 ppm sodium, and effluent number 2 more than 390 ppm sodium before the soil structure would degrade to the point of restricting water movement. Although considerably higher than normally found in effluents, these values could easily be attained under certain circumstances.

The effect of SAR and clay content of soils on hydraulic conductivity is shown by data from McNeal and Coleman (1966) and McNeal et al. (1968). At salt concentrations of 12.5 me/l and lower, the relative soil hydraulic conductivity dropped to near zero for all soils having clay contents greater than 25 percent if the SAR was greater than 50. Sandy soils with less than 5 percent clay showed only about 25 percent reduction in hydraulic conductivity even at these extreme sodium contents. Although less drastic in the effect on soil structure than sodium, other monovalent ions such as potassium or lithium will also lead to reduced infiltration rates and hydraulic conductivities.

Although they did not report SAR values or exchangeable sodium, data by Day, Stroehlein and Tucker (1972) do show the effects of irrigation with wastewater on infiltration rate. After 14 years of irrigation with wastewater at a rate recommended by agriculturalists for crop production, the infiltration rate for the areas irrigated with wastewater was 1.52 cm/hr compared with 1.91 for other areas irrigated with well water and fertilized with inorganic fertilizers. The soluble salt was 1.77 mmhos/cm $\times 10^3$ compared with 0.88 for the comparable treatments suggesting that this reduced infiltration rate was the result of accumulation of soluble salts, presumably sodium. Their data for the sodium, calcium and magnesium contents of sewage effluent were used previously for my example calculation number one of SAR values from effluents which indicated that only 6 percent exchangeable sodium should result from use of this effluent. But even this amount was sufficient to significantly reduce the infiltration rate. Secondly, it must be remembered that they applied the wastewater at a rate recommended for crop irrigation and not the maximum quantity that could be applied to soils. This reduction in infiltration rate could be attained much more quickly if higher application rates are used.

Adsorption and Precipitation Reactions

Adsorption
Although theoretically adsorption and precipitation reactions differ, they have sufficient similarities to merit their consideration under the

same general topic. Adsorption is defined as the adhesion, in an extremely thin layer, of gas molecules, dissolved substances or liquids to the surface of solids with which they are in contact. Precipitation is a term used to denote a rapid crystallization of a product of chemical reaction which is only slightly soluble in the medium in which it is formed. Adsorption differs from precipitation in that one component of the chemical reaction is already a solid. Although adsorption of gases may be an asset in spreading wastewater onto soils since the soil will eliminate many odors by this mechanism, the remaining discussion will be restricted to adsorption of ions and/or molecules from solution onto solids and the precipitation of certain chemicals in the soil. The ions of particular interest will be phosphorus, boron, sulfate and certain of the heavy metals. This does not imply that other ions or compounds may not be removed from wastewater by a similar mechanism.

Two commonly used adsorption isotherms to quantitatively describe adsorption of ions from solution onto solids are the Freundlich isotherm ($x/m = kC^{1/n}$; where x/m = the quantity of ions adsorbed per unit weight of adsorber, C = the equilibrium concentration of the adsorbate after adsorption has occurred, k = a constant, and n = a constant) and the Langmuir adsorption isotherm

$$\frac{(M)}{x/m} = \frac{1}{Kb} + \frac{(M)}{b}$$

where M = the activity of the ion in moles per liter, x/m = meq of ion M adsorbed per 100 g of adsorber, K = a constant related to bonding energy, and b = the maximum amount of ion M in meq/100 g that will be adsorbed by a given adsorber. There have been many reports concerning the applicability of both isotherms to adsorption in soils. These are summarized by Ellis and Knezek (1972).

Using the Langmuir adsorption isotherm in studying the soil's ability to adsorb ions from wastewater has several distinct advantages. First, from laboratory measurements that are easily made an adsorption maximum can be predicted. When both the adsorption maximum and K are determined, predictions can be made of the quantity of the particular ion that will be adsorbed for any input level. One disadvantage of the use of adsorption isotherms is that they give little information concerning the mechanisms of adsorption of the ions being studied.

Considerable attention has been given to the necessity to introduce some corrections into experimental data from adsorption isotherms (see Fried and Broeshart, 1967, for a summary). If appreciable quantities of the ion under study are already adsorbed on the surface, this will cause an underestimation of x/m which leads to underestimation of both the adsorption maximum and the constant K. The amount initially adsorbed on the surface has been shown to be accurately estimated by radioisotopic exchange techniques; thus, a separate determination of the already surface adsorbed ion can be made and added to the quantity of x/m determined for the adsorption isotherm. The fact that the correction has made relatively small differences in many instances (*i.e.,* less than 10 percent correction in the adsorption maximum for the data of Olsen and Watanabe, 1957) has led many researchers to the use of uncorrected data. This should only be done if it is known that the correction is small. Otherwise, serious errors will occur especially in the low range of the adsorption isotherm.

The determination of the adsorption of an anion should contain a correction for negative adsorption (anion repulsion). A discussion of this correction is given by de Haan and Bolt (1963). In general, it has been ignored in determining adsorption isotherms but this may lead to serious errors.

Phosphate Adsorption
The Langmuir adsorption isotherm has been applied to phosphorus adsorption in soils by Fried and Shapiro (1956), Olsen and Watanabe (1957), and Ellis and Erickson (1969). Values determined for adsorption maxima were generally similar. The data given in Table 4-2 were extracted from the report by Ellis and Erickson as examples of the effect of soil series and horizon on the constants from the Langmuir adsorption isotherm. Since the maximum quantity of adsorption would not be reached except for very high levels of phosphorus in solution, the percentage of the adsorption maximum that will be saturated at 10 ppm phosphorus in solution was calculated and the total pounds of phosphorus that could be adsorbed per acre foot for each horizon were calculated assuming that the bulk density of A horizons would be 1.33 g/cm^3 and that of B and C horizons would be 1.5 g/cm^3. The minimum adsorption was found in the dune sand which would adsorb only 77 pounds of phosphorus per acre foot and the maximum was for the Warsaw loam which would adsorb on the average over 900 pounds of phosphorus per acre foot. The effect of horizon is very great and is perhaps best illustrated by the data for the Rubicon sand. The A horizons adsorb a little more than 100 pounds phosphorus per acre foot. But the B horizon will adsorb more than 700 pounds of phosphorus per acre foot. The C horizon is intermediate. This correlated well with the quantity of iron in the profile in that iron has moved from the A horizon to the B horizon during the soil development making the B horizon the zone of iron accumulation. This increased iron content then accounts for the increased phosphorus adsorption by the B horizon. The high values for adsorption of

Table 4-2. Phosphorus adsorption by soils as predicted by Langmuir adsorption isotherms (data from Ellis and Erickson, 1969)

Soil Series	Texture	Horizon	$K \times 10^{-4}$	Adsorption Maximum	Adsorption at 10 ppm P % of Maximum	Amount
				mg P/100 g	%	lbs/acre-ft
Dune Sand	Sand	—	4.50	1.89	94	77
Rubicon	Sand	A_1	.77	4.23	71	108
	Sand	A_2	1.98	3.87	86	120
	Sand	B	3.99	19.27	93	731
	Sand	C	5.78	10.75	95	416
Warsaw	Loam	A_1	2.96	18.5	90	602
	Loam	B_1	3.73	40.6	92	1,523
	Clay loam	B_{21}	5.83	49.0	95	1,898
	Clay loam	B_{22}	5.20	22.4	94	858
	Gravelly clay loam	B_{23}	5.92	11.0	95	426
	Sand and Gravel	D	5.45	4.6	95	178

the Warsaw loam are apparently accounted for by a high aluminum content of this particular soil.

It is of particular interest to note that the adsorption capacity of a soil may be recovered once saturated. Ellis and Erickson (1969) found that most soils recovered in about three months once they were saturated. The number of times this saturation and recovery cycle can be completed in a soil is unknown. However, Blanchar and Kao (1972) reported that the adsorption capacity of a Mexico soil changed little after 82 years of phosphate fertilization on the Sanborn field at Columbia, Missouri.

Shapiro and Fried (1959) derived an equation describing phosphate adsorption as primarily a mass action equation by assuming that phosphate adsorption was primarily an exchange with another ion such as hydroxyl. Their data indicated that their equation was valid but that two distinct regions of adsorption occurred, one corresponding to low levels of phosphorus (*i.e.*, less than 1 ppm P in solution) and the other describing adsorption at much higher levels. Their equation is: $P(solid) = -K_p P (solid)/p + P (solid)_{max}$. This equation reduces to the Langmuir adsorption equation if the following identities are made: $P(solid) = x/m$; $K_p = 1/K_{Langmuir}$; $p = (M)$; and $P(solid)_{max} = b$.

Sulfate Adsorption

The adsorption of sulfate by soils is of less interest in applying wastewaters so it will be only briefly reviewed here. Chao, Harward and Fang (1962 and 1963) reported that sulfate adsorption by soils could be described by the Freundlich isotherm. The sulfate retained was in kinetic equilibrium with sulfate in solution. Several factors affected the adsorption including the cation accompanying the sulfate and the cation that was the exchangeable cation. As neutrality was approached, sulfate adsorption decreased considerably regardless of the type of saturating cation. Bornemisza and Llanos (1967) reported that the presence of phosphates enhanced slightly the movement of sulfate. They found no adsorption maxima even at high applications of sulfate. Aylmore, Karim and Quirk (1967) found that sulfate adsorption conformed to a Langmuir-type equation but that more than one region of adsorption existed. Barrow (1967) also found that sulfate adsorption did not always fit a Langmuir isotherm. Hasan, Fox and Boyd (1970) found adsorption maxima for several surface soils developed from volcanic ash varied from 80 to 1,500 mg S/1000 g soil. Barrow (1970) reported that the ratio of sulfate:phosphate adsorbed by soils increased three-fold as the soil pH decreased from 6 to 4. It would be concluded from this that sulfate adsorption would not be at its maximum at the pH of most wastewater.

Boron Adsorption

The adsorption of boron by soils has been recently reviewed by Ellis and Knezek (1972). Boron adsorption has been described by the Langmuir adsorption equation (Biggar and Fireman, 1960; Hingston, 1964; Hatcher and Bower, 1958). But the Langmuir adsorption equation appears to be valid only over certain limited concentrations. A development of particular interest to application of wastewater was made when several researchers (Thomas, 1944; Hiester and Vermeulen, 1952; and Vermeulen and Hiester, 1959) developed equations describing adsorption and desorption of boron during the flow of solutions through columns of exchangers where the adsorption equilibrium can be expressed by Langmuir's adsorption equation. Application of these equations to predict boron removal from soils by leaching was made by Hatcher and Bower (1958). It has been reported by Rhoades, Ingvalson, and Hatcher (1970a) that the Langmuir desorption theory underestimated the quantity of leaching required to elute toxic levels of soluble boron from soils. But, on the other hand, Tanji (1970) found good agreement and found that the chromatographic equations together with the Langmuir isotherm were adequate.

Soils chemically filter boron from solution by four mechanisms. First, iron and aluminum hydroxy compounds present in soils as coatings on or associated with clay minerals adsorb boron (Hatcher, Bower, and Clark, 1967; Sims and Bingham, 1968a,b). Secondly, iron or aluminum oxides will adsorb large quantities of boron (Scharrer, Kühn, and Lüttmer, 1956). Third, clay minerals, and particularly micaceous-type clay minerals, will absorb boron into their lattice (Couch and Grim, 1968; Fleet, 1965; and Sims and Bingham, 1967). This absorption is suggested to begin with chemical adsorption of $B(OH)_4^-$ at the tetrahedral portion of the edge of an illite flake. The anion gains stability by forming a weak ionic bond with the net positive charge expected at the mineral's edge. The second step is solid diffusion of boron into the interior of the crystal through crystal defects. Finally, magnesium-hydroxy clusters or coatings that exist on the weathering surfaces of ferromagnesium minerals have recently been shown to adsorb boron by bonding through the hydroxyl groups paralleling the bonding by iron and aluminum hydroxides (Rhoades, Ingvalson, and Hatcher, 1970b).

Heavy Metal Adsorption

The adsorption of zinc, copper, iron and manganese by soils was reviewed by Ellis and Knezek (1972). In addition, many other heavy metals, for example, nickel, chromium, cadmium, lead, mercury and cobalt, may enter into wastewater as a discharge from industry. The effects of these heavy metals are largely unknown. For those metals studied, a small fraction of the metal added appears to be bound very tightly to specific sites in the soils. These reactions for cobalt have been reported by Hodgson (1960); Hodgson and Tiller (1961); Hodgson, Geering and Fellows (1964); and Hodgson, Tiller and Fellows (1969). Zinc adsorption has been shown to be related to silicic acid by Tiller (1967). Sharpless, Wallihan and Peterson (1969) found that large quantities of zinc were rapidly adsorbed as an exchangeable cation. This was followed by a slow conversion to a non-exchangeable acid soluble form of zinc but the rate of conversion varied greatly from soil to soil. Zinc adsorption was described by the Langmuir adsorption equation by Udo, Bohn, and Tucker (1970). At moderately high levels of zinc they found that zinc was precipitated as zinc hydroxide, a subject to be discussed later in this paper. Although it was shown that adsorption of zinc was described by a Langmuir adsorption isotherm, insufficient data are now present to warrant the conclusion that the Langmuir isotherm can be used to describe adsorption of heavy metals by a wide range of soils.

Precipitation Reactions in Soils
Many of the ion species introduced in wastewater may combine with other ions in the soil solution to produce an insoluble product. If a stable, solid phase is formed, the levels of ions left in solution may be described by a solubility product. Consider the following general reaction:

$$aA + bB \ldots \rightleftharpoons lL + mM + \ldots$$

If the law of mass action is obeyed, the rate of the forward and reverse reactions will be given by:

$$\text{Rate forward} = k_f(A)^a(B)^b. \ldots \quad \text{and}$$
$$\text{Rate reverse} = k_r(L)^l(M)^m \ldots$$

The activities of each component in equations above are given by (A), (B), (L), and (M). The rate of the forward and the reverse reaction must be equal at equilibrium; therefore:

$$k_f(A)^a(B)^b \ldots = k_r(L)^l(M)^m. \ldots$$

The equilibrium constant is then given by

$$K_{eq} = k_f/k_r = \frac{(L)^l(M)^m}{(A)^a(B)^b}$$

For the specific case of the solubility product, the activity of the solid phase is assumed to be one (or not to change) and the equation reduced to:

$$K_{so} = (L)^l(M)^m \ldots$$

Solubility products have been applied to studies of soil phosphorus in many different ways. Schofield (1955) and Aslying (1954) have suggested that soil phosphorus could be characterized by the use of "lime-phosphate potentials" or the chemical potential of monocalcium phosphate. Utilizing this principle, a plot of $1/2pCa + pH_2PO_4$ as determined in a 0.01 N $CaCl_2$ solution against $pH - 1/2pCa$ should define the values of phosphorus in solution for any soil. These potentials have been measured and reported by many investigators (Henze, 1963; Ulrich, 1961; Mattingly et al., 1963; Gough and Beaton, 1963; Scheffer and Ulrich, 1960; and White and Beckett, 1964). It can be easily shown that the lime-phosphate potentials are really a rearrangement of solubility products.

Lindsay and Moreno (1960) prepared a solubility phase diagram relating pH and pH_2PO_4 to the solubility of the common phosphate minerals found in soils. While their diagram does show the points of maximum H_2PO_4 in solution under the conditions of their assumptions and point out vividly the effects of soil pH on phosphate solubility, it is also quite similar to the lime-phosphate potentials since both originate from the same solubility products.

In acid soils, points for phosphate potentials many times do not fall on solubility lines for calcium phosphates. Clark and Peech (1955) suggested the use of aluminum phosphate solubility diagrams (or iron phosphate) for acid soils and showed that experimental data fit these rather well.

Many of the heavy metals have quite insoluble hydroxides. It would be expected that heavy applications of these metals would result in saturation of adsorption sites and rapidly lead to precipitation. Table 4-3 gives solubility products from some of the compounds which might be expected to form in soils. Even though these hydroxides are very insoluble, other even more insoluble compounds may exist in soils. For example, zinc hydroxide would give 3.2 ppm zinc in solution at a pH of 8.0. But Lindsay and Norvell (1969) reported that less than 0.01 ppb Zn was actually found. The form of zinc that is controlling this low solubility is not known (Norvell and Lindsay, 1970).

Chemical Alteration of Waste

The soil not only chemically filters but chemically alters components of wastewater and sludge which it contacts. Thus, to effectively

Table 4-3. Solubility product constants for selected compounds

Chemical Formula	Solubility Expression	Solubility Product Constant
$CdCO_3$	$CdCO_3 = Cd^{++} + CO_3^{--}$	5.2×10^{-12}
$CaCO_3$	$CaCO_3 = Ca^{++} + CO_3^{--}$	6.9×10^{-5}
$CoCO_3$	$CoCO_3 = Co^{++} + CO_3^{--}$	8×10^{-13}
$CuCO_3$	$CuCO_3 = Cu^{++} + CO_3^{--}$	2.5×10^{-10}
$PbCO_3$	$PbCO_3 = Pb^{++} + CO_3^{--}$	1.5×10^{-13}
Hg_2Cl_2	$Hg_2Cl_2 = Hg_2^{+} + 2Cl^-$	1.1×10^{-14}
$Al(OH)_3$	$Al(OH)_3 = Al^{+++} + 3OH^-$	5×10^{-33}
$Cd(OH)_2$	$Cd(OH)_2 = Cd^{++} + 2OH^-$	2.0×10^{-14}
$Cr(OH)_3$	$Cr(OH)_3 = Cr^{+++} + 3OH^-$	7×10^{-31}
$Co(OH)_2$	$Co(OH)_2 = Co^{++} + 2OH^-$	2.5×10^{-16}
$Cu(OH)_2$	$Cu(OH)_2 = Cu^{++} + 2OH^-$	1.6×10^{-19}
$Fe(OH)_3$	$Fe(OH)_3 = Fe^{+++} + 3OH^-$	6×10^{-35}
$Fe(OH)_2$	$Fe(OH)_2 = Fe^{++} + 2OH^-$	2×10^{-15}
$Pb(OH)_2$	$Pb(OH)_2 = Pb^{++} + 2OH^-$	4×10^{-15}
$Mg(OH)_2$	$Mg(OH)_2 = Mg^{++} + 2OH^-$	8.9×10^{-12}
$Mn(OH)_2$	$Mn(OH)_2 = Mn^{++} + 2OH^-$	2×10^{-13}
$Hg(OH)_2$	$Hg(OH)_2 = Hg^{++} + 2OH^-$	3×10^{-26}
$Ni(OH)_2$	$Ni(OH)_2 = Ni^{++} + 2OH^-$	1.6×10^{-16}
$Zn(OH)_2$	$Zn(OH)_2 = Zn^{++} + 2OH^-$	5×10^{-17}
$CaSO_4$	$CaSO_4 = Ca^{++} + SO_4^{--}$	2.4×10^{-6}
CdS	$CdS = Cd^{++} + S^{--}$	6×10^{-27}
CoS	$CoS = Co^{++} + S^{--}$	5×10^{-22}
CuS	$CuS = Cu^{++} + S^{--}$	4×10^{-36}
PbS	$PbS = Pb^{++} + S^{--}$	4×10^{-26}
MnS	$MnS = Mn^{++} + S^{--}$	8×10^{-14}
HgS	$HgS = Hg^{++} + S^{--}$	1×10^{-60}
NiS	$NiS = Ni^{++} + S^{--}$	1×10^{-22}
ZnS	$ZnS = Zn^{++} + S^{--}$	1×10^{-20}
$AlPO_4 \cdot H_2O$	$AlPO_4 \rightleftharpoons Al^{+3} + PO_4^{-3}$	3×10^{-23}
$FePO_4 \cdot H_2O$	$FePO_4 \rightleftharpoons Fe^{+3} + PO_4^{-3}$	1×10^{-26}
$Ca_4(PO_4)_3$	$Ca_4H(PO_4)_3 = 4Ca^{2+} + H^+ + 3PO_4^{3-}$	1×10^{-47}
$Ca_{10}(PO_4)_6F_2$	$Ca_{10}(PO_4)_6F_2 = 10Ca^{2+} + 6PO_4^{3-} + 2F^-$	4×10^{-119}
$Ca_{10}(PO_4)_6(OH)_2$	$Ca_{10}(PO_4)_6(OH)_2 = 10Ca^{2+} + 6PO_4^{3-} + 2OH^-$	2×10^{-114}

understand the chemical filtration which will occur, one must also consider the changes in chemical compounds which will occur.

Wastewater and sludge materials contain many organic compounds. These organic compounds may be adsorbed by clay materials in the soil which will retard their microbiological breakdown. The nature of clay-organic complexes and reactions has been reviewed by Mortland (1970) and will not be covered here. Microorganisms will decompose the organic materials with the release of carbon dioxide and other simple compounds or ions. Organic nitrogen is released during this process as ammonia or ammonium ions. Under well aerated conditions, this ammonia will be rapidly oxidized by microorganisms to nitrate nitrogen. Both organic nitrogen and ammonium will be retained in the soil to a large extent. But nitrate nitrogen is susceptible to rapid leaching and would be expected to rapidly move into ground water or surface drainage, whichever the case may be. Under proper conditions, nitrate nitrogen will be denitrified and released back to the atmosphere in a gaseous form. This requires that the nitrate nitrogen move into an anaerobic zone with sufficient carbon as an energy source and the correct microbial population. Although this occurs occasionally in nature — in fact, denitrification is quite common in nature but only occasionally are conditions correct for nearly total denitrification of the nitrate present — the soil can be modified to favor this reaction. Thus, Erickson *et al.* (1971, 1972) produced a barriered landscape water renovation system designed to optimize this reaction. They reported more than 95 percent removal of nitrogen during the initial stages of operation.

It should be pointed out that the total nitrogen content of wastewater is usually sufficiently low that it is not likely to exceed drinking water standards for nitrate content after passing through a soil profile unless there is an input of nitrogen from another source.

Oxidation-Reduction

Oxidation is defined as the loss of electrons and reduction as the gain of electrons. When both oxidizing and reducing agents are present in the same solution the reaction will proceed until the rate of oxidation is equal to the rate of reduction and no further net change occurs.

If the following general reaction

$$aA + bB \ldots \rightleftharpoons lL \qquad mM \ldots$$

occurs in a reversible cell with e.m.f. equal to E, the free energy change is $\Delta G_r = -NFE$ for the passage of N faradays. Making substitutions into the general form for the standard free energy of a reaction yields:

$$E = E° - \frac{RT}{nF} \ln \frac{(L)^l(M)^m \ldots}{(A)^a(B)^b \ldots}$$

Although theoretically the redox potential can be measured and then the quantity of any species in solution as a function of pH and redox calculated, in practice with soils and soil solution this has not proven very successful. Bohn (1968) examined the e.m.f. of gold, graphite, and platinum electrodes in soil suspensions and concluded that gold and graphite were not useful. The platinum electrodes responded to aeration conditions, but he could not deduce a quantitative significance of his measurements to the Nernstian distribution of oxidized and reduced species.

The oxidation-reduction status of many soils will likely change under conditions of heavy application of wastewater and/or sludge materials. Reducing conditions can occur rapidly and high loading with organic materials will intensify reducing conditions.

Many chemical constituents will undergo chemical alteration because of the change in oxidation status. The reduction of nitrate nitrogen has already been discussed. Patrick (1960), in controlled redox experiments, found that nitrate nitrogen began to disappear from his soil system for redox potentials less than 300 mv. The rate of disappearance increased with decreasing redox potential so that 50 ppm nitrate nitrogen disappeared when the redox was − 100 mv as compared to 20 ppm loss for a redox of 250 mv and no change for a redox of 300 mv.

Phosphorus will also respond to changes in redox. Patrick (1964) reported that below 200 mv redox potential the extractable phosphorus increased greatly. More than threefold increases in extractable phosphorus were found when the redox was − 200 mv as compared to 200 mv. The sharp break in the phosphate release curve at 200 mv, the same point at which ferric iron begins to be reduced, indicates that the conversion of phosphorus to an extractable form is dependent upon the reduction of ferric compounds in the soil. Although limited data are available, it is expected that soil under reducing conditions would not adsorb as much phosphorus as the same soil in a well aerated condition nor would the level of phosphorus in solution be maintained at as low a level.

In addition to iron mentioned above, manganese will reduce from plus four to plus two in soils with a low redox potential. Bricker (1965) developed phase diagrams to predict manganous ion levels as a function of pH and redox potential. But Bohn (1970) found that soils with pH values less than 7.0 did not contain sufficient manganese to yield the levels of manganese in solution that were predicted.

Effect of Wastewater Applications on Phosphorus

Most wastewater is expected to contain approximately 10 ppm of total phosphorus. It is probably present in wastewater as orthophosphate, condensed phosphates and organic forms. The latter forms of phosphorus should degrade to orthophosphate rapidly in soils if not in the preliminary wastewater treatment (Murrmann and Koutz, 1972). Soils should rapidly adsorb phosphorus until their adsorbing capacity is reached. Actually, as pointed out in Table 4-2, not all of the adsorption capacity is expected to be used at the levels of phosphorus in wastewater.

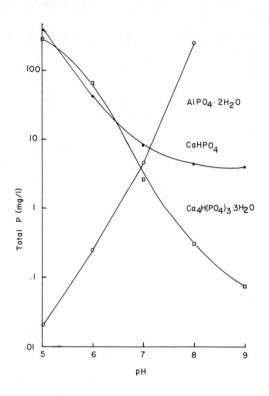

Figure 4-1. Quantity of total phosphorus in solution as a function of pH

Phosphorus compounds can precipitate in the soil. Figure 4-1 illustrates the levels of phosphorus left in solution as a function of pH. These values were found by using solubility product data from Table 4-3 and calculating total phosphate in solution by use of the Debye-Hückel equation for estimating the activity of the individual ion species in an ionic strength of 0.01 molar calcium chloride solution. The activity of the calcium ion was assumed to be $10^{-2.5}$, and it was assumed that gibbsite controlled the aluminum solubility in soils (Lindsay and Moreno, 1960). It can readily be seen the concentration of phosphorus in solution in soils with a pH less than 6.0 is limited to low levels. But the pH of most wastewaters will be above 7.0 which will cause the soil pH to rise after continued application. For pH values above 7.0, the solubility will be limited by a calcium phosphate. Two compounds are shown in Figure 4-1, dicalcium phosphate and octacalcium phosphate. It is expected that dicalcium phosphate will form rapidly but it will limit phosphorus in solution to only 4 ppm at pH 9.0 and 8.0 ppm at pH 7.0. This would effect a low percentage removal from wastewaters. Octacalcium phosphates are slower to form. They have been found to form in soils from a few weeks to several months. However, if they form in the system they will limit the solubility of phosphates to levels between 0.3 ppm at pH 8.0 and 2.7 ppm at pH 7.0. Other calcium phosphates are much less soluble (*i.e.*, hydroxapatite) but form so slowly in soils that they are not expected to have any effect on the precipitation of phosphorus from wastewater.

Effect of Wastewater Applications on Heavy Metals
If the soil pH is greater than 7.0, a condition expected after prolonged wastewater application, most of the heavy metals will precipitate as a hydroxide or a carbonate. Levels remaining in solution are expected to be quite low.

Either natural or organic chelators would increase the level of many of the heavy metals in solution. This can increase the total concentration of heavy metals in solution by many fold.

Although most of the heavy metals are expected to be retained in the soil by adsorption onto clay surfaces or organic matter or by precipitation, little is known about the effect of these heavy metals on crop growth or quality. Melton, Ellis, and Doll (1970) found that even small applications of zinc to acid soils led to excessive accumulation of zinc by bean plants and markedly reduced yield. This would suggest that the effect of heavy metals on plant growth should be carefully evaluated in wastewater disposal systems. Sludge materials are many times extremely high in heavy metals (Berrow and Webber, 1972). In addition they may contain organic materials capable of chelating these heavy metals which will result in increased uptake by plants and increased leaching through the soil profile. Again, these factors must be carefully considered.

Literature Cited

Arshad, M. A. and J. A. Carson. 1967. Ionic exchange behavior in a loam soil as indicated by movement of radio-calcium. *Soil Sci. Soc. Amer. Proc.* 31:321-324.

Aslying, H. C. 1954. The lime and phosphate potentials of soils, the solubility and availability of phosphates. Royal Vet. Agric. College Copenhagen, Yearbook, 1954, pp. 1-50.

Aylmore, L. A. G., Mesbahul Karim, and J. P. Quirk. 1967. Adsorption and desorption of sulfate ions by soil constituents. *Soil Sci.* 103:10-15.

Babcock, K. L. and R. K. Schulz. 1963. Effect of anions on the sodium-calcium exchange in soils. *Soil Sci. Soc. Amer. Proc.* 27:630-632.

Barrow, N. J. 1967. Studies on the adsorption of sulfate by soils. *Soil Sci.* 104:342-349.

Barrow, N. J. 1970. Comparison of the adsorption of molybdate, sulfate and phosphate by soils. *Soil Sci.* 109:282-288.

Berrow, M. L. and J. Webber. 1972. Trace elements in sewage sludges. *Jour. Sci. Food Agric.* 23:93-100.

Biggar, J. W. and Milton Fireman. 1960. Boron adsorption and release by soils. *Soil Sci. Soc. Amer. Proc.* 24:115-120.

Blanchar, R. W. and Chun Wei Kao. 1972. Distribution and chemistry of phosphorus in a Mexico soil after 82 years of phosphorus fertilization. From M.S. Thesis of Chun Wei Kao (1971), University of Missouri.

Bohn, H. L. 1968. Electromotive force of inert electrodes in soil suspensions. *Soil Sci. Soc. Amer. Proc.* 32:211-215.

Bohn, H. L. 1970. Comparisons of measured and theoretical Mn^{2+} concentrations in soil suspensions. *Soil Sci. Soc. Amer. Proc.* 34:195-197.

Bolt, G. H. and M. Peech. 1953. The application of the Gouy theory to soil water systems. *Soil Sci. Soc. Amer. Proc.* 17:210-213.

Bornemisza, E. and R. Llanos. 1967. Sulfate movement, adsorption, and desorption in three Costa Rican soils. *Soil Sci. Soc. Amer. Proc.* 31:356-360.

Bower, C. A., G. Ogata, and J. M. Tucker. 1968. Sodium hazard of irrigation waters as influenced by leaching fraction and by precipitation or solution of calcium carbonate. *Soil Sci.* 106:29-34.

Bower, C. A. and L. V. Wilcox. 1965. Precipitation and solution of calcium carbonate in irrigation operations. *Soil Sci. Soc. Amer. Proc.* 29:93-94.

Bower, C. A., L. V. Wilcox, G. W. Akin, and Mary G. Keyes. 1965. An index of the tendency of $CaCO_3$ to precipitate from irrigation waters. *Soil Sci. Soc. Amer. Proc.* 29:91-92.

Boyd, G. E., J. Schubert, and A. W. Adamson. 1947. The exchange adsorption of ions from aqueous solutions by organic zeolites. I. Ion exchange equilibria. *Jour. Amer. Chem. Soc.* 69:2818-2829.

Bricker, O. 1965. Some stability relations in the system $Mn-O_2-H_2O$ at 25° and one atmosphere total pressure. *Amer. Mineralogist* 50:1296-1354.

Broadbent, F. E., and G. R. Bradford. 1952. Cation exchange groups in soil organic fraction. *Soil Sci.* 74:447-457.

Brown, G. (ed.). 1961. *The X-ray identification and crystal structures of clay minerals.* Jarrold and Sons, Ltd. Norwich.

Chao, Tsun Tien, M. E. Harward, and S. C. Fang. 1962. Adsorption and desorption phenomena of sulfate ions in soils. *Soil Sci. Soc. Amer. Proc.* 26:234-237.

Chao, Tsun Tien, M. E. Harward, and S. C. Fang. 1963. Cationic effects on sulfate adsorption by soils. *Soil Sci. Soc. Amer. Proc.* 27:35-38.

Clark, J. S. and M. Peech. 1955. Solubility criteria for the existence of calcium and aluminum phosphates in soils. *Soil Sci. Soc. Amer. Proc.* 19:171-174.

Couch, Elton L. and Ralph E. Grim. 1968. Boron fixation by illites. *Clays and Clay Minerals* 16:249-256.

Day, A. D., J. L. Stroehlein, and T. C. Tucker. 1972. Effects of treatment plant effluent on soil properties. *Jour. Water Poll. Control Fed.* 44:372-375.

de Haan, F. A. M. and G. H. Bolt. 1963. Determination of anion adsorption by clays. *Soil Sci. Soc. Amer. Proc.* 27:636-640.

de Villiers, J. M. and M. L. Jackson. 1967a. Cation exchange capacity variations with pH in soil clays. *Soil Sci. Soc. Amer. Proc.* 31:473-476.

de Villiers, J. M. and M. L. Jackson. 1967b. Aluminous chlorite origin of pH-dependent cation exchange capacity variations. *Soil Sci. Soc. Amer. Proc.* 31:614-619.

Eaton, F. M. 1950. Significance of carbonates in irrigation waters. *Soil Sci.* 69:123-133.

Ellis, B. G. and A. E. Erickson. 1969. Movement and transformation of various phosphorus compounds in soils. Report to Michigan Water Resource Commission.

Ellis, Boyd G. and Bernard D. Knezek. 1972. Adsorption reactions of micronutrients in soils. Chapt. 4 in *Micronutrients in Agriculture*. Ed. J. J. Mortvedt, P. M. Giordano, and W. L. Lindsay. Soil Sci. Soc. Amer., Inc. Madison, Wisconsin.

Erickson, A. E., J. M. Tiedje, B. G. Ellis, and C. M. Hansen. 1971. A barriered landscape water renovation system for removing phosphate and nitrogen liquid feedlot waste. *Proc. of the International Symp. on Livestock Wastes*, pp. 232-234.

Erickson, A. E., J. M. Tiedje, B. G. Ellis and C. M. Hansen. 1972. Initial observations of several medium-sized barriered landscape water renovation systems for animal waste. *Proc. of the 1972 Cornell Agric. Waste Management Conf.*, pp. 405-410.

Eriksson, E. 1952. Cation-exchange equilibria on clay minerals. *Soil. Sci.* 74:103-113.

Fleet, M. E. L. 1965. Preliminary investigations into the sorption of boron by clay minerals. *Clay Minerals Bull.* 6:3-16.

Fried, Maurice and Hans Broeshart. 1967. *The soil-plant system in relation to inorganic nutrition*. Academic Press. New York.

Fried, M. and R. E. Shapiro. 1956. Phosphate supply pattern of various soils. *Soil Sci. Soc. Amer. Proc.* 20:471-475.

Gapon, E. N. 1933. On the theory of exchange adsorption in soils. *Jour. Gen. Chem. (USSR)* 3:144-163.

Gieseking, J. E. and Hans Jenny. 1936. Behavior of polyvalent cations in base exchange. *Soil Sci.* 42:273-280.

Gough, N. A. and J. D. Beaton. 1963. Influence of phosphorus source and soil moisture on the solubility of phosphorus. *Jour. Sci. Food Agric.* 14:224-266.

Grim, Ralph E. 1953. *Clay mineralogy*. McGraw-Hill Book Co., Inc. New York.

Hasan, S. M., R. L. Fox, and C. C. Boyd. 1970. Solubility and availability of sorbed sulfate in Hawaiian soils. *Soil Sci. Soc. Amer. Proc.* 34:897-901.

Hatcher, John T. and C. A. Bower. 1958. Equilibria and dynamics of boron adsorption by soils. *Soil Sci.* 85:319-323.

Hatcher, John T., C. A. Bower, and Myron Clark. 1967. Adsorption of boron by soils as influenced by hydroxy aluminum and surface area. *Soil Sci.* 104:422-426.

Henze, R. 1963. Comparison of yields from the Göttingen E-fields and the nutrient potential and supply of the soil. *I. Pflanzenbau Düng. Bodenk.* 103:9-21.

Hiester, N. K. and T. Vermeulen. 1952. Saturation performance of ion-exchange and adsorption columns. *Chem. Engr. Prog.* 48:505-516.

Hingston, F. J. 1964. Reactions between boron and clays. *Australian J. Soil Res.* 2:83-95.

Hodgson, J. F. 1960. Cobalt reactions with montmorillonite. *Soil Sci. Soc. Amer. Proc.* 24:165-168.

Hodgson, J. F., H. R. Geering and Martha Fellows. 1964. The influence of fluoride, temperature, calcium and alcohol on the reaction of cobalt with montmorillonite. *Soil Sci. Soc. Amer. Proc.* 28:39-42.

Hodgson, J. F. and K. G. Tiller. 1961. The location of bound cobalt on 2:1 layer silicates. Clays and Clay Minerals. *Proc. of the 9th National Conf.*, pp. 404-411.

Hodgson, J. F., Kevin G. Tiller and Martha Fellows. 1969. Effect of iron removal on cobalt sorption by clays. *Soil Sci.* 108:391-396.

Kerr, H. W. 1928. The nature of base exchange and soil acidity. *Jour. Amer. Soc. Agron.* 20:309-335.

Krishnamoorthy, C., L. E. Davis, and R. Overstreet. 1948. Ionic exchange equations derived from statistical thermodynamics. *Science* 108:439-440.

Krishnamoorthy, C. and R. Overstreet. 1950. An experimental evaluation of ion-exchange relationships. *Soil Sci.* 69:41-53.

Lindsay, W. L. and E. C. Moreno. 1960. Phosphate phase equilibria in soils. *Soil Sci. Soc. Amer. Proc.* 24:177-182.

Lindsay, W. L. and W. A. Norvell. 1969. Equilibrium relationships of Zn^{2+}, Fe^{3+}, Ca^{2+}, and H^+ with EDTA and DTPA in soils. *Soil Sci. Soc. Amer. Proc.* 33:62-68.

Longenecker, D. E. 1960. Influence of soluble anions on some physical and physico-chemical properties of soils. *Soil Sci.* 90:185-191.

Marshall, C. E. 1964. *The physical chemistry and mineralogy of soils.* Vol. 1. *Soil materials.* John Wiley & Sons, Inc. New York.

Mattingly, G. E. G., R. D. Russell, and B. M. Jephcott. 1963. Experiments on cumulative dressings of fertilizers on calcareous soils in southwest England. II. Phosphorus uptake by ryegrass in the greenhouse. *Jour. Sci. Food Agric.* 14:629-637.

McGeorge, W. T. 1930. The base exchange property of organic matter in soils. *Arizona Agric. Expt. Sta. Tech. Bull.* 30:181-213.

McNeal, B. L. and N. T. Coleman. 1966. Effect of solution composition on soil hydraulic conductivity. *Soil Sci. Soc. Amer. Proc.* 30:308-312.

McNeal, B. L., D. A. Layfield, W. A. Norvell, and J. D. Rhoades. 1968. Factors influencing hydraulic conductivity of soils in the presence of mixed-salts solutions. *Soil Sci. Soc. Amer. Proc.* 32:187-190.

Melton, J. R., B. G. Ellis, and E. C. Doll. 1970. Zinc, phosphorus, and lime interactions with yield and zinc uptake by *Phaseolus Vulgaris. Soil Sci. Soc. Amer. Proc.* 34:91-93.

Mitchell, J. 1932. The origin, nature, and importance of soil organic constituents having base exchange properties. *Jour. Amer. Soc. Agron.* 24:256-275.

Mortland, M. M. 1970. Clay-organic complexes and interactions. *Adv. in Agron.* 22:75-117.

Murrmann, R. P. and F. R. Koutz. 1972. Role of soil chemical processes in reclamation of wastewater applied to land. Chapt. 4 in *Wastewater management by disposal on the land.* Corps of Engineers. U.S. Army. Cold Regions Research and Engineering Laboratory. Hanover, N. H.

Norvell, W. A. and W. L. Lindsay. 1970. Lack of evidence for $ZnSiO_3$ in soils. *Soil Sci. Soc. Amer. Proc.* 34:360-361.

Olsen, Sterling R. and Frank S. Watanabe. 1957. A method to determine a phosphorus adsorption maximum of soils as measured by the Langmuir isotherm. *Soil Sci. Soc. Amer. Proc.* 21:144-149.

Patrick, W. M., Jr. 1960. Nitrate reduction rates in a submerged soil as affected by redox potential. Trans. 7th International Congress Soil Sci. Madison, Wisconsin. 2:494-500.

Patrick, W. M., Jr. 1964. Extractable iron and phosphorus in a submerged soil at controlled redox potentials. Trans. 8th International Congress Soil Sci. Bucharest, Rumania. 4:605-609.

Pratt, P. F. and F. L. Bair. 1969. Sodium hazard of bicarbonate irrigation waters. *Soil Sci. Soc. Amer. Proc.* 33:880-883.

Pratt, P. F., R. L. Branson, and H. D. Chapman. 1960. Effect of crop fertilizer and leaching on carbonate precipitation and sodium accumulation in soil. Trans. 7th International Congress Soil Sci. Madison, Wisconsin. 2:185-192.

Rao, Talur S., A. L. Page, and N. T. Coleman. 1968. The influence of ionic strength and ion-pair formation between alkaline-earth metals and sulfate on Na-divalent cation-exchange equilibria. *Soil Sci. Soc. Amer. Proc.* 32:639-643.

Rhoades, J. D., R. D. Ingvalson, and J. T. Hatcher. 1970a. Laboratory determination of leachable soil boron. *Soil Sci. Soc. Amer. Proc.* 34:871-875.

Rhoades, J. D., R. D. Ingvalson, and J. T. Hatcher. 1970b. Adsorption of boron by ferromagnesian minerals and magnesium hydroxide. *Soil Sci. Soc. Amer. Proc.* 34:938-941.

Richards, L. A. (ed.). 1954. Diagnosis and improvement of saline and alkali soils. USDA Agricultural Handbook No. 60.

Scharrer, K., H. Kühn, and J. Lüttmer. 1956. Investigations of the fixation of boron by inorganic constituents of the soil. Z. PflErnahr Düng. 73:40-48 (*Soils and Fertilizers,* 1956. 19:1501).

Scheffer, F. and B. Ulrich. 1960. Physical-chemical basis of nutrient dynamics in the soil. *Acad. Rep. Populare Romine Probl. Act. Biol. Stunte Agr.,* pp. 663-670.

Schofield, R. K. 1947. A ratio law governing the equilibrium of cations in the soil solution. *Proc. 11th International Congress Pure and Appl. Chem. (London)* 3:257-261.

Schofield, R. K. 1955. Can a precise meaning be given to "available" soil phosphorus? *Soils and Fertilizers* 18:373-375.

Shainberg, I. and W. D. Kemper. 1966. Hydration status of adsorbed cations. *Soil Sci. Soc. Amer. Proc.* 30:707-713.

Shapiro, Raymond E. and Maurice Fried. 1959. Relative release and retentiveness of soil phosphates. *Soil Sci. Soc. Amer. Proc.* 23:195-198.

Sharpless, R. G., E. F. Wallihan, and F. F. Peterson. 1969. Retention of zinc by some arid zone soil materials treated with zinc sulfate. *Soil Sci. Soc. Amer. Proc.* 33:901-904.

Sims, J. R. and F. T. Bingham. 1967. Retention of boron by layer silicates, sesquioxides, and soil materials. I. Layer silicates. *Soil Sci. Soc. Amer. Proc.* 31:728-732.

Sims, J. R. and F. T. Bingham. 1968a. Retention of boron by layer silicates, sesquioxides, and soil materials. II. Sesquioxides. *Soil Sci. Soc. Amer. Proc.* 32:364-369.

Sims, J. R. and F. T. Bingham. 1968b. Retention of boron by layer silicates, sesquioxides, and soil materials. III. Iron- and aluminum-coated layer silicates and soil materials. *Soil Sci. Soc. Amer. Proc.* 32:369-373.

Stevenson, F. J., and J. H. A. Butler. 1969. Chemistry of humic acids and related pigments. Chapt. 22 in *Organic geochemistry methods and results.* Ed. G. Eglinton and M. T. J. Murphy. Springer-Verlag. New York, Heidelberg, Berlin.

Tanji, Kenneth K. 1970. A computer analysis on the leaching of boron from stratified soil columns. *Soil Sci.* 110:44-51.

Thomas, H. C. 1944. Heterogeneous ion exchange in a flowing system. *Jour. Amer. Chem. Soc.* 66:1664-1666.

Tiller, K. G. 1967. Silicic acid and the reactions of zinc with clays. *Nature* 214:852.

Tisdale, Samuel L. and Werner L. Nelson. 1956. *Soil fertility and fertilizers.* The Macmillan Co. New York.

Udo, E. J., H. L. Bohn and T. C. Tucker. 1970. Zinc adsorption by calcareous soils. *Soil Sci. Soc. Amer. Proc.* 34:405-407.

Ulrich, B. 1961. *Soil and plants: Their interrelationships—physical-chemical view.* Ferd. Enke Verlag, Stuttgart, pp. 1-114.

Vangelern, P. von and J. Woltersdorf. 1930. *Beiträge zur Frage des Basenaustausches und der Aziditaten.* Z. Pflanzenernähr. Düng. Bodenk 15:329-342.

Vanselow, A. P. 1932. Equilibria of the base-exchange reactions of bentonites, permutites, soil colloids, and zeolites. *Soil Sci.* 33:95-113.

Vermeulen, T. and N. K. Hiester. 1959. Ion-exchange and adsorption column kinetics with uniform partial presaturation. *Jour. Chem. Phys.* 22:96-101.

White, R. E. and P. H. T. Beckett. 1964. Studies on the phosphate potentials of soils. Part I. The measurement of phosphate potential. *Plant Soil* 20:1-16.

Wiklander, Lambert. 1964. Cation and anion exchange phenomena. Chapt. 4 in *Chemistry of the soil.* Ed. Firman E. Bear. Reinhold Publishing Corp. New York.

Discussion

Hunt: I wanted to ask a question on your anaerobic denitrifica-tion. Have you had any problems in this particular sys-tem with the clogging under anaerobic conditions, and do you think that this concept has any applicability to field conditions?

Ellis: In answer to your first question, yes, there has been some trouble. Dick Thomas's slides fit exactly what we discovered. The trouble is in a very thin layer on the surface. But you can manage this. You may have difficulty in growing a crop on it. We're considering quack grass since it seems to grow about everywhere. But it does give us some difficulty. You can get away from some of this by resting and a few days later it will receive more material. Secondly, you asked do I think it has any applicability in the field? Yes, I do. The one we have built is a very detailed system where we have it all enclosed in plastics. We don't lose anything and we can analyze all the materials. Dr. Erickson in our depart-ment says we can go about and build one of these in the field very easily by using an asphalt barrier to provide the anaerobic zone. We won't worry about recycling all the water back through the swine barn to flush it a second time, we'll just let it go off into the ground water after it's all purified. The one thing I expect trouble on though, is the high levels of salt, particularly potassium which may give us difficulties and perhaps also chloride.

McKernan: I'm interested to know in your last experiment with the swine barn waste whether the burms that you have con-structed are characterized by certain kinds of vegetative cover and whether the evaporation characteristics of the cover have affected your experiment?

Ellis: We have operated these with grass covers and bare soils. I would suppose that there has been some evapo-transpiration. I realize that in Michigan, our evapotrans-piration rates are not extremely high and we were put-ting on more than 1 inch per day, so evapotranspiration should not be a large part of this.

Goydan: What method are you referring to when you mention ion adsorption tests in the laboratory?

Ellis: We've been using the Langmuir adsorption isotherm for this. It's very simple to perform. You add increasing increments of phosphorus to a series of 5 gram samples, let them come to equilibrium . . . 24 hours is sufficient to do this, determine the amount of phosphorus adsorbed, plug it back into the Langmuir equation and you can predict the adsorption maximum plus the constant K. This is what we're doing in the laboratory. There are other isotherms that can be used, but I think more work has been done with the Langmuir than anything else and it at least appears to me to give us some hope of a ballpark estimate. I certainly wouldn't want to stake my reputation or life on the fact that these are accurate but I think we're going with the best estimation we have right now without going out into the field and measuring.

Sutherland: In your incubation treatment of soils with phosphate, did you permit the soils to dry during that three-month period of time or were they allowed to remain moist?

Ellis: We maintained them relatively moist but we were doing this in polyethylene bags and brought them back up to field capacity about once a week during the three-month period, which meant there was some drying in the system. This is something I haven't pursued as much as I should have. It could be very critical to design criteria to know how many times you could go through a cycle and then give it three months in a field to recover. We know nothing except that we were able to recover the original absorption capacity in the laboratory once in a three-month period.

Craft: I have a question concerning the hog waste renovation system. How long have you researched this and also what was the type of soil? With the apparent nitrogen removals that you got, are you sure that actual nitrification and denitrification occur or is it possible that the ammonia is being absorbed by the soil and you haven't saturated the absorption complex?

Ellis: We measured the ammonia on the soil and this will not account for it. This is Erickson's experiment principally. I'm the chemist involved in it and we do the analysis work on it. I threw it in just as an illustration here, but let me say this. Yes, I think we're getting rid of it by denitrification because when we overloaded the system by accident one time, a switch blew out and we dumped a week's load in one night, immediately the nitrate values went very high and we no longer could handle it, so I think we are denitrifying the system. We've been running it off and on a little over a year now. How long we can go with it I don't know. Our soil microbiologist says indefinitely providing we maintain the carbon that we need for the denitrification. If we lose the carbon it won't work. As far as phosphate removal, we're on borrowed time there and my calculations indicate that we should go about 18 months before we start to leak phosphorus.

5
The Soil as a Biological Filter

R. H. Miller*

Renewed interest in land disposal of secondary effluents and liquid sewage sludges has stimulated the scientific community to examine in more detail than ever before the physical, chemical, and biological processes in soil which influence waste renovation. Currently the useful analogy of "soil as a filter" has been employed to simplify the discussion of the renovative capacity of soil for waste materials. Previous chapters by R. E. Thomas, "Soil as a Physical Filter" and B. G. Ellis, "Soil as a Chemical Filter" have covered the soil physical and chemical properties which influence the "soil filter." The third component of the soil filter is the biological component.

The groups of organisms comprising the soil biological filter are bacteria, actinomycetes, fungi, protozoa, algae, soil micro- and macro-animals and higher plants. The significance of higher plants to the successful renovation of liquid wastes on land has been well documented previously (Kardos, 1967, 1970; Sopper, 1971). This discussion will therefore focus on the contributions of the soil microbial population to the selectivity and success of the soil filter.

The Microbial Population of the Soil Filter

Individual groups of soil microorganisms in the plow layer of agricultural soils often reach high numerical populations. Estimates of 10^7 bacteria, 10^6 actinomycetes, and 10^5 fungi per gram of soil are typical values obtained by plate counts on various artificial media. Direct microscopic counts for soil bacteria are usually higher with about 10^9 cells per gram of soil a common figure (Clark, 1967). Soil fungi become the dominant numerical group of soil microorganisms in the litter layer (A_0) and A_1 horizons of acidic forest profiles. In both agricultural and forest soils the microbial population is concentrated primarily in the surface 15 cm organic matter rich region of the soil, and numbers decrease rapidly with depth.

Addition of organic waste materials to soil should be expected to

*Department of Agronomy, The Ohio State University.

and does increase microbial numbers (Glathe and Makawi, 1963; Miller, 1973). Representative data for changes in various groups of microorganisms during the decomposition of an aerobically digested sewage sludge are shown in Tables 5-1 and 5-2. No data is presently available on population changes induced by irrigation with secondary effluent. Presumably the increase in agricultural soils would be minimal because of the low organic loading associated with secondary effluent. The changes which might occur in the microbial population of forest soils remains an unanswered question, but would probably be more dramatic than in agricultural soils.

Numerous estimates of bacterial biomass and a few estimates of fungal biomass have been calculated and representative data are shown on Table 5-3. In most arable soils, the amount of bacterial biomass is commonly estimated to be somewhat less than that of fungi, but to exceed that of the algae, protozoa and nematodes combined (Clark, 1967). Comparative data for the biomass of actinomycetes are not available but it is generally thought to be equal to that of the true bacteria. Jenkinson (1966) used the distribution of ^{14}C in soil after decomposition of ^{14}C labeled ryegrass to estimate that the soil biomass contained 2.3 to 3.5 percent of the soil carbon.

In summary, the microbial component of the "soil filter" occupies the upper portion of the soil profile (plow layer or litter layer and A_1 horizon of a forest soil). Its mass makes up only a relatively small part of the total soil mass. The contribution of this small but significant component to waste recycling and renovation will be discussed in more detail in the paragraphs which follow.

Significance of the Biological Filter in Recycling Municipal Wastewater and Sludge

Microbial Decomposition of Organic Wastes

One of the most significant functions of the microbial component of the soil filter is the degradation of organic compounds contained in the waste materials applied to soils. Indeed, one of the primary advantages attributed to recycling of secondary effluent through soil is that soil provides an alternative to stream discharge or expensive tertiary treatments for reducing BOD and improving water quality.

Disposal of liquid sewage sludges on land presents a somewhat different problem since soil application is considered an economical method for ultimate disposal of these high organic wastes. Proper design and management of soils systems for sludge disposal by either high rate single application or repeated lower rate applications de-

Table 5-1. Plate counts[a] of bacteria and actinomycetes in soils amended with anaerobically digested sewage sludge after one month incubation

Soil	Soil Moisture[b]	Organisms/g dry soil $\times 10^{-6}$		
		Control	90 ton/ha	224 ton/ha
Ottokee	FC	7.5	33.0	46.0
sand	Sat	7.0	472	867
Celina	FC	15.5	268	88.0
silt loam	Sat	30.5	864	521
Paulding	FC	28.6	484	842
clay	Sat	13.7	37.9	96.2

a. On soil extract-sludge extract agar.
b. FC = field capacity   Sat = water saturation.

pends to a large part on the rate at which sludge organic matter is decomposed. A less rapid decomposition of sewage sludges would be advantageous for the reclamation of sandy soils or stripmine spoil. These soils would benefit from the improved physical and chemical properties associated with organic matter accumulation. In contrast, proper management of sludge disposal on finer textured agricultural soils would require a more rapid rate of decomposition of sludge carbon. Experience at both the Paris and Berlin sewage farms indicates that organic matter accumulation was associated with "exhausted" soils (Rohde, 1962). The primary reason cited for poorer plant growth in these soils was an accumulation of toxic levels of Cu and Zn associated with the organic matter. Excessive accumulation of sludge organic matter might also reduce soil aeration and cause the associated problems of odor, reduced root development, and mobility of Fe and Mn.

Table 5-2. Plate counts[a] of fungi in soils amended with anaerobically digested sewage sludge after one month incubation

Soil	Soil Moisture[b]	Organisms/g dry soil $\times 10^{-4}$		
		Control	90 ton/ha	224 ton/ha
Ottokee	FC	17.5	752	576
sand	Sat	17.5	95	303
Celina	FC	12.5	50	48
silt loam	Sat	14.0	9.0	46
Paulding	FC	11.0	419	826
clay	Sat	11.0	7.5	6.0

a. On rose-bengal-streptomycin agar.
b. FC = field capacity   Sat = water saturation.

Table 5-3. Estimates of microbial biomass in soils[a]

Reference		g/m^2	Bacterial Biomass lbs/acre	% of soil mass
Alexander	(1961)	33-330	300-3000	0.015-0.15
Jensen	(1963)	100-1000	900-9000	0.045-0.45
Russell	(1950)	170-390	1500-3600	0.077-0.18
Krasil'nikov	(1944)	67-720	600-6400	0.031-0.33
Latter &				
Cragg	(1967)	21-135	190-1200	0.010-0.06
Stockli	(1956)	160-380	1500-3500	0.075-0.17
Clark	(1967)	450	4100	0.22
Mean		300	2800	0.14
			Fungal Biomass	
Jackson	(1965)	190	1700	0.09
Clark &				
Paul	(1970)	260[b]	2400	0.19
Alexander	(1961)	55-550	500-5000	0.025-0.25

a. Values are calculated on live weight basis for 15 cm depth.
b. $g/m^2/10$ cm depth.

Those of us in agriculture are well aware of the enzymatic versatility of the heterotrophic microbial population of soil and its significance in decomposing a whole host of natural and synthetic organic compounds (Alexander, 1961; McLaren and Peterson, 1967). Soil microorganisms are actually too efficient in their catabolic activity and it has been found almost impossible to maintain the organic matter of both mineral and organic soils when used for agriculture. Hallam and Bartholomew (1953) concluded that annual additions of organic carbon of two to five tons per acre were needed just to maintain the organic carbon content of temperate region soils.

The products of microbial metabolism of organic compounds in soil under aerobic and anaerobic conditions are shown in the generalized formulae below.

Aerobic

$$(CHO)_nNS \xrightarrow{O_2} CO_2 + H_2O + \text{Microbial cells \& Storage Products}$$
$$60\%^* \qquad\qquad 40\%$$
$$+ NH_4^+ + H_2S + \text{Energy}$$
$$\downarrow \qquad \downarrow$$
$$NO_3^- \quad SO_4^{--}$$

*The percentage values are estimates of the distribution of the carbon of the original organic compound(s) after metabolism by the microbial population.

Anaerobic $-O_2$

$(CHO)_n NS \xrightarrow{} CO_2 + H_2O$ + Microbial cells & Storage Products

20%   5%

+ Organic Intermediates+ $CH_4 + H_2$

70%   5%

+ $NH_4^+ + H_2S$ + Energy

While the main products of aerobic metabolism are CO_2, H_2O and cells, in the absence of O_2 intermediate substances such as organic acids, alcohols, amines, and mercaptans accumulate. Because the energy yield during anaerobic fermentation is small, fewer microbial cells accumulate per unit of organic carbon degraded. Note also that while NO_3^- and $SO_4^=$ are the end products of organic nitrogen and sulfur compounds under aerobic conditions, H_2S and NH_4^+ are formed under anaerobic conditions.

Secondary effluent from properly operating treatment plants contains relatively low levels of organic compounds. A BOD of 25 mg/l and a COD of 70 mg/l was considered typical for secondary effluent (Reed, 1972). Very little information is available on the chemical analysis of the organic compounds of secondary effluent (Painter *et al.*, 1961; Hunter, 1973). A portion of the readily decomposable organic materials (measurable by BOD) is derived from sludge particles carried over from the treatment system. These particulates should have a chemical composition similar to that of microbial tissue. The data of Painter *et al.* (1961) although accounting for less than 50 percent of the effluent carbon, would seem to verify this assumption. Part of the BOD of wastewater effluent is also in the colloidal and soluble states and would probably differ little from the analysis given for particulate organic compounds. The protein, carbohydrates, nucleic acids, fatty acids, amino sugars and other organic materials found within microbial cells will be readily degradable by the common biochemical pathways of glycolysis, the tricarboxylic acid cycle, β-oxidation, etc.

The remainder of the organic compounds of secondary effluent are commonly called refractory organics. Refractory organics are estimated by the difference between the values of COD and BOD. As the name implies, these organic compounds are those which are considered more slowly degradable *e.g.*, phenols, detergents, fats and waxes, hydrocarbons, cellulose, lignin, tannin, plant and bile pigments, pesticides, and humic compounds. Physical entrapment and chemical adsorption of these compounds in the soil matrix should provide the necessary retention time for effective microbial degradation of most of these compounds. Since some of these refractory organics are considered toxic or problematic to different sectors of our environment their elimination from the soil by biodegradation will be discussed in greater detail in a later chapter.

Very little information is currently available on the rate at which the organic compounds of wastewater effluents are actually decomposed in soil. Thomas and Bendixen (1969) studied the rate of degradation of septic tank effluent in sand lysimeters and secondary effluent in lysimeters of sand and a silt loam soil. About 80 percent of the organic carbon from septic tank effluent was digested during 82 to 425-day dosing cycles with little difference due to duration of dosing, temperature or loading rates. Only 68 percent of the organics of secondary effluent was degraded in the sand lysimeters during 513- and 760-day dosing periods while 89 percent was degraded during a 513-day dosing of a single lysimeter containing a silt loam soil. One other aspect of these data is of significance. An average of 14 percent of the applied organic carbon was found in the percolate from the sand lysimeters (three-foot depth). These values are very large and represent a potential problem with the renovating capability of the soil filter of coarse textured soils. These high percolation rates of soluble organics may only reflect the influence of continuous dosing and do not seem to reflect data from field studies.

Application of secondary effluent to soil at a rate of two inches per week for a 40-week period (March-November) should not place any stress on the soil filter and the microorganisms of the "living filter" should effectively remove and decompose most of the organic material of the effluent. At a COD of 70 mg/l the 80 inches addition of effluent will add only 728 kg (1600 lbs) of organic matter per acre. This is far below the maintenance level of two to five tons of organic matter per acre per year noted by Hallam and Bartholomew (1953) and there should be no accumulation of organic matter in the soil. Higher and more frequent applications of secondary effluent could cause waterlogging with concomitant anaerobic conditions and slower rates of decomposition.

Anaerobically digested sewage sludges contain about 25 percent organic carbon on a dry weight basis (Burd, 1968). During the process of anaerobic digestion the waste organic solids are stabilized by the almost complete microbial fermentation of carbohydrates (the exception is cellulose) resulting in a 60 to 75 percent reduction in volatile solids. Although data on the organic analysis of anaerobically digested sludge is difficult to obtain the residual organic material consists of a mixture of microbial tissue, lignin, cellulose, lipids, organic nitrogen compounds, and humic acid-like materials (McCoy, 1971).

As might be expected, anaerobically digested sludge is not degraded rapidly in soil. A maximum of only 17 to 18 percent of the

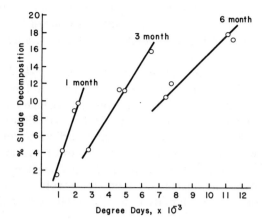

Figure 5-1. Decomposition of anaerobically digested sewage sludge in soil with time as influenced by temperature. Data points for each incubation time were calculated from measurements of CO_2-C evolution from three soils amended with 90 metric tons of sludge/ha.

$$\text{Degree days} = \sum_{i=1}^{N} \left(\frac{\overline{X}_{MT} + \overline{X}_{mt}}{2} \right) \times 30$$

Where $\overline{X}_{MT}$ = mean daily max. temp. during a month (°F)
$\overline{X}_{mt}$ = mean daily min. temp. during a month (°F)
N = No. of months

sludge carbon was evolved as CO_2 during a six-month period at soil temperatures equivalent to spring-summer or summer-autumn in Columbus, Ohio (Figure 5-1). It is also apparent that the rate of sludge decomposition is more rapid during the initial month than during the subsequent months following addition. These data certainly suggest that addition of anaerobically digested sewage sludge to soils will result in the accumulation of organic matter.

The above discussion dealt with the rate of degradation of anaerobically digested sewage sludge. Undigested primary sludge or activated sludge will contain organic residues which are much more readily degradable. Additions of the latter two sludges to soil, at comparably high rates as anaerobically digested sewage sludge, would exert a greater demand on the oxygen supplying power of soil. Anaerobic conditions, odor and reducing conditions would probably result.

Elimination of Environmental Toxins
Municipal waste effluents and sewage sludges contain a number of organic and inorganic substances which are considered potential envi-

ronmental toxins. Listed in this category are phenolic compounds, the chlorinated hydrocarbon pesticides and chlorinated biphenyls, detergent residues like ABS and NTA, petroleum products and heavy metals.

One of the important questions which must be asked when considering the feasibility of applying municipal wastes to land is the fate of these chemicals after they reach the soil. The primary environmental impact of these chemicals would occur if they would move through or off the soil surface and reach ground and surface water supplies. In this section we will discuss the participation of the microbial component of the soil filter in removing or detoxifying the organic toxins discussed above. The microbially mediated reactions which influence the mobility or plant availability of heavy metals will be discussed in a later chapter.

Phenols often reach sewage systems as wastes from oil refineries, steel mills, and chemical companies (Reed, 1972; Lake Erie Report, 1968). Secondary treatment is reported to reduce the concentration of phenolic compounds from 65 to 99 percent, the reduction being due to biological activity. The quantity of phenolic compounds in secondary effluent used for land disposal can be expected to vary greatly. Data for a typical analysis of a secondary effluent give a value of 0.3 mg/l of phenol (Reed, 1972). Assuming a 40-week period of irrigation (March to November) at two inches per week only 6.2 lbs/acre (6.9 kg/ha of phenol) would reach the soil. Even though the phenolic compounds are considered rather stable to biological degradation, considerable evidence indicates that phenolic compounds should be decomposed in soils. The enzymatic cleavage of the aromatic ring occurs by mixed function oxidases followed by subsequent metabolism of the ring carbon (Dagley, 1967; Gibson, 1968). A recent review by Horvath (1972) points out that co-metabolism might be involved in the biological metabolism of many organic compounds including some substituted phenolic compounds. Regardless of the metabolic scheme, it is doubtful if phenolic compounds will accumulate in soil when applied at or near the normal rates. The microbial portion of the soil filter should readily eliminate the phenolic compounds as long as physical and chemical adsorption provide sufficient retention time for microbial activity to proceed.

Pesticides, particularly the chlorinated hydrocarbon insecticides, DDT, aldrin, dieldrin, etc., and polychloroaromatic herbicides such as 2,3,6-TBA and 2,4,5-T have received considerable publicity as potential carcinogens or teratogenic agents. These same compounds have acquired a reputation as being recalcitrant *i.e.,* nonbiodegradable (Alexander, 1965a). Recent reports that these same pesticides may be metabolized to nontoxic intermediates under laboratory conditions by the process of co-metabolism, offer a possible approach to accelerating microbial detoxication (Horvath, 1972). It has also been suggested that "analog enrichment" which involves the addition of a biodegradable analog at the same time as the recalcitrant compound might result in a more rapid oxidation and detoxication (Horvath, 1972). Data from a lysimeter study by Robeck *et al.* (1963) would seem to support the idea that co-metabolism is indeed involved in the biodegradation of 2,4,5-T. Although 2,4,5-T is normally considered to persist in soils for periods of at least six months (Alexander, 1965b) data from this study showed that 2,4,5-T added to septic tank effluent and percolated through lysimeters was metabolized after a 14-day lag period. The more rapid degradation of 2,4,5-T in the lysimeters may be due to the organic materials of the effluent providing energy for the microbial co-metabolism of this "recalcitrant" herbicide. All of the pesticides discussed will normally be present in wastewaters in significant quantity only as a result of industrial operations. Initial low levels of pesticides coupled with strong adsorption on soil particles and eventual biodegradation make it doubtful if any environmental problems will occur.

Hydrocarbons in sewage effluents are derived from various industrial sources and oil spills. An estimate of the maximum quantity of hydrocarbons that will be present in secondary effluent can be calculated on the assumption that more than 10 to 20 mg/liter of petroleum in sewage will inhibit the microorganisms of the activated sludge system (Reed, 1972). The activated sludge process will remove between 50 to 70 percent of these hydrocarbons leaving a maximum six to ten mg/liter petroleum hydrocarbons in the effluent. Hydrocarbons which reach the soil surface can be degraded slowly by a large number of soil microorganisms (Ellis and Adams, 1961). In general, the low molecular weight hydrocarbons decompose more rapidly than those of higher molecular weight and straight chained compounds at a rate >branch chained >aromatics. β-oxidation is the mechanism proposed for the microbial degradation of aliphatic hydrocarbons and the involvement of mixed function oxidases for metabolism of the aromatic hydrocarbons (McKenna and Kallio, 1965). Strong adsorption on soil particles with slow biodegradation should eliminate any problems with hydrocarbon residues in soil.

The last group of organic environmental toxins which will be discussed and which have caused some concern when present in effluents are detergent residues. One infamous group of surface active agents, the alkylbenzene sulfonates (ABS), have been eliminated from use in detergents since 1965 because of their slow biodegradability. Although ABS has been largely removed from detergent mixtures its biodegradability in sewage systems and soils is still of considerable interest. Studies by Robeck *et al.* (1963) with sand and soil lysimeters and the Penn State group with field soils (Kardos, 1967; Kardos *et al.*, 1968) have shown that ABS can be effectively removed from waste effluents by the soil filter. Both studies have shown that adsorption in the soil surface is extremely important in providing the necessary retention time for microbial activity to occur. The Penn State experiments recorded 70 percent reduction in ABS in the top few inches of the forest floor with a 97 percent removal at the four-foot depth. Cropland was even more effective in removing ABS residues. Robeck *et al.* (1963) found that passage of effluent through three-foot lysimeters of sand was 83 to 96 percent effective in removing ABS. The importance of soil adsorption can be seen by their observation that a 21-day lag period occurred before ABS was degraded by sewage and soil microorganisms. The use of ^{35}S ABS demonstrated that ABS was degraded to $^{35}SO_4^=$ (76 percent) and short chain sulfonates (21 percent). Studies by Benarde *et al.* (1965) and Horvath (1972) suggest that ABS may be degraded by co-metabolism. This would certainly indicate the significance of an organic matter rich soil or surface horizon for the rapid decomposition of ABS.

The recent indictment of detergent phosphates as biostimulants in aquatic systems has resulted in the use of alternative compounds. Nitrilotriacetate (NTA) was one such alternative until it too was removed from detergents pending further testing to assure its safety in the environment. One aspect on which to base the approval of NTA for detergent use is the ability of sewage and soil microorganisms to degrade NTA. A recent study by Tiedje and Mason (1971) using mono-carboxyl labeled NTA has shown that the soil microflora can degrade NTA after a two-to-four-day lag period (Figure 5-2). Subsequent additions of NTA were metabolized without a lag. The pattern and rate of degradation of NTA were variable among different soils with no apparent correlation between degradation and soil texture, drainage, plant cover, or pH. Degradation was, however, dependent on aerobic conditions being maintained. Rapid degradation of the Hg, Ni, Mn, Co, Na, Cd, Pb, Cu, Fe, and Zn chelates of NTA occurred in soils which previously had been exposed to NTA.

Elimination of Pathogenic Microorganisms

Land application of sewage, primary and secondary effluent or liquid sewage sludges may present a potential health hazard because of the human and animal pathogens which these wastes contain. Among the common pathogens found in these waste materials are the bacterial pathogens *Salmonella*, *Shigella*, *Mycobacterium* and *Vibrio comma;* the hepatitis viruses, enteroviruses and adenoviruses; and the protozoan, *Endamoeba histolytica* (Foster and Engelbrecht, 1973). The

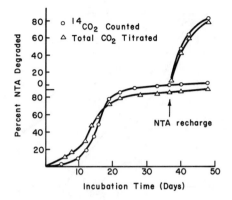

Figure 5-2. Biodegradation of nitrilotriacetic acid (NTA) in soil (Tiedje and Mason, 1971)

potential health hazards associated with land disposal of sanitary wastes without disinfection are associated with the pollution of ground water by movement of pathogenic microorganisms through the soil filter, surface runoff carrying pathogens into surface water supplied, contamination of leafy vegetables and root crops with pathogens during irrigation, and air contamination by aerosols of pathogens formed during irrigation. Of the four areas listed above, the microbial component of the soil filter will be of particular significance in the first two. Both the chance of pathogens moving through the soil column into ground water and movement off the soil surface by runoff will depend in part on their survival time in soil.

The initial soil reactions influencing the removal of pathogens from liquid wastes are physical entrapment and chemical adsorption by the soil, primarily at the soil surface (McGauhey and Krone, 1967). Once the microorganisms are retained the primary consideration is the length of survival of these organisms in the soil matrix.

An extensive compilation of scientific literature has addressed itself to the survival of pathogenic microorganisms in natural environments including the soil (Van Donsel et al., 1967; Law, 1968). Fortunately, most studies indicate a rather rapid die back of coliforms and bacterial pathogens reaching the soil so that the long term hazard to ground water or surface waters is considered minimal under normal conditions (McGauhey and Krone, 1967; Van Donsel et al., 1967). Data shown in Figure 5-3 are typical of the die back curves commonly obtained. Whether these same curves are descriptive of the die back of pathogenic viruses is still an open question, and one which should be given a high research priority. There may be instances, however,

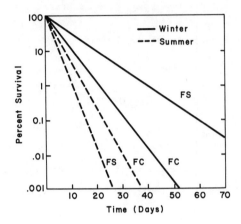

Figure 5-3. Survival of fecal coliforms (FC) and fecal streptococci (FS) in soil (Van Donsel *et al.*, 1967)

of survival for longer periods of time. A review by Rudolfs *et al.* (1950) cites reports of the survival of *Salmonella* for periods as long as six months to one year. Fecal streptococci from digested sewage sludge have been found to survive up to six months in a clay soil but not in a silt loam or sandy soil (Miller, 1973). *Escherichia coli* and *Aerobacter aerogenes* have been reported to survive up to four years in soil (Mallman and Mack, 1961).

Attempts have been made to ascertain the mechanisms by which pathogenic and coliform microorganisms are eliminated from the soil. Both abiotic and biotic factors have been considered significant. Abiotic factors considered important to the persistence of pathogenic microorganisms in soil are texture, moisture, pH, aeration, temperature and organic matter content. This paper will not review any of these aspects in detail, and readers are referred to the following references for more information (Van Donsel *et al.*, 1967; Law, 1968; Rudolfs *et al.*, 1950). The participation of the soil microorganisms of the living filter in these processes would be only indirect as microbial activity would alter soil pH, aeration, and organic matter content. More important to our discussion are the mechanisms by which soil microorganisms directly participate in the elimination of pathogenic microorganisms from the soil. Rapid die back of pathogenic microorganisms in soil would seem to be an example of a "homeostatic" reaction of the soil microbial community which maintains the constancy of the community (Alexander, 1971a). An ecological explanation of this phenomenon is that all of the potential niches are occupied in the complex environment of the soil so that the potential invaders find it difficult to gain a foothold. The exact mechanisms involved in the elimination of the foreign microorganisms *e.g.*, pathogenic bacteria, viruses and protozoa from the soil environment are difficult to ascertain. The possibilities included the production of microbial toxins; enzymatic lysis; predatory protozoa; parasitic bacteria, fungi, and phage; and the inability of the aleins to compete effectively with the indigenous community for nutrients.

In summary, it seems likely that the soil filter will effectively eliminate the pathogenic bacteria and protozoa reaching the soil from applications of secondary effluent or sewage sludge. Survival of viruses is still an open question because of the paucity of information on this topic. The limiting factor in the elimination of all pathogens may be the effectiveness of the physical and chemical processes of the soil filter in retaining the pathogens long enough for their elimination by the soil microbial population. Movement through coarse textured soils or surface cracks of fine textured soils could certainly provide a means to circumvent the effectiveness of the biological portion of the soil filter.

Microbial Reactions which Influence the
Mobility and Plant Availability of Ions in Soil

Of the many problems which would limit the usefulness of land disposal of municipal wastewaters and sludges, those involving the accumulation and movement of N, P and various heavy metal ions are potentially the most serious. For instance, movement of N or P through soil or off the soil might accelerate the processes of eutrophication in streams and lakes; accumulation of NO_3^--N at a concentration greater than 10 mg/liter in ground or surface water supplies may cause methemoglobinemia in children or nitrate toxicity in animals; movement of potentially toxic or nuisance levels of metal ions into ground water may cause a deterioration of water quality; and accumulation and increased solubility of heavy metal ions in soil may cause phytotoxic effects and reduce the renovation capacity of the plant component of the soil filter. The magnitude of the above problems should normally be greater with liquid sewage sludges than with the more dilute secondary effluents. It is the purpose of this section to discuss the influence of the soil microbial population on the mobility and solubility of nutrient and heavy metal ions in soil. The biochemical reactions of interest are mineralization, immobilization, oxidation, reduction, chelation, volatization, and precipitation.

Nitrogen. The microbial reactions involving nitrogen which are of significance to the functioning of the "soil filter" are mineralization, nitrification, and denitrification (Figure 5-4). Secondary effluent contains rather modest concentrations of both NH_4^+-N (9.8 mg/l) and

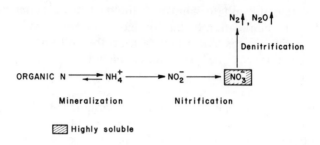

Figure 5-4. The important microbial reactions of the nitrogen cycle within the "soil filter"

NO_3^--N (8.2 mg/l) with a small amount of organic N primarily as protein (2.0 mg/l). The values given are typical values (Reed, 1972) and may differ considerably depending upon the efficiency and retention time of the treatment system.

Because secondary effluent has a low C:N ratio of< 10:1 a net mineralization of nitrogen will occur in the soil. This mineralized ammonium nitrogen as well as the ammonium nitrogen in the effluent will be held by the soil exchange sites until nitrified by the activity of the chemosynthetic autotrophs, *Nitrosomonas* and *Nitrobacter*. Nitrification should proceed at a rapid rate in all agricultural soils irrigated with secondary effluent at rates which maintain aerobic conditions. The obvious exception will be in those climatic regions where low winter temperatures will reduce microbial activity. Nitrification of ammonium nitrogen reaching acid forest soils may be limited by the absence of nitrifying bacteria. It is possible that irrigation with waste effluents may provide conditions which would allow a population of nitrifying bacteria to develop.

Once formed, NO_3^- is very mobile and will be leached from the soil as water moves through the profile. The factors affecting nitrate movement in soils have recently received a great deal of attention (Viets and Hageman, 1971). However, of considerable importance to the efficiency of the total "soil filter" will be the adsorption and utilization of NO_3^- by the actively growing agronomic crop or forest vegetation. Studies at Penn State University (Kardos, 1967; Kardos *et al.,* 1968) have demonstrated the effectiveness of vegetation in removing effluent nitrogen from soil and maintaining the integrity of the soil filter.

Activated sludge (avg 5.6 percent N) and digested sewage sludge (avg 2.4 percent N) contain a considerable quantity of nitrogen (Burd, 1968) half of which is in the ammonium form. When sewage sludge is applied to land for the purpose of disposal there is a tendency to apply as large a quantity of sludge as possible. A recent U.S.

Dept. of Interior report has recommended sludge application rates of 10 to 40 tons of dry solids per acre which would contain 480 to 1920 lbs of N per acre (Burd, 1968). Hinesly *et al.* (1971) have proposed that no more than two inches of anaerobically digested sewage sludge be added to supply the nitrogen needs of a non-leguminous crop. Even this rate of application supplies over 600 lbs of N per acre. It is apparent from these reports that one potential problem associated with disposal of liquid sludges on land will be an excess of nitrogen above that which the growing crop can assimilate. If nitrification of the excess ammonium nitrogen originally present or subsequently mineralized occurs and NO_3^- moves through the soil profile considerable nitrate enrichment of ground water or surface waters may occur. Lysimeter studies (Hinesly *et al.*, 1971) conducted on light silt loam soils by the University of Illinois have shown that nitrification does occur in soil amended with from five to ten inches (1650-3300 lbs of N/acre) of liquid digested sewage sludge. Nitrate nitrogen found in the leachate was considerably higher than unfertilized check plots or control plots receiving 200 lbs of N per acre as commercial fertilizer. The significance of the plant cover in nitrogen renovation was shown by the fact that no water and accompanying nitrate moved through the four-foot lysimeters during the summer months. It should be readily apparent from these studies that the soil filter is permeable to high applications of nitrogen in liquid wastes.

The preceding discussion has emphasized one of the more critical problems associated with the microbial component of the soil filter, namely nitrification. It is perhaps fortunate that a second microbial reaction associated with nitrogen, biological denitrification is potentially useful in alleviating the potential pollution hazard associated with the formation and movement of NO_3^-.

Biological denitrification involves the loss of N_2 and N_2O during anaerobic respiration in which NO_3^- is used as an electron acceptor. The microorganisms involved are primarily facultative anaerobic heterotrophic bacteria. Conditions which favor biological denitrification would include a near neutral pH, a readily available source of carbonaceous substrate, and anaerobic conditions ($E_h \sim +200$ MV).

The significance of biological denitrification during disposal of wastes on land is difficult to evaluate. Undoubtedly applications of secondary effluents to agricultural land, regardless of the mode of application, should provide at least temporary periods of anaerobiosis and sufficient substrate for some loss of nitrogen to the atmosphere. This will be true even though proper management of soils for waste water disposal requires that aerobic conditions be maintained. The reason for this apparent anomaly is that anaerobic microsites can occur in soils considered aerobic (Broadbent, 1973).

Denitrification losses from soils which have been amended with liquid sewage sludges should exceed that from secondary effluents because of the organic matter supplied. This author is not familiar, however, with any quantitative evaluation of denitrification from sludge amended soils.

In conclusion, it seems apparent that biological denitrification will remove some NO_3^- from soils during waste renovation on agriculture soils. If the pH of forest soils will allow a build-up of nitrifying bacteria with subsequent nitrification, it is also likely that the heterotrophic denitrifying bacteria will also be present. It is doubtful that much can be done to increase biological denitrification on spray irrigation sites where growing crops are being maintained. Rapid infiltration systems such as that at Flushing Meadows (Bouwer, 1973) and the overland flow systems for waste disposal should be able to take greater advantage of denitrification for NO_3^- removal.

Phosphorus. Phosphorus will be present in secondary effluent (10 mg/l) primarily as orthophosphate; as the condensed phosphates, meta and polyphosphates; and as organic phosphate (Reed, 1972). Sewage sludges contain high concentrations of phosphorus (0.7-3.9 percent) (Burd, 1968). Although the chemical identity of sludge phosphorus has not been determined it probably corresponds closely to that of secondary effluent.

Chemical fixation of orthophosphate by Fe, Al, Ca, and clay minerals in soil and plant removal provide the primary mechanisms for the renovation of waste phosphorus by the soil filter. Soil microorganisms influence the effectiveness of soil renovation primarily by mineralizing orthophosphorus from the more mobile organic and condensed phosphates so that the fixation reactions can occur (Figure 5-5). The significance of the microbial reduction of ortho P to volatile

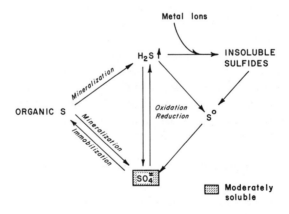

Figure 5-5. The important microbial reactions involving sulfur within the "soil filter"

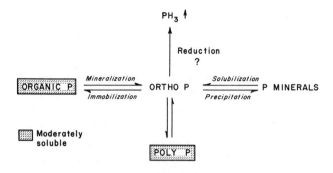

Figure 5-6. The important microbial reactions involving phosphorus within the "soil filter"

PH_3 and the synthesis of inorganic poly P in soils (Ghonsikar and Miller, 1973) has presently not been evaluated.

Sulfur. The primary chemical form of sulfur in secondary effluent will be $SO_4^=$ with small amounts as organic sulfur. Sewage sludges will be higher in organic sulfur but will also contain some insoluble metal sulfides and hydrogen sulfide. If aerobic conditions are maintained in the soil during waste disposal the microbial reactions of primary interest are the oxidation of metal sulfides and H_2S to $SO_4^=$ which is both mobile and available to higher plants (Figure 5-6). Mineralization of organic sulfur will probably be of greater significance than immobilization when waste materials are added to soils with the result that the pool of soluble $SO_4^=$ will increase.

Improper management of liquid waste disposal on land which creates anaerobic soil conditions will result in $SO_4^=$ reduction to H_2S. Hydrogen sulfide can in turn react with various metal ions to form insoluble sulfides. Ferrous sulfide has been implicated as one of the chemical components responsible for intensifying soil clogging during wastewater irrigation (Reed, 1972).

Inorganic ions. Waste effluents contain relatively low concentrations and sewage sludges high concentrations of metallic and non-metallic cations and anions (Ewing and Dick, 1970; Lagerwerff, 1967). The exact composition of these wastes with regard to inorganic constituents is extremely variable and dependent upon the industrial sources which contribute wastes to the sanitary treatment system as well as the treatment processes themselves.

When secondary effluents are applied to soils most of the heavy metals are retained within the surface horizon by interactions with soil organic matter and colloidal clay minerals; or by precipitation as insoluble oxides, hydroxides, phosphates, or sulfides. In the case of applied sewage sludge, the sludge solids will retain most of the metal ions until released by the microbial decomposition of the sludge organic matter.

Addition of these inorganic constituents to soils in liquid wastes presents a potential problem because of their movement into ground water, destroying water quality; or by their accumulation to phytotoxic levels in the soil. The latter effect would reduce the efficiency of the higher plant component of the "soil filter" for waste renovation. In addition, a particular element may be taken up in such concentration that the intended use of the harvested plant material for human or animal consumption may be curtailed.

Soil reactions of iron and manganese are similar in many ways and thus will be discussed together. The microbial reactions in soil which affect the success of the "soil filter" with respect to Fe and Mn are shown in Figure 5-7. A detailed discussion of the relative significance of each reaction to the mobility of Fe and Mn is beyond the scope of this chapter, but a few salient remarks will be made about each. The readers are referred to an excellent symposium, Mortvedt *et al.* (1972), for further information on the soil reactions of these and other micronutrient ions. Unfortunately, much of this information is based on soil reactions at rather low concentrations of inorganic ions. Considerably more information is needed on the interactions of inorganic ions in soils at the high concentrations likely to be encountered after prolonged applications of waste effluents and sewage sludges.

The iron and manganese in well aerated soils and at near neutral pH's will be primarily found in the oxidized state as insoluble organic matter complexes and insoluble oxides, hydroxides, and phosphates

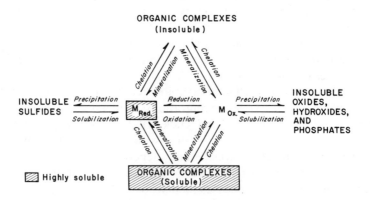

Figure 5-7. Microbial reactions which influence the solubility and mobility of Fe and Mn in soils

(Figure 5-7). The concentration of these individual ions in the aqueous phase is normally very low, often in the parts per billion range. The ions which are found are considered to be primarily in organic combination as soluble metal-organic matter complexes (Lindsay, 1972; Geering et al., 1969). Organic compounds capable of forming chelates are continuously being produced in soil by microbial activity. Most of these compounds can in turn be decomposed so the amount present in the soil solution represents a balance between synthesis and destruction. Since chelating agents have the ability to transform solid phase forms of Fe and Mn (hydroxides, phosphates, etc.) into soluble metal complexes, their production during decay of organic waste materials is likely to increase the availability of these ions to plants, and their mobility through the profile. The degradation of the soluble organic matter-metal complexes, as well as the in-soluble organic matter complexes will again release Fe and Mn ions which will again be precipitated or recomplexed. Some micro-organisms can also form mineral acids (nitric and sulfuric) which would solubilize some of the oxides, hydroxides, or phosphates.

Another microbial process of considerable significance to the mo-bility of Fe and Mn is that of reduction. If a soil becomes waterlogged during irrigation with liquid wastes the Fe^{2+} and Mn^{2+} level in soil rises rapidly. Ferrous and manganous ions are highly mobile in soil and may, under prolonged anaerobic condition, move through the soil profile into water supplies or form a water impermeable layer in the B horizon (Döring, 1960; Bocko, 1965). The presence of available or-ganic substrates enhances the reduction of both ions. The reduction of Fe^{3+} has been shown to be entirely a result of microbial activity, while Mn^{4+} reduction is almost exclusively microbial at a pH >6.0 (Alexander, 1961). The reduction of both ions may occur as an indirect result of microbial activity in lowering soil pH, or of the E_h by depletion of O_2; or by direct reduction with both Fe^{3+} and Mn^{4+} serving as electron acceptors in cell respiration. Biological reoxida-tion of both Fe^{2+} and Mn^{2+} has been shown to occur in soils (Aristovskaya and Zavarzin, 1971; Ehrlich, 1971) although chemical oxidation of Fe^{2+} can occur at a near neutral pH, and Mn^{2+} at a pH >8.0.

Under anaerobic conditions and in the presence of high concentra-tions of H_2S, insoluble sulfides of both Fe and Mn can be formed in soil (see section on sulfur). The effect of sulfide formation will be to reduce the mobility of Fe and Mn.

The microbial reactions which influence various heavy metal ions are shown in Figure 5-8. Basically, the reactions are like those of Fe and Mn but do not include oxidation-reduction reactions. As with Fe and Mn a very large percentage of the ion present in solution prob-

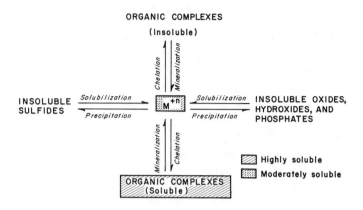

Figure 5-8. Microbial reactions which influence the solubility and mobility of Zn, Cu, Ni, Cd, Hg, Cr, Ag, and Co in soils

ably occurs as soluble organic complexes (Lindsay, 1972). The quantity of all of these heavy metals which will be retained by the "soil filter" after repeated application of metal containing wastes will be largely related to the organic matter content of the soil. Unfortunately very little is known concerning the relative amounts of the various metal ions which will occur as organic-metal complexes or of the factors affecting the availability of the organically bound nutrients to plants. Experiences at the Paris and Berlin sewage farms have indicated that "exhausted" soils high in organic matter retained a larger total amount as well as soluble Cu and Zn (Rohde, 1962). Studies at the University of Illinois by Hinesly *et al.* (1971) have shown that plants grown in soil amended with liquid digested sewage sludge contained a greater concentration of Zn, Mn and Fe but not Ni and Cu. They attributed the enhanced uptake in part to the addition of the elements in the sludge as well as the indirect effect of sludge on increasing the availability of the metal ions.

A third group of inorganic ions, K^+, Mg^{2+}, Ca^{2+}, and Na^+, is also found in waste effluents and sewage sludges. None of these cations are complexed strongly by soil organic matter and their retention in soil is related to normal exchange reactions on clay minerals and organic colloids. The microbial population of soils has little effect on the reactions of these ions except indirectly in the formation and degradation of soil organic matter (Figure 5-9).

A couple of other microbial reactions could possibly influence the mobility of metal ions in soils. One involves the alkylation of certain metals to volatile derivatives. Thus far, the microbial alkylation of Hg, Se, Te, and As has been demonstrated to occur (Figure 5-10;

Slightly soluble

Figure 5-9. Microbial reactions which influence the solubility and mobility of Ca, Mg, K, and Na in soils

Alexander, 1971b; Ehrlich, 1971). Whether these laboratory phenomena have any significance in the soil environment remains to be evaluated. A second reaction would be the immobilization of metal ions within microbial cells. Although there are some examples of very large accumulations of metal ions within microbial cells in culture it is doubtful if this reaction will be of any significance in the soil reactions of metal ions.

Conclusions

The preceding discussion has reviewed in moderate detail the various microbial reactions which influence the success of soil as a filter for renovating municipal wastewater and sludge. The majority of these activities are beneficial, actually essential, for maintaining the integrity and effectiveness of the soil filter. Only one reaction, nitrification, can be considered detrimental to the success of the soil filter when the disposal method maintains adequate soil aeration.

It should also be emphasized that prolonged periods of anaerobiosis must be avoided for the proper functioning of the microbial component of the soil filter. Proper management of land disposal systems for liquid waste regardless of the mode of application must provide for periods of adequate aeration. Failure to do so will result in reduced decomposition of organic wastes, odors, reduction and mobilization of Fe and Mn, changes in the solubility of other in-

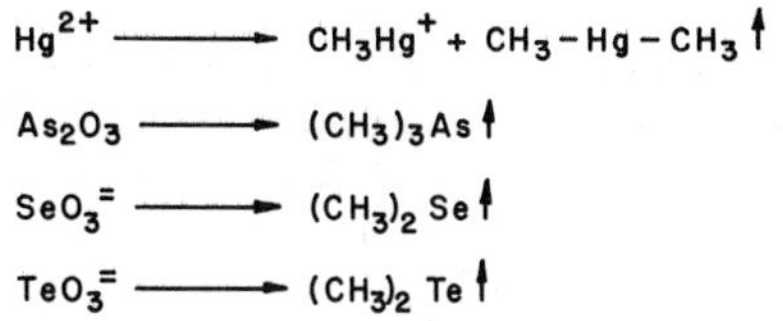

$$Hg^{2+} \longrightarrow CH_3Hg^+ + CH_3-Hg-CH_3 \uparrow$$
$$As_2O_3 \longrightarrow (CH_3)_3As \uparrow$$
$$SeO_3^= \longrightarrow (CH_3)_2Se \uparrow$$
$$TeO_3^= \longrightarrow (CH_3)_2Te \uparrow$$

Figure 5-10. Microbial alkylation of Hg, As, Te, and Se

organic ions, and inundation of vegetative cover. In addition, anaerobic conditions in the soil seem to intensify the clogging of the soil surface with microbial cells, polysaccharides, and ferrous and manganous sulfides which reduces water infiltration.

Literature Cited

Alexander, M. 1961. *Introduction to Soil Microbiology.* John Wiley and Sons, Inc., N.Y.

Alexander, M. 1965a. Biodegradation problems of molecular recalcitrance and microbial fallibility. *Adv. Appl. Microbiol.* 7:35-80.

Alexander, M. 1965b. Persistence and biological reactions of pesticides in soils. *Soil Sci. Soc. Amer. Proc.* 29:1-7.

Alexander, M. 1971a. *Microbial Ecology.* John Wiley and Sons, Inc., N.Y.

Alexander, M. 1971b. Biochemical ecology of microorganisms. *Ann. Rev. Microbiol.* 25:361-392.

Aristovskaya, T. V. and G. A. Zavarzin. 1971. Biochemistry of iron in soil. Ch. 13. In *Soil Biochemistry,* Vol. 2., A. D. McLaren and J. Skujins (ed.). Marcel Dekker, Inc., N.Y.

Benarde, M. A., B. W. Doft, R. Horvath, and L. Shaulis. 1965. Microbial degradation of the sulfonate of dodecyl benzene sulfonate. *Appl. Microbiol.* 13:103-105.

Bocko, J. 1965. Displacement of iron in soil irrigated with sewage. *Zesz. nauk. Wyzsz. Szk. roln. Wrocl. Melior.* 10: No. 61, 209-217. Abstract only, *Soils & Fertilizers* 29: No. 527.

Bouwer, H. 1973. Renovating secondary sewage effluent by groundwater recharge with infiltration basins. *Recycling Treated Municipal Wastewater and Sludge through Forest and Cropland.* The Pennsylvania State University Press.

Broadbent, F. E. 1973. Factors affecting nitrification-denitrification in soils. *Recycling Treated Municipal Wastewater and Sludge through Forest and Cropland.* The Pennsylvania State University Press.

Burd, R. S. 1968. A study of sludge handling and disposal. Water Pollution Control Research Series Publication No. WP-20-4, U.S. Department of the Interior.

Clark, F. E. 1967. Bacteria in soil. In *Soil Biology.* A. Burges and F. Raw (ed). Academic Press, N.Y.

Clark, F. E. and E. A. Paul. 1970. The microflora of grassland. *Adv. Agronomy* 22:375-435.

Dagley, S. 1967. The microbial metabolism of phenolics. In *Soil Biochemistry,* Vol. 1, A. D. McLaren and G. H. Peterson (ed), pp. 287-318. Marcel Dekker, Inc., N.Y.

Döring, H. 1960. Chemical causes of soil fatigue following irrigation with sewage water in Berlin, and possibilities of preventing the decrease in crop yields. *Dtsch. Landw.* 11:342-345.

Ehrlich, H. L. 1971. Biogeochemistry of the minor elements in soil. Ch. 12. In *Soil Biochemistry,* Vol. 2, A. D. McLaren and J. Skujins (ed). Marcel Dekker, Inc., N.Y.

Ellis, R., Jr. and R. S. Adams, Jr. 1961. Contamination of soils by petroleum hydrocarbons. *Adv. Agronomy* 13:197-216.

Ewing, B. B. and R. I. Dick. 1970. Disposal of sludge on land. In *Water Quality Improvement by Physical and Chemical Processes.* University of Texas, Austin.

Foster, D. H. and R. S. Engelbrecht. 1973. Microbial hazards in disposing of waste-water on soil. *Recycling Treated Municipal Wastewater and Sludge through Forest and Cropland*. The Pennsylvania State University Press.

Geering, H. R., J. F. Hodgson, and C. Sdano. 1969. Micronutrient cation complexes in soil solution: IV. The chemical state of manganese in soil solution. *Soil Sci. Soc. Amer. Proc.* 33:81-85.

Ghonsikar, C. P. and R. H. Miller. 1973. Soil inorganic polyphosphates of microbial origin. *Plant and Soil* 38. (In Press).

Gibson, D. T. 1968. Microbial degradation of aromatic compounds. *Sci.* 161:1093-1097.

Glathe, H. and A. A. M. Makawi. 1963. Uber die Wirkung von Klarschlanm auf Boden und Mikroorganismen. *Z Pfl Ernahr Düng.* 101:109-121.

Hallam, M. J. and Bartholomew, W. V. 1953. Influence of rate of plant residue addition in accelerating the decomposition of soil organic matter. *Soil Sci. Soc. Amer. Proc.* 17:365-368.

Hinesly, T. D., O. C. Braids, and J. E. Molina. 1971. Agricultural benefits and environmental changes resulting from the use of digested sewage sludge on field crops. Report SW-30d, U.S. Environmental Protection Agency.

Horvath, R. S. 1972. Microbial co-metabolism and the degradation of organic compounds in nature. *Bacteriol. Rev.* 36:146-155.

Hunter, J. V. and T. A. Kotalik. 1973. Chemical and biological quality of treated sewage effluent. *Recycling Treated Municipal Wastewater and Sludge through Forest and Cropland*. The Pennsylvania State University Press.

Jackson, R. M. 1965. Studies of fungi in pasture soils. 2. Fungi associated with plant debris and fungal hyphae in soil. *New Zealand Jour. Agric. Res.* 8:865-877.

Jenkinson, D. S. 1966. Studies on the decomposition of plant material in soil. II. Partial sterilization of soil and soil biomass. *Jour. Soil Sci.* 17:280-302.

Jensen, H. L. 1963. Recent advances in soil microbiology. *Sci. Hort.* 15-21.

Kardos, L. T. 1967. Wastewater renovation by the land—a living filter. In *Agriculture and the Quality of Our Environment*. N. C. Brady (ed). AAAS Publication 85, Washington, D.C.

Kardos, L. T. 1970. A new prospect. *Environment* 12:20-21, 27.

Kardos, L. T., W. E. Sopper, and E. A. Myers. 1968. A living filter for sewage. In *Science for Better Living*, pp. 197-201. U.S. Dept. of Agriculture, Yearbook of Agriculture, Washington, D.C.

Krasilnikov, N. A. 1944. The bacterial mass of the rhizosphere of plants. *Mikrobiologia* 13:144-146.

Lagerwerff, J. V. 1967. Heavy-metal contamination of soils. In *Agriculture and the Quality of Our Environment*. N. C. Brady (ed). AAAS Publication 85, Washington, D.C.

Lake Erie report—A plan for water pollution control. U.S. Dept. Interior, Fed. Water Poll. Control Admin. 1968.

Latter, P. M. and J. B. Cragg. 1967. The decomposition of *Juncus squarrosus* leaves and microbiological changes in the profile of *Juncus* moor. *Jour. Ecol.* 55:465-482.

Law, J. P., Jr. 1968. Agricultural utilization of sewage effluent and sludge. An annotated bibliography. Fed. Water Poll. Control Admin. U.S. Dept. Interior.

Lindsay, W. L. 1972. Role of chelation in micronutrient availability. Ch. 17. In E. W. Carson (ed). *The Plant Root and Its Environment*. University of Virginia Press, Charlottesville.

Mallman, W. L. and W. N. Mack. 1961. Biological contamination of ground water. Ground Water Contamination, U.S. Public Health Service Tech. Rept. W61-5, pp. 35-43.

McCoy, J. H. 1971. Sewage pollution of natural waters. In *Microbial Aspects of Pollution*. G. Sykes and F. A. Skinner (ed). Academic Press, N.Y.

McGauhey, P. H. and R. G. Krone. 1967. Soil mantle as a wastewater treatment system. Engineering Research Laboratory Report No. 67-11, Univ. of Calif., Berkeley.

McKenna, E. J. and R. E. Kallio. 1965. The biology of hydrocarbons. *Ann. Rev. Microbiol.* 19:183-208.

McLaren, A. D. and G. H. Peterson. 1967. *Soil Biochemistry*, Vol. 1. Marcel Dekker, Inc., N.Y.

Miller, R. H. 1973. The microbiology of sewage sludge decomposition in soil. Unpublished report. Dept. of Agronomy, The Ohio State University.

Mortvedt, J. J., P. M. Giordano and W. L. Lindsay (ed). 1972. *Micronutrients in Agriculture*. Soil Sci. Soc. Amer., Inc. Madison, Wisc.

Painter, H. A., M. Viney and A. Bywaters. 1961. Composition of sewage and sewage effluents. *Jour. Inst. Sew. Purif.* Pt. 4, 302.

Reed, S. C. 1972. Wastewater management by disposal on the land. Special Report 171, Cold Regions Research and Engineering Laboratory, Hanover, N. H.

Robeck, G. G., J. M. Cohen, W. T. Sayers, and R. L. Woodward. 1963. Degradation of ABS and other organics in unsaturated soils. *Jour. Water Poll. Control Fed.* 35:1225-1236.

Rohde, G. 1962. The effects of trace elements on the exhaustion of sewage irrigated land. *Jour. Inst. Sew. Purif.* Pt. 6, 581-585.

Rudolfs, W., L. L. Falk and R. A. Ragotzkie. 1950. Literature review of the occurrence and survival of enteric, pathogenic and relative organisms in soil, water, sewage, sludges and on vegetation. *Sewage Ind. Waste* 22:1261-1281.

Russell, E. J. 1950. *Soil Conditions and Plant Growth*, 8th Ed., Longmans, Green and Co., London.

Sopper, W. E. 1971. Effects of trees and forests in neutralizing waste. Institute for Research on Land and Water Resources, The Pennsylvania State University, University Park, Pa. Reprint Series No. 23.

Stockli, A. 1956. Mitt. Schiveiz. Landwirt. 8:125-130. In F. E. Clark and E. A. Paul. 1970. The microflora of grassland. *Adv. Agronomy* 22: 404.

Thomas, R. E. and T. W. Bendixen. 1969. Degradation of wastewater organics in soil. *Jour. Water Poll. Control Fed.* 41:808-813.

Tiedje, J. M. and B. B. Mason. 1971. Biodegradation of nitrilotriacetic acid (NTA) in soils. Bacteriol. Proc., p. 1.

Van Donsel, D. J., E. E. Geldreich and N. A. Clarke. 1967. Seasonal variations in survival of indicator bacteria in soil and their contribution to storm-water pollution. *Appl. Microbiol.* 15:1362-1370.

Viets, F. G., Jr. and R. H. Hageman. 1971. Factors affecting the accumulation of nitrate in soil, water, and plants. Agriculture Handbook No. 413, ARS, USDA, Washington, D.C.

6
Site Selection Criteria for Wastewater Disposal — Soils and Hydrogeologic Considerations

Richard R. Parizek*

Site selection criteria for sewage effluent spray irrigation sites are discussed. Soils, geology, hydrology, topography, project management and other factors are considered to maximize the chances for achieving a high degree of renovation of waste constituents while at the same time minimizing secondary environmental problems that can result such as degradation of groundwater quality, water logging of soils, surface runoff and erosion, and local flooding. Site conditions suitable and unsuitable for groundwater recharge and reuse are pointed out as are factors to be considered when designing monitoring programs necessary to prove the degree of treatment being achieved, hence the success or failure of a particular irrigation operation. Finally, the importance of the hydrogeologic-soil condition is discussed for the benefit of administrators who are responsible for defining environmental policy and preparing guidelines for design, regulation and enforcement procedures to be used for wastewater irrigation projects.

Comments are not based solely on experience gained with the Penn State Wastewater Project. Rather, basic principles are considered which should apply when selecting irrigation sites or designing and operating irrigation systems in many areas. Experiences from our own project as well as other successful and unsuccessful projects in Pennsylvania and elsewhere are used for illustration.

Significance of the Soils, Geologic, and Hydrologic Conditions

Significance of various physical and geochemical factors to be considered when selecting irrigation sites varies depending on the quality of wastewater to be applied, acreage required, amount and duration of wastewater application, water quality standards to be met for the receiving body of water, climate, other uses to be made of the irrigation site, seasons of year water is to be applied, attention that is likely

*Department of Geosciences and The Mineral Conservation Section, The Pennsylvania State University.

to be given to managing the irrigation project, and a number of other factors.

For example, where effluent is being used primarily as a source of irrigation water and is being applied solely as a benefit to crops, the amount and quality of water best suited to plant growth and the intended use of the crop may be the limiting factors. How often and how much water should be applied and by what method to achieve the best growth response at least cost? Almost any soil and cover crop condition can beneficiate sewage effluent when application rates are equal to or less than evapotranspiration rates because under these conditions little if any effluent moves through the soil. The soil moisture reservoir becomes a physical barrier to water movement whenever the soil-water content drops below field capacity. The residence time of effluent in the biologically active zone is prolonged in such a climatic setting and effluent is depleted mainly by evapotranspiration rather than deep percolation. In more humid regions this procedure would be impractical because water could be applied only from time to time as weather conditions dictate. More frequent applications would be possible in arid to semi-arid regions.

Prolonged use of this practice in more arid regions, balancing application rates with evapotranspiration rates, however, would result in a salt or total dissolved solids build-up in shallow soils, an increase in the salinity of return flow and occasional groundwater recharge of poor quality. This normally would not be a problem in humid regions because precipitation is available to provide dilution.

When planning to apply wastewater in arid to semi-arid regions, considerable attention must be given to site selection and land management to be assured the irrigation area will not be chemically degraded and the agricultural productivity destroyed. Considerable experience has been gained in applying waters with a high total dissolved solids content in arid and semi-arid regions with both favorable and devastating results. This general problem has been studied by others and is well documented in the literature, for example, Fireman and Haywood (1955). Several points are obvious. Application rates combined with precipitation must exceed evapotranspiration rates to insure that soluble salts are leached from the soil. Good subsurface drainage is desirable as is a rather deep water table to minimize groundwater evapotranspiration losses and a resulting salinity build-up. There is a limit, particularly for large projects, to the number of times reclaimed effluent should be recycled from the community to the treatment site to avoid a long term increase in total dissolved solids. It is desirable to have thorough drainage of return flow or an open rather than a closed geochemical system (Figure 6-1a and 6-1b). In the latter, the total dissolved solids will accumulate and ultimately may cause problems (Figure 6-1c).

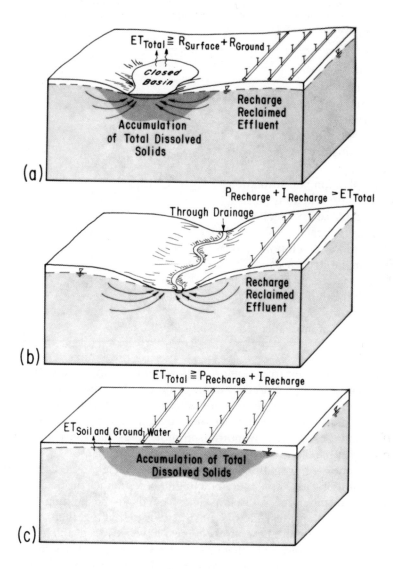

Figure 6-1. Locally open (a), open (b) and closed (c) geochemical systems. In (a), total evapotranspiration from the basin equals or exceeds total surface- and groundwater runoff causing a local increase in the total dissolved solids in the discharge area. In (b), recharge from precipitation and irrigation exceeds evapotranspiration and groundwater is discharged to a through going stream. In (c), soil- and groundwater evapotranspiration nearly equals or exceeds recharge from precipitation and irrigation and total dissolved solids increase.

Table 6-1. Summary of physical, geochemical and biochemical processes that contribute to the renovation of solid and liquid waste materials (after Parizek and Langmuir, 1971)

Physical Processes
   Filtration
   Dispersion
   Dilution
   Adsorption-desorption
   Gas transfer
Geochemical Processes
   Complex ion pair formation
   Acid-base reactions
   Inorganic redox reactions
   Ion exchange
   Precipitation-solution
Biochemical Processes
   Solute uptake in biosynthesis
   Solubilization of cellulose, etc.
   Mineralization of organics
   Catalysis of inorganic redox reactions

Most wastewater irrigation projects will not be operated only when irrigation water is required. Rather, to be feasible, they must operate during periods when soil moisture is in excess of plant requirements, and the moisture content is at or above field capacity. The more irrigation rates exceed evapotranspiration rates the more important topography, soils, geologic, hydrologic and other factors become in the selection of irrigation sites to insure sufficient and long term renovation of waste constituents. No one of a number of factors to be considered under these circumstances needs to be limiting or controlling but rather these factors must be considered together.

Other authors in these proceedings have stressed the role and importance of biological, chemical and physical processes in wastewater renovation which must work in tandem to provide a maximum degree of renovation. The basic processes involved are summarized in Table 6-1. These processes operate primarily within the biologically active zone of shallow soils and in deeper soils and rock above and below the water table. The soil and rock substrate and the soil-water and groundwater they contain serve more than just as a substrate for the biological community — the living filter which accounts for most of the renovation achieved. Rather they exert an active physical and geochemical role as well which helps to increase the efficiency of the treatment system and provide protection or a factor of safety against the premature or eventual break-through of waste constituents to the groundwater or surface water reservoir. This can occur during prolonged use of irrigation sites, during periods of excessive application accompanying pipe line breaks or leaks, where runoff and local ponding at the surface and in the subsurface redistributes effluent and causes heavy loadings, during heavy precipitation, during winter irrigation, and melting of snow and ice packs.

It is desirable, therefore, in site selection studies to consider those aspects of the soils, geologic and hydrologic conditions that will help to maximize and prolong the renovation process, hopefully, indefinitely.

Characteristics of an Ideal Site
There is little point in defining site characteristics so specifically and rigidly that they can rarely be met under the great variety of conditions likely to be encountered in the field. It is desirable to outline conditions that should be striven for when selecting wastewater renovation sites. The very best and most conservative sites should always be selected when choices are available. In this manner secondary environmental problems can be minimized or eliminated and the life of the renovation system, hence the project, prolonged indefinitely. Fewer choices are available for small projects where effluent must be treated close to its source. If site conditions are poor at these locations, land application may not be the answer. For larger projects where millions to tens of millions of gallons of effluent a day are involved, proximity to the source is far less important than obtaining a suitable site.

It is equally important that regulatory officials responsible for adopting policy guidelines for irrigation projects or for reviewing, approving and policing irrigation projects maintain a flexible viewpoint as well because many sites that may appear to depart drastically from the ideal may in fact be found to be suitable under actual use. For example, poorly drained soils may actually provide a higher degree of nitrate removal when compared to better drained soils. Control of nitrate concentrations in groundwater at irrigation sites is one of the main challenges that users of the irrigation system face. Nitrate removal can be one of the weakest links in the irrigation concept.

It is possible to engineer some sites to improve infiltration and drainage, improve renovation, control groundwater levels, prevent trespass of wastewater by overland or subsurface flow, control wind drift of effluent, etc. Regulatory officials should encourage innovation and originality among those designing and operating irrigation projects because each project must be designed as a separate unit and each will have its own special problems and challenges that must be worked out. There is no single fixed blue print for wastewater irrigation systems that can be used under all field circumstances.

Infiltration and Drainage

Sewage effluent must infiltrate into soil and be retained for a sufficient period within the biologically active zone to be acted upon by renovation agents. Some renovation may be achieved during overland flow but this is not as effective as when effluent enters and is retained within the soil. Reduction in BOD, removal or reduction of suspended solids and bacteria, etc. can be expected during overland flow. After infiltrating into the soil, some of the effluent may be withdrawn and consumed by evapotranspiration, some may percolate to the water table or move laterally as interflow and be returned to surface. Lateral flow need not be bad at irrigation sites provided the effluent has been renovated prior to being discharged to the surface and provided that other wastewater is not being applied to these soil-water discharge areas, particularly the larger ones. Some lateral flow is inevitable particularly when effluent is being applied in humid regions, on sloping ground or on soils where the B-horizon, caliche layers, plow soles and stratification within or below the C-horizon help promote lateral movement (Figure 6-2). Effluent has been sampled at the Penn State research facility after having moved laterally through soil for 25 to more than 250 feet before being discharged to the surface or intercepted in a 17-foot deep trench lysimeter (Figure 6-3). Water was found to be of favorable quality wherever it had entered the soil and had a residence time sufficiently long to permit renovation.

Natural soil or at least fine-grained unconsolidated material is always preferred at irrigation sites over mechanically weathered bedrock, quarry wastes, artificial fills containing a wide variety of waste materials and grain sizes. The latter can have high or excessive infiltration capacities and may be too well drained to favor renovation when compared to most natural soils. A moderately well drained to well drained soil would appear to meet both infiltration and drainage requirements for an irrigation area. However, even less well drained soils can be considered provided that effluent is not being applied during prolonged rainy periods, periods of heavy rainfall or freezing weather.

Values of hydraulic conductivity of different soils have been reported by O'Neil (1949), and Smith and Browning (1946). These may serve as a guide when considering soils for irrigation projects (Table 6-2).

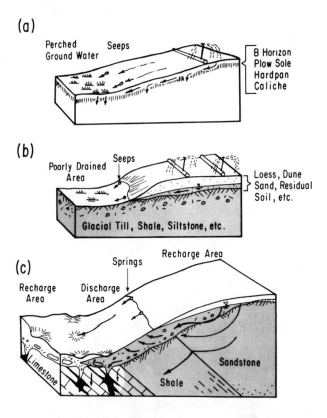

Figure 6-2. Three cases favoring lateral flow of reclaimed effluent. In (a) flow is
mainly downslope and occurs above the B-horizon, plow sole, hardpan or
caliche layer. In (b), a deeper penetration of effluent may be possible but
due to the stratification, most water moves laterally to seeps and springs.
In (c), effluent may be applied to the recharge area at the left, be renovated and discharged to surface and again be recharged. Effluent would
not be renovated if applied to the discharge area in (c). (After Parizek and
Myers, 1968.)

Figure 6-3.

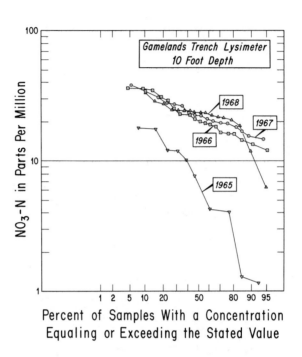

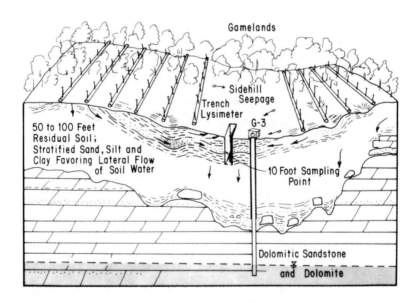

Figure 6-3. (Continued)

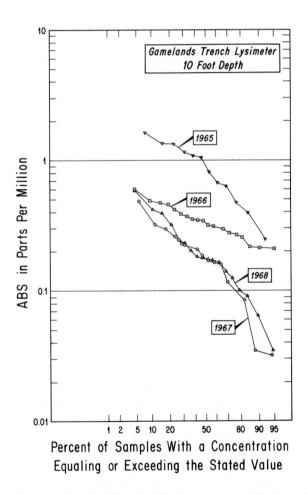

Figure 6-3. Concentration of ABS and NO_3-N (parts per million) equaled or exceeded for effluent that has migrated laterally through sandy clay and sandy loam and been collected in a 10-foot deep pan lysimeter located above a clay confining layer. Irrigation began in November 1965 at a rate of 6 inches per week until August 1966 and was continued at 4 inches per week November-April each succeeding year. Note the reduction in ABS following 1966. Schematic diagram shows location of sampling point.

Table 6-2. Classes of permeability or percolation rates for saturated subsoils (expanded from Smith and Browning, 1946)

Class	Hydraulic Conductivity or Percolation Rate	Comments
	inches/hour	
Extremely slow	<0.001	So nearly impervious that leaching process is insignificant. Unsuitable for wastewater renovation under most circumstances.
Very slow	0.001-0.01	Poor drainage results in staining; too slow for artificial drainage. Wastewater renovation possible under restricted conditions.
Slow	0.01-0.1	Too slow for favorable air-water relations and for deep root development. Usable under controlled conditions; drainage facilities may be required; runoff likely to be a problem. Good nitrate removal possible.
Moderate	0.1-1.0	Adequate permeability (conductivity). Ideal for most irrigation systems.
Rapid	1-10	Excellent waterholding relations as well as excellent permeability (conductivity). Ideal for most irrigation systems. Application rates may have to be reduced to insure renovation.
Very rapid	>10	Associated with poor waterholding conditions. Infiltration and drainage may be too rapid to achieve complete renovation. Extreme caution required.

Soils in the extremely slow to very slow class are bound to create water logging and runoff problems at irrigation sites and neither can be drained effectively to control the water table position. Soils in the slow class may require artificial drainage to control water levels, and improve on aeration conditions. These soils may prove to afford better nitrate removal when compared with better drained soils. Soils in the moderate to rapid class should be ideal. For soils in the very rapid class, flow rates may be excessive thus precluding a high degree of renovation. Effluent must be retained within the soil profile and subsoil for a sufficient period to allow the renovation processes to be effective. This is measured in days, not hours and will vary with climate, season of year, crop cover, etc.

At our winter irrigation site, for example, a six-inch per week application rate (water applied during a single day) was not excessive from an infiltration standpoint. However, nitrates and MBAS were rapidly driven to depths of 17 feet in the soil after six months of winter irrigation, were below the biological zone and could not be renovated during the following growing season by biological processes. These constituents were free to migrate to the water table after adsorption requirements were met.

Where highly permeable sand and gravel, mechanically weathered bedrock, fractured bedrock, conduits and cavity systems are present beneath the soil, little if any additional treatment except dilution and dispersion should be anticipated. Renovation must be achieved within the overlying soil.

Irrigation techniques and equipment are so well advanced today that it is possible to select and achieve a $\frac{1}{4}$-, $\frac{1}{6}$-, $\frac{1}{8}$-inch or even lower application rate per hour. Where, for example, a two-inch per week amount is called for, it is possible to apply the water at a low rate over a one to two day period or at a higher rate for briefer periods but on two separate days following one or two days of rest. Many sites with poorly drained soils could be considered suitable for irrigation provided that application rates are lower than for well drained soils assuming all other factors were equal.

The infiltration capacity can be maintained or improved by adopting good farm management practices at the irrigation site. If effluent is to be applied in winter or on soils with low infiltration rates, plowed ground should be avoided. Rather, forested areas or hay fields with well established cover crops should be used. Even under favorable site conditions, local runoff is possible from time to time particularly in the winter, early spring or late fall when evapotranspiration requirements are low, soil-water contents are high, water temperatures are low, and effluent is applied during periods of precipitation.

When winter irrigation is required in northern latitudes, careful attention must be given to selecting irrigation sites that have good infiltration capacities and subsurface drainage. Forested areas are desirable. Root holes, animal burrows and thick organic litter on the forest floor tend to provide higher infiltration capacities when compared to the same soil type in adjacent grasslands or cultivated areas. Also it has been shown that a honeycomb-type structure or more open structure tends to form in forested areas compared to the less permeable concrete-type frost that develops in plowed ground (Storey, 1955).

At the Penn State site, runoff from melting snow and ice packs composed of effluent is more pronounced in open fields than from ice packs in woodlands having the same soil type. Runoff may be traced across sloping hayfields for 100 to more than 500 feet to where it enters forest border lands that surround our fields. Here it is lost by infiltration within 500 to 1,000 feet from the irrigation plots even during periods of quick thaw.

Runoff from the Penn State irrigation plots is less than might be expected for other facilities because closed surface sags and depressions reflecting the differential solution of underlying dolomite bedrock provide surface detention storage in fields and forests alike. These depressions trap surface water, minimize runoff, and help to promote infiltration.

Measurement of Infiltration

The infiltration process is complex and influenced by a number of variables. The problem is to assess the infiltration rate not at isolated test plots, within the area of interest, but rather for the entire project area. This is a difficult task in advance of irrigation because test plots that have adequate infiltration characteristics when tested by themselves may in fact prove to be soil-water or even groundwater discharge areas or become water logged after water is applied to a more general area for prolonged periods. It is as important to know how the proposed site behaves in the presence of excess water in advance of irrigation—as in the spring—as it is to know the infiltration capacity at a number of test plots. Potential drainage problem areas need not be obvious when observing soil characteristics or type of vegetation present. Frequently problem areas can be isolated by field study following spring thaws, prolonged periods of heavy rainfall and recharge. Runoff, standing water and near saturation conditions may be observed for brief periods at sites where drainage problems are likely to occur after extensive irrigation begins.

Even experiences gained with normal agricultural irrigation practices may not prove to be foolproof in selecting irrigation sites and isolating problem areas. Normally, water is applied when there is a moisture deficit, hence, potential drainage problem areas are not as likely to be revealed. Wastewater treatment by irrigation normally requires that water be supplied in excess of evapotranspiration requirements and during periods of excess water even if winter storage is planned. Infiltration and drainage problems are maximized under these circumstances.

Infiltrometers either of the flooding or sprinkler type may be used to evaluate infiltration rates at test plots with the reservations mentioned. Methods involved have been described by Chow (1964), Gray, Norum and Wigham (1970) and others. Parizek and Myers (1968) pointed out that preliminary estimates of drainage problems can be obtained from experience or by conducting trial irrigation operations on site using potable water. Areas with poorest drainage might be tested at rates in excess of what is planned during normal operation to determine the worst possible drainage conditions that might result. Problem areas can be avoided in the final design of the distribution lines, receive less water on a weekly basis, be used only seasonally, or drained artificially. Even then, it may be difficult to anticipate subsurface drainage conditions that may develop in the long term within deeper soil or rock both above and below the water table.

For these reasons, all irrigation projects should undergo a shakedown period when they are first put into operation. During this time problem areas can be isolated and necessary adjustments made in the irrigation system. This may require changing the application schedule. Spray heads may have to be removed, or even segments of distribution lines discontinued at troublesome areas. If corrective action is taken, many of the drainage problems usually observed at irrigation sites can be minimized or eliminated. Unfortunately, irrigation systems are often viewed as rigid systems that once designed and constructed, no longer need to be altered. Economic and poor enforcement considerations dictate this to be so.

At our Gamelands site for example, effluent was applied on hill slopes underlain by stratified soils comprised of interbedded clay, silt and sand. Lateral flow and surface discharge were excessive at four-inch and six-inch per week winter application rates when effluent was applied from line to line in sequence going from top to bottom or bottom to top of a particular slope. Surface discharge and runoff were reduced when lower application amounts were used (decreasing from six inches to four inches per week) and when effluent was applied in a staggered manner, *i.e.*, first using a line on one slope, then a line on an adjacent slope before returning to the initial slope. This procedure allowed more time for subsoil drainage between applications, hence, lateral surges of soil-water movement were reduced. This simple management procedure can be adopted for manually operated or automated systems even after the project has been initiated.

Factors Commonly Ignored
Infiltration and drainage rates are influenced by water temperature and water quality among many other important factors. Infiltration rates determined in advance of irrigation may bear little resemblance to those encountered when effluent is applied. The hydraulic conductivity, K, of a soil varies with the physical properties of the soil together with the density and viscosity of water applied. This is expressed by the equation

$$K = k\rho g/n \qquad (1)$$

where ρ = density of water in gm/cm^3
n = viscosity of water in dyne-sec/cm^2
k = intrinsic permeability of soil or rock in cm^2
g = acceleration due to gravity in cm/sec^2
K = hydraulic conductivity of soil or rock in cm/sec.

This equation has been applied to soil-water flow in unsaturated and saturated conditions.

The rate of flow is determined by Darcy's law

$$V = -Ki \qquad (2)$$

where V= volume of flux of water per unit cross-sectional area
K= hydraulic conductivity in cm/sec
i = hydraulic gradient.

Frequently K is treated as a constant in field studies despite the fact that it varies with the properties of the soil as well as of the intrained water as noted above. Also intrinsic permeability of soil or rock commonly is assumed to be constant unless there is a change in soil characteristics. The fact that significant changes in intrinsic permeability can occur is frequently ignored when evaluating infiltration and drainage characteristics of soils at proposed irrigation sites. The mineralogy of soils together with quality of effluent to be disposed of must be considered because clay soils can expand in the presence of increased volumes of water or with changes in water quality. Also changes in cations and anions in soils resulting from exchange reactions can bring about dispersion reactions that break up soil aggregates and plug soil pores. Swelling and dispersion phenomena both can drastically influence intrinsic permeability, hence the infiltration capacity of a soil and its drainage characteristics. Irrigation sites that initially had favorable drainage characteristics experienced serious runoff problems with use for these and other reasons.

Temperature has a drastic effect on infiltration and drainage. It influences the viscosity of water as well as its surface tension. Eisenberg and Kauzmann (1969) have shown that the viscosity of water changes from 1.798 centipoises at 0°C to 0.8904 at 25°C. Equation 1 instructs us that the hydraulic conductivity responds to changes in temperature. Lowering the water temperature from 25°C to 0°C can decrease the hydraulic conductivity by one-half (Klock, 1972). The effect of changes in density accompanying water temperature changes is insignificant by comparison (equation 1). Weast (1968) has shown how surface tension is affected by temperature which influences both infiltration and drainage. Surface tension is 75.60 dynes per cm at 0°C and 71.97 dynes per cm at 25°C.

In his experiments, for example, he calculated from the capillary rise equation that 19 percent of the water in a soil column would remain after drainage at 0.3°C and observed 15.5 percent to remain in experiments. An additional 1.7 percent of total available water would be lost if the temperature increased from 0.3°C to 25°C. The water content of a soil greatly influences its water transmission properties

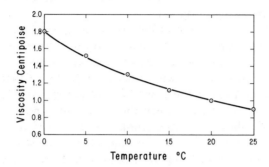

Figure 6-4. Water viscosity as a function of water temperature.

which Bruce and Klute (1956) show to be a maximum when the moisture content approaches 75-80 percent of pore saturation.

The range in water temperatures likely to be encountered at irrigation sites must be considered when evaluating proposed or potential irrigation sites and application rates. Figure 6-4 can be used to predict infiltration to be expected at 0°C or slightly warmer temperatures when infiltration measurements were made at some warmer temperature. This is important if year around irrigation is planned because water temperatures may vary from near freezing during winter to more than 80 to 90°F in summer. Klock (1972) instructs us in the use of the graph in Figure 6-4. The measured infiltration or hydraulic conductivity is multiplied by the viscosity given on the graph for a known water temperature. Dividing this new value (the intrinsic permeability) by the viscosity value, given at 0°C (1.787 centipoises) or any other temperature, the predicted infiltration rate or hydraulic conductivity at the new temperature is obtained. An example is provided where an infiltration rate was measured at 15°C and found to be 2.42 cm/hour. The question arises, what will be the infiltration rate at 0°C?

$$k = I_{15°C} \, n_{15°C} = (2.42)(1.139) = 2.756 \tag{3}$$

$$I_{0°C} \; \frac{k}{n_{0°C}} = \frac{2.756}{1.787} = 1.54 \text{ cm/hr.} \tag{4}$$

The rate obtained, 1.54 cm/hour, represents a 63 percent reduction in the infiltration rate due to a viscosity change alone. A 63 percent reduction in infiltration is sufficient to produce runoff from some soils in the late fall, winter and early spring. Similar corrections for temperature must be made when estimating the infiltration rate from holding ponds, diversion ditches and similar features used to collect and trap runoff at irrigation sites.

Less well-known are the infiltration characteristics of frozen soils which are important in year around irrigation projects in northern latitudes. At our winter irrigation site, six inches and four inches per week were applied the first winter partly in the belief that more water may be required to keep the ground from freezing. Also less land area and pipes were required to keep the system in continuous operation to prevent ice damage to the trunk and distribution lines. We observed that whenever effluent was applied at freezing to below freezing conditions (wet bulb temperatures near 32°F) ice began to develop first on twigs, tree trunks, needles, grass, etc., until more massive ice packs developed. As long as water was applied at below freezing temperatures, ice continued to build to the point that it encrusted tree trunks and branches and even began to encroach on spray heads. Where spray heads were close to trees, ice grew around and over an occasional head which continued to supply water. Snow trapped in ice packs added to the total amount of water in storage. Any day that effluent was applied at above 32°F, the ice pack began to melt and water was available for infiltration or runoff. Surprisingly, much of this melt water stayed in close proximity to the ice packs indicating that some of the water was stored in adjacent snow packs when snow was available and some infiltrated into the soil beneath and adjacent to the ice packs. Two points are clear. Ground frost development must be limited or poorly developed below ice packs near spray heads. Adjacent soils, although exposed and frozen, must retain some of their infiltration and permeability characteristics. The water content of soil near spray heads increases following the growing season and should be sufficient to produce a rather tight ground frost. However, the moment that an ice pack begins to accumulate an insulation layer is formed which helps to prevent the further development of frost. As the pack thickens and migrates laterally around the spray head, it serves as a more effective insulator. Water applied during thaws is available to permeate the ice pack and help break up what ground frost may be present.

Significant runoff may be observed particularly in the spring when effluent is being applied, during warm rainy periods when ice packs are still present. Adjacent soils, although frozen, cannot be impermeable during these periods. Runoff has been observed to enter forested border areas not receiving effluent and pond in shallow depressions where it later infiltrates the soil or it infiltrates during overland flow.

Most investigators interested in the infiltration phenomenon in fro-

zen soils agree that the quantity and size of ice-free pores are important. Work by Larkin (1962), Kuznik and Bezmenov (1963), Post and
Dreibelbis (1942) and others shows that if a soil is frozen when its
moisture content is greater than field capacity, its infiltration rate will
be very low and if saturated, the intake rate may be virtually zero.
Gray *et al.* (1970) report that other experiments have shown that
whenever an extremely wet layer within the soil profile is frozen,
downward movement of water through the layer is impeded until the
zone is thawed. Zavodchikov (1962) showed that the infiltration rate
of frozen soil may be increased six to eight times its initial rate during
the melting period which implies that heat is added to the deeper
frozen layers and helps to thaw this ice. At our own site, heat
contained in the effluent may be sufficient to cause the repeated and
early break-up of ground frost. Even in areas that are flooded from
time to time, free from snow and later are exposed to below freezing
temperatures, infiltration continues during the next period of runoff.
Ground frost may be nearly impermeable at first in these areas, but it
must thaw quickly during the next runoff-ponding cycle.

It is also possible that not all voids are occupied by ice but rather
as the freezing process continues, the total dissolved solids content
increases to the point that the final "brine" produced does not freeze.
Small conductive channels may remain for this reason.

Recent studies by Jame and Norum (1972) support the conclusion
that in a frozen soil, unfrozen liquid water can exist in equilibrium
with ice over a large temperature range below 0°C. Equations developed by them using a concept of soil-water potential help to explain
the freezing point depression of pore water that is brought about in
frozen soil. At a fixed value of soil-water suction, or soil-water potential, there is a corresponding freezing point depression which implies
that for each moisture content there is a corresponding freezing point
depression. They explain that as freezing occurs in the soil-water
system, water is transformed into ice lenses; the amount of water
remaining in the pores thus comes under increasing suction or potential. This suction or potential is believed responsible for the reduction
of the freezing point of the remaining pore water. Presumably the
remaining water is free liquid water which can account for soil conductivities observed below freezing temperatures.

Whatever the mechanisms are that help to maintain infiltration,
excessive runoff should be anticipated at most project sites whenever
irrigating in winter. Levees or small dams will have to be provided to
prevent the trespass of these waters. Forest border lands, natural
depressions, or engineered interception structures all can help infiltration and control runoff.

Ion Exchange Capacity

Physical-chemical processes operating in the soil that can add to the renovation process are discussed by others in these proceedings. It is sufficient to state that a high cation-anion exchange capacity is desirable. Clay minerals, sesquioxides, abundant organic matter, and other fine-grained mineral matter contribute to the exchange capacity. The exchange capacity is relied upon to retain and store exchangeable waste constituents within the shallow soil until they can be assimilated by the biologic system at a later date. Exchange and other physical-chemical reactions may also be relied upon to store nutrients within the soil indefinitely. Phosphorus removal by soil is a case in point. Even at the winter irrigation site where six inches per week of effluent were applied November through April, the first year on sandy soils, phosphorus was not detected above background concentrations even at shallow depths (3 to 17 feet) (Figure 6-5). Kardos has indicated that given our phosphorus concentrations and two-inch per week year around application rate, 100 years would be required to saturate even a five-foot thick column of our soil with phosphorus. If phosphorus were our only concern, higher application rates could be used year around (>2 inches per week) successfully for a prolonged period.

A soil's ability to physically retain effluent within the biologically active zone is largely dependent upon its drainage characteristics and its water content. Once the water content is in excess of field capacity, water is free to move through the soil after each new increment of water is applied. This moisture condition is prevalent during the late fall, winter and early spring when the biologic system is less active and evaporation rates are low. During this time, the adsorption capacity of the soil must be relied upon to retain nutrients within the shallow soil. This is one of the principal roles of the soil system during winter irrigation and when applying effluent during periods of heavy rainfall. Swelling and dispersion characteristics of soils are related to the mineralogy and exchange capacity of soils and quality of water applied as has been pointed out.

Soil Thickness

Evidence provided by Sopper and Kardos in this volume supports the conclusion that most renovation is achieved within the upper three to four feet of land surface where biological activity is at a maximum. Some would debate, therefore, that a three- to four-foot thick soil column should be adequate to provide the degree of treatment required.

In carbonate terranes where bedrock is covered by thin residual or transported soils, shallow voids and cavities are common near the

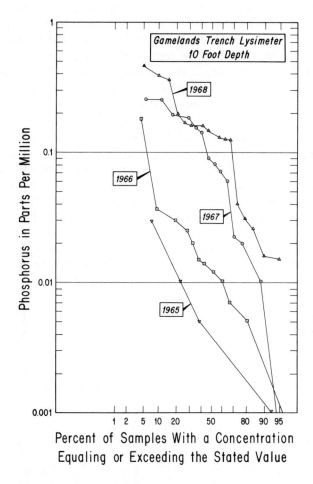

Figure 6-5. Concentration of phosphorus (ppm) equaled or exceeded for effluent that has migrated laterally through sandy clay and sandy loam and been collected in a 10-foot deep pan lysimeter located above a clay confining bed. Irrigation began in November 1965 at a rate of 6 inches per week until August 1966 and was continued at 4 inches per week November-April each succeeding year.

bedrock surface. Thin soils are especially prone to being washed or piped into these voids under natural conditions. The process is speeded up when additional water is added to the soil (Figure 6-6). Soil may be eroded away and the soil and renovation media eliminated. Sinkholes and piping voids become avenues for quick recharge that short circuit unrenovated water to the water table. Two large piping holes developed at our reed canarygrass plot where a two-inch per week application rate has been maintained since 1965. Both occurred where soil was 40 to 60 feet thick. Similar but more numerous sink holes developed at the Morgan Paper Company spray field near Lititz, Pennsylvania where residual soils derived from carbonate bedrock average less than 10 feet in thickness. Sink holes can be backfilled as they develop and covered with soil. This adds to the management responsibilities where this problem applies. Subsurface erosion problems are not normally experienced in most other geologic settings.

More than three to four feet of soil is desirable at irrigation sites in humid regions located on other soil and rock types for other reasons as well. Any site found to contain only three to four feet of soil cover on the average is bound to contain a significant land area where soils are likely to be even thinner than three feet. Most designers of wastewater irrigation projects are likely to irrigate the entire site rather than try to isolate numerous thin soil areas unless required to do so. A detailed soil exploration program is required at any site to be used for wastewater renovation but this program can prove to be

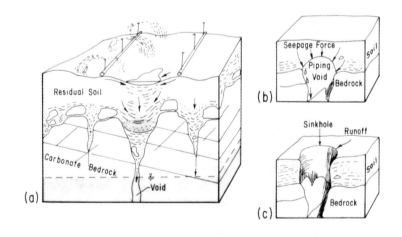

Figure 6-6. Development of piping voids and sinkholes when irrigating residual soils in carbonate terranes. In (a), soil water is channeled to voids in bedrock. Seepage forces help to erode overlying soil into voids (b) and sinkholes may finally develop allowing for recharge of unrenovated effluent (c).

costly as test borings, test pits, seismic shot lines, etc. have to be closely spaced. Even then, many thin soil areas may be overlooked. I prefer to see 20 or more feet of soil (unconsolidated deposits) above bedrock or a thick cover of fine-grained soil above coarse gravel or boulder gravel because animal burrows often extend to bedrock and provide open channels for surface runoff, application rates are always uneven in actual practice and surface ponding, runoff, and subsurface lateral flow, stem and trunk flow, and pipeline leaks all help to re-distribute effluent in an uneven manner at irrigation sites. Some parts of the soil system, therefore, are called upon to handle application rates measured in feet of water per week rather than inches per week as intended. Operational problems also arise from time to time requir-ing that more water be applied than the designed amount. All of these conditions increase the likelihood of break-throughs of incompletely treated effluent, hence, degradation of groundwater and ultimately surface water quality in the vicinity of irrigation projects.

At winter irrigation sites three to four feet of soil is totally in-adequate in northern latitudes because the nutrient storage potential of thin soils is apt to be inadequate and nutrients (pollutants) will be flushed to the water table.

The thickness of the soil cover can be artificially increased using top soil or suitable subsoil materials. Some would argue that soil structure is important to the infiltration process, hence, artificial fills should not be considered for irrigation. However, even artificial fills can be designed to insure suitable infiltration and optimum drainage through careful selection and placement of cover materials. Research work with coal mine spoil restoration using sewage effluent and sludge show that it will not take long to develop a lush cover of trees or grass even when comparatively poor material (rock fragments) is being irrigated (Sopper and Kardos, 1972). A higher degree of reno-vation would be achieved the first year if fine-grained material were used as cover material.

Topographic Setting
Slope is related to soil characteristics and runoff. Steeper slopes will promote overland flow and subsurface lateral flow more so than gentle slopes all other factors being equal. However, so long as overland flow can be avoided, it should be possible to irrigate rather steep slopes successfully under some field circumstances. It depends upon the amount of slope to be irrigated, subsoil and water table conditions, design of laterals, application rates, land use, and other factors. Also some projects will provide for lagoon storage during winter and wet periods when slope begins to exert a dominant influence on runoff.

Slopes can be engineered to some extent to provide contour

ditches, terraces, etc., to increase detention storage and infiltration. In addition to overland flow, subsurface seepage problems are more likely to develop on steep slopes where groundwater discharge areas begin to develop.

In more humid regions groundwater mounds tend to develop beneath topographic highs in response to groundwater recharge. Groundwater gradients are thereby increased during recharge periods with the result that a greater amount of water is induced to flow through an increased saturated thickness of soil or rock to regions of discharge. Irrigation projects located where there is some local relief and favorable permeability in the substrate can take advantage of the fact that there is space available for a water table build-up beneath topographic highs. Also as gradients increase, flow rates may be sufficient to transport recharge waters naturally to points of discharge.

In low relief to nearly flat areas water tables are commonly at or very near land surface and there is little if any space for additional recharge. Subsoil drainage must be provided artificially to insure adequate drainage and aerobic conditions in the biologically active zone.

Drainage ditches, tile fields, drainage wells or water supply wells may be used for this purpose (Figure 6-7) but often at a considerable additional expense to the project. Tile fields and drainage ditches are preferable where they can be used because once they have been installed they operate by gravity. Drainage wells and water supply wells have pumping lift costs to contend with in addition to construction, operation, and maintenance costs, which can add significantly to total project costs. These factors should be considered when selecting irrigation sites in low relief and poorly drained areas.

Characteristics of the Groundwater Reservoir
Parizek and Myers (1968) stressed the importance of knowing location of groundwater recharge and discharge areas when selecting wastewater renovation sites using land disposal methods. Irrigating natural groundwater discharge areas with the intent of achieving recharge should produce a negative result (Figure 6-8). Renovated water is soon rejected by the groundwater reservoir and lost by runoff and evapotranspiration. Still worse, poor drainage conditions and runoff result, and soils may become water logged. This could cause the biologically active zone to shift from an aerobic to anaerobic state, cause a destruction or alteration of the physical-chemical-biological treatment processes, and ultimately a degradation of soil-, ground-, and surface-water quality (Parizek and Myers, 1968). This basic concern is complicated by the fact that recharge-discharge relationships are not fixed. Rather, the boundary separating the two is

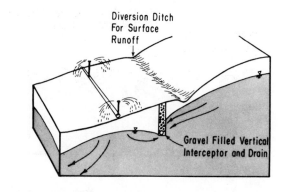

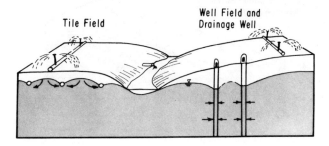

Figure 6-7. Control of surface runoff by diversion ditches, and groundwater levels by gravel-filled interceptor drains on steep slopes (a); and by tile fields, drainage wells, or water supply wells (b). Drainage ditches also may be used.

transient. Significant increases in the rates of recharge accompanying irrigation can greatly expand discharge areas, particularly for large projects. Areas that were formerly well drained recharge areas may become poorly drained discharge areas. These areas can occur several hundred to thousands of feet beyond stream channels or appear as discontinuous upland patches remote from nearby streams.

Advantages of having relief on the water table have been discussed. In addition, there should be space available for a seasonal build-up of the water table beyond natural conditions. Permeability characteristics of saturated soil and rock should be sufficient to convey reclaimed effluent to groundwater discharge areas. Where both gradients and permeability are sufficient to facilitate lateral movement of reclaimed effluent and natural recharge, a considerable savings can be achieved when compared to sites where this must be done artificially.

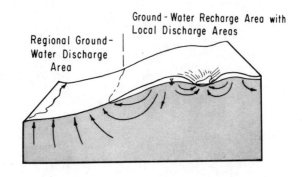

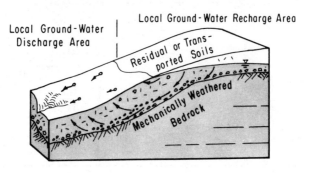

Figure 6-8. Groundwater flow systems showing regional and local groundwater discharge areas, and regional recharge areas (a); and a local groundwater flow system common on many slopes in humid regions (b). Groundwater flow in (b) may be concentrated within more permeable beds of colluvium, alluvium or within highly jointed top of bedrock. Shallow artesian systems are common in the setting. (After Parizek and Myers, 1968.)

The question frequently arises, how deep should the water table be at an irrigation site used for wastewater renovation? More importantly, what is the seasonal range in water table position and how will this be modified by additional recharge accompanying irrigation? The latter questions can be answered only by examining soils at the site to see if they formed under conditions of a seasonally high water table, by observing water table fluctuations on site or similar adjacent sites at least a year in advance of irrigation and by computing water table changes likely to be brought about by irrigation. Soils are one of the most important and reliable indices to the natural drainage (Table 6-3). As they formed they integrated and thus reflect the results of years of favorable or unfavorable drainage conditions. Soil properties are related to both the depth of the water table and number of months during the year that water is in contact with the soil profile. Schneider

Table 6-3. Soil class by drainage, color appearance, and water table position (from Schneider and Erickson, 1972)

Soil Class	Color	Water Table Conditions
Well-drained	Bright red, yellow, and brown. Free of mottles to a depth of 36 to 42 inches or more.	Water table commonly greater than 60 inches during most months.
Moderately well-drained	Uniform red, yellow or brown colors in the surface and upper subsoil horizons. Mottles present in the lower subsoil and parent or underlying materials.	
Somewhat poorly drained (imperfectly drained)	Generally mottled directly below surface horizon. Color matrix below surface layer is dominantly yellow and brown with gray, rust brown, and orange mottles.	Mottled conditions indicate the presence of a high water table during some parts of the year, usually spring, late fall and winter months. Seasonally, water table ranges from 24 to 120 inches in depth.
Poorly drained	Dark-colored surface layer high in organic matter. Horizon below the surface layer predominantly gray with orange, brown, rust brown or yellow mottles.	High water table at or within 30 inches of surface most of the year unless artificially drained.

and Erickson (1972) stress that even in dry months of the year the natural soil drainage can be predicted by observing the color and color pattern of each soil horizon, natural vegetation — whether it is water-tolerant or water-loving, and position on the landscape. This is important because water tables may fail to rise to their maximum level during a particular series of dry years or during the brief period of field study when irrigation sites are being selected.

The decision to artificially drain a site using wells, tile fields, or ditches immediately limits the concern for the position of water table because its position will be controlled or engineered as required. Even when one is willing to do so, this does not mean that artificial drainage can always be achieved at a reasonable expense. Soils, for example, that are in the "extremely slow" to "very slow" permeability class (Table 6-2) may be so nearly impervious that leaching and artificial drainage are impossible using conventional artificial means. Sites must be examined carefully with this point in mind.

It would not be rational for regulatory agencies to arbitrarily set a depth of water table position, for example, at 6 or 10 feet, as a requisite condition of irrigation sites. If this were done vast areas in the United States with water tables less than this would be eliminated from consideration. This would involve great expanses of the midwest with little or no relief that had to be drained to be farmed, and a significant percentage of areas covered by glacial till. Farm lands now being drained by tiles need not be suitable in their present form, however, because a closer spacing and even a deeper tile setting may be required to control both rainfall and reclaimed effluent. On the other hand, where enforcement personnel responsible for environmental protection are few in number and overtaxed with work, more stringent site requirements are justified.

Sites can be selected with wastewater renovation as the sole purpose. Under these circumstances, renovation is to be achieved in advance of a more distant present or possible future water use. Parizek and Myers (1968) indicated that site selection criteria for a renovation system favoring distant reuse will depart from those favoring local reuse as groundwater. Shallow penetration of renovated effluent and rapid return to the surface may be acceptable. This can be achieved by irrigating side hill slopes and local uplands that favor the surface return of waters after a sufficient degree of treatment has been achieved. Irrigation on local uplands surrounded by nearby valleys and on stratified deposits favoring the development and lateral movement of perched groundwater are common settings where this can be achieved (Figure 6-2). Loess overlying glacial till, shale or siltstone bedrock, lake clay, lake silts and sands, fluvitile silts and sands, dune sand, residual and other transported soils that overlie deposits with low permeability characteristics are cases in point. The percentage of land area that would favor renovation but unimportant groundwater recharge is greater for many states than is land that would favor significant increases in groundwater recharge for local reuse.

Groundwater recharge for local reuse may be an important objective at some project sites. Examples have been cited above where infiltration, renovation, and quick return to land surface can be achieved. In these cases, reclaimed effluent may be available for reuse off-site as surface water, it may be recaptured by wells located downstream by induced streambed infiltration, or used for recreational purposes or wildlife propagation (Parizek and Myers, 1968).

Water supply wells may be located beneath or adjacent to irrigation sites to derive benefits of reclaimed water. Wells may be planned to improve drainage as well as to supply water. In both instances, the number and spacing of wells required to provide the necessary amount of water will depend upon aquifer characteristics — storage, transmission properties, boundary conditions, recharge rates — and degree of treatment anticipated, amount of land to be irrigated, application rates and evapotranspiration requirements.

The number and spacing of on-site wells necessary to insure drainage may depend upon the volume of water required from the well field, depth and extent of pumping cones of depression developed for each well, economic considerations, and aquifer hydrologic characteristics.

Parizek and Myers (1968) point out that pumping cones of depression within the free-water surface or water table are ideal for dewatering some unconfined soil and rock aquifers and for deriving direct benefit from artificial recharge. Five plans of action are possible: (1) a wastewater renovation facility can be located adjacent to an existing well field where site conditions are suitable for irrigation, and effluent used is free of toxic or harmful nondegradable substances that otherwise are not likely to be removed in the renovation media, (2) a well field can be placed in close proximity of the site after it has been established that adequate renovation is being achieved, (3) reclaimed water discharged to surface can be re-collected in wells relying upon induced streambed infiltration, or (4) drainage wells can be placed within the irrigation area with no beneficial use planned for the water except to insure adequate drainage. Where there is doubt that adequate renovation can be achieved without relying upon dilution as well, (5) the irrigation site should be located remote from areas of existing or potential groundwater development.

For cases 1 through 4, to be effective, unconfined aquifers, or at least, semi-unconfined aquifers should underlie the irrigation site (Parizek and Myers, 1968) (Figure 6-9). These may be of diverse origin and be composed of fractured bedrock — sandstones, siltstones, carbonate rocks, gneisses and schists — sedimentary rocks containing favorable intergranular or primary permeability — sandstone, siltstone, carbonate rocks — or of permeable unconsolidated sediments such as sand and gravel.

Where confining beds are thick or relatively low in permeability, confined aquifers may derive little additional recharge than was being achieved under natural conditions. Once the maximum hydraulic gradient has been developed between the source bed and confined aquifer in response to recharge and pumpage, vertical leakage rates are fixed (Figure 6-10). Where recharge rates to source beds are in excess of the vertical leakage rate to the confined aquifer, water is rejected from the shallow system and no additional recharge benefits are achieved.

The following example should illustrate the point. Where a two-inch per week year around application rate is used in a humid

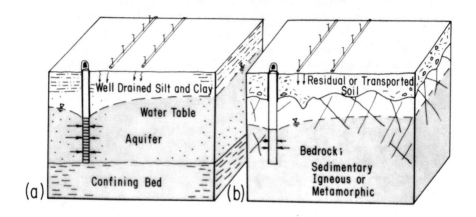

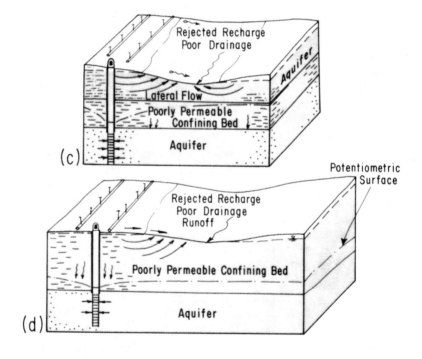

Figure 6-9. Example hydrogeologic settings favoring recharge to unconfined and semiconfined aquifers undergoing development (a and b) and conditions where recharge may be minimal (c and d). In (c) infiltration to an unconfined silt deposit or aquifer may be favorable initially, but recharge exceeds vertical leakage through the confining bed and lateral flow and poor drainage result. In (d), the confining bed extends to surface, promotes runoff, poor drainage and prevents significant recharge to the underlying aquifer.

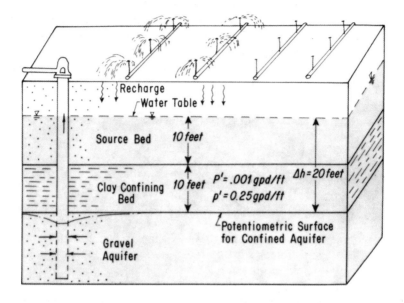

Figure 6-10. Hypothetical field conditions for which two vertical leakage rates were computed for a 10-foot thick clay confining bed assumed to have a vertical coefficient of permeability of 0.001 and 0.25 gallons per day per square foot. A mean hydraulic head of 20 feet was assumed between the water table and potentiometric surface for the confined aquifer.

region, between 976,000 to 1,475,000 gallons per year per acre of recharge might be expected. Figure 6-10 shows a confined aquifer pumped to the extent that its potentiometric surface has just reached the base of an overlying clay confining bed 10 feet thick. Above the confining bed is a slightly more permeable source bed that is receiving reclaimed effluent but does not serve as an aquifer because it has a saturated thickness of only 10 feet, and is not particularly permeable.

Assuming coefficients of vertical permeability for the clay confining bed of 0.001 and 0.25 gallons per day per square foot which is within the range of a clay-rich glacial till, vertical leakage rates of 31,937.5 and 7,982,550 gallons per year per acre might be expected. In the case where the coefficient of vertical permeability for the confining bed was 0.25 gallons per day per square foot the average annual leakage rate through the clay confining bed for the example cited would greatly exceed the recharge rate to the overlying source bed derived from reclaimed effluent which is taken as 1,500,000 gallons per year per acre. Most of the effluent would be potentially available to recharge the aquifer under development. For the case where the coefficient of vertical permeability was in the order of 0.001 gallons per day per square foot, the vertical leakage rate only would represent a fraction of the total recharge derived from the irrigation system. A variety of drainage problems might develop near the land surface within the upper source bed and significant benefits of recharge to the underlying aquifer would not necessarily be achieved.

Vertical flow rates through such confining beds can be computed using a form of Darcy's law

$$Q = \left(\frac{P'}{m'}\right) \Delta h \, Ac \qquad (5)$$

where   Q   = leakage rate through the confining bed in gallons per day (gpd).

       P'   = vertical hydraulic conductivity of confining bed, in gallons per day per square foot (gpd/ft²).

       m'   = saturated thickness of confining bed in feet.

       Δh   = difference in the mean hydraulic head in the aquifer and in the source bed overlying the confining layer, in feet.

       Ac   = area of confining bed through which leakage is occurring in square feet.

Selected vertical hydraulic conductivities for soil and rock units are presented in Table 6-4 as a guide.

One point cannot be overstressed. A large volume of recharge should be expected when irrigating in humid regions even when only a two-inch per week rate is used during the growing season. Even more recharge is achieved with year around irrigation.

Over 78 feet of effluent has been applied at the Penn State facility to plots irrigated at a rate of two inches per week, 12 months a year starting in 1964. Based on calculated evapotranspiration losses, between 59 to 100 percent of the applied water was potentially available for recharge depending upon the rate of application used, length of irrigation period and weather conditions experienced that year. The lesser amount occurred when effluent was applied April through November during a drought year, whereas, the 100 percent value was for a year when rainfall exceeded evapotranspiration by 6.01 inches (Table 6-5).

Recharge rates were higher at all plots irrigated on a 12-month per year basis and during years of normal to above normal precipitation. As evapotranspiration rates diminish during the late fall, winter and spring, nearly all applied effluent and precipitation are available for recharge at our site. Losses by runoff are negligible.

Annual recharge rates might approximate 2.9 million gallons per year where two inches per week are applied on a year around basis to

Table 6-4. Vertical hydraulic conductivities for soil and rock units determined from field testing procedures

Vertical Hydraulic Conductivity in gpd/ft²		Material Examined	Source
Range	Avg.		
1.02-1.60	1.31	Glacial drift in Illinois; sand and gravel, some clay and silt	Walton (1965)
0.10-0.63	0.25	Glacial drift in Illinois; clay and silt with considerable sand and gravel	"
0.01-0.08	0.03	Glacial drift in Illinois; clay and silt with some sand and gravel	"
0.005-0.011	0.008	Glacial drift in Illinois; clay and silt with some sand and gravel and dolomite	"
–	0.005	Glacial drift in Illinois; clay and silt with some sand and gravel and shaley dolomite	"

Range	Material Examined	Source
0.00005-.00007	Dolomite, with shale	Norris (1962)
0.00005-.0007	Maquoketa shale, northern Illinois	"
0.00008-0.9	Glacial till in northeastern Ohio	"
0.01-0.5	Surficial till, Montgomery Co. Ohio	"
0.03-0.16	Buried till, Montgomery Co. Ohio	"
0.08-0.02	Glacial till, southern Illinois	"
0.0003-0.5	Glacial till, South Dakota	"

Hydraulic Conductivity in gpd/ft²	Material Examined	Source
0.001-2.0	Clay, silt	Walton (1970)
100-3,000	Sand	"
1,000-15,000	Gravel	"
200-5,000	Sand and gravel	"
0.1-50	Sandstone	"
0.00001-0.1	Shale	"

135 acres, 1.5 billion gallons for a 600-acre project, etc. For projects involving thousands of acres (Muskegon County, Michigan, various projects proposed by the U.S. Army Corps of Engineers) vast amounts of recharge would be involved. These projects will, and have required detailed hydrogeologic investigations of proposed irrigation sites and a hydrogeologic systems analysis to determine what effect irrigation waters are likely to have on recharge and regional water table configurations. Such analyses will help to delineate areas likely to be flooded both on and adjacent to irrigation plots, the need for, and density and distribution of drainage facilities, and their effect on water tables during irrigation. For some projects, potential problem

Table 6-5. Recharge by sewage effluent for one-inch and two-inch application rates by year at the Pennsylvania State University project site

Year	Application Rate Inches per Week (April through November)	Percent Potential Recovery	Remarks	Recharge (g/acre/yr)
1963	1	65.5	Agronomic	427,000
1963	2	82.7	crops: Blaney-	1,078,000
1964	1	59.8	Criddle method	–
1964	2	79.9		–
1965	2	–		1,493,000
		Inches of Recharge		
1963	1	18	Forestry plots:	488,700
1963	2	41	Thornthwaite	1,113,000
1964	1	26	method	706,000
1964	2	59		1,602,000
1965	2	–		1,493,000
1967	2	–		1,859,000

(After Parizek *et al.*, 1967; Kardos, 1970; and Sopper, 1971).

areas will be delineated that may or may not cause problems once the project has been placed into operation. Contingency plans to eliminate potential drainage problems can be included at the time irrigation projects are designed and submitted for approval to regulatory agencies. Control measures, in turn, would be added to the system only after it has been shown that they are required through actual experience.

Large irrigation projects involving hundreds or thousands of acres of land are more difficult to analyze because as the land requirement increases the soils, geologic and hydrologic diversity and complexity are more likely to increase. Water table level responses at these sites will require analyses using electrical analog or digital modeling techniques rather than conventional analytical methods which assume more nearly ideal conditions. Data requirements for modeling soil-water and groundwater flow under complex field conditions also become more demanding because all elements required in the models must be accounted for during field studies either through actual measurement or "educated" guesswork. Fortunately, computers are now available that allow solution of large sets of simultaneous equations that can predict cause and effect phenomena in heterogeneous aquifer and confining bed systems under a wide variety of recharge and no flow boundary conditions. Generalized digital computer programs have been written to simulate one-, two- and three-dimensional steady and nonsteady flow of groundwater in heterogeneous deposits under water table, nonleaky and leaky artesian conditions. Programming techniques allow for varying pumpage from wells, varying natural or artificial recharge rates, relationship between exchange between surface waters and the groundwater reservoir, influence of drainage facilities on water table level, groundwater evapotranspiration and similar other complexities frequently encountered in the field (Douglas and Rachford, 1956; Zienkiewicz and Cheung, 1965; Zienkiewicz, Mayer and Cheung, 1966; Pinder and Bredehoeft, 1968; Bittinger, Duke and Longenbaugh, 1967; Bredehoeft, 1970; Cooley and Peters, 1970; Cooley, 1970; Prickett and Lonnquist, 1971; and Pinder, 1971).

These analytical procedures make it possible to determine the water table configuration that will develop in response to natural recharge and various schemes of groundwater development. The problem is identical for sewage effluent irrigation projects with the exception that recharge rates are greatly increased. However, basic data requirements must be met through detailed hydrogeologic investigations frequently involving geologic mapping, test drilling programs, control pumping tests, etc. Most project areas will require definition of the following variables:

1. Coefficient of vertical and horizontal permeability distributions for aquifers and confining beds.
2. Specific yield of deposits saturated or dewatered by water table fluctuations, and coefficients of storage for confined aquifers.
3. Thickness and distribution of aquifer and confining units.
4. Location and character of hydraulic boundary conditions, including recharge and nonflow boundaries.
5. Water table and potentiometric surface configurations for unconfined and confined aquifers with seasonal changes.
6. Location and amount of natural recharge and artificial recharge expected from the applied effluent.
7. Location of groundwater withdrawal points and annual pumping schedule.
8. Estimated groundwater evapotranspiration losses for the area where water tables are within 10 or less feet of land surface.

Analyses of groundwater systems can now be made for rather complex field situations. These analyses should be demanded by regulatory agencies responsible for evaluating proposals for large scale irrigation projects. These same analysis procedures may be used to determine drawdowns likely to be brought about by drainage ditches, tile fields, water supply and relief wells proposed to control water levels.

Hydrologic Isolation, Dilution and Dispersion
The groundwater reservoir can serve other roles as well. Some waste constituents are likely to be contained in sewage effluent that cannot be renovated by biological or biochemical processes or physical-chemical processes operating within the soil. Ultimately these will find their way to the groundwater reservoir. Difficult or impossible to renovate trace elements and other substances that are likely to pass through the renovation system unaltered or little altered can be isolated within groundwater flow systems (Figure 6-11). These remaining substances, in turn, can be diluted to acceptable concentrations within nearby streams and lakes. A groundwater hydrologic isolation system will work only as long as groundwater flow systems are more or less in a steady state condition. Any change in the nearby groundwater recharge-discharge regimen, change in hydrologic boundary conditions brought about by new groundwater development, excavations, or mining can cause a shift in the flow regimen, therefore a change in the system being relied upon to achieve isolation. It should be remembered that these waste constituents may survive for years to tens of years within the groundwater reservoir once they have been introduced and a procedure of "controlled contamination pollution, or degredation" is being adopted.

A more detailed hydrologic analysis is justified where such a system is to be used compared to a system where renovation is likely to be more complete.

Aside from a hydrologic isolation role, the soil-water and groundwater reservoirs may be relied upon to provide dilution and dispersion of waste materials (Figures 6-12 and 6-13). In Figure 6-12, effluent is added to a regional groundwater mound to achieve maximum dilution as groundwater flows radially away in all directions. In Figure 6-13, a site has been selected where effluent will be diluted and dispersed within a highly permeable aquifer located below the project site. Such a system should be used with extreme caution.

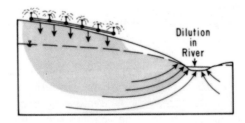

Figure 6-11. Isolation of toxic substances within groundwater flow systems. Groundwater flow is from an area of recharge beneath the irrigation site to the river which is being relied upon for dilution.

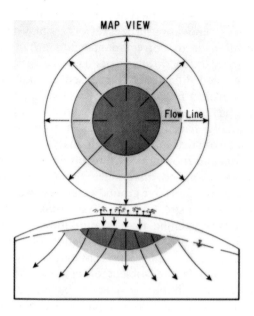

Figure 6-12. Reclaimed effluent is being recharged to a groundwater mound where radial flow maximized dilution and dispersion of toxic substances.

All nonbiodegradable substances and wastes not involved in physical-chemical reactions within the soil-water and groundwater reservoirs must be accounted for in this manner whether intended or not. A basic question arises. If waste substances cannot be removed within the renovation media by any of a combination of processes involved, should they be allowed in sewage or other effluents applied to the land and if so in what concentrations? Trace elements, heavy metals, and other more difficult to handle wastes derived from industrial processes may have to be excluded from irrigation systems or at least strictly controlled and monitored. Many of these same wastes do not belong in our rivers or lakes either.

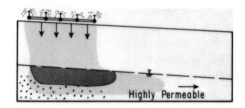

Figure 6-13. Reclaimed effluent is being recharged to an aquifer with high permeability favoring dilution and dispersion.

Toxic wastes pose a problem. They may poison biological systems responsible for key renovation processes. They may cause slow, but long term and difficult to correct damage to groundwater quality. They may be concentrated within plants used for agricultural production and cause related difficulties when used as food or feed. Spectacular irrigation project failures may be cited where oil field brine or chemical wastes have been applied to the land.

Where potentially harmful substances are included in sewage effluent that will be applied to the land, an analysis should be made to determine the concentration that may result as a function of volume and quality of water applied, time since application and distance of travel within the soil-water and groundwater reservoirs beneath and adjacent to the irrigation site. Conservative estimates can be made for design purposes by assuming that only dilution and dispersion are being relied upon to reduce the concentration of a particular substance. A more complete and representative analysis of the real complexities involved is the subject of ongoing study by various people. Ultimately it will be possible to include biochemical and geochemical reactions in addition to physical processes now being used in these analyses to study flow in saturated and unsaturated systems.

It is first necessary to determine the seepage velocity within all reference elements of the groundwater reservoir that influence groundwater flow in the vicinity of an irrigation site. All of the basic data requirements specified earlier that are required in groundwater systems analyses must be met. In addition, the porosity of saturated soil and rock must be known to determine the average seepage velocity for the deposits in question. Also the waste concentration, total waste load applied with time and area of application must be known. Horizontal and longitudinal dispersion coefficients must be known for all saturated soil and rock encountered. These hydrologic parameters are essentially unknown for most naturally occurring soil and rock and this further complicates these analyses.

The theoretical basis and derivations of dispersion equations are presented by Bear, Zaslavsky and Irmay (1968), Reddell and Sunada (1970), Ogata (1970) and Bredehoeft and Pinder (1972).

If no chemical reactions occur between the water and the aquifer or soil materials which affect the dissolved-solids concentration, then equation 6 describes the mass transport and dispersion of dissolved chemical constituents in a saturated porous media.

$$n \frac{\partial C}{\partial t} = \frac{\partial}{\partial x_i} \left(D_{ij} \frac{\partial C}{\partial x_j} \right) - \frac{\partial (q_i C)}{\partial x_i} + C_p Q \qquad (6)$$

where: C is the mass concentration of dissolved solids (m/L³),
        Dij is the coefficient of hydrodynamic dispersion (L²/T),
        Cp is the mass concentration of dissolved solids at a source
        or sink (m/L³,
    and Q is the rate of production of a source (L³/T).

The first term on the right hand represents movement of dissolved solids due to hydrodynamic dispersion, and is assumed to be proportional to the concentration gradient. The second term represents convective transport, which is proportional to the seepage velocity. The third term is a fluid source or sink.

Bear, Zaslavsky, and Irmay (1968) conclude that two processes account for hydrodynamic dispersion. One is mechanical dispersion, which depends upon both the flow of the fluid and the nature of the pore system through which flow takes place. The second is molecular diffusion which is time dependent and becomes significant at low flow velocities. In two recent field studies, Bredehoeft and Pinder (1972) and Konikow (1973) showed diffusion to be of little consequence.

Scheidegger (1961) expressed the relationship between the dispersion coefficient, fluid flow, and the pore system as

$$\text{Dij} = \alpha \text{ijmn} \; \frac{\text{Vm Vn}}{\text{V}} \tag{7}$$

where: αijmn is the dispersivity of the porous medium (L),
        Vm and Vn are the components of velocity in the m
        and n directions (L/T), and
        V is the magnitude of velocity (L/T).

Further, for isotropic porous medium the dispersivity tensor is defined by the constant α_I, the longitudinal dispersivity of the medium, and α_{II}, the transverse dispersivity. These are related to the longitudinal and transverse dispersion coefficients by

$$D_L = \alpha_I V \tag{8}$$
$$D_T = \alpha_{II} V \tag{9}$$

The method of characteristics is used to solve equation (6): Pinder and Cooper (1970), Reddell and Sunada (1970), and Bredehoeft and Pinder (1972).

Konikow (1973) presented the most complete field study that demonstrated the applicability of the theory in predicting shallow groundwater quality changes resulting from irrigation practice in a semi-arid region.

Digital solution of complex groundwater flow and chemical transport equations involved will provide a conservative estimate of the waste concentration that will result if no other renovation processes are involved.

These analyses should be demanded of designers of wastewater irrigation projects where there is doubt about the water quality conditions that may result in response to prolonged irrigation. These analyses will provide some estimate of how much of a buffer zone should be allowed between spray fields and wells and springs used as water supplies.

Design of Monitoring Facilities

All wastewater irrigation projects must contain appropriate monitoring facilities so that the designers' claims and expectations can be verified through actual experience. Wastewaters, soils, geologic and hydrologic settings, operating and management procedures are so varied that it is not safe to assume that if the irrigation method worked in one area it will automatically work in an adjacent area with a similar setting. Operator and management variations alone can cause the demise of a particular project. Cases can be cited where the recommended total annual application amount was applied to a plot within a two- or three-week period rather than on a weekly year around basis. Groundwater pollution, vegetation kills, water logging of soils, surface runoff and soil erosion resulted at these sites. The simple act of irrigating wastewaters is not sufficient to insure renovation. A misapplication of the technique can do a disservice to the living filter-irrigation concept.

Regulatory agencies should demand the installation of monitoring facilities at all wastewater irrigation projects and require routine performance reports of the operator. Some would argue that since only one sample point is required to evaluate the performance of sewage treatment plants, the effluent outflow line, only one point should be required at irrigation project sites. This is absurd in view of the field complexities involved. Questions arise. How many monitoring points are necessary, how should they be constructed, where should they be located, how frequently should samples be taken, for what waste constituents should one examine, for how long should sampling continue, what analysis techniques should be applied, etc.? For example, soil-water samples collected from six feet below an irrigation site will produce different results when compared to samples taken from monitoring wells completed in the water table below irrigation plots or when compared to samples collected from wells located in the direction of groundwater flow but adjacent to irrigated areas. It is also necessary to determine how representative a sample station is when compared to the general conditions encountered at the site. Regulatory agencies must determine what water quality standards should be met for each of the sampling regimes — on-site soil-water and groundwater, and groundwater adjacent to the site.

Only several hydrogeologic factors are considered here to illustrate the caution that must be exercised. A variety of monitoring devices and sampling stations were designed and installed at the Penn State Waste Water Renovation and Research Facility (Parizek *et al.,* 1967). These were intended for research purposes, hence the number and diversity of stations and frequency of sampling were considerably greater than would be required for routine projects.

Sampling water within the soil-moisture reservoir — above the water table — poses special problems because water is normally under tension and will not enter bore holes unless perched groundwater lenses develop. Shallow and deep pan and pressure-vacuum lysimeters were used to collect soil-water samples at the Penn State facility as well as sand-point wells, and soil samples. The advantages and disadvantages of pan and pressure-vacuum lysimeters, design and construction procedures used are described by Parizek and Lane (1970). Pressure-vacuum lysimeters represent the single best approach to sampling soil-water or water under tension. They are inexpensive, easy to install, provide samples long after other sampling devices fail as the moisture content is reduced and can be used at depths of six inches to more than 60 feet. Commercial lysimeters are available and can be modified to provide water samples below 20 or more feet (Parizek and Lane, 1970). These can be stacked within individual bore holes and provide soil-water samples at any interval within soil. It is possible, therefore, to determine the degree of renovation being achieved with time and depth on a systematic basis below irrigation plots.

Sampling water within unsaturated bedrock poses other problems where deep water tables are encountered within bedrock. A variety of well types and pumps can be used to obtain effluent samples from the groundwater reservoir. Ideally, monitoring wells should be pumped long enough to induce flow from adjacent soil or rock deposits, thereby increasing the chance of providing a more representative sample of groundwater within the vicinity of the well. Hand bailing a few gallons from a six-inch diameter well, for example, might represent only a 1/4,000,000 or less part or sample of water recharged at a 100-acre irrigation site.

Groundwater flow systems must also be considered when designing monitoring wells. Wells may be located above (Figure 6-14) or below (Figure 6-15) flow channels containing effluent, hence, they may fail to provide samples of effluent recharged to the groundwater reservoir. Depending upon the hydrogeologic setting involved, pumping may increase the chance of obtaining representative samples or have little

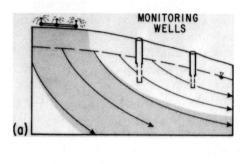

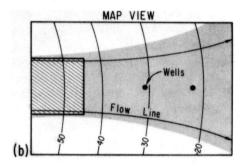

Figure 6-14. Monitoring wells located above flow channels containing sewage effluent (a). In map view (b), monitoring wells appear to be properly located.

effect. In both cases shown in Figures 6-14 and 6-15, water table maps constructed for the region could lead one to believe that the monitoring wells shown should intercept reclaimed effluent. Chances of bypassing are greatly increased where monitoring wells are completed in fractured rocks. Fractures greatly increase the permeability of rock over that of the more massive blocks of rock they enclose. The number, distribution, orientation and aperture size of rock fractures or joints and bedding plane separations rarely can be determined for irrigation sites because these sites should contain a soil cover even to be considered for irrigation. Hence, there is risk that unclaimed effluent may escape the site undetected.

Zones of fracture concentration revealed by fracture traces, on the other hand, can be routinely mapped on aerial photographs. These delineated zones of intensive jointing and physical and chemical weathering have increased permeability and porosity that may be 10 to 1,000 times greater than in the adjacent rock (Lattman and Parizek, 1964; Parizek and Voight, 1970; Siddiqui and Parizek, 1971; Parizek, 1971a, b).

Monitoring wells located on fracture traces can greatly increase the

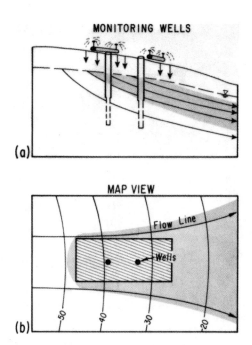

Figure 6-15. Monitoring wells drilled and cased below flow channels containing sewage effluent (a). In map view (b), monitoring wells appear to be properly located.

chances of obtaining a representative sample of groundwater beneath and adjacent to irrigation sites because they concentrate flow and serve as conduit-like systems that are interconnected on a regional basis (Figure 6-16). Monitoring wells located remote from these zones may fail to reveal pollution problems developing on site, either because they channel effluent away from irrigation sites (Figure 6-17a) or provide dilution where adjacent groundwater enters the site (Figure 6-17b). The case shown in Figure 6-17b might be important for small irrigation projects or where monitoring wells are located on the fringe of irrigation plots on the upslope side of the water table.

Zones of fracture concentration can serve another important function where well dewatering or groundwater reuse is planned in areas underlain by fractured rocks. These zones serve as efficient groundwater collector channels when tapped by wells. Fewer dewatering wells would be required to control groundwater levels in fractured rocks where wells are placed at fracture trace intersections compared with cases where wells would be drilled without knowledge of these zones. Zones of fracture concentration are narrow, hence are

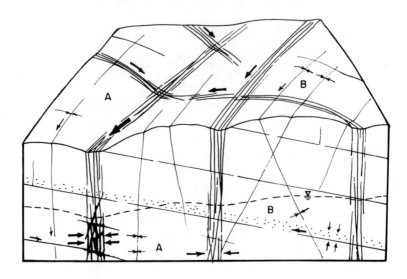

Figure 6-16. Intersecting zones of fracture concentration that increase rock per-
meabilities 10 to 1,000 fold when compared with adjacent massive blocks
of rock (A and B) that may contain systematic and non-systematic joints,
bedding plane partings, primary permeability, etc. (From Parizek, 1971.)

not often penetrated by chance. This would be of vital importance in
large projects where dozens of dewatering wells might be involved.
Dewatering using zones of fracture concentrations can be achieved
with a fraction of the total number of wells that otherwise might be
required.

These same zones greatly increase the yield potential of water
supply wells. Siddiqui and Parizek (1971) showed the percent of
fracture trace wells whose yield values equalled or exceeded specific
values when compared with wells located remote from fracture traces
(Figure 6-18). Data presented are for wells completed in shale, shaley
limestone, limestone, dolomites, with various textures and sandy
dolomites located in central Pennsylvania. Similar relationships are
being found for other rock types in Pennsylvania and elsewhere as
well. Fracture trace and fracture-trace intersection wells in all cases
are among the most productive wells being drilled within various rock
types when compared to wells drilled off these zones in the same
terrane.

Administrative Considerations
A wealth of experience is available on applying irrigation water to
crops. However, data are still scant on the use of sewage effluent as

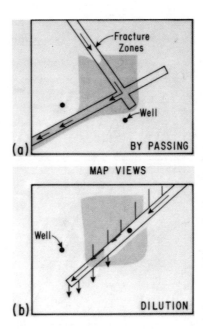

Figure 6-17. Map view of zones of fracture concentration, direction of groundwater flow, and location of monitoring wells. In (a), incompletely renovated effluent is channeled along zones of fracture concentration and bypasses monitoring wells. In (b) dilution is occurring along the zone of fracture concentration and overly optimistic monitoring data may be obtained.

irrigation water to determine the degree of renovation that may be achieved under varied crop and climatic conditions. Many have irrigated with sewage effluent but with little concern of the pollution potential involved. A number of questions become obvious when one considers land disposal and treatment of wastewaters. Many of these were considered in the design of the Penn State research project and must be considered by others who are seeking alternative solutions to wastewater treatment and disposal problems. Some of these have been listed and discussed by Parizek *et al.* (1967), Parizek and Myers (1968), and Parizek (1971c).

Regulatory agencies charged with the responsibility of reviewing waste treatment and disposal applications and with enforcement are or will be forced to decide often with scanty data whether to grant operating permits for wastewater irrigation systems. Some states may grant one-year experimental or provisional permits until they are assured projects are performing up to expectation.

Soil-water and groundwater flow rates frequently are so slow that

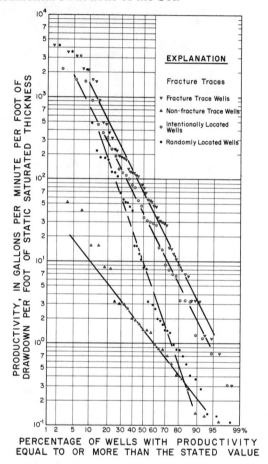

Figure 6-18. Comparison of well yields for wells located at fracture trace intersections, single fracture traces and at nonfracture trace sites. Data are for shale, shaley limestone, limestone, dolomite and sandy dolomite. (From Siddiqui and Parizek, 1971.)

months or even years may be required before applied effluent reaches a particular monitoring station. This is shown in Figure 6-19 where soil-water was being sampled from a perched groundwater lens within a loamy soil. The monitoring point is located at a depth of 33 feet below surface where effluent is applied April through November. Chlorides, which serve as our best tracer, did not begin to increase above background concentrations until 13 months after irrigation began (Figure 6-19).

Nearly two years were required before detectable changes in chloride and nitrate were noted in groundwater monitoring wells located 275 feet below irrigation sites containing nearly 50 to 100 feet of clay to sandy clay soil and 50 to 200 feet of unsaturated cavernous

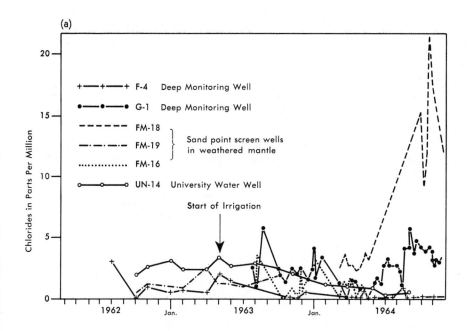

Figure 6.19. Concentration of chloride in water from selected deep and shallow on-site wells at the Pennsylvania State University Research Facility. Note that more than a year was required to detect chloride increases in FM-18, a shallow soil-water sampling station. No changes were observed within the first year and a half at the other stations. (After Parizek *et al.,* 1967)

dolomite bedrock (Figure 6-20). Monitoring wells in each case were open to the top of the water table and equipped with pumps.

Monitoring installations must be planned to allow an early evaluation of irrigation projects as well as the long term response of these systems. Both were allowed for in the Penn State project with the result that water quality changes within the deep groundwater reservoir have been noted after nine years of irrigation but the quality changes are entirely acceptable. In fact it is of better quality than the average groundwater supply being used for domestic and farm purposes within the adjacent valley area.

Other problems arise when attempting to evaluate monitoring results. Seasonal changes in land use, weather, recharge, rates of physical, chemical and biological processes produce erratic graphical plots of water quality when a given constituent is considered (Figure 6-21). It is difficult to establish meaningful trends in such data even after two or more years of irrigation let alone account for the possible sources and reasons for the variability observed. In short, the success or ultimate failure of a particular project cannot be judged in the short term. Monitoring must be continued for the life of the project even if to a limited extent once initial success has been established.

Conclusions

1. Knowledge of the soils, geology and hydrology can help when selecting sites for wastewater renovation to insure that a high degree of renovation is achieved for a prolonged period, to insure that groundwater recharge and/or reuse can be achieved and to minimize secondary environmental problems that can result from wastewater irrigation projects.

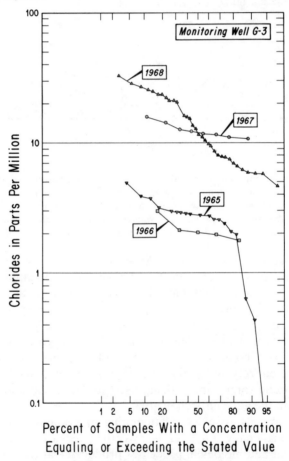

Figure 6-20. Concentration of chloride, NO_3-N and ABS (ppm) equaled or exceeded for effluent that has migrated vertically through 50 to more than 100 feet of sandy clay and sandy loam, and 50 to 200 feet of unsaturated dolomite bedrock. Nearly two years were required to establish changes in groundwater quality due to recharge of effluent. Irrigation began in November 1965 at a rate of 6 inches per week until August 1966 and was continued at 4 inches per week November-April each succeeding year.

2. This same knowledge must be applied to the design of monitoring systems used to evaluate these projects.

3. Regulatory agencies responsible for the evaluation of irrigation proposals and policing and enforcement work need diversified personnel to deal with wastewater irrigation projects. Aside from sanitarians, soil scientists, groundwater geologists and related personnel are required. Regulation and enforcement are mandatory to insure the success of irrigation projects.

4. As the size of irrigation projects increases, the likelihood for major failures will increase. Numerous small scale projects have already failed due to poor design, improper site selection and poor management. More attention will have to be given to details of site selection, use of a conservative design, and continued project management. Management is the key to achieving a high degree of reno-

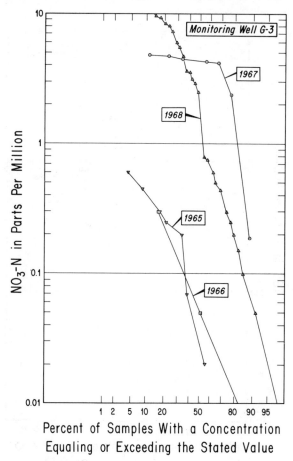

Figure 6-20. (Continued)

vation over the long term at good sites and to making the best of poor sites.

5. Wastewater irrigation projects are different from normal fresh water irrigation projects. Many sites are entirely unsuited for wastewater treatment using the irrigation method.

6. Many sites that may appear to be unsuited for wastewater irrigation may in fact be made suitable through the use of imaginative engineering practices.

7. The concentrations of harmful trace elements and toxic substances not likely to be removed in the renovation media may well have to be controlled in irrigation waters or reduced or eliminated in advance of land disposal. Extensive soil-water and groundwater pollution is a much more difficult condition to correct than surface water pollution and pollutants can persist for generations within the subsurface.

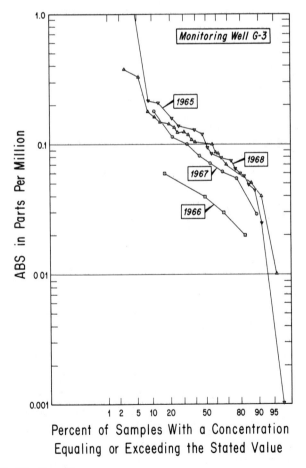

Figure 6-20. (Continued)

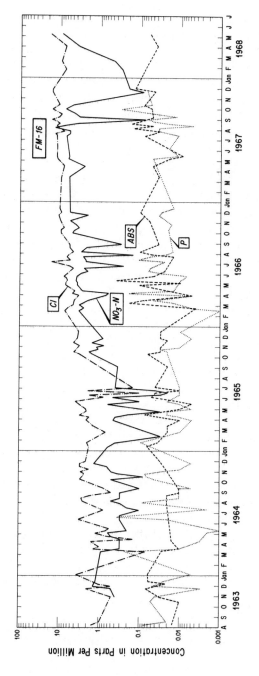

Figure 6-21. Concentration of chlorides, ABS, phosphorus and nitrate nitrogen in sand point well FM-16 at a site receiving 2 inches of effluent per week April through November since 1963. Note the erratic plots obtained. Significant quality changes can be difficult to establish in the short term.

8. Recent theoretical developments and increased size of computers make it possible to evaluate regional water level changes likely to be brought about by large irrigation projects under complex field sites as well as to estimate quality changes likely to result from dilution, dispersion and other mechanisms operating within the soil-water and groundwater reservoirs. This capability should be exploited when designing large projects as our total documented experience with wastewater irrigation projects is still limited despite the number of irrigation projects in use.

9. Regulatory agencies should not be shortsighted in the levels of treatment they require of spray irrigation projects. If only phosphorus is to be removed, high application volumes — two, six or more inches per week — might be used on a variety of soils with success. However, pollution may result from other points of view, MBAS, nitrates, etc. The physical-chemical-biological processes operating in the soil can be relied upon to provide a high degree of renovation of a number of constituents from the outset if allowed to do so.

10. Land ownership will greatly increase the cost of spray irrigation projects when compared to other methods of treatment particularly where real estate values are high. It would appear reasonable that long term lease agreements would be a suitable basis for state and federal funding of irrigation projects. Arrangements might be possible where land owners are paid for the use of their land where water and nutrients are in excess of their needs but pay for these when they need them.

11. Hopefully the idea that irrigation projects are only suitable for small towns, trailer courts, and small industries is dead. The concept is applicable to major metropolitan centers as well. Public water supplies for these major centers are rarely derived from within city limits. Rather, water may be imported from sources 50 or more miles away. By contrast, wastewater treatment facilities have traditionally been located in the topographically low end of town for economic reasons. Large scale projects being planned or dreamed about show that these waters can be returned to their region of origin so that they might be renovated and made available for reuse. The problems involved are more apt to be political than technical or economical.

Acknowledgments
Portions of this research were supported by funds from Demonstration Project Grant WPD 95-01 received initially from the Division of Water Supply and Pollution Control of the Department of Health, Education, and Welfare and subsequently from the Federal Water Pollution Control Administration, Department of the Interior. Partial support was also provided by the Office of Water Resources Research, USDI, as authorized under the Water Resources Research

Act of 1964, Public Law 88-379 and the Mineral Conservation Section, College of Earth and Mineral Sciences, The Pennsylvania State University.

Literature Cited

Bear, J., D. Zaslavsky and S. Irmay.1968. *Physical Principles of Water Percolation and Seepage*, UNESCO, 465p.

Bittinger, M. W., H. R. Duke, and R. A. Longenbaugh. 1967. Mathematical simulations for better aquifer management, International Assoc. Scientific Hydrology, Symposium of Haifa, publ. 72.

Bredehoeft, A. D. 1970. Digital analysis of areal flow in multiaquifer groundwater system, a quasi three-dimensional model, *Water Resources Research*, Vol. 6, No. 30, p. 883-888.

Bredehoeft, J. D. and G. F. Pinder. 1972. The application of the transport equations to a groundwater system, 24th International Geol. Congress, Montreal, Canada, Section 2, Hydrogeology, p. 255-263.

Bruce, R. R. and A. Klute. 1956. The measurement of soil moisture diffusivity, *Proc. Soil Sci. Soc. Amer.*, Vol. 20: 458-462.

Chow, V. T. 1964. *Handbook of Applied Hydrology*, McGraw-Hill Book Co., New York, N.Y.

Cooley, R. L. 1970. A finite difference method for analyzing liquid flow in variably saturated porous media, Tech. Paper 22, The Hydrologic Engineering Center, Corps of Engineers, Sacramento, California, 44p.

Cooley, R. L. and J. Peters. 1970. Finite element solutions of steady state potential flow problems, Hydrologic Engineering Center, U.S. Army Corps of Engineers, Publ. 723-440.

Douglas, J. and H. H. Rachford, Jr. 1956. On the numerical solution of head conduction problems in two and three space variables, *Trans. Amer. Math. Soc.* 82: 421-439.

Eisenberg, D. and K. Kauzmann. 1969. *The Structure and Properties of Water*, Oxford Univ. Press, New York, N.Y., 296p.

Fireman, M., and H. E. Haywood. 1955. Irrigation water and saline and alkali soils, p. 321-327, 1955 *Yearbook of Agriculture*, U.S. Dept. of Agriculture, 751p.

Gray, D. M., D. I. Norum, and J. M. Wigham. 1970. Infiltration and the Physics of Flow of Water Through Porous Media, Section V, in *Handbook on the Principles of Hydrology*, Edited by D. M. Gray, National Research Council of Canada, p. 5.1-5.58.

Jame, Y. W. and D. I. Norum. 1972. Phase composition of a partly frozen soil, Research Paper No. 11, Div. Hydrol., College of Eng., Univ. of Sask., Saskatoon, Saskatchewan.

Kardos, L. T. 1970. A new prospect: preventing eutrophication of our lakes and streams, *Environment*, Vol. 12 (2): 10-27.

Klock, G. O. 1972. Snowmelt temperature influence on infiltration and soil water retention, *Jour. of Soil and Water Conservation*, Vol. 27 (1): 12-14.

Konikow, L. F. 1973. Simulation of hydrologic and chemical-quality variations in an irrigated stream-aquifer system, Arkansas River Valley, Colorado, PhD dissertation, The Pennsylvania State University, University Park, Pa., 79p.

Kuznik, I. A. and A. I. Bezmenov. 1963. Infiltration of melt water in frozen soils, *Soviet Soil Sci.*, No. 7, p. 665-670, Translation Scripta Technica, Ind.

Larkin, P. A. 1962. Permeability of frozen soils as a function of their moisture content and fall tillage, *Soviet Hydrol. Selected Papers,* No. 4: 445-460, Amer. Geophys. Union Publishers.

Lattman, L. H. and R. R. Parizek. 1964. Relationship between fracture traces and the occurrence of groundwater in carbonate rocks, *Jour. of Hydrology,* Vol. 2: 73-91.

Norris, S. E. 1962. Permeability of glacial till, U.S. Geol. Survey Research.

Ogata, A. 1970. Theory of dispersion in a granular medium, U.S. Geol. Survey Prof. Paper 411-I, 34p.

O'Neil, A. M. 1949. Soil characteristics significant in evaluating permeability, *Soil Sci.,* Vol. 67: 403-409.

Parizek, R. R., L. T. Kardos, W. E. Sopper *et al.* 1967. Wastewater renovation and conservation, Penn State Studies No. 23, The Penn. State University, University Park, Pennsylvania, 71p.

Parizek, R. R. and E. A. Myers. 1968. Recharge of groundwater from renovated sewage effluent by spray irrigation, *Proc. of 4th American Water Resources Conference,* New York, p. 426-443.

Parizek, R. R. and B. E. Lane. 1970. Soil-water sampling using pan and deep pressure-vacuum lysimeters, *Jour. Hydrology,* Vol. 11: 1-21.

Parizek, R. R. and B. Voight. 1970. Question 37: on remote sensing investigations for dam and reservoir construction in kart-terranes, Commission Internationale des Grands Barrages, Montreal, G. R. Q. 37, Vol. 6: 538-541.

Parizek, R. R. 1971a. Prevention of coal mine drainage formation by well dewatering, Special Res. Report, Coal Research Section, The Pennsylvania State University, University Park, Pennsylvania.

Parizek, R. R. 1971b. Hydrogeologic framework of folded and faulted carbonates — influence of structure, p. 28-34, in *Hydrogeology and Geochemistry of Folded and Faulted Carbonate Rocks of the Central Appalachian Type and Related Land Use Problems,* Parizek, R. R., W. B. White and D. Langmuir, Guidebook, The Geological Society of America, 184p.

Parizek, R. R. 1971c. Land use problems in carbonate terranes — waste water renovation and conservation, p. 153-170, in *Hydrogeology and Geochemistry of Folded and Faulted Carbonate Rocks of the Central Appalachian Type and Related Land Use Problems,* Parizek, R. R., W. B. White and D. Langmuir, Guidebook, The Geological Society of America, 184p.

Parizek, R. R. and D. Langmuir. 1971. Management of leachates from sanitary landfills, Penna. Geol. Survey Bull. (in press).

Pinder, G. F. and J. D. Bredehoeft. 1968. Application of the digital computer for aquifer evaluation, *Water Resources Res.,* Vol. 4 (5): 1069-1093.

Pinder, G. F. and H. H. Cooper. 1970. A numerical technique for calculating the transient position of the salt water front, *Water Resources Res.,* Vol. 6 (3): 875-882.

Pinder, G. F. 1971. An iterative digital model for aquifer evaluation, U.S. Geol. Survey, Open File Report, 44p.

Post, F. A. and F. R. Dreibelbis. 1942. Some influences of frost penetration and micro-climate on the water relationships of woodland pasture and cultivated soils, *Proc. Soil Sci. Soc. Amer.,* Vol. 7: 95-104.

Prickett, T. A. and C. G. Lonnquist. 1971. Selected digital computer techniques for groundwater resource evaluation, Illinois State Water Survey, Bull. 55, Urbana, Illinois, 62p.

Reddell, D. L. and D. K. Sunada. 1970. Numerical simulation of dispersion in groundwater aquifers, hydrology paper, Colorado State University, No. 41, 79p.

Scheidegger, A. E. 1961. General theory of dispersion in porous media, *Jour. Geophys. Res.,* Vol. 66 (10): 3273-3278.

Schneider, I. F. and A. E. Erickson. 1972. Soil limitations for disposal of municipal wastewater, Research Rept. 195, Farm Science, Michigan State University, Agric. Expt. Station, East Lansing, Michigan, 54p.

Siddiqui, S. H. and R. R. Parizek. 1971. Hydrogeologic factors influencing well yields in folded and faulted carbonate rocks in central Pennsylvania, *Water Resources Res.*, Vol. 7 (5): 1295-1312.

Smith, R. M. and D. R. Browning. 1946. Some suggested laboratory standards of subsoil permeability, *Proc. Soil Sci. Soc. Amer.*, Vol. 11: 21-26.

Sopper, W. E. and L. T. Kardos. 1972. Effects of municipal wastewater disposal on the forest ecosystem, *Jour. of Forestry* 70 (9): 540-545.

Storey, H. D. 1955. Frozen soil and spring and winter floods, p. 179-184, *Water, Yearbook of Agriculture*, U.S. Dept. of Agriculture, 751p.

Walton, W. C. 1965. Ground water recharge and runoff in Illinois, Illinois State Water Survey Rept. of Investigation 48, Urbana, Ill., 55p.

Walton, W. C. 1970. *Groundwater Resource Evaluation*, McGraw-Hill, Inc., 664p.

Weast, R. C. 1968. *Handbook of Chemistry and Physics* (49th edition), Chem. Rubber Co., Cleveland, Ohio, 2120p.

Zavodchikov, A. B. 1962. Snowmelt losses to infiltration and retention on drainage basins during snow melting period in Northern Kazakhstam, *Soviet Hydrol. Selected Papers*, No. 1, p. 37-42, Amer. Geophys. Union.

Zienkiewicz, O. C. and Y. K. Cheung. 1965. Finite elements in the solution of field problems, *The Engineer*, Vol. 220 (5722): 507-510.

Zienkiewicz, O. C., P. Mayer, and Y. K. Cheung. 1966. Solution of anisotropic seepage by finite elements, Amer. Soc. Civil Engineers, *Engin. Mech. Div. Jour.*, Vol. 92, No. EM1, p. 111-120.

III / WASTEWATER QUALITY CHANGES DURING RECYCLING

7

Renovation of Municipal Wastewater through Land Disposal by Spray Irrigation

Louis T. Kardos and William E. Sopper*

Diversion of treated municipal wastewater from its usual disposal medium, surface waters, to the land means that the diverted wastewater with all its constituents must ultimately reside in the soil or be removed from the soil in harvested vegetation, by vapor loss to the atmosphere, or by movement in the soil solution to the groundwater. The latter in turn may cycle as base flow to the surface waters or be reused as a pumped water supply. It is imperative therefore that the quality changes in the wastewater as it passes through the living filter, the soil and its associated biosystems, be documented and evaluated.

In the Penn State project this was accomplished by extracting soil solution samples with suction lysimeters installed at various depths in the soil profile. Soil water samplers were obtained from Soil Moisture Equipment Co., Santa Barbara, California. Details concerning the method of installation and operation of these and other monitoring systems are given in Penn State Studies No. 23 (Parizek et al., 1967). The chemical quality of the chlorinated secondary treated wastewater was monitored by obtaining a composite of the wastewater being applied through the sprinklers during each irrigation sequence. Irrigation application rates were 0.25 inches per hour and amounts applied were 0, 1, 2, or 4 inches at weekly intervals. Various sites received irrigation ranging from 16 to 32 weeks (Apr.-Nov.) on the corn rotation area, 40 to 50 weeks (Jan.-Dec.) on the reed canarygrass area and 23 to 52 weeks (either Apr.-Nov. or Jan.-Dec.) on forested areas. The irrigation programs and soil types for these areas are shown in Table 7-1. Detailed descriptions of the soil types are given in Parizek et al. (1967). Average annual concentrations of various constituents in the applied wastewater are shown for the corn rotation area for

*Department of Agronomy and School of Forest Resources, The Pennsylvania State University

Table 7-1. Irrigation programs for agronomy and forestry areas

Vegetative Cover	Soil[a]	Weekly Application in Inches	Seasonal Irrigation Amounts in Inches								Total
			1963 June-Dec.	1964 March-Nov.	1965 April-Nov.	1966 April-Nov.	1967 April-Nov.	1968 April-Oct.	1969 April-Oct.	1970 April-Oct.	
Rotation-Corn	H	1	24	33	29	32	26	20	16	16	196
Rotation-Corn	H	2	48	66	58	64	52	40	32	32	392
Hardwoods	H	1	23	33	30	32	28	31	28	25	230
Red Pine	H	1	23	33	30	32	28	31	28	25	230
Red Pine	H	2	46	66	60	64	56	62	56	50	460
Old Field	H	2	46	66	60	64	56	62	56	50	460
Reed canarygrass	H	2	–	July-Nov. 36	Apr.-Dec. 80	Jan.-Dec. 78	Jan.-Dec. 94	Jan.-Dec. 98	Jan.-Dec. 100	Jan.-Dec. 86	572
Hardwoods	M	2	–	–	Nov. 23-Dec. 12	Jan.-Dec. 104	Jan.-Dec. 104	Jan.-Dec. 102	Jan.-Dec. 104	Jan.-Dec. 90	516

a. H = Hublersburg silt loam or clay loam. M = Morrison sandy loam.

Table 7-2. Average concentration of various constituents in wastewater applied to the corn rotation area at rates of one and two inches per week during the period 1963 to 1970

Constituent	1963 1	1963 2	1964 1	1964 2	1965 1	1965 2	1966 1	1966 2	1967 1	1967 2
					Concentration (mg/l)					
Phosphorus	9.680	9.720	8.620	8.545	6.310	6.935	5.970	5.370	4.930	6.725
MBAS	3.17	3.20	1.47	1.54	1.09	0.98	0.33	0.36	0.26	0.30
Nitrate-N	5.7	5.8	14.9	13.8	6.3	5.9	8.1	8.0	5.4	5.2
Organic-N*	7.3	7.3	3.7	2.8	2.9	2.5	6.5	4.6	4.0	4.0
Potassium	17.1	16.8	16.4	15.3	19.9	20.6	20.6	19.2	18.4	18.6
Calcium	32.4	32.3	35.6	35.0	24.8	25.3	30.1	28.9	22.6	22.6
Magnesium	18.5	19.0	19.2	19.1	13.4	14.0	19.8	18.4	11.3	12.2
Sodium	46.0	46.9	32.2	34.2	36.0	35.7	41.4	38.6	39.5	40.0
Manganese	†	†	†	†	†	†	0.08	0.08	0.16	0.12
Chloride	43.4	43.9	40.0	38.9	42.7	43.8	54.4	51.4	48.9	45.0
Boron	†	†	0.40	0.40	0.32	0.32	0.36	0.36	0.42	0.41
pH	7.3	7.3	7.2	7.3	7.5	7.6	7.6	7.7	7.6	7.8

Table 7-2. (continued)

Constituent	1968		1969		1970	
	1	2	1	2	1	2
	Concentration (mg/l)					
Phosphorus	5.345	7.105	4.675	6.560	4.265	4.135
MBAS	0.50	0.57	0.57	0.54	0.44	0.44
Nitrate-N	4.7	4.2	5.8	5.1	5.8	4.9
Organic-N	2.9	3.8	7.8	4.8	3.3	4.1
Ammoniacal-N	15.7	14.6	11.4	12.8	5.3	6.3
Potassium	16.7	17.1	15.2	13.8	13.5	13.7
Calcium	20.9	20.2	34.6	32.0	29.8	24.2
Magnesium	10.6	10.4	17.4	16.3	14.3	11.8
Sodium	37.4	40.8	51.5	52.8	34.3	32.7
Manganese	0.36	0.18	0.12	0.10	0.14	0.11
Chloride	50.6	41.2	60.6	44.4	48.1	45.0
Boron	0.38	0.40	0.34	0.38	0.29	0.29
pH	7.6	7.7	7.8	7.9	7.9	8.0

*Values included ammoniacal nitrogen. For the period 1965-1967, values are underestimated due to loss of undetermined amounts of ammoniacal nitrogen during analysis. Method of analysis changed in 1968.
†Values not determined.

1963-70 in Table 7-2 and are representative of the concentrations in wastewater applied to the other areas.

The extent of renovation of the applied wastewater may be expressed as the change in mean annual concentration of a particular constituent in the applied wastewater when compared with that found in the soil solution in the suction lysimeters. However this computation is not applicable to the nitrogen components since they are biologically changed from one form to another. Because nitrate-N is a widely used limiting parameter for drinking water, the overall renovation for the nitrogen fractions will be discussed in terms of the limiting concentration of 10 mg NO_3-N per liter being exceeded or not.

Since phosphorus and nitrogen are the two key eutrophic elements, most of the discussion in this paper will be focused on them. Table 7-3 shows the mean annual concentration of phosphorus in the applied effluent and at the 6- , 24- and 48-inch depths in the corn rotation area from 1965 through 1970. The Duncan's separations shown are between treatments within years and within depths. The wastewater treatments began in 1963 but suction lysimeter samples for a complete season were not obtained until 1965. These results show that on the wastewater treated areas, P concentration decreases drastically between the upper six inches and the 24-inch depth, remains essentially constant at the 24- and 48-inch depths, does not differ or is erratically different from the control area at the deeper positions, but is significantly greater than the control (P = 0.01) at the six-inch depth on the two-inch per week wastewater area each year beginning in 1965. Differences between the control and one-inch per week area were generally not significant at the six-inch depth.

For the two-inch treatment the minimum decrease in concentration at the six-inch depth was 91 percent in 1967 and the maximum was 98 percent in 1965. On the one-inch treatment area, the minimum decrease at the six-inch depth was 97.1 percent in 1967 and the maximum was 99.1 percent in 1965. In 1970 the decrease was 96.7 percent for the two-inch treatment and 98.4 percent for the one-inch treatment at the six-inch depth. At the 48-inch depth, decrease in concentration ranged from 98.1 percent to 99.6 percent for the two-inch treatment and from 98.6 to 99.8 percent for the one-inch treatment. The data indicate that phosphorus is not leaking out of the soil profile into the groundwater at a higher concentration from the wastewater treated area than from the control area and that excellent removals of phosphorus are continuing through the eighth year of treatment on the corn rotation area. A more detailed description of the phosphorus retention mechanisms is given in an unpublished Ph.D. thesis (Edwards, 1968) and in the chapter by Hook, Kardos and Sopper (1973).

The reed canarygrass area, which is on the same soil type and has

Table 7-3. Mean annual concentration (mg/l) of phosphorus in suction lysimeter samples at three depths in corn rotation plots receiving various levels of wastewater, 1965 to 1970

Depth in Inches	1965			1966			1967		
	Wastewater Application—Inches Per Week								
	0	1	2	0	1	2	0	1	2
6	0.035a**[1]	0.047a	0.118b	0.044a**	0.077a	0.269b	0.046a**	0.149a	0.571b
24	0.025a**	0.020a	0.044b	0.045N.S.	0.036	0.055	0.039a**	0.039a	0.086b
48	0.032b**	0.016a	0.022ab	0.045b*	0.028a	0.036ab	0.039a**	0.030a	0.054b

Depth in Inches	1968			1969			1970		
	Wastewater Application—Inches Per Week								
	0	1	2	0	1	2	0	1	2
6	0.035a**	0.160a	0.586b	0.022a**	0.073a	0.557b	0.042a**	0.060a	0.138b
24	0.048a*	0.063ab	0.078b	0.079N.S.	0.046	0.058	0.054N.S.	0.064	0.094
48	0.041N.S.	0.052	0.060	0.066N.S.	0.066	0.070	0.034a**	0.052ab	0.075b

1. The Duncan's separations are between wastewater treatments within depths and within years.
** = P(0.01), * = P(0.05), N.S. = not significant.

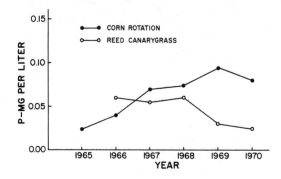

Figure 7-1. Mean annual phosphorus concentration in lysimeter samples at the 48-inch depth in corn rotation and reed canarygrass areas. Corn areas received 2 inches of effluent weekly from April to November since 1963. Reed canarygrass areas received 2 inches of effluent from January to December since 1964.

been receiving two inches of effluent weekly, year around, since 1964, and hence almost twice as much phosphorus annually as the corn rotation area, is much more effective in removing phosphorus. Figure 7-1 indicates the mean annual phosphorus concentration at the 48-inch depth in the two-inch corn rotation area as contrasted with the two-inch reed canarygrass area. Detailed phosphorus data for the reed canarygrass area are in Table 7-4. The mean annual phosphorus concentrations at each depth were not significantly different from year to year. Through 1970, the reed canarygrass area had received 180 inches more wastewater than the corn rotation area but lysimeter concentration at the six-inch depth was only 0.186 mg/l compared to 0.557 mg/l in the corn area.

Comparative data for phosphorus in the forest areas are given in Table 7-5 and Figure 7-2. The irrigation programs and soil types for these areas are given in Table 7-1. Although there are variations in time of initiation of wastewater irrigation and total irrigation load on the various areas, Figure 7-2 shows that in 1970 phosphorus concen-

Table 7-4. Mean annual concentration of phosphorus in suction lysimeter samples at three depths and in the applied wastewater in the reed canarygrass area receiving two inches of wastewater weekly from 1966 to 1970

Lysimeter Depth	1966	1967	1968	1969	1970
inches			concentration (mg/l)		
6	0.164	0.128	0.218	0.186	0.161
24	0.091	0.110	0.120	0.089	0.067
48	0.055	0.053	0.052	0.035	0.038
Wastewater	7.690	7.695	8.450	4.185	3.490

Table 7-5. Mean annual concentration (mg/l) of phosphorus in suction lysimeter samples at three depths in forest areas receiving various levels of wastewater during the period 1965 to 1970

Red Pine — Hublersburg Soil

| | 6-inch depth | | | 24-inch depth | | | 48-inch depth | | |
| | inches per week | | | inches per week | | | inches per week | | |
Year	0	1	2	0	1	2	0	1	2
1965	0.450	0.178	0.335	–	0.190	0.517	0.040	0.300	0.400
1966	0.157	0.202	0.373	0.064	0.024	0.049	0.043	0.134	0.143
1967	0.065	0.149	0.242	0.040	0.108	0.072	0.053	0.092	0.031
1968	0.024	0.562	1.007	0.013	0.253	0.109	0.075	0.089	0.044
1969	0.020	0.056	0.261	0.040	0.068	0.040	0.010	0.064	0.037
1970	0.171	0.094	0.235	0.076	0.053	0.065	0.065	0.076	0.070
Av.	0.148	0.207	0.409	0.047	0.116	0.142	0.048	0.126	0.121

Hardwood — Hublersburg Soil

| | 6-inch depth | | 24-inch depth | | 48-inch depth | |
| | inches per week | | inches per week | | inches per week | |
Year	0	1	0	1	0	1
1965	0.065	–	0.010	0.390	0.050	0.250
1966	0.048	0.429	0.034	0.077	0.037	0.043
1967	0.053	0.068	0.030	0.078	0.044	0.077
1968	0.064	0.166	0.044	0.388	0.106	0.222
1969	0.023	0.212	0.025	0.065	0.072	0.047
1970	0.047	0.244	0.046	0.087	0.033	0.143
Av.	0.050	0.224	0.032	0.181	0.057	0.130

Old Field — Hublersburg Soil

| | 6-inch depth | | 24-inch depth | | 48-inch depth | |
| | inches per week | | inches per week | | inches per week | |
Year	0	2	0	2	0	2
1965	0.065	–	–	0.116	–	0.460
1966	0.038	0.091	0.030	0.069	0.030	0.140
1967	0.045	0.136	0.032	0.097	0.039	0.068
1968	–	0.275	0.122	0.125	0.040	0.053
1969	0.036	0.293	–	0.122	0.051	0.098
1970	0.035	0.342	0.102	0.119	0.042	0.114
Av.	0.044	0.227	0.072	0.108	0.040	0.156

Hardwood — Morrison Soil

| | 6-inch depth | | 24-inch depth | | 48-inch depth | |
| | inches per week | | inches per week | | inches per week | |
Year	0	2	0	2	0	2
1966	0.076	0.255	0.091	0.030	0.059	0.042
1967	0.049	0.113	0.223	0.057	0.068	0.063
1968	0.020	0.452	0.050	0.129	0.071	0.116
1969	0.031	0.319	0.032	0.104	0.059	0.137
1970	0.052	0.277	0.026	0.119	0.051	0.209
Av.	0.046	0.283	0.084	0.088	0.062	0.113

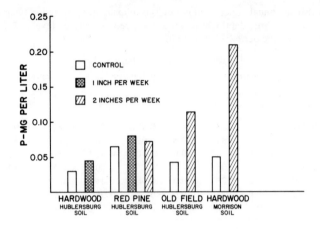

Figure 7-2. Mean annual phosphorus concentration in lysimeter samples at the 48-inch depth in forest areas receiving various levels of wastewater during 1970

tration at the 48-inch depth on the Morrison sandy soil area is substantially higher than on the finer textured Hublersburg soil areas. The detailed data in Table 7-5 show some erratic fluctuations at any one depth from year to year but the grand averages over years show the greatest effect of wastewater additions on the phosphorus concentration in the six-inch zone, with diminishing effect in the deeper zones.

Although the concentration of phosphorus in the percolating soil water was adequately small on all of the sites, the same cannot be said for nitrate-nitrogen. Both Table 7-6 and Figure 7-3 demonstrate

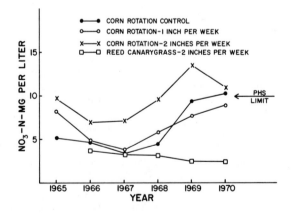

Figure 7-3. Mean annual nitrate-nitrogen concentration in lysimeters at the 48-inch depth in corn and reed canarygrass areas receiving various levels of wastewater

Table 7-6. Mean annual concentration (mg/l) of nitrate-nitrogen in suction lysimeter samples at three depths in corn rotation plots receiving various levels of wastewater during the period 1965 to 1970.

Depth in Inches	1965			1966			1967		
	Wastewater Application — Inches Per Week								
	0	1	2	0	1	2	0	1	2
6	6.8N.S.	4.2	4.7	4.6b**[1]	1.7a	5.0b	1.1a**	2.4b	5.2c
24	6.1N.S.	6.8	7.7	3.3b**	1.8a	4.0b	3.1b**	2.2a	6.6c
48	5.2a**	8.2b	9.7c	4.7a**	4.9a	7.0b	3.4a**	3.8a	7.1b

Depth in Inches	1968			1969			1970		
	Wastewater Application — Inches Per Week								
	0	1	2	0	1	2	0	1	2
6	12.6N.S.	12.0	10.5	14.7N.S.	11.9	17.3	9.6N.S.	8.5	6.5
24	2.6a**	4.5b	10.6c	10.0b**	5.3a	14.0c	7.3N.S.	6.0	8.1
48	4.5a**	5.8b	9.5c	9.4b**	7.7a	13.5c	10.3N.S.	8.9	10.9

1. The Duncan's separations are between wastewater treatments within depths and within years.
** = P(0.01); N.S. = not significant.

Table 7-7. Mean annual concentration of nitrate-nitrogen in suction lysimeter samples at three depths in the reed canarygrass area receiving two inches of wastewater weekly during the period 1966 to 1970

Lysimeter Depth	1966	1967	1968	1969	1970
inches		concentration — mg/l			
6	0.8N.S.[1]	0.6	0.7	0.6	1.2
24	2.2N.S.	1.5	1.8	1.1	0.8
48	3.7b*	3.3ab	3.1ab	2.5a	2.4a

1. The Duncan's seperations are between years within depths.
* = P(0.05), N.S. = not significant.

that the corn rotation area held nitrate-nitrogen levels below the recommended Public Health Service limit for drinking water, 10 mg NO_3-N per liter, on the control and one-inch per week treatments quite well. However, at the two-inch per week level, the mean annual concentration remained below the limit only when grass-legume hays occupied from 28 to 68 percent of the site in 1965 through 1968. In 1969 and 1970 when the entire site was occupied by corn the mean annual concentration exceeded the Public Health Service limit. On the reed canarygrass area, where more than twice as much nitrogen was added annually in the year-around two-inch application, the mean annual NO_3-N concentration remained well below the Public Health Service limit (Table 7-7).

The nitrate data for the forested areas are given in Table 7-8 and Figure 7-4. It is clear that the forested areas can handle a one-inch per week application without having the mean annual concentration at the 48-inch depth exceed the Public Health Service limit. However, when two inches were applied per week either in the April through November period with red pine on the Hublersburg soil or year-around with hardwoods on the Morrison soil the NO_3-N concen-

Table 7-8. Mean annual concentration (mg/l) of nitrate-nitrogen in suction lysimeter samples at three depths in forest areas receiving various levels of wastewater, 1965-1970

	Red Pine — Hublersburg Soil								
	6-inch depth			24-inch depth			48-inch depth		
	inches per week			inches per week			inches per week		
Year	0	1	2	0	1	2	0	1	2
1965	0.2	1.7	9.2	—	0.4	10.7	0.9	2.2	3.9
1966	0.1	1.5	26.8	0.2	0.2	14.6	0.1	2.1	9.3
1967	0.9	6.9	9.6	0.4	5.1	10.6	0.9	1.7	13.8
1968	0.5	18.7	21.8	0.2	6.1	17.6	0.9	2.7	19.9
1969	0.1	17.6	10.5	0.2	9.0	19.6	0.2	4.2	24.2
1970	<1	11.0	4.8	1.7	5.5	3.3	<1	5.3	8.3
Av.	0.3	9.6	13.8	0.5	4.4	12.7	0.6	3.0	13.2

Hardwood — Hublersburg Soil

Year	6-inch depth inches per week 0	6-inch depth inches per week 1	24-inch depth inches per week 0	24-inch depth inches per week 1	48-inch depth inches per week 0	48-inch depth inches per week 1
1965	0.1	1.0	—	0.2	—	0.0
1966	0.1	3.3	0.1	2.1	0.1	0.2
1967	0.4	13.3	0.4	5.4	0.3	1.4
1968	0.4	10.9	0.2	10.0	0.1	8.0
1969	0.4	6.8	0.3	4.9	0.1	7.2
1970	< 1	9.5	< 1	4.7	< 1	5.0
Av.	0.3	7.5	0.3	4.6	0.2	3.6

Old Field — Hublersburg Soil

Year	6-inch depth inches per week 0	6-inch depth inches per week 2	24-inch depth inches per week 0	24-inch depth inches per week 2	48-inch depth inches per week 0	48-inch depth inches per week 2
1965	0.1	5.1	0.1	8.4	0.3	8.0
1966	0.1	4.3	0.4	7.5	0.1	5.0
1967	0.4	4.6	0.4	12.0	0.3	6.1
1968	0.0	4.8	0.2	4.9	0.2	3.7
1969	0.4	7.3	0.4	8.3	0.2	2.3
1970	< 1	5.2	1.0	2.4	< 1	3.5
Av.	0.3	5.2	0.4	7.3	0.2	4.8

Hardwood — Morrison Soil

Year	6-inch depth inches per week 0	6-inch depth inches per week 2	24-inch depth inches per week 0	24-inch depth inches per week 2	48-inch depth inches per week 0	48-inch depth inches per week 2
1966	0.2	12.5	0.5	14.9	0.1	10.6
1967	—	16.9	0.5	20.4	1.4	19.2
1968	0.1	22.3	0.2	26.0	0.1	25.9
1969	0.4	17.0	0.1	24.4	0.3	23.7
1970	1.1	21.0	< 1	34.8	1.0	42.8
Av.	0.5	17.9	0.3	24.1	0.6	24.4

Hardwood — Hublersburg Soil

Year	6-inch depth inches per week 0	6-inch depth inches per week 4	24-inch depth inches per week 0	24-inch depth inches per week 4	48-inch depth inches per week 0	48-inch depth inches per week 4	72-inch depth inches per week 0	72-inch depth inches per week 4
1965	0.1	7.3	—	4.2	—	2.3	—	5.2
1966	0.1	11.1	0.1	9.3	0.1	9.1	—	9.5
1967	0.4	8.6	0.4	5.1	0.3	3.4	—	8.3
1968	0.4	8.8	0.2	3.2	0.1	0.9	—	8.2
Av.	0.3	9.0	0.2	5.5	0.2	3.9	—	7.8

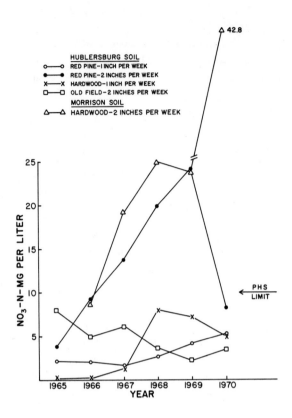

Figure 7-4. Mean annual nitrate-nitrogen concentration in lysimeters at 48-inch depth in forested areas receiving various levels of wastewater

tration at the 48-inch depth rapidly exceeded the Public Health Service limit. On the other hand, two inches of wastewater applied weekly on the old field area in the April through November period did not result in excessive NO_3-N values at the 48-inch depth.

The difference between the two-inch red pine and two-inch old field areas on the same soil type probably resides in the difference in the recycling of the nitrogen through the two vegetative covers. In the red pine relatively less nitrogen is assimilated in the annual growth than in the herbaceous annuals and perennials in the old field and larger amounts of readily decomposable organic residues are deposited annually in the old field. The larger quantities of carbonaceous material in the old field area may also promote a higher degree of denitrification in this fine textured soil. The sandiness of the soil on the two-inch hardwood area would not be conducive to denitrification of the larger nitrogen load applied in a year-around irrigation period and the hardwood leaf litter although more decomposable than the red pine needle litter would not be as decomposable as the old field residues.

The explanation above was serendipitously corroborated when the two-inch red pine area was clearcut after many of the trees were felled by a heavy wet snow and windstorm in November, 1968. After the clearcutting in 1969 the area grew up to a dense cover of herbaceous vegetation similar to that on the irrigated old field area. A large mass of carbonaceous material was deposited on the surface that fall and in 1970 another dense cover of herbaceous vegetation was produced and the mean annual concentration of NO_3-N dropped from a value of 24.2 mg NO_3-N/l in 1969 to a value of 8.3 mg NO_3-N/l in 1970 and to 3.8 mg NO_3-N/l in 1971.

Further support for the importance of denitrification in decreasing the inputs of nitrate to the groundwater was obtained in the data from the hardwood area on the Hublersburg soil which received four inches of wastewater, weekly, in the April through November period (Table 7-8). In spite of doubling the nitrogen load, the NO_3-N concentration at 48 inches remained below 10mg/l, probably because the larger hydraulic load encouraged more denitrification.

Changes in concentration of other chemical constituents in the wastewater which have been examined are shown in the histograms of Figures 7-5 and 7-6 for lysimeter samples at the 48-inch depth on the corn rotation area during 1970. For every constituent, the concentration in the applied wastewater was greater than in the lysimeter samples at the 48-inch depth. By the time the percolate reached the 48-inch depth some degree of renovation was secured for all con-

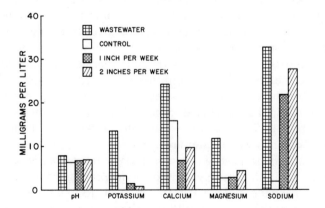

Figure 7-5. Mean annual concentration of potassium, calcium, magnesium, sodium, and pH in the wastewater and in lysimeters at the 48-inch depth in the corn rotation area during 1970

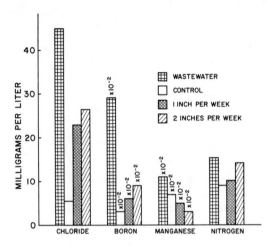

Figure 7-6. Mean annual concentration of chloride, boron, manganese, and total nitrogen in the wastewater and in lysimeters at the 48-inch depth in the corn
rotation area during 1970

stituents. However, if one compares the concentrations in the control
area with those in the wastewater treated areas the pattern is not
consistent. For example concentrations of K, Ca and Mn were higher
in the control area at 48 inches than in the wastewater treated areas,
while the reverse was true for Mg, Na, Cl, B and total-N
(NO_3-N + Org.-N + NH_4-N). It should be pointed out that the control
area did receive substantial amounts of K and Ca in the commercial
fertilizer that was applied to that area but not to the wastewater areas.
The greatest increase in concentration as a result of the wastewater
treatment occurred with Na and Cl. The sodium concentration increased almost 14-fold on the two-inch treatment compared to the
control and the chloride concentration increased to a value almost 5
times that of the control. The largest relative decrease in concentration from that in the wastewater occurred with potassium as a 15-fold
decrease from 13.7 mg/l in the wastewater to 0.9 mg/l at the 48-inch
depth in the 2-inch wastewater area.

Boron and manganese were substantially decreased in concentration from that in the wastewater, boron decreasing from 0.29 to 0.09
mg/l and manganese decreasing from 0.11 to 0.03 mg/l. Both of
these concentrations as well as those of the other constituents, except
nitrate-nitrogen, are well below the recommended limits for drinking
water. The nitrate-nitrogen, which constitutes about 83 percent of the
total nitrogen in the percolate on the corn area can be substantially

decreased below the NO_3-N limit by using a perennial grass as the vegetative cover rather than an annual crop such as corn. These nitrogen relationships were discussed earlier and the problem of handling the excess nitrogen should not be an unsurmountable one.

The data allow one to conclude that with appropriate management of nitrogen loads to maximize utilization by the vegetation and with hydraulic loads adjusted to the soil site to maximize denitrification it should be possible to recharge water of drinking quality into the aquifer below a wastewater disposal site.

Acknowledgments
Research reported here is part of the program of the Waste Water Renovation and Conservation Project of the Institute for Research on Land and Water Resources, and Hatch Projects No. 1481 and 1809 of the Agricultural Experiment Station, The Pennsylvania State University, University Park, Pennsylvania.

Portions of this research were supported by funds from Demonstration Project Grant WPD 95-01 received initially from the Division of Water Supply and Pollution Control of the United States Department of Health, Education, and Welfare and subsequently from the Federal Water Pollution Control Administration, United States Department of the Interior. Partial support was also provided by the Office of Water Resources Research, United States Department of the Interior, as authorized under the Water Resources Research Act of 1964, Public Law 88-379.

Literature Cited

Edwards, Ivor K. The Renovation of Sewage Plant Effluent by the Soil and by Agronomic Crops. Ph.D. Thesis in Agronomy. 174 pp. Sept. 1968.

Hook, James E., L. T. Kardos and W. E. Sopper. 1973. Effect of Land Disposal of Wastewaters on Soil Phosphorus Relations. *Recycling Treated Municipal Wastewater and Sludge through Forest and Cropland*. The Pennsylvania State University Press, University Park, Pa.

Parizek, R. R., L. T. Kardos, W. E. Sopper, E. A. Myers, D. E. Davis, M. A. Farrell and J. B. Nesbitt. 1967. Waste Water Renovation and Conservation. Penn State Studies No. 23, 71 pp. The Pennsylvania State University Press, University Park, Pa.

8
Renovating Secondary Effluent by Groundwater Recharge with Infiltration Basins

Herman Bouwer*

The Salt River Valley in Central Arizona is changing from a predominantly agricultural to a predominantly urban valley. Groundwater currently supplies about one-third of the municipal and agricultural water needs in the area of the Salt River Project, which is the main irrigation district in the Valley. The resulting depletion of the groundwater can be reduced if the sewage effluent produced by the increasing population (presently about one million) can be reused. The principal contenders for the sewage effluent would be irrigated agriculture and recreation (parks, golf courses, and lakes). Certain industrial applications may also be possible, but reuse for drinking water is still far off (Long and Bell, 1972).

Unrestricted use of sewage effluent for recreational lakes and irrigation requires tertiary treatment. A promising technique for such treatment in the Salt River Valley would be by groundwater recharge, with spreading basins in the Salt River bed. This normally dry bed traverses the valley from east to west, attains a width of one-half to one mile, and consists mostly of a loamy sand top layer underlain by coarse sand and gravel strata. The groundwater table is at a depth of 10 to 50 feet in the western part of the valley. A chain of infiltration basins could be constructed on each side of the riverbed. After infiltration, the sewage water would move to the center of the riverbed where it would be pumped from a series of wells (Figure 8-1).

Because the performance of a land-filtration system depends so much on the local conditions of climate, soil, and groundwater, a pilot system should precede any large-scale development. For the Salt River bed, such a system was installed in 1967. The study is in cooperation with the Salt River Project, which received a demonstration grant from the Environmental Protection Agency for partial support of the first three years of the study. The findings obtained and their use in the design of a large-scale system will be presented in the following sections.

*U.S. Water Conservation Laboratory, Agriculture Research Service, USDA

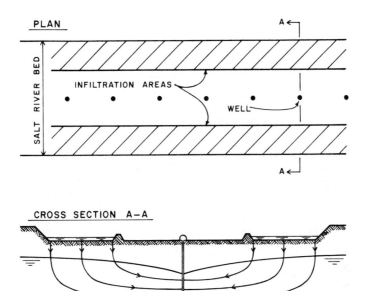

Figure 8-1. Schematic plan and cross section of infiltration basins and wells for Salt River bed

Experimental Project

Description of System
The experimental system, called the Flushing Meadows Project, is located in the Salt River bed west of Phoenix, about 1.5 miles west of 91st Avenue. The project contains six parallel infiltration basins of 20 by 700 feet each and 20 feet apart, and a number of observation wells (Figure 8-2). Secondary effluent from the 91st Avenue sewage treatment plant (activated sludge process) is pumped into the basins from the effluent channel on the north side of the project.

The first 50 feet of each infiltration basin were made into a sedimentation pond by excavating the bottom of the basin and constructing a gravel dam 50 feet from the inlet. Constant water depth in each basin is maintained by an overflow structure at the lower end of the basin. Infiltration rates in the basins are calculated from the inflow at the upper end and the outflow at the lower end measured with critical depth flumes (Replogle, 1971).

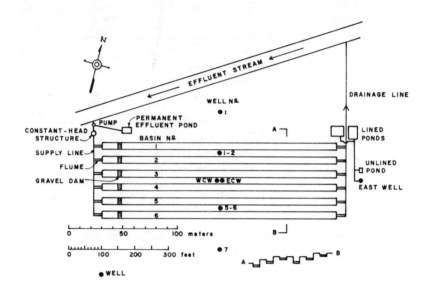

Figure 8-2. Schematic of Flushing Meadows Project

The soil profile beneath the basins consists of about three feet of fine, loamy sand (saturated hydraulic conductivity about four feet/day) underlain by coarse sand and gravel layers to a depth of about 240 feet, where a clay layer begins. The profile has been described in detail (Bouwer, 1970). The static water table is at a depth of about 10 feet. The observation wells are 20 feet deep, with the exception of the East Center Well (ECW), which is 30 feet deep, and the West Center Well (WCW), which is 100 feet deep (Figure 8-2). All wells are cased with nonperforated steel pipe, open at the bottom.

Infiltration Rates and Flooding Schedules
The infiltration rates generally ranged between two and three feet per day at the beginning to between one and two feet per day at the end of an inundation period, at a water depth of one foot. The decrease in infiltration was due to clogging of the surface layer of the soil and it was essentially linear with time. Drying the basins restored the infiltration rate. The infiltration recovery during dry-up was S-shaped, and essentially complete recovery of the infiltration rate was generally

obtained after 10 days of drying in the summer and 20 days in the winter.

Maximum long-term "hydraulic loading" was obtained with flooding periods of two to three weeks, alternated with dry periods of about 10 days in summer and 20 days in winter. With this schedule, an annual infiltration of 400 feet has been obtained. Regular drying of the basins was also necessary to provide oxygen in the soil for BOD removal and nitrification of ammonium.

Suspended solids had a significant effect on infiltration rates. In the summer and fall, the suspended solids content was generally in the 10 to 20 mg/l range, which was acceptable for infiltration. In the winter and spring, however, the suspended solids content was often in the 50 to 100 mg/l range. This caused a buildup of sludge in the basins, which was removed each year in late spring or early summer by "shaving" the basins with a front-end loader. Best infiltration results were obtained if the suspended solids content was less than 10 mg/l (Rice, 1972).

Infiltration rates in basins with an established grass cover (bermudagrass) were about 25% higher, and those in a gravel-covered basin (two inches of concrete sand topped by four inches of 3/8-inch rock) were about 50% lower, than those in a bare soil basin, when the soil variability between the basins was taken into account. In the spring, however, short flooding periods had to be used for the grassed basins to allow the grass to grow to a mature stand. During this sequence of short flooding periods, the infiltration amounts were less than those in the bare soil basin where flooding periods of two to three weeks could be used for the entire year. Moreover, the increased infiltration obtained for a complete grass cover could also have been obtained in the basins without vegetation by increasing the water depth. Thus, over a long period, nonvegetated basins can yield similar or even higher infiltration rates than vegetated basins.

Vegetation may be desirable where the wastewater is applied with sprinklers to protect the soil surface against the impact of the drops. Also, vegetated basins may remove more nitrogen from the effluent than nonvegetated basins (see section on *Nitrogen*). The low infiltration rates in the gravel-covered basin are attributed to accumulation of solids at the surface of the underlying soil, and to poor drying of this soil during dry periods caused by a mulching effect of the gravel layer.

Water Table Response
The static depth of the groundwater table was about 10 feet below the bottom of the infiltration basins. The water table beneath the basins rose during infiltration and reached a pseudoequilibrium posi-

tion which, in the center, was about two to four feet (depending on the infiltration rates) above the static water table level. During dry periods, the water table receded to its static level.

Based on the assumption that the sand and gravel layers of the aquifer formed a uniform anisotropic medium, the hydraulic conductivity of the aquifer was evaluated as 282 feet/day horizontally and 17.6 feet/day vertically. These values were obtained with an electrical resistance network analog from the response of the water levels in the East Center Well and the West Center Well to infiltration, and they agreed with directional hydraulic conductivity data obtained from permeability tests on the observation wells (Bouwer, 1970).

Water Quality Improvement

Quality parameters of the secondary effluent and the water pumped from the 30-foot deep East Center Well (ECW), mostly obtained in 1971, are shown in Table 8-1. The effluent was sampled continuously for 24-hour periods. Grab samples were obtained almost daily from ECW. The water obtained from ECW is effluent water that infiltrated in basins 3 and 4 (Figure 8-2), then moved through about six feet of unsaturated soil to the water table, after which it traveled about 30 feet below the water table to the intake of the well. The underground detention time of ECW-water was about five to ten days, depending on the infiltration rate in the basins.

Table 8-1. General range of quality parameters of secondary sewage effluent and renovated water from East Center Well

Constituent	Effluent	East Center Well
	mg/l	mg/l
BOD	10-20	0-1
COD	30-60	10-20
TOC	10-25	1-7
Org.-N	2-6	0.3-0.7
NO_3-N	0-1	0.1-50
NO_2-N	0-3	0-1
NH_4-N	20-40	5-20
PO_4-P	7-12	4-8
F	3-5	2-2.5
B	0.7-0.9	0.7-0.9
Cu	0.1	0.02
Zn	0.2	0.1
Cd	0.008	0.007
Pb	0.08	0.07
Total salts	1,000-1,200	1,000-1,200
pH	7.7-8.1	6.9-7.2
Fecal coliforms per 100 ml	10^5-10^6	0-100

Oxygen demand. The BOD of the renovated water from ECW was essentially zero (Table 8-1). The COD of ECW-water was in the 10- to 20-mg/l range, which was about the same as the COD of the native groundwater in the area. The total organic carbon content (TOC) of the renovated water averaged about 4 mg/l, indicating some residual organic matter.

Nitrogen. The nitrogen in the effluent was mostly in the ammonium form (Table 8-1). Total nitrogen levels in the effluent ranged from around 25 mg/l in the summer to around 35 mg/l in the winter. The form and concentration of the nitrogen in the renovated water depended on the length of the inundation periods of the basins and on whether the basins were vegetated.

When short, frequent flooding periods were used for the basins (*e.g.,* two days wet-two days dry), the oxygen levels in the soil were sufficiently high for complete nitrification of the ammonium. In that case, the renovated water from the wells contained NH_4-N levels of 1-5 mg/l and NO_3-N levels of 20-30 mg/l.

If medium inundation periods were used (*e.g.,* two weeks wet-two weeks dry), NO_3-N levels were close to zero in the renovated water, except for NO_3-N peaks which occurred a few days after the start of each new inundation (Figure 8-3). These peaks were due to the

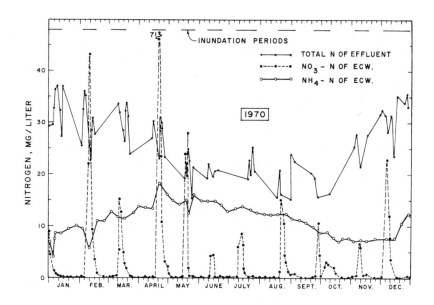

Figure 8-3. Nitrogen in secondary effluent and renovated water

arrival of effluent water that was held as capillary water in the soil during the preceding dry period. Because of the aerobic conditions in the upper layers of the soil during drying, ammonium adsorbed by the clay and organic matter during inundation, plus the ammonium in the capillary effluent water itself, could be converted to nitrate. When the basins were flooded again, this nitrate-rich effluent water was then pushed down by the newly infiltrated water, and when it arrived at a well caused an NO_3-peak in the water samples from that well. The arrival time of the NO_3-peak at ECW ranged between five and 10 days, depending on the infiltration rate in basins 3 and 4.

If very long inundation periods are used (*e.g.*, several months), the nitrogen can be expected to remain in the ammonium form as the effluent moves through the soil. This has not been tested in the field system, but it was observed in parallel laboratory studies where columns filled with soil from the infiltration basins were flooded with the same secondary effluent (Lance and Whisler, 1972).

When sequences of medium inundation periods were first used in 1968, the NH_4-N concentration in the renovated water was in the 2-3 mg/l range. Thus, after the passage of the NO_3-peak, the total nitrogen level in the renovated water was 90% less than that in the sewage effluent. However, continued use of medium inundation periods caused a gradual increase in the NH_4-N level in the renovated water. In 1969, for example, the NH_4-N level in ECW water increased from 4 mg/l in January to about 10 mg/l in July. Then it gradually dropped to 4 mg/l in November, and increased again to reach about 15 mg/l in June 1970. After that, the NH_4-N level in the water from ECW decreased to 7.5 mg/l in November 1970 (Figure 8-3). In 1970, the total-N level in the renovated water after the passage of the NO_3-peak was only 30% to 60% less than that in the sewage effluent.

The gradual increase in the NH_4-N level was probably due to the application of more ammonium during flooding than could be nitrified during drying, causing the cation exchange complex in the soil to remain essentially saturated with NH_4. The limiting factor is probably the amount of oxygen entering the soil during drying (Lance *et al.*, 1972). During the summer months, higher temperatures and better drying of the soil may cause a temporary increase in the nitrifier activity. This could explain the decrease in the NH_4-N concentration of the renovated water from May until December (Figure 8-3).

The tendency of the NH_4-level in the renovated water to gradually increase with continued use of two- to three-week flooding periods was reversed by changing to a sequence of short, frequent floodings (*e.g.*, two days wet-five days dry). This was done in 1971 for basins 1, 2, 5, and 6, while basins 3 and 4 were continued to be flooded with two-three week periods (Figure 8-2). While the NH_4-N level in the renovated water below basins 3 and 4 stayed at a plateau of about 18 mg/l for most of 1971, the NH_4-N levels below basins 1, 2, 5, and 6 gradually decreased to about 5 mg/l at the end of 1971. During the first few months of 1971, when short inundation periods were used for basins 1, 2, 5, and 6, the renovated water below basins 1 and 2, which were not vegetated, contained much higher NO_3-N levels than the renovated water below basins 5 and 6, which were covered by native grasses (mainly Mexican sprangletop and barnyard grass) and bermudagrass. This NO_3-N was probably due to nitrification of ammonium stored in the soil during the preceding sequences of medium flooding periods. The lower NO_3-N releases from the vegetated basins could be attributed to increased denitrification in the root zone, or to decreased nitrification which would cause the ammonium to remain adsorbed to the clay and organic matter.

With high-rate land disposal systems, such as the Flushing Meadows Project with loading rates of 300 to 400 feet per year, the nitrogen loading is so high (24,000 to 32,000 pounds per acre per year at Flushing Meadows), that crop uptake of nitrogen is insignificant as a removal process. Some nitrogen can be stored in the soil by adsorption of ammonium to clay and organic matter, fixation in microbial tissue, etc., but this is only temporary. Consistent nitrogen removal can be obtained mainly by denitrification. This requires the presence of nitrate and organic carbon under anaerobic conditions. If nitrogen removal from the effluent water is desired, the system should be managed so as to create conditions that promote denitrification.

For example, the pattern of nitrogen removal with sequences of two- to three-week flooding periods (Figure 8-3) is probably due to denitrification. During dry-up, and probably also during the initial stages of inundation, the upper three feet of soil are aerobic and the ammonium nitrogen in the capillary water and that adsorbed on the clay and organic matter can be nitrified. Some of the nitrate thus formed may move into micro-anaerobic pockets in the soil, where denitrification can occur. Also, when flooding is resumed, the nitrates may mix with the incoming sewage effluent and become denitrified in anaerobic zones. When all nitrates are flushed out and oxygen is depleted, the nitrogen in the effluent water will probably stay in the ammonium form and can be adsorbed by the clay and organic matter, after which it will be nitrified during the following dry-up period.

The overall nitrogen removal is difficult to predict from Figure 8-3 because the volumes represented by the samples from ECW are not known. However, the N levels in the renovated water from the wells outside the basin area, where the NO_3-peaks are not as distinct as in Figure 8-3, indicate that total nitrogen removals of around 30% can be obtained with medium flooding periods (two weeks wet-two weeks dry). This agrees with results from laboratory studies using soil columns, where a complete nitrogen balance could be developed for the system (Lance and Whisler, 1972).

There is some evidence that vegetation had a beneficial effect on denitrification. For example, in 1968, the NO_3-N levels after the passage of the NO_3-peaks were about 6 mg/l in the renovated water below the bare soil basins, but less than 0.5 mg/l in the renovated water below the basins with a mature stand of bermudagrass. Also, the grassed basins released much less nitrate than bare soil basins when, after three years of using primarily two- to three-week flooding periods, the schedule was changed to a sequence of two days flooding-five days dry to lower the ammonium level in the renovated water. Direct uptake of N by the crop could not account for the difference in nitrate levels in the renovated water. The beneficial effects of vegetation on denitrification are probably due to the organic carbon exuded by live roots and that returned to the soil by decaying roots (which supplied energy for the denitrifying organisms) and to the more anaerobic environments due to oxygen uptake by the root system (Woldendorp et al., 1965). More research is needed on the effect of vegetation on denitrification and the system management needed to obtain maximum nitrogen removal.

Phosphate. The PO_4-P levels in the secondary sewage effluent averaged about 10 mg/l in 1970 and 1971. The PO_4-P concentrations in the renovated water from ECW were low when the project was first started, but gradually increased to about the 5 mg/l level, where they have remained for the last two years. The renovated water yielded by the "outlying" wells 1 and 8 (Figure 8-2) had lower PO_4-P levels. The main mechanism for P-removal is probably precipitation of calcium-phosphate compounds, such as apatite, and precipitation of magnesium ammonium phosphate. Analysis of the top soil from the infiltration basins with an electron microprobe indicated phosphorus-rich clumps and coatings of soil particles. Phosphate-fixing materials, such as iron and aluminum oxides, are not present in large quantities in the sands and gravels of the Salt River bed.

Fluoride. The fluoride content was reduced from about 4 mg/l in the effluent to about 2 mg/l in the renovated water from ECW. Like the phosphates, the water from the outlying wells was lower in fluoride. The removal of fluoride paralleled that of phosphate, suggesting the formation of fluorapatites as a probable mechanism for its decrease.

Boron. The boron concentration in the effluent gradually increased from about 0.4 mg/l in 1968 to about 0.9 mg/l in 1971. Boron is not removed as the effluent moves through the sands and gravels of the Salt River bed (Table 8-1).

Metals. Metal analyses were carried out in the fall of 1971 on six samples taken biweekly over a two-month period. The concentrations of copper and zinc in the renovated water from ECW were considerably less than those in the effluent, but the concentrations of lead and cadmium remained essentially unchanged (Table 8-1). A combination of high pH and aerobic environment apparently favors immobilization of metallic ions in the soil.

Total salts. The concentration of total dissolved salts in the effluent was generally in the 1000-1200 mg/l range. The salt concentration in the renovated water was slightly higher, as a result of evaporation from the infiltration basins. The annual evaporation from a free water surface in central Arizona is about six feet. The evaporation at Flushing Meadows can be expected to be slightly less, because evaporation from the soil is reduced at the end of a dry period. When the annual evaporation is about five feet and the annual infiltration is 350 feet, the salt content of the renovated water can be expected to be about 1.4 % higher than that of the effluent.

The concentrations of the more important ions in the effluent were as follows:

Ion	Concentration	Ion	Concentration
	mg/l		mg/l
Na^+	200	HCO_3^-	381
Ca^{++}	82	Cl^-	213
Mg^{++}	36	SO_4^{--}	107
K^+	8	CO_3^{--}	0

pH. The pH of the renovated water was about seven, which is one unit less than that of the sewage effluent (Table 8-1). This is probably due to bacterial action in the soil, which produces carbon dioxide and organic acids.

Fecal coliforms. Most of the reduction in fecal coliform density (Table 8-1) occurred in the first three feet of travel through the soil. This was determined by samples of effluent water taken at different depths in the soil profile with ceramic cups to which a vacuum was applied. For inundation periods of two to three weeks, the fecal coliform density in the renovated water from ECW increased after the start of a new flooding period, when newly infiltrated water reached the well. The fecal coliform density then decreased to low values (often zero) until the next flooding period. The fecal coliform density for the outlying wells was lower than for ECW, *i.e.*, a general range of 0-10 per 100 ml for well 7 (Figure 8-2), and a complete absence of fecal coliforms for well 8.

Operational System

The infiltration studies at the Flushing Meadows Project have shown that a full-scale operational system can be designed on the basis of a hydraulic loading of about 300 feet per year. Thus, one acre of infiltration basin can handle 300 acre-feet of sewage effluent per year, or about 0.27 mgd. To renovate the total present flow of around 80 mgd would thus require about 300 acres of basins. The projected sewage flow for the year 2000 is some 300,000 acre-feet per year, which would require about 1,000 acres of basins.

Because of the many existing wells in the Salt River Valley, the wastewater renovation system should be designed and operated in such a way as to prevent the renovated water from moving into the aquifer outside the system of infiltration basins and wells. This can be achieved by locating the infiltration basins along both edges of the riverbed (which is about 0.5 mile wide) and placing the wells for pumping the renovated water in the center of the riverbed (Figure 8-1). To insure that renovated water will not move into the aquifer outside the riverbed, the system should be operated to keep the water table below the outer edges of the basin areas at a level equal to, or slightly below, the water table in the rest of the aquifer. Thus, the renovated water should be pumped from the wells at the same or a slightly higher rate than the infiltration rates in the basins.

From the response of the water levels in the observation wells to infiltration at the Flushing Meadows Project, the effective transmissibility of the aquifer for recharge was evaluated by resistance network analog and horizontal flow theory (Bouwer, 1970). This transmissibility was then used in an analog study of the system in Figure 8-1 to predict water table positions and underground detention times for various geometries. The results showed that the conditions in the Salt River bed enable a system with underground detention times of at least several weeks and underground travel distances of at least several hundred feet (Bouwer, 1970). The quality of the renovated water from the wells should be better than that shown in Table 8-1 for the water from ECW, for which the underground detention time was only about one week and the underground travel distance about 40 feet. Thus, the large-scale operational system should yield renovated water that can be used for unrestricted irrigation, primary contact recreation, and certain industrial applications (Environmental Protection Agency, 1968, and Arizona State Dept. of Health, 1972).

Economic Aspects

Preliminary estimates indicate that the total cost of putting the sewage effluent into the ground and pumping it up as renovated water with the system of Figure 8-1 in the Salt River bed will be around $5 per acre-foot (Buxton, 1969). The cost of in-plant tertiary treatment to obtain renovated water of similar quality will be an order of magnitude higher. Moreover, a significant part of the investment for a land treatment system is in land. Since land values tend to increase with time, an additional cost benefit can be obtained with the sale or different use of the land once the infiltration system has become obsolete. Wastewater renovation by groundwater recharge is aesthetically more attractive to the public than in-plant treatment. Also, land treatment systems are essentially 100% fail-safe.

Acknowledgments

The author acknowledges the valuable contributions to this project by E. D. Escarcega, J. C. Lance, and R. C. Rice of the U.S. Water Conservation Laboratory. The cooperation of the Salt River Project and its support of M. S. Riggs, who performed the water analyses, are gratefully acknowledged. The metal analyses were done by J. V. Lagerwerff of the U.S. Soils Laboratory, ARS-USDA, in Beltsville, Md. P. R. Buseck of Arizona State University performed the electron microprobe analyses of the soil.

Literature Cited

Arizona State Department of Health, Phoenix, Ariz. 1972. Rules and regulations for reclaimed wastes.

Bouwer, Herman. 1970. Groundwater recharge design for renovating wastewater. *Jour. Sanitary Engr. Div., ASCE,* Vol. 96 SA1, 59-74.

Buxton, J. L. 1969. Determination of a cost for reclaiming sewage effluent by groundwater recharge in Phoenix, Ariz. M.S. thesis, Arizona State University, College of Engineering Science.

Environmental Protection Agency, Washington, D.C. 1968. Water quality criteria. Report of Natl. Tech. Adv. Comm. to Secretary of Interior.

Lance, J. C. and F. D. Whisler. 1972. Nitrogen balance in soil columns intermittently flooded with secondary sewage effluent. *Jour. of Environmental Quality* 1:180-186.

Lance, J. C., F. D. Whisler, and H. Bouwer. 1973. Oxygen utilization in soils flooded with sewage water. *Jour Environmental Quality* (in press).

Long, W. N., and F. A. Bell. 1972. Health factors and reused waters. *Jour. Amer. Water Works Assoc. 64,* 220-226.

Replogle, J. A. 1971. Critical-depth flumes for determining flow in canals and natural channels. *Amer. Soc. Agric. Engr. Trans. 14,* 428-433.

Rice, R. C. 1972. Soil clogging during infiltration with secondary sewage effluent. Paper presented at Annual Meeting Amer. Soc. Agric. Engr., Hot Springs, Ark.

Woldendorp, J. W., K. Dilz, and G. J. Kolenbrander. 1965. The fate of fertilizer nitrogen on permanent grassland soils. Proc. 1st General Meeting European Grassland Fed., 53-76.

9
Phosphorus and Nitrate Levels in Groundwater as Related to Irrigation of Jack Pine with Sewage Effluent

Dean H. Urie*

In response to requests from municipalities to use forest lands for sewage disposal sites, the North Central Forest Experiment Station has begun research on the effects of sewage effluent on groundwater nutrient levels. This report covers results from an initial test conducted near Cadillac, Michigan, under conditions similar to those found on a site that has been selected for sewage renovation near Traverse City, Michigan. The test was conducted on a sand soil with a shallow water table where groundwater contamination could be a serious hazard. The treatment area was covered with a pole-sized jack pine (*Pinus banksiana* Lamb.) stand having a sparse understory vegetation.

This exploratory test was conducted to gain background information on the methods which could be used to conduct field tests of sewage effluent renovation where only small volumes of effluent are available.

Little research on sewage renovation in forests has been done (Sopper, 1971). Reports by Rudolph and Dils (1955) and Rudolph (1957) are perhaps most applicable to the study reported here, as their tests of tree survival and growth under irrigation by cannery wastewater was conducted on sand soils at Fremont, Michigan. Groundwater under those tests was found to meet potable water standards after three years of irrigation.

Irrigation with secondary effluent has resulted in a high degree of phosphorus removal in loam and sandy loam soils under pine and hardwood forests at The Pennsylvania State University. Nitrate in soil water at 60-cm (24-inch) and 120-cm (48-inch) depths has increased during the study although no report of increases in groundwater nitrate concentrations has yet been found. Water table levels are approximately 60 m (200 feet) below the surface in contrast to the shallow water tables in the study reported here.

Pure red pine (*Pinus resinosa* Ait.) removed less nitrate in The Pennsylvania State University studies than hardwood and white spruce forests. The pine plantation used for the test described here

*North Central Forest Experiment Station, Forest Service, USDA

was similarly expected to remove the smallest amount of nitrogen of all forest types on the Traverse City project area.

Despite the poor removal of nitrates on sand forest land, the availability, low cost, high infiltration, and remoteness of such soils have created a demand for them for sewage disposal with and without the forest cover (Shaeffer, 1970; Urie, 1971).

Methods of Study

Secondary-treated municipal sewage effluent from the Cadillac, Michigan, treatment plant was used to irrigate a small plot in a 35-year-old jack pine plantation. The plantation is located on a Kalkaska loamy sand soil which is a Typic Haplorthod developed on deep sand drift. During the test period, water table depth varied from 1.3 m (4 feet) to 3 m (10 feet), which is shallower than normal for Kalkaska sands on the proposed Traverse City disposal site. The test site is located on the Cadillac District, Manistee National Forest, NE¼, NW¼, Sec. 14, Selma Township, Wexford County, Michigan.

The plantation had been thinned by removing every fourth row in 1968. Slash from this cut was still present, with little decomposition of twigs over 5 cm (⅕ inch) diameter. The residual stand is about 10 m (40 feet) in height, with an average diameter of 16 cm (6.3 inches). Ground cover is sparse except in the cleared strips where a few hardwood seedlings have become established. *Lycopodium* covered about 12 percent of the surface of the plot prior to irrigation. Needle litter was 2.5 cm (1 inch) in depth before irrigation.

Observation wells were installed to depths of 1.5 m (5 feet) below the water table on the irrigation test site. Measurements of static water levels showed that the water table sloped toward Pleasant Lake (Figure 9-1). Three wells were then installed within the irrigated area. Two 1¼-inch-diameter wells were driven to the level of the lowest annual water table fluctuation. Well No. 1 was located at the center of the irrigated plot and Well No. 2 was located on the edge of the plot in the direction of groundwater flow, as determined from the surrounding wells. A recorder was installed in a six-inch-diameter well near the center of the irrigated plot. Previous groundwater studies in the area have shown that the annual cycle of water table fluctuation experienced during the 1972 growing season was similar to those occurring in two previous years.

A standard rain gage was installed in a nearby forest opening. Water quality samples were removed from the two treatment wells (No. 1 and No. 2) and two control wells (No. 3 and No. 4) (Figure 9-1), using a pitcher pump. All wells were capped during irrigation.

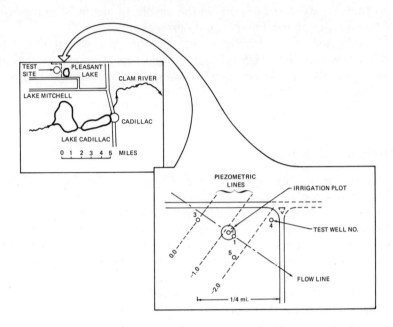

Figure 9-1. Location and groundwater gradients, Cadillac test site

Treatment

Effluent Application

The effluent was trucked from the plant and temporarily stored during the irrigation period. Irrigation began immediately upon delivery. Sewage effluent was applied at an average rate of 64 mm (2.5 inches) over a 10-hour period one day per week to an area averaging 6.1 m (20 feet) in radius. Two applications were made during November 1970. Treatments were renewed April 26, 1971, when the ground was free of snow and frost, and continued until October 19, 1971. A total of 162 cm (64 inches) was applied during the 1971 growing season. Distribution of the single rotary sprinkler used was checked with temporary gages. Application was relatively uniform from 2 to 5 m (7 to 16 feet), except in tree shadows and splash zones.

Field Measurements

Water quality samples were removed from four wells about 12 hours after irrigation ended. This timing coincided with the recharge peak shown by the recording well.

A liter sample was collected from Wells 1, 2, 3, and 4 at each sampling date. The samples were preserved with HgCl (10 mg/l) and

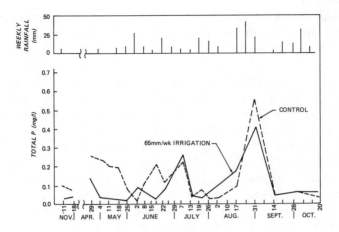

Figure 9-2. Average levels of total phosphorus in groundwater from Cadillac tests, 1970-71

refrigerated. Storage did not exceed 30 days. Liter samples of irrigated effluent were drawn from the temporary storage tank during irrigation.

Rainfall during the week previous to each irrigation was measured in the open using a standard eight-inch gage. Rainfall for seven-day periods is shown in Figures 9-2 and 9-3. The pattern of water table levels in the center of the irrigated plot was determined from the water level recorder record.

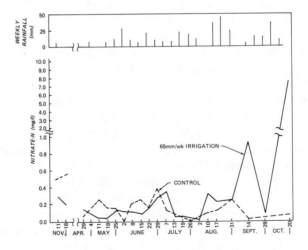

Figure 9-3. Average levels of nitrate-N in groundwater from Cadillac tests, 1970-71

Lab Analyses

Chemical analyses of nitrate-N and total phosphorus in water samples were performed by the Institute of Water Research, Michigan State University, using standard Environmental Protection Agency methods.

Additional measurements of ammonia-N and total Kjeldahl-N in the sewage effluent from the Cadillac treatment plant were made from samples collected during May and June 1972. These samples showed similar nitrate-N and phosphorus levels to those measured during the treatment period. The average level of total nitrogen was used to estimate the total nitrogen applied during the test period.

Soil samples were removed from 0- to 23-cm (0- to 9-inch) and 23- to 53-cm (9- to 21-inch) layers in the irrigated plot and from an equal number of points in the surrounding unirrigated control area. Analyses of phosphorus and nitrate, as well as other standard soil fertility tests were performed by the Michigan State University Soil Testing Laboratory.

Suction lysimeters were installed at 61- and 122-cm depths (24 and 48 inches) in September 1971. Samples of soil water were removed on seven dates and analyzed for nitrate-N, ammonia-N, and total phosphorus.

Results

Phosphorus

The average concentration of phosphorus in the effluent was 7.52 mg/l for the first 24 weeks of the 25-week season in 1972. An excessively high value (58 mg/l) on the last treatment date was associated with a temporary failure in the sewage treatment process. This input boosted the average to 9.67 mg/l, a total phosphorus loading of 141 pounds per acre.

The phosphorus level in groundwater sampled at the four wells is shown in Figure 9-2. The mean total phosphorus level in the two treatment wells was 0.09 mg/l for 25 sampling dates (Table 9-1). The mean level in the control wells was 0.14 mg/l. There was no significant difference between the treatment and control wells. The two control wells were in shallower water table situations, which may have caused a small increase in average phosphorus content.

There was no evidence of phosphorus enrichment of the groundwater. High levels in two wells on August 31 may have been due to sampling errors as one treatment well and one control well were anomalously high (0.72 and 0.99 mg/l, respectively).

Phosphorus levels in soil water at 60-cm (24-inch) and 120-cm

Table 9-1. Total phosphorus and nitrate levels in groundwater samples collected in the Pleasant Lake study, 1971

Date	Total Phosphorus Treatment Mean	Control Mean	Nitrate-N Treatment Mean	Control Mean
	mg/l	mg/l	mg/l	mg/l
11/10/70	0.04	0.07	0.16	0.63
11/11/70	.03	.13	.32	.63
11/18/70	.04	.08	.22	.57
4/27/71	.15	.18	.11	.12
4/29/71	.14	.26	.16	.08
5/ 4/71	.03	.24	.10	.18
5/11/71	.03	.20	.06	.28
5/18/71	.02	.20	.06	.18
5/25/71	.02	.08	.14	.18
6/ 2/71	.09	–	.12	–
6/ 8/71	.06	.12	.12	.24
6/15/71	.02	.22	.09	.28
6/22/71	.08	.12	.18	.17
6/29/71	.16	.17	.30	.40
7/ 7/71	.26	.29	.36	.14
7/13/71	.04	.04	.06	.10
7/19/71	.03	.08	.06	.06
7/26/71	.06	.03	.04	.02
8/ 2/71	.10	.04	.03	.06
8/10/71	.14	.07	.32	.11
8/17/71	.18	.10	.23	.14
8/31/71	.42	.56	.26	.26
9/14/71	.04	.04	.93	.04
9/28/71	.06	.06	.10	.05
10/20/71	.06	–	7.60	–
Mean	.09	.14	.48	.19

(48-inch) depths were sampled with tension lysimeters during September and October. Total phosphorus in the soil water was below 0.2 mg/l in all samples.

Soil analyses were made on a rather gross basis. An increase of 27 pounds per acre of total phosphorus was found in the 0- to 15-cm (0- to 6-inch) layer of the irrigated plot (Table 9-2). Phosphorus contents of litter and foliage were not determined.

Nitrogen
Nitrate levels in the effluent were low, approximately the same as in the groundwater public water supply source. 0.3 mg/l. Most of the nitrogen was in ammonia and organic form, approximately 8.0 mg/l and 2.9 mg/l, respectively. The total nitrogen applied was about 170 pounds per acre.

Groundwater samples were tested for nitrate during the entire

Table 9-2. Nitrate-N and total P in the soils on the irrigated and control areas of the Pleasant Lake study, October 20, 1971

Soil Depth	Total P		Nitrate-N	
	Irrigated	Control	Irrigated	Control
inches	lbs/a	lbs/a	lbs/a	lbs/a
0-6	36	9	8	2
6-12	12	8	2	2
12-21	21	18	4	4

study. Tests for other forms of nitrogen were conducted only during the final weeks of treatment. Definite increases in mean nitrate levels appeared in September and continued through the end of the irrigation (Figure 9-3). The test well on the downslope edge of the treatment plot produced samples with the highest NO_3-N levels. The highest NO_3-N level of 14.3 mg/l was measured on October 20, 10 days after the last irrigation.

Tension lysimeters at 60-cm (24-inch) and 120-cm (48-inch) depths were used to collect samples during September and October in which nitrate-N levels ranged from 25 to 30 mg/l. By mid-November, nitrate levels at these depths in treatment and control areas were below 5 mg/l.

Soil analyses showed increases of approximately six pounds per acre of nitrate-N in the surface six inches (Table 9-2) on October 20, 1971. After 10 days, no changes were found in deeper soil layers despite the high soil-water nitrate level measured on this date from suction lysimeters.

Vegetation Response

A comparison of 1971 annual growth on the 15 irrigated and 15 control jack pine was made in November. Increment borings showed a mean annual radial growth of 0.14 cm (0.055 inch) on irrigated trees in comparison to 0.10 cm (0.040 inch) on control trees. Dominant trees showed greatest effects and irrigated trees had nearly twice the annual ring width of controls. The 1971 growing season was rather dry (May-September precipitation was 95 mm (3.7 inches) below normal; thus, the supplemental water may have been the main cause for the growth increase.

Subordinate vegetation increased in frequency due to irrigation, mostly through survival of *Prunus* and *Fraxinus* seedlings. Several species of flowers and vegetables were introduced, apparently from seeds contained in the sewage effluent.

Conclusions

The single plot test described here illustrated that the nitrates added in sewage effluent irrigation may reach shallow water tables under sand-soil, forest conditions. Phosphorus renovation was complete during the initial year. Public health considerations may limit the permissible dosage levels in such highly permeable soils. Further tests will be needed to determine whether hardwood forest types or shrub-herb cover conditions may be more satisfactory for sewage renovation purposes on sandy soils. Alternative methods of cropping or volatilization of nitrogen may be a necessary pretreatment before economic volumes of sewage effluents can be renovated satisfactorily. Dilution of nitrate levels during groundwater flow may be a satisfactory solution in remote areas, with small sewage irrigation loads, and where domestic water supplies are protected.

Experience with this single plot test has resulted in the adoption of a different type of field test in locations where sewage effluent must be trucked to the test site. Tests now in progress utilize plots about 0.001 hectare in area using gravity methods of application. Tension lysimeters (soil water samplers) are being used instead of wells to test the degree of renovation under various treatments. These micro plots do not permit tests of response of large trees to sewage treatments. Replicated tests of renovation are possible with small volumes of effluent on a variety of soils and understory vegetation types.

Literature Cited

Rudolph, V. J. 1957. Further observations on irrigating trees with cannery waste water. *Mich. Agric. Expt. Sta. Q. Bull.* 39: 416-423.

Rudolph, V. J., and R. E. Dils. 1955. Irrigating trees with cannery waste water. *Mich. Agric. Expt. Sta. Q. Bull.* 37: 407-411.

Shaeffer, J. R. 1970. Reviving the Great Lakes. *Saturday Rev.,* Nov. 9, 1970, p. 62-65.

Sopper, William E. 1971. Effects of trees and forests on neutralizing wastes. In Trees and Forests in an Urbanizing Environment, *Symposium on Urban Forestry,* Amherst, Mass., p 43-57.

Urie, Dean H. 1971. Opportunities and plans for sewage renovation on forest and wildlands in Michigan. *Mich. Acad.* IV (1): 115-124.

10
Restoration of Acid Spoil Banks with Treated Sewage Sludge

Terrence R. Lejcher and Samuel H. Kunkle*

In many areas where strip mining has occurred there is a critical need for land reclamation, both to return wasteland to productivity and to reduce water pollution problems. Strip mining of coal often causes a significant degradation of water quality, aquatic environment and riparian wildlife habitat (Udall, 1967). In some cases, traditional strip mine reclamation techniques are apparently ineffective for correcting water quality impacts (Anderson *et al.*, 1972); therefore, new land reclamation techniques are needed.

Studies at The Pennsylvania State University (Hunt, Sopper and Kardos, 1971), and at other locations (Peterson and Gschwind, 1971), indicate that the utilization of treated municipal wastes may offer a potential technique for land reclamation in strip mined areas. Simultaneously, many cities are faced with the question of sludge disposal from their treatment plants. For example, Chicago is producing over 900 metric tons per day (dry weight) of solids from its sewage treatment plants. Disposal of the digested solids or sludge includes the following alternatives and costs:

Dewatering and incineration	$63/metric ton
Wet air oxidation	$55/metric ton
Digestion and permanent lagoons	$54/metric ton
Drying and sale as fertilizer	$50/metric ton
Digestion, and reclamation of strip mines	$18/metric ton
Digestion, and reclamation of farmlands	$16/metric ton

In the case of Chicago, the sludge is disposed of primarily by the first four processes above. The disadvantages of these particular disposal methods include cost, air pollution, and the scarcity of storage space. Sludge storage costs for the Metropolitan Sanitary District of Greater Chicago are over 1.5 million dollars per year (Dalton *et al.*, 1968). On the other hand, sludge disposal on strip mined lands offers an opportunity to reduce disposal costs while making a beneficial use of the sludge.

*Shawnee National Forest, Eastern Region, Forest Service, USDA

Little information is available regarding the practicality or environmental consequences of sludge treatment of strip mined sites. Therefore, the Shawnee National Forest in Illinois, in conjunction with the Metropolitan Sanitary District of Greater Chicago, established a demonstration site in 1970 to evaluate sludge treatment on strip mined land. The demonstration site, a 77 hectare stripped area, is known as the Palzo Tract. Within the Palzo Tract, four plots (500 square meters each) were set up to monitor water quality runoff and to observe plant growth following sludge treatment. Monitoring of the plots has continued since 1970. Land reshaping of the entire 77 hectares is underway in 1972 in preparation for sludge application to the entire tract. These efforts are in cooperation with Forest Service Research and university personnel. This paper presents the 1970-1972 water, vegetative, and soil observations from the small plots and considers the sampling design for the larger area and an adjacent stream which is affected by runoff from the tract.

The Chemical Processes in Spoil
Chemical oxidation of pyrite in shales of stripped areas is somewhat complex and not completely understood. The general reactions, however, are described by Hill (1971) as follows:

$$2FeS_2 + 2H_2O + 7O_2 \longrightarrow 2FeSO_4 + 2H_2SO_4 \qquad (1)$$

Oxidation of the pyrite (equation 1) produces ferrous sulfate and sulfuric acid. The reaction continues as follows:

$$4FeSO_4 + 2O_2 + 2H_2SO_4 \longrightarrow 2Fe_2(SO_4)_3 + 2H_2O \qquad (2)$$

$$Fe_2(SO_4)_3 + 6H_2O \longrightarrow 2Fe(OH)_3 + 3H_2SO_4 \qquad (3)$$

Oxidation of the ferrous iron procedes slowly. However, the resultant ferric iron is reduced by the pyrite to release more acid and ferrous iron (equation 4).

$$FeS_2 + 14Fe^{3+} + 8H_2O \longrightarrow 15Fe^{2+} + 2SO_4^{2-} + 16H^+ \qquad (4)$$

Singer and Stumm (1968) and others also present evidence that microbes possibly play an important role in the oxidation process. Smith and Shumate (1971) indicate the reaction rates are a function of pH, temperature and oxygen concentration conditions at the pyrite surface. Erosion of stripped areas also continually exposes fresh pyrite for oxidation.

Plot Vegetative Response
The four 500 square meter plots on the demonstration tract were designed to sample subsurface flow. Each plot was treated with sludge in November 1970 at treatment levels of 304, 178 and 78 dry

metric tons of sludge per hectare. The fourth plot remained as a control. The following spring, the plots were seeded with K-31 tall fescue (*Festuca arundinacea*) and weeping lovegrass (*Eragrostis curvula*) at the rates of 22 and 8 kilograms per hectare, respectively. Within 30 days germination had occurred on all but the control plot. At the end of the first growing season, there was a ninety percent vegetative cover on the most heavily treated plot, whereas the plots with lower treatments were less than 50 percent covered. In the second growing season only the 304 ton per hectare treatment continued to support as much vegetation as in the first growing season.

Plot Runoff Response
Water samples collected from subsurface drains in the plots have been analyzed for chemical and bacterial contamination since the study began. The average acidity levels and concentrations of various metals observed in runoff from the plots appear in Figure 10-1 and Table 10-1. The heaviest treatment (304 metric tons per hectare) reduced acidity as well as aluminum and iron concentrations in the runoff by more than 60 percent and manganese concentrations by more than 50 percent. Slight increases in chromium, cadmium and zinc concentrations were observed, however, as shown in Table 10-1 and Figure 10-2. (All of these elements also naturally appear in acid runoff from the tract.)

Within the period of observation, a cyclic trend in metal concentra-

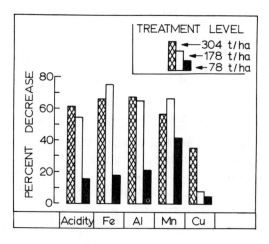

Figure 10-1. Percent decrease in acidity and certain metals in runoff from the plots following sludge treatment at the three levels of application.

Table 10-1. Average concentration of certain parameters in subsurface runoff from the sludge treated plots before and after treatment ("after" values based on 1970-1972 averages)

| Element | Treatment (metric tons/hectare) | | | | | | |
| | -304- | | -178- | | -78- | | -0- |
	Before	After	Before	After	Before	After	Average
				-milligrams per liter-			
Al	1,240	402	395	138	440	346	548
Cd	1.14	1.92	0.31	1.18	0.70	1.13	0.66
Cr	3.5	4.8	1.3	1.6	2.3	3.4	2.1
Cu	11.6	7.5	3.8	3.3	4.0	3.6	4.5
Fe	3,700	1,260	1,280	320	1,000	822	1,620
Mn	70	30	51	17	71	42	36
Pb	0.33	0.23	0.16	0.18	0.42	0.18	0.22
SO$_4$	11,000	7,740	8,400	3,730	7,100	6,770	7,980
Zn	24.4	36.4	8.1	24.8	14.1	26.0	13.3
Acidity	22,940	8,900	7,310	3,320	7,040	5,900	9,770

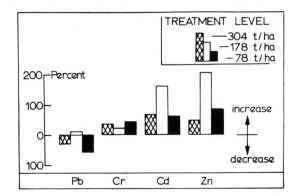

Figure 10-2. Percent change in concentrations of certain metals in runoff from the plots following sludge treatment at the three levels of application.

tions has been noted. From November 1970 through September 1971, a sharp decrease in metal concentrations was observed in the runoff. During the dormant season of 1971-1972, a slight rise in concentrations occurred. With the onset of the growing season during the spring of 1972, metal concentrations began decreasing again. This cyclical pattern of concentrations is perhaps associated with the seasonal availability of water and with plant uptake of metals. The dormant season in the area coincides with the period of higher rainfall and lower evapotranspiration rates. The initial decrease in metal concentrations in the runoff was likely due to neutralization of the spoil's acidity by the highly alkaline sludge. The sludge, which contains about 40 percent organic matter, also has a high cation exchange and buffering capacity which may complex many of the metal cations in the acid spoil. Also, uptake by plants during the growing season was indicated by analyses conducted on the weeping lovegrass. The observed increase in lead, chromium, cadmium and zinc, particularly noted in runoff from the 178-ton treatment, implies that the lower treatment rates are incapable of providing sufficient buffering to help tie up certain metals (Figure 10-2). These metals, whose solubility is pH dependent, probably passed through the inadequately neutralized spoil, to appear in the runoff. In summary, these initial results indicate that sludge treatment of acid spoils apparently must be at a high enough level to neutralize the spoil in order to prevent additional water pollution by metals and to maintain a vegetative cover. The heaviest treatment of 304 metric tons per hectare appeared to be most desirable.

Nutrients

Although the sludge contains about five percent dry weight of nitrogen, only one to two percent are in the water soluble form of ammonia and nitrate. Merz (1959) indicates that as much as 80 percent of the nitrogen in sludge may remain in the organic form the first year. The slow availability of the nitrogen is highly desirable for plant growth and water quality considerations. Analysis for NO_3-N and NO_2-N in runoff from the test plots has shown no concentrations exceeding State water quality standards. Concentrations of NH_3-N ranged from 54.0 mg/l immediately after treatment to 8.0 mg/l 10 months after treatment on the most heavily treated plot. The high levels of NH_3-N and O-N, in conjunction with no consistent increases of NO_2-N and NO_3-N, indicate that the acidity of the spoil material and/or the heavy metal concentrations probably are preventing nitrification. Once a high enough pH is established, nitrification could be anticipated and NH_3-N concentrations presumably would decrease. Establishment of sorghum and millet, both high nitrogen demanders, possibly would minimize nitrogen concentrations in the runoff.

Bacteria

No fecal coliform bacteria were found in runoff from the sludge treated plots during the year immediately following application. A digestion period of seven to ten days during municipal treatment kills pathogenic organisms, according to Burd (1966). Also, lagooning of a sludge for 30 days after digestion further reduces fecal coliforms by 99 percent (Braids *et al.*, 1970). The sludge used by Palzo has been logooned for over two years. Exposure to ultraviolet radiation by spreading the sludge on the ground is detrimental to bacteria. Finally, fecal coliforms in contact with acid water with a pH of 2.5 for 24 hours exhibit a die-off of greater than 99 percent (Joseph and Shay, 1952). Considering all of these factors, it appears unlikely that pathogens would survive in the runoff.

Spoil Observations

The maximum level sludge treatment effectively raised the pH of the acid spoil. Figure 10-3 shows the subsurface pH profile of the most heavily treated plot versus the control plot 18 months after treatment (July 1972). As would be expected, the major difference in pH between the treatment and control plot spoil is in the top 20-25 centimeters. The average pH based on nine observations per plot taken at various times during the first year following treatment showed the following:

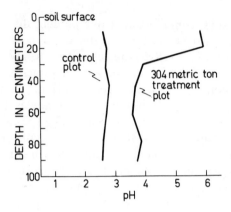

Figure 10-3. Effect of sludge treatment on pH of spoil within the plots.

Treatment rate	Plot average soil surface pH
(dry metric tons/hectare)	
304	6.2
178	5.2
78	4.7
0	2.3

Laboratory analyses of percolate from the spoil were made to supplement the field runoff and spoil pH observations. Columns of spoil approximately one meter by five centimeters were augered from the most heavily treated and the control plots in 1972. The spoil cores then were transported in two layers to the laboratory (0-50 centimeter and 50-100 centimeter layers) and leached with distilled water. About one-half year's equivalent of precipitation (1000 ml) was percolated through the individual columns during a ten-day period. The percolate was analyzed for the parameters shown in Tables 10-2 and 10-3, plus calcium and magnesium.

These preliminary percolate analyses of July 1972 indicate that mixing of the sludge into the spoil was apparently more effective than simple surface application in terms of water quality improvements. As shown in Tables 10-2 and 10-3, acidity was reduced in percolate from the treated plot's spoil when sludge was mixed into the spoil (note hydrogen ion concentration). Likewise, iron concentrations in the percolate were greatly reduced by the sludge incorporation. Less impressive reductions appeared for sulfur, manganese, aluminum, and copper.

Table 10-2. Concentrations of chemical constituents in the percolate collected from the 0-50 cm column of spoil material

Treatment	Constituent											
	Zn	Pb	Fe	S	Mn	Cu	Na	Al	K	H	Co	Ni
	mg/l	mg/l	mg/l	%	mg/l	mg/l	mg/l	mg/l	mg/l	meq/l	mg/l	mg/l
304 t/ha plot	28.4	3.5	trace	0.058	2.0	0.5	7.1	105	28.0	1.38	0.2	3.5
Mixed	22.0	4.5	trace	0.060	1.0	–	5.8	155	16.0	1.92	0.1	2.8
	62.4	20	42	0.135	2.8	3.2	3.2	960	0.2	54.15	0.1	4.2
Unmixed	22.6	4.5	1.9	0.063	13.0	1.2	3.8	1300	0.5	11.35	0.2	2.8
	1.9	5.0	5400	0.082	3.3	0.6	0.9	210	0.1	36.96	0.5	1.0
Control Plot	1.4	5.0	11	0.071	2.2	0.2	1.8	1300	–	11.97	0.1	0.5

Table 10-3. Concentrations of chemical constituents in the percolate collected from the 50-100 cm column of spoil material

Treatment	Constituent											
	Zn	Pb	Fe	S	Mn	Cu	Na	Al	K	H	Co	Ni
	mg/l	mg/l	mg/l	%	mg/l	mg/l	mg/l	mg/l	mg/l	meq/l	mg/l	mg/l
304 t/ha plot	37.4	4.6	trace	0.077	3.0	0.4	9.9	370	78.0	4.49	0.2	4.5
Mixed	4.8	5.0	trace	0.045	0.5	–	4.3	250	22.0	2.11	0.2	1.0
	48.4	5.5	196	0.098	17.5	2.2	2.7	2500	0.2	30.92	0.2	3.8
Unmixed	29.6	4.7	14	0.055	4.0	1.0	4.5	920	0.4	11.70	0.4	2.5
Control	40.4	6.5	2600	0.229	12.8	1.2	8.7	12600	0.1	33.14	0.1	7.7
Plot	1.2	4.9	4600	0.069	2.8	0.6	0.8	1200	0.2	28.71	0.2	0.5

Sludge application apparently increased zinc and sodium levels in the percolate water, as shown in Table 10-2. Hunt *et al.* (1971) noted that zinc apparently was weathered out of spoil when treated effluent was applied in irrigation. Further observations are needed to assess the significance of any metal releases that are associated with sludge application.

If the zone of highest oxidation rates in the spoil can be effectively neutralized and stabilized, the acid production should be decreased. The zone of major oxidation in the spoil is recognized by Good *et al.* (1970) to be in the top 25 centimeters. This zone has the clay removed by leaching and is most permeable to air and water.

Infiltration capacities averaging 7,400 cm/hr have been measured in the top 40 cm of Palzo spoil. The second zone, immediately below this highly permeable zone, has a lower permeability due to clay fines precipitated by rain. However, the permeability of the deeper zone is not strikingly lower in the samples studied at this site. Below 40 cm, permeability averages 6,200 cm/hr. A very wide range of permeability in these samples suggests more samples are needed to increase the precision of the estimate. A third zone suggested by Good *et al.* (1970), is the deepest area where little, if any, oxidation occurs.

Large Scale Operations

Following the results of the plot work discussed above and considering the results of researchers in the same subject area, the Forest Service has decided to apply sludge on the larger tract surrounding the test plots.

The entire 77 hectare acid producing watershed, where the spoil pH ranges from 1.9 to 4.0, will be treated with anaerobically digested sludge. The purpose of the demonstration is to test the practicality of sludge treatment on a large scale.

The sludge will probably be obtained from the Metropolitan Sanitary District of Greater Chicago. It will be shipped, by rail, unloaded in a receiving lagoon, and piped to a storage lagoon on the site, which will hold 1.020×10^5 cubic meters of sludge.

The 77 hectare area has been extensively leveled and reshaped in June-July 1972. Digested sludge will be applied to the site at a rate of 626 dry metric tons per hectare over a two or three year period. Either an irrigation sprinkler system or gated irrigation pipe will be used to apply the sludge. Before and during sludge application, the site will be disked to increase infiltration. Infiltration tests run on the most heavily treated test plot indicate that upon saturation, infiltration capacities average only about 25 cm/hr. Thus, successful irrigation must be intermittent to allow soil drainage.

The planned rate of application is twice that of the most heavily treated test plot. The 304 metric ton per hectare plot had sludge mixed to a depth of about 8.0 cm. However, since the upper 25 cm is reported to be the zone of most extensive oxidation by Good *et al.* (1970), it seems desirable to mix the sludge to this depth, if possible. Complete disking on the entire tract will mix the sludge to the first 15 to 20 cm. Although the amount of sludge applied will be about twice that of the most heavily treated plot, it will be mixed to about twice the depth. This sludge-spoil combination will contain about 20 percent sludge and should provide a good rooting zone for plant establishment.

The nutrient value of the sludge is high enough to support plant growth. Hinesly (1972) claims the N:P:K ratio to be 33:18:4. The nutrient loading rate for the suggested application rate will be: nitrogen—7,670 kilograms per hectare, phosphorus—4,180 kilograms per hectare and potassium—930 kilograms per hectare. As previously discussed, most of the nitrogen is in the organic form and thus, will be available to the plants over a long period of time. Supplemental potash may be required.

The immediate establishment of K-31 tall fescue (*Festuca arundinacea*), weeping lovegrass (*Eragrostis curvula*), and orchard grass (*Dactylis glomerata*) should provide erosion protection. The planting of shortleaf pine (*Pinus echinata*), Virginia Pine (*Pinus virginiana*), cottonwood (*Populus deltoides*) and black locust (*Robinia pseudoacacia*) should provide further stabilization. If vegetation can be well established and erosion controlled, acid production from the site should basically be reduced by a combination of the following factors:

1. Neutralization of the surface acid producing spoil (and chelation of the metals).
2. Erosion control to prevent exposure of fresh pyritic material.
3. A decrease of surface and subsurface water flow from the site, due to increased evapotranspiration losses.

The Receiving Stream
The acid water leaving the tract has a very low pH and high acidity concentration. Calculations based on sampling observations and average stream discharge data indicate that approximately 9,000 metric tons per year of acidity are contributed to the adjacent receiving stream. This acid runoff is generally considered to be one of the worst in the State of Illinois. Table 10-4 describes the impact of the Palzo runoff upon the chemistry of the stream.

In addition to stream sampling above and below the Palzo Tract, a water quality survey was made every 75 to 100 meters along the 1.5 kilometer section of the adjacent stream. The purpose of the stream survey was: (1) to identify apparent acid input points; (2) to describe

Table 10-4. Impact of Plazo runoff on Sugar Creek as shown by the 1969 to 1971 stream samples

Pollutant	Sugar Creek above Palzo[a]	Palzo Runoff[b]	Sugar Creek below Palzo[a]
	mg/l	mg/l	mg/l
Al	59	2,075	306
Fe	49	3,955	529
Mn	5.7	320.0	51.4
SO_4	558	23,675	3,731
Acidity	338	20,100	3,232
Specific			
Conductance	825	14,885	3,329
(umhos/cm)			

a. Upper 40 cm layers of stream only.
b. Surface flow emerging from the tract.

patterns of stratification, mixing and assimilation of the acid into the stream; and (3) to determine the range of water quality within individual cross sections of the stream. These survey data serve both as pretreatment information and as a basis for stream sampling design. One stream survey, taken during stable, summer flow conditions, is shown in Figure 10-4. Continuing surveys should determine the patterns of stratification as related to stream discharge.

As illustrated in Figure 10-4, water quality changes along the stream (Sugar Creek) are most striking. For example, values of pH and conductivity change from around 6.0 pH units and 500 micromhos per centimeter upstream, to less than 3.0 pH units and over 11,000 micromhos per centimeter downstream.

The stream cross sections above the stripped tract are fairly uniform in water quality (Section A, Figure 10-4). However, once acid inputs occur, a distinct and stable stratification appears (Sections K and P, Figure 10-4). The location of cross sections A and P also are shown on the map of Figure 10-5.

Inputs of acid water into upstream reaches of the creek by the Palzo Tract appear to be neutralized, presumably because of dilution and buffering effects. However, once the stream's moderate buffering capability is overwhelmed, stratification becomes continuous.

The extreme water quality stratification in the receiving stream emphasizes the need for integrated or layered sampling, if one is to correctly evaluate water quality changes occurring in the stream.

Monitoring Design

A monitoring system will be initiated on the site to determine the large scale effect of treating the spoil banks with digested sewage

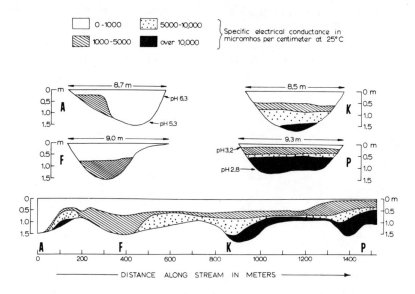

Figure 10-4. Water quality changes and stratification in Sugar Creek as it flows past the Palzo Tract. One of the stream surveys is shown, with the longitudinal profile (bottom) and four of the sixteen cross sections (above). Each cross section was profiled vertically at three points. Flow was 200 to 300 liters per second. Points A and P appear on Figure 10-5.

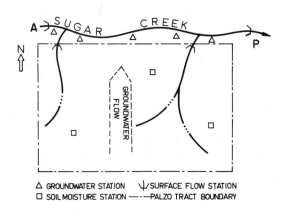

Figure 10-5. Schematic map of the 77 hectare strip mined tract to be treated showing major features of the monitoring layout. Points A and P correspond to Figure 10-4.

sludge. Water, spoil and plant responses will be observed in a variety of ways.

Since the Palzo Tract is now causing severe pollution problems, as shown in Table 10-4, monitoring the water leaving the area will be most important. Figure 10-5 is a simplified model of the entire study area, showing the direction of water movement and location of monitoring equipment. The following main sites will be monitored:

a. Two Palzo surface runoff stations on the tract, with continuous pH, electrical conductance and flow measurements. Weekly samples will be analyzed for chemicals and bacteria.

b. Two Sugar Creek stream stations, with continuous pH, electrical conductance and flow measurements. Weekly samples will be analyzed for chemicals and bacteria.

c. Twenty-two shallow groundwater stations, spaced about 65 meters apart along the saturated zone. Bi-weekly samples will be taken after treatment begins and analyzed for selected parameters.

d. Twenty soil moisture stations randomly located at 20 to 100 cm depths throughout tract. Monthly observations will be made for selected parameters.

The basic objectives of the above design are:

a. To determine if runoff from the tract is in compliance with Federal and State water quality standards.

b. To establish a good baseline record of water quality parameters before sludge treatment.

c. To determine the pattern and relationship of individual elements entering Sugar Creek. This information should allow composite sampling and analysis of index parameters, in order to reduce the number of observations.

Monitoring in subwatersheds (within the tract) will be used to determine effects of particular treatments on selected areas. Important measurements in the subwatersheds will include observation of the hydrologic response of the area due to treatment, monitoring of fecal coliform counts during and after sludge application, and evaluation of chemical parameters in runoff following selected levels of treatment.

Cooperative Research

In addition to the demonstration work, the North Central Forest Experiment Station will utilize a randomized block design to study the effects of various levels of sludge and limestone applications upon soil chemistry, water quality and plant growth.

The Forestry Department of Southern Illinois University, supported by the National Science Foundation, also is studying plant and soil response of sludge and limestone treatments upon acid spoil as it varies with depth of incorporation into the spoil. They are investigating vegetative response of 12 grasses and six tree species.

The Agronomy Department of the University of Illinois presently is studying pyrite and other forms of sulfur in the acid spoil. They will examine redox potential of the spoil at various depths to describe the rate of change in surface and subsurface spoil materials resulting from sludge treatments.

Summary
This report details the preliminary results of a strip mined reclamation demonstration project in Southern Illinois. The initial observations indicate that treated municipal sludge, when applied to the spoil in sufficient amounts, improves spoil pH, allows establishment of vegetation and reduces acidity and concentrations of some of the chemicals in the runoff issuing from the tract.

The proposed application of sludge to a larger 77 hectare area should provide some insight into the practicality of sludge treatment on strip mined areas. If such treatment is practical, three main advantages could possibly result: (1) reclamation of useless stripped areas, (2) reduction of water pollution associated with these areas, and (3) the disposal of municipal sludge.

Literature Cited

Anderson, D. A., S. H. Kunkle and D. R. Hedrich. 1972. Affluence, effluence, and new roles for forest hydrology in the East. *Proc. Amer. Water Resources Assoc.*, Fort Collins, Colorado, June 1972. 14 pp.

Braids, O. C., M. Sobhan-Ardakani and J. A. E. Molina. 1970. Liquid digested sewage sludge gives field crop necessary nutrients. *Illinois Res.* 12(3):6-7.

Burd, R. S. 1966. A study of sludge handling and disposal. Publication WP-20-4. Federal Water Poll. Control Admin. USDI. Cincinnati, Ohio.

Dalton, Frank E., J. E. Stein and B. T. Lynam. 1968. Land reclamation—A complete solution of the sludge and solids disposal problem. *Jour. Water Poll. Control.* 40:5. 789-800.

Good, D. M., U. T. Ricca and K. S. Shumate. 1970. The relation of refuse pile hydrology to acid production. *Third Symposium on Coal Mine Drainage Research.* 145-149.

Hill, Ronald D. 1971. Restoration of the terrestrial environment. *The ASB Bulletin.* 16:3. 107-116.

Hinesly, Thomas D. 1972. Personal contact. Department of Agronomy. University of Illinois.

Hunt, Clifford F., W. E. Sopper and L. T. Kardos. 1971. Renovation of treated municipal sewage effluent and digested liquid sludge through irrigation of bituminous coal strip mine spoil. The Pennsylvania State University. Technical Paper, Institute for Research on Land and Water Resources. 118 pp.

Joseph, J. M. and D. E. Shay. 1952. Viability of *Escherichia coli* in acid mine waters. *Amer. Jour. of Pub. Health.* 42:795-800.

Merz, Robert C. 1959. Utilization of liquid sludge. *Water and Sewage Works.* 106:489-493.

Peterson, J. R. and J. Gschwind. 1971. Human and animal wastes as fertilizers. *Fertilizer Technology and Use.* 577-594.

Singer, P. C. and W. Stumm. 1968. Kinetics of the oxidation of ferrous iron. *Second Symposium on Coal Mine Drainage Research.* Mellon Institute. 12-34.

Smith, E. E. and K. S. Shumate. 1971. Rate of pyrite oxidation and acid production rate in the field. Presented at Acid Mine Drainage Workshop. Athens, Ohio. 11 pp.

Sopper, W. E. 1970. Revegetation of strip mine spoil banks through irrigation with municipal sewage effluent and sludge. *Compost Science.* 6-11.

Udall, Stewart L. 1967. Surface mining and our environment. U.S. Department of the Interior. 124 pp.

11
Effects of Land Disposal of Wastewaters on Soil Phosphorus Relations

J. E. Hook, L. T. Kardos and W. E. Sopper*

At present there is an increasing usage of soil and soil-plant systems as a final treatment and disposal system for municipal and industrial wastewaters. The success of a land disposal site depends upon the ability of the soil to temporarily fix and store effluent constituents for use by plants and microbes and to prevent the migration of contaminants to the groundwater (Sopper, 1971). The movement and the fixation of phosphorus, a major constituent of many wastewaters, are important considerations in these disposal systems. In the Wastewater Renovation and Conservation Research Project at The Pennsylvania State University, the fate of phosphorus has been monitored as treated municipal sewage effluent was applied to cropland and forested areas. Ten years of monitoring have indicated a high degree of efficiency of the soil-plant system to retain and use phosphorus. The purpose of this report is to describe the chemical forms in which the phosphorus was being retained and to what depth in the soil it was accumulating.

Method of Study

To evaluate phosphorus, as well as other constituents, of the treated wastewater, an extensive monitoring network was established. Its purpose was to collect water samples in the soil and underlying substratum. This network is described in detail elsewhere (Parizek *et al.*, 1967). Yields of harvested crops were measured and samples

*Department of Agronomy and School of Forest Resources, The Pennsylvania State University

were analyzed for phosphorus content by the methods reported by Baker *et al.* (1964).

Soil samples from the various treatment and control areas were analyzed for pH, organic matter, free iron, free aluminum, and available phosphorus. Organic matter and pH were determined by the methods of Peech *et al.* (1947). Available phosphorus was determined using the dilute hydrochloric acid, dilute NH_4F extractant of Bray as described by Jackson (1956). Phosphorus in the soil samples was fractionated according to the scheme of Chang and Jackson (1957) with modifications of Glenn *et al.* (1959) and Peterson and Corey (1965). Free iron was determined in the citrate-dithionite extract of the phosphorus fractionation scheme. Basically it was the extractant described by Aguilera and Jackson (1953). Free aluminum was the aluminum extracted by the NH_4F (pH 8.2) extract of the phosphorus fractionation scheme.

The areas which received effluent included two major soil series, the Morrison sandy loam and the Hublersburg clay loam. These series have quite different properties and represent two possible extremes of the range of deep well drained Pennsylvania soils. Several properties of these soils which affect movement and fixation of soluble phosphorus are presented in Table 11-1.

Treatments of these areas included variations of effluent levels, usually zero, one and two inches per week and variations of vegetative cover. Although as many as 42 plots have been studied, only four treatment and three control plots will be considered in this paper. Each of the treated areas considered here was irrigated with two inches of effluent per week.

The agronomy area, located on Hublersburg clay loam was divided into seven crop rotation strips. The crop sequence is presented in Table 11-2.

Treatment was two inches of effluent per week and a control which received fertilizer phosphorus. The amount of effluent applied, concentration of phosphorus in the effluent and the amount of phosphorus applied for the eight years of treatment are presented in Table 11-3. From the phosphorus content and yield data, the average removal of phosphorus on the treated site was calculated and is also presented in Table 11-3.

The net amount remaining—the total applied, 620.7, minus the removal by crops, 206.3 or about 414 pounds per acre per year—is a measure of the amount which is being held by the soil.

The reed canarygrass area, located on Hublersburg clay loam, was irrigated with effluent year round. The grass was established in 1964, and since 1965 three cuttings were made each year except in 1968

Table 11-1. Some properties of the two soils at the areas which were used in the effluent irrigation project

Area	Soil depth	pH	Organic matter	Free iron	Clay content
	inches		%	% Fe_2O_3	%
	Hublersburg clay loam				
Agronomy control	0-12	5.6	2.96	3.44	—
	12-24	5.1	0.86	4.54	—
	24-36	5.1	0.40	5.70	—
	36-48	5.0	0.20	6.15	—
	48-60	4.9	0.15	6.75	—
Reed canarygrass irrigated	0-12	6.4	3.01	3.62	43
	12-24	5.8	0.82	5.00	52
	24-36	5.4	0.34	5.25	49
	36-48	5.3	0.18	5.35	45
	48-60	5.1	0.09	5.42	41
Old field control	0-12	5.2	2.39	3.94	—
	12-24	5.2	0.54	5.30	—
	24-36	5.1	0.23	5.80	—
	36-48	5.1	0.21	5.80	—
	48-60	5.1	0.21	5.80	—
	Morrison sandy loam				
Gamelands forest control	0-12	4.8	1.67	1.66	15
	12-24	4.9	0.31	2.14	28
	24-36	5.0	0.25	2.31	28
	36-48	5.0	0.19	2.22	16
	48-60	4.9	0.19	2.71	36
Gamelands forest irrigated	0-12	5.5	1.43	1.21	—
	12-24	5.2	0.30	2.08	—
	24-36	5.0	0.14	2.17	—
	36-48	4.7	0.12	2.32	—
	48-60	4.7	0.12	2.37	—

when only two cuttings were made. The amount of phosphorus removed yearly by the grass is shown in Table 11-4. Also presented in that Table are the amount of effluent applied, concentration of phosphorus in the effluent and amount of phosphorus applied.

The old field area, located on Hublersburg clay loam, was usually irrigated from May through November each year. This field, abandoned in the early 1930's, has received no commercial fertilizer. Growth responses of the vegetation have been measured (Sopper, 1971) but none of the vegetation has been removed. The area is covered with a variety of weeds and has a scattered stand of white

Table 11-2. Yearly crop sequence for the seven strips in the agronomy area

Strip number	1963	1964	1965	Year 1966	1967	1968	1969	1970	1971
1	corn	oats	alfalfa	alfalfa	alfalfa	corn	corn	corn	corn
2	wheat	red clover	corn	corn	corn	corn	corn	corn	corn
3	red clover	corn	oats	alfalfa	alfalfa	corn	corn	corn	corn
4	wheat	red clover	corn	corn	corn	corn	corn	corn	corn
5	corn	oats	alfalfa	alfalfa	alfalfa	corn	corn	corn	corn
6	red clover	corn	oats	alfalfa	alfalfa	corn	corn	corn	corn
7	alfalfa	corn	oats	alfalfa	alfalfa	corn	corn	corn	corn

Table 11-3. Concentration of phosphorus in the effluent and amounts of phosphorus added by effluent irrigation and removed by crop harvest in the agronomy area receiving two inches of effluent at weekly intervals

	Year								
	1963	1964	1965	1966	1967	1968	1969	1970	Total
Average concentration of P in effluent (mg/l)	9.70	8.55	6.95	5.35	6.75	7.10	6.55	4.15	—
Amount of effluent applied (inches/year)	48	66	58	64	52	40	32	32	392
Total phosphorus applied (lbs/acre/year)	105.7	127.8	91.1	77.9	76.2	64.4	47.6	30	620.7
Average amount of phosphorus removed by all crops (lbs/acre/year)	26.3	18.5	27.1	31.8	24.8	[a]	43.1	34.7	206.3

a. No harvest

Table 11-4. Concentration of phosphorus in the effluent and amounts of phosphorus added by effluent irrigation and removed by crop harvest in the reed canarygrass area

	1964	1965	1966	1967	Year 1968	1969	1970	Total
Average concentration of P in the effluent (mg/l)								
	8.55	6.95	7.70	7.70	8.45	4.20	4.05	—
Amount of effluent applied (inches/year)								
	36	80	78	94	98	100	86	572
Total phosphorus applied (lbs/acre/year)								
	69.5	125.7	135.9	163.9	187.6	94.8	88.8	866.2
Average amount of phosphorus removed by reed canarygrass (lbs/acre/year)								
	a	40.0	33.4	55.9	47.2	47.2	56.0	279.7

a. No harvest

spruce (*Picea glaucus* M.). The old field control plot is similar but has received no effluent.

The gamelands area, located on Morrison sandy loam soil, has a mixed hardwood forest vegetation. The plot (new gamelands) for which lysimeter data is presented has been irrigated on a year-round basis since 1965. The control, adjacent to this plot has not been irrigated or fertilized. For analysis of total soil phosphorus (the fractionation data) a nearby plot (old gamelands) which has been irrigated since 1963 was used. This plot has received various levels of effluent irrigation and prior to sampling in 1970 had received a total of 600 inches of effluent.

Results

One of the first questions to be considered was that of how much phosphorus was leached through the soil. The concentration of phosphorus in the percolating soil water was derived from the suction lysimeter data. These lysimeters sampled water in and just below the plant root zone. The mean annual concentrations of phosphorus in the soil water of the treated and control areas are presented in Table 11-5.

In the agronomy area, mean annual concentration in samples from the control site at a depth of 48 inches varied within a range of 0.030 to 0.080 ppm. These concentrations represent the normal background phosphorus which is in equilibrium with the soil phosphorus. These concentrations are considered typical for this heavy textured soil. The mean annual concentration in samples from the old field control area also fell within this range.

When treated with effluent from 1963 to 1971 the percolate in the agronomy area has shown no increase in phosphorus concentration at the 48-inch depth. Only a slight inconsistent increase occurred at 24 inches. At six inches the percolate concentration in the treated area varied considerably but was consistently higher than in the control area. Since the effluent concentration was about seven ppm and the highest percolate concentration was about 0.6 ppm a reduction of greater than 90 percent occurred after water percolated through only six inches of soil.

The reed canarygrass area was as effective as the agronomy area in reducing phosphorus concentrations in the soil percolate. The concentration at the 24-inch depth in the reed canarygrass area was only slightly higher than in either agronomy control or the treated area, and has remained nearly constant. The increase which occurred in

Table 11-5. Mean annual concentration of phosphorus (mg/l) in soil percolate samples taken at three depths from both effluent treated and control areas

Area	Soil	Effluent amount in./wk.	Year 1965	1966	1967	1968	1969	1970	1971
				6-Inch depth					
Agronomy	clay loam	0	.035	.050	.045	.060	.025	.035	.045
Agronomy	clay loam	2	.145	.250	.600	.620	.500	.135	.120
Reed canarygrass	clay loam	2	—	.165	.140	.190	.205	.135	.210
Old field	clay loam	0	—	.040*	.045*	.000*	.035	.035	.030*
Old field	clay loam	2	—	.090	.140	.260	.295	.340*	.995
New gamelands	sandy loam	0	—	.050*	.050*	–	.045	.050	.090*
New gamelands	sandy loam	2	—	.265	.115	.450	.320	.630	.965
				24-Inch depth					
Agronomy	clay loam	0	.055	.045	.045	.045	.070	.060	.040
Agronomy	clay loam	2	.040	.060	.090	.080	.060	.090	.065
Reed canarygrass	clay loam	2	.025*	.085	.100	.105	.100	.075	.105
Old field	clay loam	0	—	.030*	.032	.120*	.220*	.100*	.025*
Old field	clay loam	2	—	.070	.095	.125*	.120	.120*	.250*
New gamelands	sandy loam	0	—	.090*	.225*	.035*	.030*	.025*	.040*
New gamelands	sandy loam	2	—	.030	.050	.130	.105	.130	.090
				48-Inch depth					
Agronomy	clay loam	0	.030	.040	.040	.040	.080	.045	.035
Agronomy	clay loam	2	.025	.040	.070	.075	.095	.080	.060
Reed canarygrass	clay loam	2	.010*	.055	.055	.060	.030	.045	.060
Old field	clay loam	0	—	.030	.040	.040	.050	.040	.040*
Old field	clay loam	2	—	.060	.070	.055	.100	.115*	.420*
New gamelands	sandy loam	0	—	.060*	.070	.075*	.105*	.050*	.025
New gamelands	sandy loam	2	—	.040	.055	.115	.140	.155	.265

*Indicates mean computed from fewer than 10 samples.

1971 at the six-inch depth was a result of a substantial increase in both concentration and amount of applied phosphorus. During most of that year effluent containing stabilized digested sludge (approximately one part of sludge slurry to eleven parts of effluent) was applied to that area. This effluent-sludge mixture had a total phosphorus level of 20 to 25 mg/l and an orthophosphate level of 10 to 15 mg/l.

In the old field treated area, though located on the Hublersburg clay loam soil, the percolate has increased in phosphorus concentration more than in the treated agronomy and reed canarygrass areas. This greater increase occurred to the 48-inch depth. The factor which may have contributed most to this increase was that phosphorus was not removed in a harvested crop. The phosphorus cycled through the soil rather than being removed. The old field was also treated with effluent each year for as many as ten weeks longer than the agronomy area.

At the gamelands treated area, located on the Morrison sandy loam soil, effluent irrigation has resulted in a substantially greater increase in phosphorus concentration in the soil percolate. This can best be seen in the Figures showing mean phosphorus concentration in the percolate at 48 inches (Figures 11-1 and 11-2). While treated sites on the Hublersburg soil have concentrations about the same as the agronomy control (Figure 11-1), the gamelands treated area has shown a steady increase above that of the control area since the irrigation began in 1965 (Figure 11-2). One reason for this greater increase is the recycling of phosphorus through the forest litter. A more important reason is the lower clay content and lower content of sesquioxides in the soil (Table 11-1). The effect of these properties will be discussed in greater detail later.

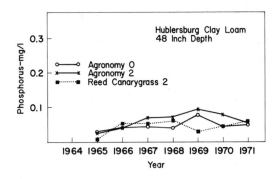

Figure 11-1. Mean annual concentration of phosphorus in percolate samples from Hublersburg clay loam soil at several areas receiving zero and two inches of effluent per week

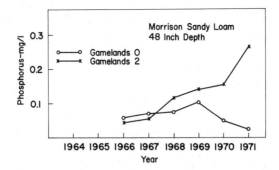

Figure 11-2. Mean annual concentration of phosphorus in percolate samples from the Morrison sandy loam soil at areas receiving zero and two inches of effluent per week

If a few assumptions are made concerning the movement of water, these concentrations of phosphorus in the soil water can be used to calculate the amount of phosphorus which may be leaching into the substratum. In 1970, for example, 86 inches of effluent were applied to the reed canarygrass area. The total rainfall that year was 47 inches. Of that, approximately 26 inches[1] were lost by evapotranspiration. Assuming that the total of effluent and recharge — 107 inches — percolates downward (no interflow or runoff) at the mean concentration of phosphorus found in the six-inch lysimeter — 0.135 mg/l — then a total of 3.3 lbs/acre/year would move downward. By the time this reaches four feet the concentration is reduced to 0.060 mg/l. From this depth only 1.4 lbs/acre/year would leave the irrigated area. This is only 1.7 percent of the 89 lbs/acre added that year.

Very little of the phosphorus added with effluent has been lost by leaching. The remainder, 98.3%, has been removed by crops, has been held by the soil and has been lost in runoff. The amount of runoff is not exactly known for each treated area, but it has not been excessive. The agronomy and old field areas were irrigated during the driest part of the year. Runoff occurred only during heavy rainstorms. The reed canarygrass area had a considerable amount of runoff during winter and spring. The amount of water lost as runoff from a sub-watershed of this area occasionally exceeded the amount applied as effluent (Myers, 1967). Ice covered ground, saturated soils, negligible evaporation and increased precipitation led to higher runoff during winter irrigation. Myers showed that the runoff which passed

1. This value represents the potential evapotranspiration as calculated by the Thornthwaite equation. Taylor, S.A. and Ashcroft, G.L. 1972. *Physical Edaphology*. W.H. Freeman and Co., San Francisco. Pp. 64-66.

the weir below this sub-watershed of the reed canarygrass area had a lower phosphorus concentration than the applied effluent even when no precipitation was available to dilute the runoff. This was interpreted as indicating that a portion of the effluent had entered the soil, moved downslope as interflow and seeped back to the surface with a lowered phosphorus content.

Runoff losses of phosphorus from the irrigated areas on the sandy Morrison soil were probably very low. Even during winter a thick leaf mulch and sandy surface soil prevented runoff. Interflow on top of clay layers in the soil contributed most downslope movement of irrigated water. Rebuck (1967) intercepted runoff and shallow interflow from an effluent irrigated area located on this soil. He found an average eight percent loss of irrigation water when application rates were between one and three inches per week. Since much of this water was from interflow, the effluent had contact with the soil for enough time to substantially lower the phosphorus concentration.

The amount of phosphorus removed by crops is a large and important part of the total phosphorus added. The data in Table 11-3 indicate that the crops removed from 14 to 115 percent of the phosphorus added annually to the agronomy area. The net phosphorus added since the beginning of effluent treatment increased until 1968 after which it has actually decreased. This was due to the decrease in added phosphorus and increase of phosphorus removed by the crop. Ideally, if the amount added would just equal the amount removed in harvest, phosphorus would not build up in the soil and the concentration of phosphorus in the percolate would be expected to remain constant or decrease.

In the reed canarygrass area (Table 11-4), higher phosphorus applications have resulted in a continued net increase in phosphorus not removed by the crop since irrigation began. Though the reed canarygrass removes slightly more phosphorus than the agronomic crops (Table 11-2), it has removed only 30 to 60 percent of the total added. At this site it is expected that the gradual increase in net phosphorus, which represents primarily the amount which is building up in the soil, will result in a gradual increase in phosphorus in the percolating water.

In the old field and gamelands forest areas no harvest was made. Some of the added phosphorus is taken up by the plants and trees in these areas. Sopper (1971) reported higher concentrations of phosphorus in foliar material of irrigated hardwoods in the gamelands than in the control. Similarly ground vegetation in the irrigated old field area had a higher phosphorus content than in the control. The forest vegetation in these treated areas did take up phosphorus, but the extent to which this uptake contributes to renovation of the effluent is

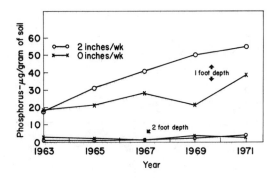

Figure 11-3. Bray extractable phosphorus in the effluent irrigated and control plots of the Agronomy area

not certain. Most of the phosphorus taken up by the trees and ground vegetation is recycled in the litter. This must obviously result in buildup of phosphorus in the soil and an eventual increase of phosphorus in the percolating water. This was found to occur in both the old field and gameland areas as discussed earlier.

When phosphorus is added to soils it usually is in the form of orthophosphate anions. Even organic phosphates are mineralized to this soluble form before being taken up by plants or reacting with the soil. These anions bond chemically with surfaces of iron and aluminum oxyhydroxides and will form precipitates with iron and aluminum when these are in solution. The bonds formed from surface and precipitation reactions vary in strength. The most weakly bonded, that is the most soluble phosphates, readily equilibrate with the soil solution and, hence, would be considered available to plants. A good measure of the amount of this available phosphorus is the Bray dilute acid-dilute fluoride extraction. This test was carried out periodically with soils from the treatment plots. The results of the Bray test are shown in Figures 11-3 and 11-4 for the agronomy and old field areas.

Soil from the agronomy area showed an increase in Bray extractable phosphorus over the nine years of treatment, although this increase occurred only in the upper one foot of soil. The control plot which received about 40 lbs P/acre/year as commercial fertilizer, showed a smaller increase. Below the top foot of soil no increase was observed. In the reed canarygrass area (not shown) soils were analyzed only two years — 1969 and 1971. The amount of Bray extractable phosphorus in the upper foot was 29.8 and 42.3 μg P/gram of soil for the two years, respectively. Again there was no increase below the upper foot of soil.

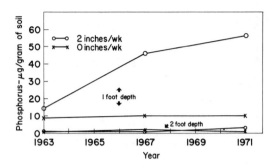

Figure 11-4. Bray extractable phosphorus in the effluent irrigated and control plots of the Old Field area

Bray phosphorus in the old field area (see Figure 11-8) increased approximately the same as in the agronomy area. The control plot of this area, which received no fertilizer, remained almost constant. In the second foot of both control and effluent treated plots, the Bray phosphorus remained constant at less than 3.0 μg P/gram of soil. These plots are all located on the Hublersburg clay loam. Effluent additions have not increased Bray extractable phosphorus significantly below the upper foot of this soil. As was pointed out earlier, the effluent has caused increases in water soluble phosphorus of percolate samples below the upper foot. This apparent discrepancy is due to the fact that the concentration in the percolate is measuring the equilibrium phosphorus in transit whereas the Bray extract measures both equilibrium and reserve phosphorus with the latter dominating in relative quantity.

In the old gamelands area on the Morrison sandy loam, however, there was evidence that an increase of Bray phosphorus has occurred to a depth of three feet. Samples were analyzed only in 1967 and 1971. In 1967, just 2½ years after effluent irrigation began, Bray phosphorus had reached 75.6, 4.9 and 2.2 μg P/gram of soil for the first, second, and third feet, respectively. This compared to 16.5, 2.1 and 1.2 μg P/gram of soil for the respective depths of the control plot. In 1971 the irrigated area had 143.8, 31.6 and 9.9 μg P/gram of soil and the control had 6.3, 1.5 and 0.7 μg P/gram of soil in the respective depths. The Morrison sandy loam soil on which this treatment area was located has shown a very large increase in Bray extractable phosphorus in response to year-round effluent irrigation.

A difficulty with the Bray extractable phosphorus test is that this test does not measure all of the native or retained phosphorus. It does indicate changes in the amount of phosphorus which is available to plants, and, as shown in Figures 11-3 and 11-4, this amount is affected by treatments. However, for many soils the Bray test measures less than 5% of the total soil phosphorus.

To evaluate changes in the phosphorus content more completely a fractionation of the soil phosphorus was carried out on soils from those treatment plots for which certain chemical properties are given in Table 11-1. The procedure was used to explain what has happened to the applied phosphorus and to relate this to other measured properties of the soils.

The fractionation procedure separates the soil phosphorus into four fractions: the NH_4F soluble fraction, the NaOH soluble fraction, the reductant-soluble fraction and the H_2SO_4 soluble fraction. While these phosphorus fractions do not represent discrete chemical compounds, they do result from groups of related compounds. The NH_4F (pH 8.2) extracts phosphorus which is bound to aluminum and aluminum compounds. NaOH extracts phosphorus bound to the surfaces of iron compounds. The reductant solution dissolves phosphorus compounds enmeshed within iron oxyhydroxides, and the sulfuric acid extracts calcium and magnesium phosphates.

In a typical untreated soil the phosphorus fractions were distributed as shown in Figure 11-5. The fractions are expressed as percent of the total extracted. This total varied from 300 to 600 μg P/g soil. The NaOH plus the reductant fractions made up 80 to 90 percent of the total extracted soil phosphorus. These are the fractions associated with iron. This was not surprising since total iron oxides expressed as Fe_2O_3 made up two to six percent of those soils; whereas, aluminum oxyhydroxides made up less than one half of one percent. Calcium and magnesium in these soils exist primarily as

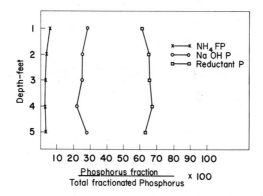

Figure 11-5. Percentage distribution of phosphorus fractions within the profile of the Old Field control plot

exchangeable cations. Only a small portion, less than six percent, of the total extracted soil phosphorus was associated with calcium and magnesium. It is, in fact, possible that this small percentage was actually related to aluminum which was released after the iron reduction treatment.

NH_4F phosphorus made up less than five percent of the total extracted phosphorus for most untreated soils, particularly subsoils. In the upper foot of the reed canarygrass effluent treated plot it constituted 13 percent. In the upper foot of the agronomy area control plot it was 16 percent. In the gamelands treated plot NH_4F phosphorus made up 43, 27, 17 and 11 percent of the total fractions of the first through fourth feet, respectively. This fraction, though not the most abundant, was probably the most important. This was demonstrated first by its relation to Bray extractable phosphorus. It was found to be highly correlated with this Bray test for plant available phosphorus. Its importance was further demonstrated by its relation to effluent and fertilizer treatments.

In Figures 11-6 and 11-7 the distribution of the NH_4F phosphorus is shown for soils of several plots. Those in Figure 11-6 are located on the Hublersburg clay loam. The greatest amounts of NH_4F phosphorus occurred in the upper foot of all three areas, decreased sharply in the second foot and then remained relatively constant in the deeper layers. Statistically significant differences between the three areas were only present in the upper foot. The reed canarygrass area which had been treated with effluent had the greatest amount of NH_4F phosphorus in the upper foot and was followed in order by the agronomy area control plot which has been receiving commercial

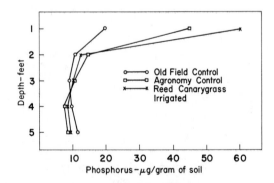

Figure 11-6. The mean distribution of phosphorus in the NH_4F fraction of one effluent treated and two control areas located on Hublersburg clay loam soil. The Agronomy control area is fertilized but the Old Field control area is not fertilized.

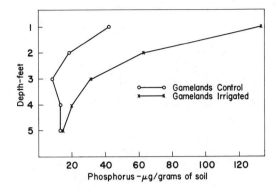

Figure 11-7. The mean distribution of phosphorus in the NH₄F fraction of the effluent irrigated and control areas located on Morrison sandy loam soil

fertilizer, and by the old field control plot which has received neither effluent nor commercial fertilizer.

In the forested plots located on Morrison sandy loam, Figure 11-7, effluent additions have significantly increased the amount of NH_4F phosphorus extracted when compared to the control. This increase occurred in the second and third as well as the first foot. This movement of applied phosphorus was similarly indicated by the Bray test.

There are several reasons why phosphorus has penetrated deeper in this hardwood area of the Morrison soil. First, there is no removal of harvested crops. As mentioned earlier phosphorus taken up by growing plants is later released as the leaf litter mineralizes. Secondly, the sandy soil of this area has a greater hydraulic conductivity; as a consequence the phosphorus in soil solution has less time to react with particle surfaces. Third, the mineral composition of the Morrison soil (Table 11-1) shows about one half as much free iron as the Hublersburg soil. Further it has less aluminum oxyhydroxides and has less clay which would result in less reactivity with phosphorus.

In addition to the noted effect of effluent treatments on the NH_4F fraction of the soils there was one other significant treatment effect. This was with respect to the NaOH fraction of the reed canarygrass plot, shown in Figure 11-8. The effluent additions of phosphorus have resulted in a slight increase of NaOH phosphorus, though only in the upper foot. This should be expected. The fractions as separated are in equilibrium with each other. Aluminum phosphate compounds generally have a higher solubility than iron phosphates. As the aluminum phosphates try to maintain their solubility, phosphate in solution reacts with iron surfaces and iron in solution as these become avail-

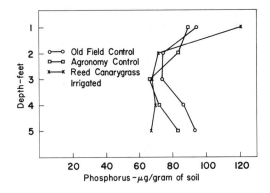

Figure 11-8. The mean distribution of phosphorus in the NaOH fraction of one effluent irrigated and two control areas located on Hublersburg clay loam soil. The Agronomy control area is fertilized but the Old Field control area is not fertilized.

able for phosphate reactions. The long range effect is to form the less soluble iron phosphates at the expense of the aluminum phosphates.

By calculating the amounts of phosphorus added to the reed canarygrass plot and by estimating the amounts lost by leaching, runoff and crop harvest, a mass balance indicated that 500 pounds of phosphorus per acre were retained by the plot in six years. This amount was equal to the amount of phosphorus extracted in the NH_4F and NaOH fractions of the reed canarygrass topsoil minus the amount extracted in these fractions from the untreated old field topsoil. This mass balance indicates that most of the added effluent phosphorus can be accounted for in the NH_4F and NaOH fractions.

Conclusions

Soils and soil plant systems may be effectively used to renovate wastewaters. Applications must be managed so that the constituents of the wastewater remain at the disposal site or leave in harmless or beneficial forms. The water which leaves the disposal site should have concentrations below USPHS recommended limits for drinking water and below stream standards where applicable. In the case of phosphorus, a major constituent of municipal wastewaters, the soil-plant system proves to be an excellent renovating medium. When the system is properly managed most of the added phosphorus remains in the soil at the disposal site or leaves as a nutrient in harvested crops. Soils differ in their ability to hold phosphorus. In a heavy textured soil high in sesquioxides, phosphorus from effluent irrigation did not increase in the soil below a depth of one foot after seven years of irrigation. In a light textured soil with half as much sesquioxides phosphorus content of soils increased to a depth of three feet after six years of treatment. The Bray test for available phosphorus was suitable for determining zones of accumulation of added phosphorus. The fractionation of total soil phosphorus enabled a rough mass balance to be made for the phosphorus within the disposal system.

Acknowledgments

Portions of this research were supported by funds from Demonstration Project Grant WPD 95-01 received initially from the division of Water Supply and Pollution Control of the Department of Health, Education, and Welfare and subsequently from the Federal Water Pollution Control Administration, Department of the Interior. Partial support was also provided by the Office of Water Resources Research, USDI, as authorized under the Water Resources Research Act of 1964, Public Law 88-379.

Literature Cited

Aguilera, N. H. and M. L. Jackson. 1953. Iron oxide removal from soils and clays. *Soil Sci. Soc. Amer. Proc.* 17:359-364.

Baker, D. E., G. W. Gorsline, C. B. Smith, W. I. Thomas, W. E. Grube, and J. L. Ragland. 1964. Technique for rapid analysis of corn leaves for eleven elements. *Agron. Jour.* 56:133-136.

Chang, S. C. and M. L. Jackson. 1957. Fractionation of soil phosphorus. *Soil Sci.* 84:133-144.

Glenn, R. C., P. H. Hsu, M. L. Jackson, and R. B. Corey. 1959. Flow sheet for soil phosphate fractionation. *Agronomy Abstracts,* p. 9.

Jackson, M. L. 1956. *Soil Chemical Analysis.* Prentice-Hall. Englewood Cliffs, New Jersey, 498 pp.

Myers, J. C. 1967. A study of drainage conditions on a hillside receiving sewage effluent at weekly intervals. M. S. Thesis. The Pennsylvania State University, University Park, Pennsylvania.

Parizek, R. R., L. T. Kardos, W. E. Sopper, E. A. Myers, D. F. Davis, M. A. Farrell, and J. B. Nesbitt. 1967. Waste Water Renovation and Conservation. Penn State Studies No. 23, The Pennsylvania State University, 71 pp.

Peech, M., L. T. Alexander, L. A. Dean, and J. F. Reed. 1947. Method of Soil Analysis for Soil Fertility Investigations. United States Dept. of Agric. Circular No. 757. Wash., D. C.

Peterson, G. W. and R. B. Corey. 1965. Modified Chang and Jackson procedure for routine fractionation of inorganic phosphorus. *Soil Sci. Soc. Amer. Proc.* 30:563.

Rebuck, E. C. 1967. The hydrologic regime due to sprinkler irrigation of treated municipal effluent on sloping land. M. S. Thesis. The Pennsylvania State University. University Park, Pennsylvania.

Sopper, W. E. 1971. Disposal of municipal waste through forest irrigation. *Environ. Pollution* 1:263-284.

Discussion

Hortenstine: You described your method on soil phosphorus, that is your chemical method, but nothing on the method of determining soil solution phosphorus. What method did you use on this?

Hook: The technique we used is one of the standard methods, the ammonium molybdate-sulfuric acid procedure.

Pearce: Are there levels of phosphorus that can build up in the soil that will be toxic to plants?

Hook: We certainly haven't come anywhere near levels that would be toxic to plants and I don't know even what level would be that high. There might be others here that have an idea of what would be toxic levels . . . Dr. Kardos says there's probably never any toxicity with phosphorus. The phosphorus is just not available enough in the soils although you may have a lot of it there. For example, I mentioned, or I might have mentioned, there were about 600 micrograms of phosphorus per gram of soil extracted in the total fractionation procedure. Of this only a very small fraction was actually in solution at any one time.

Goydan: How can one estimate the phosphorus requirement for the bacteria so that you would be able to achieve optimum degradation?

Hook: Again, I don't know that I'm really qualified to answer that. The concentration is maintained in the soils, that is background concentration has always been sufficient for any bacteria. What minimal levels you could get, I don't know. I've never seen concentrations lower than about 0.005 ppm, and I don't know that even that would be below the level microbes would need. The phosphorus is there in very low concentration and it's a matter normally, at least for higher organisms, of how fast it can come into solution and get to the plants. Similarly it would be how fast it would get to the microbes. I doubt that it would ever be limiting.

Goydan: In some industrial effluents where you don't have phosphorus inherent in the waste, sludge or effluent, and in other cases where you may not even have the necessary nitrogen requirements, would you need a means to predict the fertilizer requirements, say if you're preparing the field?

Kardos: I'll have to go along with what Mr. Hook said. I don't think there's ever going to be a situation with wastewater renovation where phosphorus will be limiting. The actual amount which the soil micro population will need will be absolutely supplied by anything that the effluent will have. Does that answer the question?

Unknown: If the effluent doesn't have phosphorus. In that case, I would still say that the natural soil process which is there should be quite sufficient to supply the needs. I can only remember one case that I noticed where there was a response to phosphorus, a microbial response to phosphorus in soils, and that was a sandy soil. Again, I think the soil phosphorus would be quite available and adequate.

Ellis: In response to the question before the last one. I've never seen a case where we've had what I consider phosphorus toxicity but the literature is full of examples of phosphate-induced deficiencies. For example, I've seen field beans that at zero phosphate levels yield 30 to 34 bushels per acre and at 800 lbs. of phosphorus per acre, they'll yield six. It turns out to be a zinc deficiency. So we might have to really be careful of our management if we get into areas of high phosphate applications.

12
Effect of Land Disposal of Wastewater on Exchangeable Cations and Other Chemical Elements in the Soil

Louis T. Kardos and William E. Sopper*

The chemical changes that occur in soil through which the applied wastewater percolates have usually been given less attention than the changes occurring in the wastewater itself. This is understandable since most investigations of land disposal of wastewater have been directed by sanitary engineers rather than soil scientists. In a review of the literature by Edwards (1968) it was indicated that most of the concern about soil chemical changes focused on changes in the amounts of sodium relative to the other exchangeable cations in the soil. This concern with exchangeable sodium stems from the well-documented research in irrigation agriculture which has shown that when the exchangeable sodium percentage reaches a value of about 15 a deterioration of soil structure and adverse effects on infiltration can be expected in medium and fine textured soils.

Henry *et al.* (1954) in a three-year experiment using sewage effluent containing 680 ppm of Na increased the exchangeable Na level to 2.37 m.e./100 g and significantly decreased the exchangeable Ca and Mg, but exchangeable K was unaffected. In spite of the high exchangeable Na content there was no mention of any difficulty with infiltration.

In an investigation of primary sewage effluent spreading on five California soils with relatively low clay content (3 to 10 percent), Sanitary Engineering Research Laboratory (1955), it was reported that exchangeable calcium and magnesium decreased while exchangeable sodium, potassium and ammonium increased. Permeability of the soil was not affected, probably because of the low clay content.

Edwards (1968) in soil samples taken in 1966 after 236 inches of wastewater had been applied to the corn rotation area of the Penn State Waste Water Renovation Project found no significant change in the status of the exchangeable cations from that found in 1963 after 48 inches of wastewater had been applied. By 1966 the exchangeable sodium percentage (ESP) in the wastewater treated areas had increased with respect to the control area about four-fold in the upper

*Department of Agronomy and School of Forest Resources, The Pennsylvania State University

foot and one and a half to two-fold in the next four feet. However the maximum ESP value in 1966 was only 3.3 and occurred in the upper foot of the two-inch-per-week treatment area. In 1966 exchangeable hydrogen, calcium and magnesium still occupied 93 percent of the total exchange capacity in the upper foot and 95 to 96 percent in the next four feet. The sodium adsorption ratio (SAR) value in the wastewater defined as

$$SAR = \frac{Na^+}{\sqrt{\dfrac{Ca^{++} + Mg^{++}}{2}}}$$

ranged from 1.20 to 1.62 in the period 1963-66. Ion concentrations are expressed as milliequivalents per liter. Agricultural Handbook No. 60 (1954) defines an irrigation water as having a low sodium hazard if the SAR value is less than ten. On this basis, the Penn State wastewater would qualify as an excellent irrigation water.

Kline (1967) examined soil samples from the forested areas taken in the fall, 1963; spring, 1964; and fall, 1965. He found larger differences between 1963 and 1965 samples for exchangeable Na on the treated plots but differences between control and treated areas in 1965 were similar to those found in 1963. Differences in exchangeable Na between control and treated areas were significant to a greater depth in the soil where two inches were applied weekly to red pine than where only one inch was applied. Exchangeable Na was significantly greater to a depth of five feet in the two-inch red pine area but only to a depth of three feet in the one-inch red pine. In all cases exchangeable Na remained below 0.5 m.e./100 g and did not exceed an ESP value of 3.0. There was no consistent pattern of differences in the other exchangeable cations except that exchangeable Ca tended to be higher than the control on the two-inch red pine treated area and exchangeable K tended to be higher than the control on the one-inch red pine area.

The present report extends the information given by Edwards (1968) through the soil sampling in 1969 and also reports on changes in the status of exchangeable Mn, adsorbed chloride and boron, kjeldahl nitrogen and organic matter in the crop rotation area and in some of the forested areas.

Summarized over the five soil depths (one foot increments to a depth of five feet), Figure 12-1 indicates that in the corn rotation area only in the case of exchangeable Mg and Na was there a significant change due to wastewater treatment. The Mg increases occurred most strongly in the upper foot, as seen in Figure 12-2. Below the

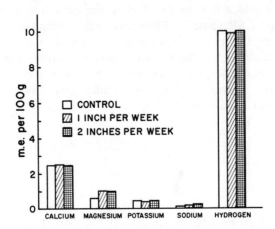

Figure 12-1. Exchangeable cations in soil samples from corn rotation area which has been receiving 0, 1, and 2 inches of wastewater, averaged over five one-foot depth intervals and over six sampling years, 1963, 1965-69.

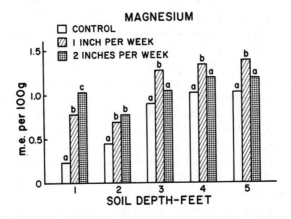

Figure 12-2. Exchangeable magnesium at one-foot depth intervals in soil samples from the corn rotation area which has been receiving 0, 1, and 2 inches of wastewater weekly, averaged over six sampling years, 1963, 1965-69. Bars having a common letter at any depth are not significantly different, P = 0.01.

second foot greater increases occurred with the one-inch-per-week treatment than with the two-inch treatment. Exchangeable Mg increased in a similar manner in the forest areas.

The Na increases were also greatest in the upper foot (Figure 12-3) and in this upper zone it appears that both the one- and two-inch-per-week treatments have peaked at a value of approximately 0.5 m.e. per 100 grams of soil, equivalent to an ESP value of approximately 2.5 to 3.0 percent. Samples taken in 1971 from the forested areas (Table 12-1) showed a range in maximum exchangeable Na from 0.5 m.e./100 g in the one-inch red pine area on the fine textured Hublersburg soil to 0.2 m.e./100 g in the two-inch hardwood area on the sandy Morrison soil. These values were equivalent, respectively, to ESP values of 2.9 and 3.2. Thus it appears highly probable that with the present effluent quality, with an SAR value less than 2.0, one need not be concerned about a sodium hazard to soil structure and permeability.

With respect to the other principal exchangeable cations, K, Ca and H, there were no significant treatment effects in the corn rotation area (Figure 12-1). Since this area had been limed during the farm management program prior to its use in the wastewater experiment a sharp decrease of Ca with depth was present originally and this depth effect has persisted. In the unlimed forest areas (Table 12-1) the depth difference in initial exchangeable Ca content between the upper foot and the deeper layers was not as great and some increase in Ca in the upper foot occurred as a result of both the two-inch- and

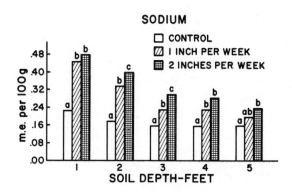

Figure 12-3. Exchangeable sodium at one-foot depth intervals in soil samples from the corn rotation area which has been receiving 0, 1, and 2 inches of wastewater weekly, averaged over six sampling years, 1963, 1965-69. Bars having a common letter at any depth are not significantly different, $P = 0.01$.

Table 12-1. Exchangeable cations in 1971 in soils at five depths from forest areas which have been receiving 0 and 1 or 2 inches at weekly intervals

Area	Soil Depth (feet)	K		Ca		Mg (m.e./100 grams)		Na		H		Mn (µg/g)	
		0	1	0	1	0	1	0	1	0	1	0	1
						Wastewater applied – inches per week							
Red Pine[a]	1	0.1	0.3	1.8	3.1	0.4	1.3	0.2	0.3	15.9	16.8	34.4	22.9
	2	0.3	0.1	1.9	1.7	1.2	0.7	0.2	0.3	11.1	10.3	12.9	18.4
	3	0.1	0.3	1.3	0.7	1.5	0.7	0.3	0.5	11.8	16.4	12.0	19.9
	4	0.5	0.4	1.6	0.5	1.5	0.6	0.2	0.4	–	–	10.5	13.0
	5	0.4	0.4	1.4	0.4	1.5	0.5	0.3	0.4	–	–	9.6	17.4
						Wastewater applied – inches per week							
Hardwood[a]	1	0.1	0.2	1.0	1.9	0.2	1.1	0.2	0.3	25.3	16.2	52.9	26.9
	2	0.3	0.3	1.2	1.1	1.2	1.5	0.2	0.3	18.2	14.7	32.7	18.9
	3	0.2	0.3	1.1	1.0	1.7	1.4	0.2	0.4	12.6	12.9	23.5	17.4
	4	0.2	0.4	1.0	1.4	2.1	1.2	0.2	0.4	–	–	14.9	16.3
	5	0.3	0.4	0.8	1.1	1.7	1.3	0.2	0.4	–	–	13.1	21.4

	Wastewater applied—inches per week											
	0	2	0	2	0	2	0	2	0	2	0	2
Old Field[a]												
1	0.1	0.4	2.0	3.3	0.2	1.7	0.2	0.3	14.9	15.5	15.9	14.5
2	0.0	0.2	2.2	2.0	0.8	1.3	0.2	0.3	11.6	16.4	12.1	17.2
3	0.0	0.1	1.1	1.4	1.4	1.2	0.2	0.3	12.0	16.7	10.6	15.8
4	0.0	0.2	1.5	1.0	1.6	1.4	0.2	0.3	—	—	9.5	15.7
5	0.0	0.1	1.2	1.1	1.5	1.4	0.2	0.3	—	—	8.7	16.1
	Wastewater applied—inches per week											
	0	2	0	2	0	2	0	2	0	2	0	2
Hardwood[b]												
1	0.0	0.1	0.5	1.9	0.1	0.5	0.2	0.2	13.7	7.3	32.7	4.1
2	0.2	0.0	1.1	1.0	0.8	0.4	0.2	0.2	13.4	5.2	11.0	4.9
3	0.3	0.1	0.8	1.3	1.0	0.7	0.2	0.2	11.5	9.4	10.9	5.7
4	0.2	0.0	0.5	1.0	0.8	0.8	0.2	0.2	—	—	9.9	6.4
5	0.0	0.1	0.5	0.7	1.0	0.8	0.2	0.2	—	—	7.3	4.2

a. On Hublersburg silt loam soil with irrigation during the April through Nov. period since 1963.
b. On Morrison sandy loam soil with irrigation year round since Nov. 23, 1965.

one-inch-per-week wastewater treatment. Effects of wastewater treatment on exchangeable K in the forest areas were small and nonsignificant. Exchangeable H in the forest area was inconsistently affected by wastewater treatment except on the sandy Morrison soil which received the greatest amounts of wastewater. On this site the exchangeable H in 1971 in the upper foot was 13.7 m.e./100 g in the control area and only 7.3 m.e./100 g in the wastewater area.

In the corn rotation area the small increase in exchangeable Mg and Na was reflected in an increase in base saturation which in turn was reflected in a significant increase in pH in the upper two feet for both the one- and two-inch treatments (Figure 12-4).

Although manganese is not commonly measured among the exchangeable cations it was included because of the possible effect of the increased wetness on the solubilization of manganese by oxidation-reduction reactions. The data in Figure 12-5 indicate that differences due to wastewater treatments were not significant in the more aerobic and less acid upper two feet but that wastewater treatment did increase exchangeable Mn in the next three feet, with the differences being significant at the 1 percent level with the one-inch-per-week and at the 5 percent level with the two-inch-per-week treatment. On the forested areas the one-inch wastewater additions decreased the exchangeable Mn in the upper foot in the red pine area and in the upper three feet in the hardwood area, however, exchangeable Mn increased in the deeper layers. In

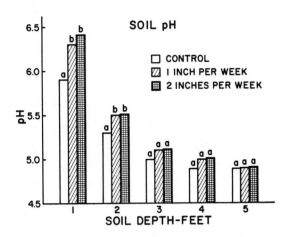

Figure 12-4. Soil pH at one-foot depth intervals in corn rotation area which has been receiving 0, 1, and 2 inches of wastewater weekly, averaged over six sampling years, 1963, 1965-69. Bars having a common letter are not significantly different, P = 0.01.

the two-inch treatment areas, exchangeable Mn increased below the upper foot in the old field area on the fine textured Hublersburg soil but decreased at all depths in the hardwood area on the sandy Morrison soil. This situation conforms to the nitrification-denitrification activity described for these two sites in the chapter by Kardos and Sopper (1973). The nitrate data indicate that anaerobic conditions occur in the Hublersburg soil but not in the Morrison. As a consequence of the reducing conditions, oxides of manganese would be expected to become more soluble and interact with the exchange sites in the Hublersburg soil. On the other hand, the large decrease in exchangeable hydrogen in the Morrison soil combined with its strongly aerobic character should result in a decreased solubility of the oxides of manganese.

Kardos and Sopper (1973) reported that chloride concentration in the soil water was five-fold higher in the wastewater treated corn rotation area than in the control area. Since the Hublersburg soil has been shown to contain substantial amounts of free iron oxides (Hook, Kardos, and Sopper, 1973) and such oxides have a substantial capacity for adsorbing anions, soil samples were extracted with hot, $0.05N \cdot NH_4NO_3$ to determine the adsorbed chloride content. Figure 12-6 shows that the adsorbed chloride increased with soil depth and that the differences between the wastewater treatments were not

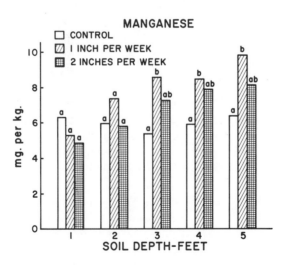

Figure 12-5. Exchangeable manganese at one-foot depth intervals in soil samples from the corn rotation area which has been receiving 0, 1, and 2 inches of wastewater weekly, averaged over six sampling years, 1963, 1965-69. Bars having a common letter at any depth are not significantly different, $P = 0.01$.

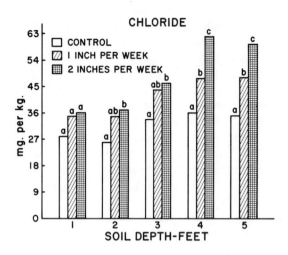

Figure 12-6. Extractable chloride at one-foot depth intervals in soil samples from the corn rotation area which has been receiving 0, 1, and 2 inches of wastewater weekly, averaged over six sampling years, 1963, 1965-69. Bars having a common letter at any depth are not significantly different, P = 0.01.

significant in the first foot but that chloride in the two-inch treatment at the second and third foot was significantly greater than in the control and chloride in the fourth and fifth foot was significantly different for all three wastewater treatments. The average chloride content of the two-inch wastewater area at the fourth and fifth foot was approximately 40 percent greater than that of the control area. The relatively large values in the control area compared to values found in forested control areas by Kline (1967) are probably due to chlorides from the muriate of potash in the commercial fertilizer which was added annually to the corn rotation control area.

The amount of adsorbed chloride found in 1969 was surprisingly large and the total for the five-foot depth, 1216 pounds per acre, was approximately 3.8 times as much as was added in the two-inch wastewater treatment that year. Soils with less free iron oxides like the Morrison sandy loam which contains only one-half to one-third as much as the Hublersburg silt loam (Hook, Kardos, and Sopper, 1973), would not retain as much chloride.

Other soil constituents which were examined were ammonium acetate extractable boron which increased as wastewater treatment level increased but the slight differences were not significant. Kjeldahl nitrogen and organic matter were erratically variable from year to year and differences were not significant.

In conclusion, changes in soil chemical quality have occurred as a result of the wastewater treatments but these changes have been relatively small and do not appear to pose any problems for the future.

Acknowledgments
Research reported here is part of the program of the Waste Water Renovation and Conservation Project of the Institute for Research on Land and Water Resources, and Hatch Projects No. 1481 and 1809 of the Agricultural Experiment Station, The Pennsylvania State University, University Park, Pennsylvania. Portions of this research were supported by funds from Demonstration Project Grant WPD 95-01 received initially from the Division of Water Supply and Pollution Control of the Department of Health, Education, and Welfare and subsequently from the Federal Water Pollution Control Administration, Department of the Interior. Partial support was also provided by the Office of Water Resources Research, USDI, as authorized under the Water Resources Research Act of 1964, Public Law 88-379 and by the Pinchot Institute for Environmental Research, Forest Service, USDA.

Literature Cited

Edwards, Ivor K. The Renovation of Sewage Plant Effluent by the Soil and by Agronomic Crops. Ph.D. thesis in Agronomy. 174 pp. Sept. 1968. The Pennsylvania State University.

Henry, C. D., R. E. Moldenhauer, L. E. Engelbert, and E. Truog. 1954. Sewage effluent disposal through crop irrigation. *Sewage and Industrial Wastes* 26: 123-133.

Hook, James E., L. T. Kardos and W. E. Sopper. 1973. Effect of Land Disposal of Wastewaters on Soil Phosphorus Relations. *Recycling Treated Municipal Wastewater and Sludge through Forest and Cropland*. The Pennsylvania State University Press.

Kardos, Louis T. and W. E. Sopper. 1973. Renovation of Municipal Wastewater through Land Disposal by Spray Irrigation. *Recycling Treated Municipal Wastewater and Sludge through Forest and Cropland*. The Pennsylvania State University Press.

Kline, Glenn N. Effect of Sewage Effluent on the Chemical Properties of the Soil in a Hardwood Stand, Red Pine Plantation and Open Old Field. M.Sc. thesis in Forestry. 78 pp. Sept. 1967. The Pennsylvania State University.

Sanitary Engineering Research Laboratory. 1955. An Investigation of Sewage Spreading on Five California Soils. Tech. Bul. 12. I.E.R. Series 37. Sanitary Engineering Laboratory, University of California, Berkeley, California.

United States Salinity Laboratory Staff. 1954. Diagnosis and Improvement of Saline and Alkali Soils. U.S. Dept. of Agric., Agricultural Handbook No. 60. L. A. Richards, Editor.

Discussion

Unknown: I'd like to ask a question that I don't think has been addressed, or at least not explicitly so far. If we can assume that in forests you have acid conditions, perhaps, therefore, it's safe to assume that the plant and the microorganism species are acidophilic in nature. Do you have any kind of information or are you concerned with what extent any change in the ion species ratio in the pH, ionic balance or whatever is affecting certain kinds of pH specific microorganisms?

Kardos: No. We have done very little work along that line. We had one study done by a post-doctoral fellow in 1968 and 1969 in which he looked at the qualitative characteristics of the micro-flora and the quantitative amounts. He could find no significant differences between the treatment area and the control area in the cropland area. In earlier studies in the forested area, by a microbiologist on the staff, no differences were found in total microbiological activity between the control and treated areas. This was measured by the dehydrogenase total biological activity method. We don't have really as much data as we'd like to have in this regard. The post-doctoral fellow did get some samples, core samples, and then aseptically went into the center of the core and examined these samples for presence of organisms. He found that when he got below the second foot that he couldn't find organisms in that material which was aseptically separated from those core samples. From there down to five feet you find an occasional organism, that's about all, but the numbers were very, very low below the second foot.

Hunt: I'd like to make a comment on the question about the industrial waste deficient in phosphorus. I have found a response to phosphorus on industrial waste in the soil. This was with Prudhoe Bay crude oil added at a 15 percent level in a Fairbanks silt. The pH was about 4.9 to 5 and I found a significant response in the microbial activity as additional phosphorus was added.

Kardos: The effect there may be confounded again because your significant response may be due to detoxification of something which would affect the organisms. In other words, the amount of soluble aluminum or manganese may have been suppressing the activity and in adding the phosphorus you may not have really been supplying phosphorus for the organisms but you were detoxifying something else. It's hard sometimes to separate these out.

Hunt: In this case it was a primary response.

Kardos: It could very well be.

Unknown: Your abstract states that there were no significant increases in organic matter. Can you explain that please?

Kardos: Yes. We're not loading on that much organic material. We have a very low BOD material. The only increase in organic matter we might expect might be from increases in organic inputs from the increased vegetative growth. But when you have started out with a little over three percent organic matter, it's pretty hard to find any significant differences in changes in that organic matter content. We're not adding that much organic matter really to expect to find much of a change.

13
Factors Affecting Nitrification-Denitrification in Soils

F. E. Broadbent*

The oxidation of ammonium to nitrate in soils by microorganisms has been the subject of a great many research efforts dating back to the beginning of scientific agriculture. The nature of the nitrifying bacteria and their responses to a broad range of environmental conditions have been amply documented in the literature. It is not my intention to review this literature in any detail here today. Suffice it to say that nitrifying bacteria are present in almost all soils and that they are active over a wide range of moisture and temperature conditions (Frederick, 1956; Justice and Smith, 1962; Reichman et al., 1966; Robinson, 1957; Tyler et al., 1959).

Although the nitrifiers are obligate aerobes they are able to function in oxygen concentrations substantially lower than that of the atmosphere. For example, Amer and Bartholomew (1951) measured nitrification rates in a soil in relation to the oxygen concentration of the ambient atmosphere. As expected, rate of nitrate production decreased with decreasing oxygen concentration. About half as much nitrification occurred at 2.1 percent oxygen as at 20 percent. Below 0.4 percent oxygen nitrification essentially ceased and at 0.2 percent there was a net loss of nitrate indicating that denitrification was taking place. The activities of nitrifying bacteria may also be curtailed by low pH which frequently may result from acid produced by the nitrifiers themselves.

Although a number of heterotrophic microorganisms have been found capable of oxidizing ammonium to nitrite and a few to nitrate, present evidence indicates that their activity is minimal in relation to that of the autotrophic nitrifying bacteria. It can be said for all practical purposes that nitrification does not require organic materials as a source of energy.

Denitrification, also recognized quite early as a microbial process, has not been studied quite so intensively as has nitrification, but recent concern over the presence of nitrate in waters has revived interest in it. The capacity of denitrifying bacteria to convert a potential pollutant to an innocuous gas which is a normal atmospheric constituent suggests denitrification as an ideal decontamination process. Whereas even such an eminent soil microbiologist as Waksman

*Department of Soils and Plant Nutrition, University of California, Davis

(1932) once dismissed denitrification as "of no economic significance in well aerated not too moist soils in the presence of moderate amounts of organic matter or nitrate," today this process is being studied and utilized by people representing a range of interests varying all the way from engineering to medicine.

Conditions for Nitrification-Denitrification

Whereas nitrifying bacteria are autotrophic, denitrifiers are heterotrophic. Nitrifiers are obligate aerobes, denitrifiers are facultative anaerobes. Denitrification cannot take place in the presence of any significant concentration of oxygen. Nitrification is an energy yielding process, denitrification an energy requiring one. It would seem then that by virtue of their contrasting environmental requirements nitrification and denitrification would be mutually exclusive processes. My remarks here today will be concerned primarily with variations on the theme that in fact nitrification and denitrification can and do occur simultaneously in the same soil, lake, pond or stream, often in locations which are physically separated by only very short distances.

The classical case is the rice paddy. Flooded soils are known to develop two distinct layers after submergence; a surface oxidizing layer only a few millimeters thick and a deep subsurface layer which is in a chemically reduced state (Pearsall, 1950; Shiori and Tanada, 1954). In the shallow surface layer of soil and in the flood water above the soil nitrification readily proceeds because oxygen is present. However, if nitrate so formed diffuses into the reduced layer, it is utilized as an electron acceptor and nitrogen gas is released. Indirect evidence for this sequence of events is provided by the data of Table 13-1 which shows that when tagged ammonium sulfate was

Table 13-1. Recovery of tagged N from flooded Maahas clay incubated in air and in N_2 after addition of 100 ppm N as $(NH_4)_2SO_4$[a]

Incubation time	NH_4-N	Organic N	Total
days	ppm	ppm	ppm
	Incubated in Air		
0	97.0	1.1	98.1
14	76.2	15.3	91.5
30	47.8	18.0	65.8
	Incubated in N_2		
0	97.0	1.1	98.1
14	68.9	31.8	100.1
30	41.5	58.2	99.7

a. From Broadbent and Tusneem (1971)

added to a flooded soil nitrogen was lost if the surface of the flood water was in contact with the atmosphere. However, when oxygen was excluded by substitution of pure nitrogen gas for air in contact with the flood water surface so as to prevent nitrification, no loss of nitrogen from the system occurred.

More direct evidence is given in Table 13-2, which shows that nitrogen gas evolved from a flooded soil in an oxygen atmosphere was derived from added ammonium sulfate. In a krypton atmosphere virtually no evolution of nitrogen was observed, because nitrate was not produced.

Greenland (1962) suggested the possibility of simultaneous nitrification and denitrification in Ghanian soils several years ago. In many situations both in soils and waters there exists the possibility of oxygen depleted layers or microenvironments where the rate of oxygen utilization exceeds the rate of diffusion of oxygen to the site. For example, the vertical distribution of oxygen in bodies of water frequently reflects the transition from an aerated surface layer to anoxic conditions at some depth below. Ammonia-containing water flowing into a lake, pond or artificial lagoon might undergo nitrification near the surface and the nitrate so produced could become subjected to denitrification through diffusion into anoxic zones, provided the organic matter content were sufficiently high to support the growth of denitrifying bacteria.

Meek et al. (1970) measured nitrate concentrations and E_h values as a function of depth in a cotton field of high water table in the Imperial Valley, California, after application of 280 kg anhydrous ammonia per hectare. There was a reduction in nitrate concentration and a drop in E_h as the soil solution approached the water table. In another study with soil columns with controlled water tables Meek et al. (1970) found that disappearance of nitrate near the water table was associated with decreases in redox potential, oxygen content of the soil solution, and oxygen levels in the soil atmosphere. They concluded that the quantity of soluble carbon down to the saturated zone was also important.

Table 13-2. Tagged N in various fractions in flooded Sacramento clay 24 days after addition of 100 ppm tagged N as $(NH_4)_2SO_4$ [a]

Atmosphere	NH_4-N	NO_3-N	Organic + clay-fixed N	N_2 gas	Total
	ppm	ppm	ppm	ppm	ppm
Oxygen	4.9	8.1	68.4	9.3	90.7
Krypton	13.3	0.2	83.9	0.2	97.6

a. From Broadbent and Tusneem (1971)

Experimental Evidence of
Nitrification-Denitrification in Soils

Denitrification in Soils of High Water Table

Much of the evidence of nitrification-denitrification and related nitrogen transformations under field conditions has been reviewed recently by Viets and Hageman (1971) who concluded that much unwanted nitrate can be eliminated by managed denitrification in treatment plants and on land that receives large amounts of animal waste. Some of the difficulties attendant to obtaining good quantitative estimates of the extent of denitrification under field conditions are illustrated in an experiment in California with Tulare sandy loam, a soil with a water table at about a four-foot depth. Manure waste from a large dairy, after dilution with a considerable volume of wash water, was passed through a separator to remove solids, which were recycled by using them as bedding for the cows. The liquid effluent containing 50 to 120 ppm soluble N, almost entirely in the ammonium form, was spread on half-acre field plots by three methods of flooding. Analyses of the distribution of ammonium and nitrate nitrogen in quadruplicate plots showed that nitrification was rapid, since the values for NH_4-N were very low, below three ppm in most instances and never exceeding five ppm. Nitrate-N values given in Figure 13-1 suggest denitrification below the surface layer, since there was a tendency for nitrate concentration to decrease with depth. However, this distribution can also be explained on the basis of concentration of adsorbed ammonium from the dairy effluent near the soil surface. Another difficulty is that field data of this kind are very variable. For example, the coefficient of variation of the data of Figure 13-1 is 75 percent. Of particular interest are the low nitrate levels in the intermittently flooded plots, which received more nitrogen than the single flooded plots. The alternation between flooded and unflooded conditions is particularly favorable to the nitrification-denitrification sequence. For example, three rice soils at the International Rice Research Institute kept in flood fallow lost no nitrogen with no mid-season drying, but lost 120 to 320 kg N/hectare with mid-season drying (IRRI, 1969).

In a laboratory experiment a one-meter column of Tulare sandy loam was set up to maintain the water table at 70 cm depth while collecting the effluent from the 100 cm depth. Dairy waste containing 65 ppm N as tagged ammonium was applied in amounts equivalent to 156 kg N per hectare (139 lbs N/acre). Subsequently 0.001 M $CaCl_2$ solution was applied to the column at five to seven day intervals in increments of 12 cm and the column effluent analyzed for soluble nitrogen containing the tracer. A total of 67 cm of water passed

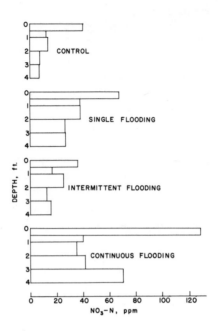

Figure 13-1. Distribution of nitrate in field plots of Tulare sandy loam receiving dairy effluent

through the column. Figure 13-2 shows that untagged nitrate initially present in the soil leached out quickly before anaerobic conditions were established. Some tagged nitrate came through as a small pulse near the end of the leaching period. Tagged nitrogen in the leachate was 1.97 percent of the N added. Analysis of residual N in the soil at the conclusion of the experiment indicated 15.4 percent of the applied nitrogen remained, making an overall recovery of only 17.4 percent. Presumably the remainder was denitrified.

A similar experiment with the very sandy subsoil found below the water table in this same area was conducted to evaluate the extent of denitrification in an environment low in available carbon. Total organic C in the subsoil is 0.49 percent. Tagged nitrate equivalent to 80 kg N/hectare (71 lbs/acre) was applied to the column, which was then leached with 0.001 M $CaCl_2$ intermittently over a period of six weeks until a total of 45 cm effluent had been collected. In this case (Figure 13-3) 6.33 mg or 41 percent of the tagged nitrate passed through the column. Residual tracer nitrogen in the column was not determined, but was undoubtedly less than the 15.4 percent found in the experiment cited previously because of the very coarse texture of the subsoil.

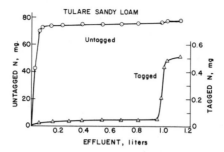

Figure 13-2. Nitrate in effluent from a 1-meter column of Tulare sandy loam after addition of 25.9 mg tagged NH_4-N in dairy wastewater. Water table maintained at 70 cm depth

Denitrification in Unsaturated Soils

Denitrification in saturated soil is, of course, to be expected. A question of perhaps greater interest is whether denitrification occurs to a significant extent in unsaturated soil profiles. One can readily visualize conditions favorable for denitrification in the micropores of an unsaturated soil, or even in the macropores at depths where the diffusion of oxygen is too slow to meet the oxygen demand. Again, the use of tracer sources of nitrogen provides an answer to the question.

In a preliminary experiment tagged KNO_3 was placed at the sur-

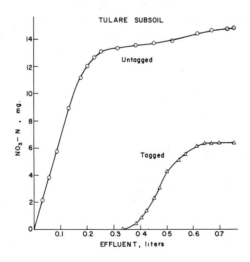

Figure 13-3. Nitrate in effluent from a 1-meter column of Tulare subsoil after addition of 15.2 mg N as tagged nitrate. Water table maintained at 70 cm depth

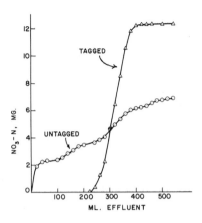

Figure 13-4. Nitrate in effluent from a 1-meter column of Yolo fine sandy loam after addition of 27.1 mg N as tagged KNO_3

face of a one-meter column of Yolo fine sandy loam. The column was then leached intermittently with saturated $CaSO_4$ solution over a two-week period until the effluent contained no more tagged nitrate. Saturation occurred only at the soil-air interface at the bottom of the column. The elution curves shown in Figure 13-4 indicate that 12.3 mg or 45.6 percent of the tagged nitrate-N passed through the column. The gradual increase in untagged N eluted from the column can be attributed to mineralization of organic N. A more detailed accounting of nitrification-denitrification in the Yolo soil was obtained in a larger column containing six feet of soil and equipped with porous ceramic probes at one-foot intervals which allowed withdrawal of a small volume of soil solution when desired. The soil was initially brought to field moisture capacity, then tagged $(NH_4)_2SO_4$ equivalent to 100 kg N/hectare (89 lbs/acre) was applied at a depth of two inches. Thereafter three inches (7.5 cm) of water was applied at biweekly intervals over a period of 28 weeks. One day after each water application soil solution samples were taken at each depth and analyzed. After eight weeks when effluent appeared at the bottom of the column the leachate was regularly collected and analyzed. Progress of the nitrification process and gradual disappearance of tagged nitrogen from the column are shown in Figure 13-5. No significant concentration of nitrate penetrated below five feet and at no time did the column effluent contain more than a trace of nitrate, either tagged or untagged. An accounting of the tracer N (Table 13-3) indicates that the soluble nitrogen which disappeared was largely denitrified.

A striking contrast between a partly saturated and an unsaturated

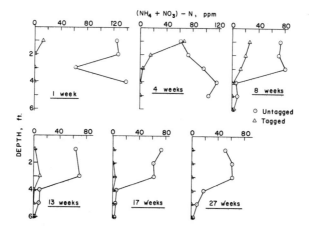

Figure 13-5. Distribution of soluble nitrogen in extracts from a 6-foot column of Yolo fine sandy loam at various times following addition of tagged $(NH_4)_2SO_4$

column was observed with Venice peat, a very permeable soil containing about 40 percent organic carbon. One column was free-draining; the other had the water table maintained at 70 cm from the surface. Elution curves shown in Figure 13-6 indicate that 12.1 mg or 79 percent of the added nitrate-N was recovered in the effluent from the unsaturated column, whereas 0.06 mg or 0.4 percent of the added nitrate passed through the column with a 30 cm saturated layer. It may be observed that only about half as much untagged N passed through the latter column as the unsaturated one and that most of this amount was leached early in the experiment before anaerobic conditions could be established. Denitrification of untagged N undoubtedly occurred.

Table 13-3. Balance sheet of tagged nitrogen added as $(NH_4)_2SO_4$ to a free-draining column of Yolo fine sandy loam

	N	Percent of total
	mg	%
Added initially	182.0	100.0
In column leachate	0.0	0.0
Removed in samples	10.7	5.9
Residual NH_4^+ and NO_3^-	2.3	1.3
In soil organic matter	12.8	7.0
Not accounted for (denitrified)	156.2	85.8

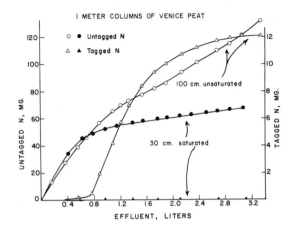

Figure 13-6. Soluble nitrogen in effluents from columns of Venice peat after addition of 15.2 mg tagged N as $Ca(NO_3)_2$

Direct Evidence of Denitrification of Unsaturated Soil

A shortcoming of all the experiments previously cited is that none of them provides direct evidence of denitrification. Disappearance of tracer nitrogen from a soil is convincing evidence of loss, but the evidence that denitrification is responsible is only presumptive. It would be desirable to provide a complete accounting of all forms of nitrogen by direct analysis, but the experimental difficulties involved in trapping and analyzing gaseous forms of nitrogen without drastic alteration of the soil environment are formidable. A major problem is that of detecting a relatively small quantity of N_2 resulting from nitrate reduction in a vast sea of atmospheric N_2.

Direct evidence that some N_2 in the soil pore space is indeed the end product of the nitrification-denitrification sequence is given in Tables 13-4 and 13-5. These give the composition of soil gases and of the soil solution at various depths in a column of Hanford sandy loam which was continuously leached with a solution of tagged NH_4Cl containing 50 ppm N. The column was designed to permit control of the hydraulic head at all depths, which in practice varied from -3 to -13 cm of water at various depths.

The data of Table 13-4 show depletion of oxygen and increase of CO_2 and N_2 with increasing depth. Nitrification occurred readily, but may have been confined primarily to the top 28 cm since NH_4^+ in soil solution is very low below that depth. The presence of absorbed NH_4^+ at lower depths is still a possibility. Decreasing nitrate concen-

Table 13-4. Composition of the soil atmosphere at various depths in a column of Hanford sandy loam continuously leached with a solution containing 50 ppm N as tagged NH_4Cl on day 46

Depth	Air-filled pores	CO_2	O_2	N_2
cm	%	%	%	%
8	10.7	0.77	17.3	81.9
28	8.1	1.65	8.64	89.7
48	5.5	2.05	2.30	95.6
68	3.4	3.03	1.62	95.3
88	10.3	3.18	2.21	94.6

tration with depth below 28 cm strongly suggests denitrification. Unequivocal evidence is provided by the detection of ^{15}N-tagged nitrogen gas at all depths below eight cm.

Practical Significance of Nitrification-Denitrification

Although definitive field data are still scarce, it seems clear that application of water containing nitrate or a potential source of nitrate such as organic N or ammonium salts to the surface of a soil will probably not result in that nitrate moving unimpeded to the water table, having been diminished only by those quantities which are intercepted by plant roots. Indeed, the well known poor uptake efficiency of fertilizer nitrogen by crops, usually not much better than 50 percent, may be due in part to the stimulating effect of plant roots on denitrification. Woldendorp *et al.* (1966) noted that 15 to 20 percent of the nitrate passing through the rhizosphere may be denitrified. A recent report by Kolenbrander (1972) of nitrate and chloride concentrations in well water at a number of pumping stations in Holland over a 45-year period provides some very interesting evidence of widespread denitrification. The wells are located in agricul-

Table 13-5. Nitrate-N and nitrogen gas derived from tagged NH_4Cl in a column of Hanford sandy loam on day 46

Depth	NH_4^+-N	NO_3^--N	NO_3^--N tagged	N_2 tagged
cm	ppm	ppm	%	%
8	16.3	14.2	79	0.1
28	3.7	38.9	87	4.10
48	0.5	29.1	91	7.46
68	0.0	23.2	89	8.21
88	0.0	17.2	85	8.30

tural areas where the annual input of fertilizers has increased substantially over the years. When the concentrations of nitrate and chloride in the wells were plotted against average annual fertilizer applications it was found that the proportion of chloride which ended up in the ground water was approximately five times the proportion of nitrogen. He concluded that low concentrations of nitrate in deep-level ground water point to the likelihood of considerable further denitrification during infiltration of drainage water into deeper strata.

In another recent study Pratt *et al.* (1972) determined nitrate concentrations in saturation extracts of soil in three-meter profiles of a long term fertility trail with citrus. Assuming no net immobilization or mineralization and that the amount of N denitrified was equal to the total N input, minus that found in the soil, minus removal in the fruit, they found that up to 43 percent of the total nitrogen input was lost.

Any precise attempt to follow the course of nitrification-denitrification on a field scale requires a method of discriminating between input nitrogen from fertilizers, wastewater, or other sources, and that which results from decomposition of soil organic matter, which typically contains five to six percent N. This can be accomplished by use of ^{15}N-tagged materials, as illustrated in some of the soil column data presented here, but the cost of materials enriched with this isotope has been prohibitive for field work. Recently the Atomic Energy Commission's Los Alamos Scientific Laboratory has begun producing ^{15}N-depleted material which can also be used as a nitrogen tracer in natural systems, with the limitation that the amount of dilution which can be tolerated is substantially less than is feasible with highly enriched ^{15}N compounds. However, essentially pure ^{14}N compounds are expected to become available in ton quantities at costs which permit their utilization in field trials. It is expected that experiments with isotopically tagged materials in the natural environment, some of which are already underway, will permit a complete accounting of the fate of nitrogen applied to soils and will provide better quantitative measures of nitrification-denitrification and related nitrogen transformations under a variety of environmental conditions.

Literature Cited

Amer, F. M. and W. V. Bartholomew. 1951. Influence of oxygen concentration in soil air on nitrification. *Soil Sci.* 71:215-219.
Broadbent, F. E. and M. E. Tusneem. 1971. Losses of nitrogen from some flooded soils in tracer experiments. *Soil Sci. Soc. Amer. Proc.* 35:922-926.
Frederick, L. R. 1956. The formation of nitrate from ammonium nitrogen in soils. I. Effect of temperature. *Soil Sci. Soc. Amer. Proc.* 20:496-500.

Greenland, D. J. 1962. Denitrification in some tropical soils. *Agric. Sci.* 58:227-233.

International Rice Research Institute Annual Report 1969. Pp. 139-140.

Justice, J. K. and R. L. Smith. 1962. Nitrification of ammonium sulfate in a calcareous soil as influenced by combination of moisture, temperature and levels of nitrogen. *Soil Sci. Soc. Amer. Proc.* 26:246-250.

Kolenbrander, G. J. 1972. Does leaching of fertilizers affect the quality of ground water at the waterworks? *Stikstof* 15:8-15.

Meek, B. D., Grass, L. B., and A. J. MacKenzie. 1969. Applied nitrogen losses in relation to oxygen status of soils. *Soil Sci. Soc. Amer. Proc.* 33:575-578.

Meek, B. D., Grass, L. B., Willardson, L. S. and A. J. MacKenzie. 1970. Nitrate transformations in a column with controlled water table. *Soil Sci. Soc. Amer. Proc.* 34:235-239.

Pearsall, W. H. 1950. The investigation of wet soils and its agricultural implications. *Emp. Jour. Expt. Agric.* 18 (72):289-298.

Pratt, P. F., Jones, W. W. and V. E. Hunsaker. 1972. Nitrate in deep soil profiles in relation to fertilizer rates and leaching volume. *Jour. Environ. Quality* 1:97-102.

Reichman, G. A., Grunes, D. L. and F. G. Viets, Jr. 1966. Effect of soil moisture on ammonification and nitrification in two northern plains soils. *Soil Sci. Soc. Amer. Proc.* 30:363-366.

Robinson, J. B. D. 1957. The critical relationship between soil moisture content in the region of the wilting point and mineralization of soil nitrogen. *Jour. Agric. Sci.* 49:100-105.

Shiori, M., and T. Tanada. 1954. The chemistry of paddy soils in Japan. Min. Agric. and Forestry. Japanese Gov't. Tokyo. 45 p.

Tyler, K. B., Broadbent, F. E. and G. N. Hill. 1959. Low temperature effects on nitrification in four California soils. *Soil Sci.* 87:123-129.

Viets, F. G., Jr. and R. H. Hageman. 1971. Factors affecting the accumulation of nitrate in soil, water, and plants. Agric. Handbook No. 43, ARS, USDA.

Waksman, S. A. 1932. *Principles of soil microbiology* (2nd ed.). Williams and Wilkins Co., Baltimore.

Woldendorp, J. W., Dilz, K. and G. J. Kolenbrander. 1966. The fate of fertilizer nitrogen on permanent grassland soils. *Proc. 1st Gen. Mtg. Europ. Grassland Fed.* 1965:53-76.

Discussion

Hanson: Was the six-foot column of Hanford sandy loam a mixed soil with organic matter all the way through the column supplying an energy source for the bacteria?

Broadbent: Yes. It had organic matter all the way down. This is extremely deep soil. The organic matter tails off to about 30 percent of the surface layer at around six feet.

Hanson: Did you attempt to simulate the field soil in terms of the profile?

Broadbent: Yes. This was an attempted simulation of field distribution.

Overman: Obviously in turning the nitrogen cycle, you had to turn the carbon cycle also. Do you feel that decomposing organic matter in the upper profile will supply carbon several feet down near the water table?

Broadbent: This, of course, depends on a great many soil properties. But, in general, I would say yes.

14
Biotoxic Elements in Soils[1]

T. D. Hinesly and R. L. Jones*

Application of stabilized municipal waste treatment plant residues on agricultural lands is the most economically viable solution to a growing solids disposal problem. Yet, it is a small problem from the standpoint of its utilization by agriculture. If all municipal wastewaters generated in the continental United States were given secondary treatment and the resulting solids stabilized for utilization as a fertilizer and soil amendment, about 10 to 12 million dry tons of solids would be available each year. The utilization of the solids in amounts just sufficient to meet the needs of nonleguminous crops for supplemental nitrogen would require an annual application of about 10 dry tons per acre. Thus, not much over one million acres of land would be required at one time to utilize the total continental United States production of sludge solids. Only enough sludge solids would be available to treat slightly more than 0.2 percent of the 465 million acres of crop land or slightly less than 0.06 percent of the total 1,904 million acres contained in the continental United States. However, because of its potential as a source of sorely needed stable organic matter, municipal sludge exhibits its greatest value as a resource when used as an amendment for the reclamation of surface-mined lands. Since over 0.5 million acres of land strip-mined for coal already exist in various states of devastation while another 0.5 million acres have been or will be stripped during the twenty-year period from 1964 to 1984, there is no scarcity of land which needs the nutrients and organic matter supplied in sludge. If properly used in the reclamation of such lands, a discussion of the accumulation of biotoxic elements in soils as a result of sludge recycling would be purely academic. For example, unusual concentration levels of chemical elements are released by weathering of shales in strip-mine spoil banks where, in the absence of adequate contents of organic matter, problems already exist which can be ameliorated with applications of stabilized municipal sludges.

It is recognized that the solids from many small wastewater treatment plants will probably continue to be recycled to crop land. Also, the number of proponents for using land for the disposal or renovation of partially treated wastewater appears to be growing. Therefore,

1. No manuscript was received from the authors.
*Department of Agronomy, University of Illinois

it is essential to review what is known with regard to the accumulation of biotoxic elements in soils because in either case the growing of crops will be part of the system. Nearly all chemical elements, whether classed as essential or nonessential for the life processes of plants and/or animals can be considered as biotoxic at some concentration levels. It is necessary to attempt to identify those chemical elements which tend to be ubiquitously present in relatively high concentration in municipal wastewaters and sludges and might accumulate in soils in forms available to crop plants at concentrations which may be injurious to plants or to animals consuming the produce.

15
Microbial Hazards in Disposing of Wastewater on Soil

D. H. Foster and R. S. Engelbrecht*

Those who are considering land disposal of wastewater and sludges are faced with a peculiar dilemma. On the one hand, they may be applauded for recovering a resource and applying it in useful ways—to irrigate crops and restore despoiled areas such as strip mines. On the other hand, they are damned for spreading a host of pollutants including pathogenic organisms around in the environment. It is the purpose of this paper to explore the public health dangers that may arise from the ultimate disposal of wastes on land and to assess how well founded is the public apprehension concerning health hazards. The paper is not intended to be an alarming account of hypothetical hazards designed to downgrade the potential benefits to be derived from land application of wastewater and sludges. Rather, it is felt that engineers, agriculturists, and governmental officials should be provided with the type of information that will allow a rational, unemotional, and realistic assessment of the potential public health problems associated with the application of wastewater to land.

If one were to catalog the species of pathogens of men and animals which could be present in raw wastewater, the list would be a long one indeed. The tremendous variety of pathogens which may occur in domestic wastewater is derived principally from the feces and urine of infected human and animal hosts finding a direct route into the sewer. Surface runoff in areas provided with combined sewer systems will result in mammalian and avian pathogens reaching the waste-water collection system. The relative densities of the pathogens present in the wastewater will depend on a number of complex factors; and, therefore, it is difficult to say with any degree of assurance what the general pathogenic character of a particular wastewater will be. A thorough knowledge of the health of the population in a given situation, the possibility of "disease carrier" states in the population, an understanding of the sources contributing to the wastewater, and a knowledge of the relative ability of the pathogen to survive outside its host under a variety of environmental conditions is necessary. The literature can establish guidelines but each situation should be evaluated individually.

*Department of Civil Engineering, University of Illinois

Survival of Pathogens in Wastewater

The principal pathogens present in wastewater may be divided into four convenient groups (Table 15-1). Far more is known about the occurrence of bacteria in wastewater than any of the other groups. Massive outbreaks of bacterial disease due to sewage polluted water have long been considered by many to be a thing of the past. Yet one has only to look back as recently as 1965 to find a waterborne bacterial epidemic of large proportions (Greenberg and Ongerth, 1966). Enough is not yet known to pinpoint the cause of sporadic isolated cases of typhoid and other potentially waterborne diseases so as to be able to definitely eliminate fecally polluted water from the list of possible causes. Use of wastewater for irrigation in the vicinity of isolated cases of enteric disease could lead to the suspicion in the public's mind that the two are somehow related, whether or not this is in fact the case. This subject should receive a closer examination.

Pathogenic Bacteria in Wastewater

Over 400 serotypes of the genus *Salmonella* have thus far been identified (Salle, 1967). Members of this group have frequently been isolated from feces, sewage, receiving waters and have even been found in finished drinking water supplies (Beard, 1938; Browning and Mankin, 1966; Salle, 1967; and Seligman and Reitler, 1965). The most important member of this group is *Salmonella typhosa,* the agent of typhoid fever. *Salmonella paratyphi* and *Salmonella schott-muelleri,* the agents of paratyphoid, may also be present in wastewater. Several other members of the *Salmonella* group have been pointed out as causative agents of gastrointestinal disturbances and, as a result, have been found in the feces of infected persons (Browning and Mankin, 1966; and Seligman and Reitler, 1965). The survival

Table 15-1. Major groups of wastewater pathogens

1. Bacteria
   Salmonella
   Shigella
   Mycobacterium
2. Protoxa
   Entamoeba histolytica
   Naegleria
3. Helminth parasites
   Ascaris
   Ancylostoma
   Necator
   Taenia
   Trichuris
4. Viruses

of *Salmonellae* in wastewater is dependent on temperature, the presence of organic matter and predation. Survival of typhoid organisms in wastewater for more than 35 days at room temperature has been reported by Wilson and Blair (1931), but generally survival for shorter periods of time has been noted. Heukelekian and Schulhoff (1935) found survival to be related to temperature with 99 percent destruction of typhoid organisms in wastewater occurring within six to ten days at both 22° and 37°C, while persistence increased to 17 days at 2°C. Green and Beard (1938) found survival to be up to 19 days and 27 days at indoor (20°C) and lower outdoor temperatures (7°C), respectively. A 99.9 percent kill occurred within 12 days under these conditions.

Others (Heukelekian and Schulhoff, 1935; and Rochaix, 1930) have demonstrated that organic matter and the presence of predator organisms can have a significant effect on the survival of *Salmonella* bacteria. When organic matter in the form of feces or urine was added to unpolluted water, growth of *Salmonella* was observed. In the presence of competitive organisms, survival of *Salmonella* is reduced. Survival in typical wastewater was reported in one study to be from a few hours to 11 days while survival was increased to as much as 20 months when competing organisms were removed from sewage by sterilization (Rochaix, 1930).

In summary, it may be stated that survival of typhoid and related organisms is relatively brief in wastewater. It should be noted, though, that constant inputs of these organisms are possible and it has been indicated that they were found in wastewater whenever they were sought (Kabler, 1959; and Northington et al., 1970).

Shigella organisms are one of the chief causes of bacillary dysentery but fortunately their presence in wastewater is considered rare (Wang et al., 1956). During a five-year study of irrigation water in Colorado, no *Shigella* organisms were isolated despite frequent isolations of *Salmonella*. When competitors were removed by sterilization, *Shigella* organisms inoculated into wastewater increased rapidly in numbers. However, in unsterilized stools they did not survive long (Wang et al., 1956). *Shigella flexneri* was implicated in a waterborne outbreak of gastroenteritis involving the irrigation of wastewater on pasture land (Browning and Mankin, 1966); and thus, while its survival may be limited outside the human body, the potential danger of *Shigella* in wastewater effluents applied to soil must be recognized.

Mycobacteria have been extensively studied in wastewater since the time of the first findings of *M. tuberculosum* in feces around 1900. Tubercle bacilli appear to reach wastewater from feces containing swallowed sputum of infected individuals and from undisinfected sputum in sanitoria wastewater. Müller (1959) reported that raw wastewater contained 5 to 100 tubercle bacilli per liter compared to 100 times as many *Salmonella* organisms in the same volume. The tubercle organisms may be considered to be a regular component of urban wastewater, even without known sanitoria sources, since 90 percent of the raw wastewater samples examined were positive for tubercle bacilli. Of chief concern with these acid-fast bacilli is their ability to withstand a wide variety of environmental conditions for prolonged periods. Musehold (1900) exposed infected river water and wastewater to prevailing outdoor environmental conditions and was able to recover viable tubercle bacilli for up to five months. Others (Kroger and Trettin, 1950; Mannsfeld, 1937; and Rhines, 1935) have demonstrated survival times in sewage from 48 days up to 6½ months. Greenberg and Kupka (1957) reviewed the findings of several survival studies and concluded that tubercle bacilli survived natural conditions in sewage and other contaminated materials for relatively long periods of time.

The majority of the studies carried out on *Mycobacteria* have focused on the presence of *M. tuberculosum* in sanitoria wastes. These studies may not provide a realistic picture of the danger of infection from contaminated waters. While *M. tuberculosum* is perhaps the most important potentially waterborne human pathogen of the genus *Mycobacterium,* other species of this group are capable of infecting men and animals. For example, granuloma may be caused by *M. balnei* which may be present in chlorinated water used for swimming pools (Cleere, 1960). Agents of bovine tuberculosis may be present in milk and slaughterhouse wastes (Greenberg and Kupka, 1957). On the other hand, sanitoria wastes would generally be expected to contain variable but higher concentrations of tubercle bacilli than general domestic wastes and, therefore, may overestimate the importance of this disease agent. The quantity of these organisms excreted by nonsanitoria patients is a matter of dispute. While nearly all fecal samples examined from sanitoria patients with pulmonary tuberculosis have been shown to contain viable *M. tuberculosum* (Jensen and Jensen, 1942), reports of these organisms in stools of apparently healthy individuals range from positive findings in under two percent of fecal specimens examined in one study to 21 percent in another (Laird *et al.,* 1913; and Wilson and Rosenberger, 1909). Therefore, one could expect the tubercle organisms to be present in domestic wastewater but in quantities which may be expected to be highly variable.

Pathogenic Protozoa in Wastewater

Protozoans pathogenic to man and capable of transmission by the water route are *Entamoeba histolytica,* the agent of amoebic dysentery, and members of the *Hartmanella-Naegleria* group, a free-living amoeba causing meningo-encephalitis (Stringer and Kruse, 1970). The cyst stage in the life cycle of protozoa is the principal means of dissemination of dysentery since motile amoebae are fragile entities, dying quickly once they are outside the body (Noble and Noble, 1964). Cysts must be kept moist in order to remain viable for any extended period in the environment. Each mature cyst, upon excysting, is capable of producing four motile amoebae. However, laboratory studies have shown that as many as eight and possibly more cysts may be required to establish an active culture containing adult motile amoebae (Rudolfs *et al.*, 1950). The efficiency of cysts in producing pathogenic adults does not, therefore, appear to be great. Kott and Kott (1967) found the sewage in Haifa, Israel to contain a maximum of nine *E. histolytica* cysts per liter with a median value of four per liter. Others have estimated that cysts may occur in contaminated waters at levels not likely to be greater than 5000 cysts per liter (Chang and Kabler, 1956). Since many cysts found in wastewater are derived from nonpathogenic protozoans, studies limited to *E. histolytica* cysts probably are more representative of health hazards from wastewater application on land than estimates of total cyst populations in wastewater. If a maximum of 20 cysts constitutes an infective dose (Rudolfs *et al.*, 1950), the data of the Kotts (1967) would indicate that one infective dose may be contained in five liters of wastewater. The actual cyst concentration in wastewater will probably depend on the percentage of carriers in the population. Therefore, the agents of amoebic dysentery should be considered whenever cyst carrier rates in the population are 10 percent or higher (Northington *et al.*, 1970).

Helminth Parasites in Wastewater
The ova of intestinal parasitic worms are excreted in the feces of infected individuals and may be spread by a wastewater-crop-human chain (Chang, 1965). Liebman (1965) reported ova of *Ascaris lumbricoides*, the pinworm *Oxyuris vermicularis*, the whipworm *Trichuris trichiura*, and the tapeworm *Taenia saginata* to be present in wastewater at high levels. Cram (1943) noted that hookworm eggs may also be present but others have rarely found the eggs of either *Necator americanus* or *Ancylostoma duodenale* in wastewater (Aiba and Sudo, 1965). Since hookworm larvae enter their host from fecally contaminated soil, it could be disseminated by wastewater application on soil. In moderate climates the human contribution of ova to wastewater would appear to be no greater than 10 percent but may reach 30 percent in subtropical regions such as the southern extremities of the United States (Liebman, 1965). The remainder of the ova are of

animal origin. Various authors have reported 59 to 80 worm eggs per liter of sewage (Aiba and Sudo, 1965; and Liebman, 1965). Translated into terms familiar to the engineer, this could mean millions and perhaps billions of eggs reaching a wastewater treatment facility daily. The eggs are generally resistant to environmental conditions, having a thick outer covering to protect them against dessication (Noble and Noble, 1964). Fifteen days at 29°C were required in one study to destroy 90 percent of *Ascaris* ova and they may survive 40°C for up to 60 days (Komiya and Kutsumi, 1965; and Liebman, 1965). In summary, it may be stated that a large quantity of a variety of ova from parasitic worms may be present in wastewater and that they possess a high degree of resistance to many environmental stresses.

Viruses in Wastewater

Over 100 distinct serotypes of viruses (Table 15-2) may be present in wastewater on a worldwide basis, regardless of climate (Grabow, 1968). They are the smallest of the wastewater pathogens, a fact which may have some bearing on their removal in wastewater treatment and soil percolation.

Of the enteroviruses, evidence of waterborne disease transmission exists only for polio virus (Mosley, 1965). Of the other viruses listed, infectious hepatitis and gastroenteritis warrant special attention. The agents of both diseases have yet to be isolated but both are thought to be viral in origin since they can be transmitted by bacteria-free filtrates of wastewater or fecal suspensions (Dolin *et al.*, 1971; Gordon *et al.*, 1947; and Neefe *et al.*, 1947). The actual concentration of these agents in wastewater is, of course, unknown but they appear to be relatively prevalent if one can use their disease incidence as a yardstick. From 1946 to 1960 there were 142 reported waterborne outbreaks of gastroenteritis and 23 infectious hepatitis epidemics (Weibel *et al.*, 1964). Together they involved nearly 19,000 disease cases. These are only the reported epidemics and it is likely that many more unreported waterborne epidemics and sporadic cases oc-

Table 15-2. Viruses in wastewater

Group	No. of types	Associated diseases
Enterovirus		
Polio	3	Poliomyelitis
Coxsackie	30	Aseptic meningitis, myocarditis
Echo	31	Aseptic meningitis, enteritis
Reovirus	3	Enteritis
Adenovirus	31	Respiratory illnesses
Infectious hepatitis	Unknown	Jaundice
"Viral" gastroenteritis	Unknown	Gastroenteritis

curred. Furthermore, disease is only a clinical manifestation of establishment of a parasitic infection. It has been estimated that far more viral infections occur than actual disease incidences (Mosley, 1965). Clearly then, a large quantity of virus may be present in the wastewater, and surviving the multiple treatment and natural barriers in their path to finally result in disease. The initial concentration in wastewater must be high for the chance contact of man and virus to have any chance of successful infection. Viruses as a group are generally more resistant to environmental stresses than many of the bacteria. For example, Clarke *et al.* (1964) compared the survival of viruses in wastewater to three enteric bacteria. Survival of virus in wastewater at 20°C was longer in all cases than the bacteria studied and ranged from 23 to 41 days. The time required for 99.9 percent reduction of viral numbers reportedly ranges from 2 to 100 days for various members of the enteric virus group (Akin *et al.*, 1971). Virus survival was inversely related to temperature. Other factors, such as pH value, which could conceivably affect virus survival have not been thoroughly investigated.

It has been estimated that the virus concentration of raw wastewater is approximately 7000 units per liter (Clarke *et al.*, 1964). Kelly and Sanderson (1960), using a semiquantitative technique for virus recovery, reported the virus density in raw wastewater to be 4000 units per liter during the warmer months of the year and 200 units during the colder months. Shuval (1969) recently found the virus density in raw wastewater in five Israeli cities to average 1050 virus units per liter and to range from as few as five to as many as 11,184 units per liter. Lund *et al.* (1969) observed maximum values of 100,000 virus units per liter. One problem in interpreting these various findings is that viruses are rather fastidious in their growth requirements. The techniques for sample concentration, the host cell system, and the type of culture technique used will all be selective with respect to the viruses enumerated. No universal procedure or system is presently available for cultivation of all viruses. It is likely, therefore, that many of the investigations of virus density in wastewater have not included all viruses present due to the selectivity of techniques employed. In addition, many of the previous studies involved centrifugation or filtration of samples to remove particulates associated with the wastewater before enumerating the viruses present (Lund *et al.*, 1969). Lund's work did not involve these forms of sample treatment and the higher values for virus density obtained indicate that other workers may have lost many viruses in the sediment they removed. If Lund's values for the virus density of raw wastewater are correct, it is readily apparent that tremendous quantities of virus arrive at wastewater treatment plants daily.

Removal of Pathogens in Wastewater Treatment Processes

In order to assess the importance of pathogens in land application of wastewater and sludges, one must not only know how many are present in the raw wastewater or in the settled sludges, but also the efficiency of various treatment processes in removing or destroying them. The degree of treatment and types of unit operations used in treating wastewater for application on soil may vary and, therefore, the approach adopted here will be to discuss each treatment operation or process separately. It should be noted that much of the information available in the literature on the efficiency of various treatment steps is derived from laboratory studies. Where available data exist comparison of laboratory and field data would suggest that laboratory research often overestimates the efficiency that can be obtained in the field. Therefore, some mental adjustment of laboratory data to be presented may be appropriate.

Primary Sedimentation

Primary treatment of wastewater appears to exhibit a variable efficiency in removing pathogens depending in part on the type of pathogen studied (Table 15-3). Bloom et al. (1958) isolated Salmonellae from six of seven different primary effluent samples. The raw sludge also contained members of this genus with 19 of 20 samples being positive for Salmonella organisms. McKinney et al. (1958) were unable to isolate S. typhosa from raw wastewater sludge. Müller (1959) found tubercle bacilli to be reduced by 50 percent by primary sedimentation while Kelly et al. (1955) found a 57 percent reduction. Reductions of tubercle bacilli from 48 to 54 percent during settling of raw sewage have been reported by others (Heukelekian and Albanese, 1956). Considerable quantities of the Mycobacterium may occur in the sludge produced in primary sedimentation. Pramer et al. (1950) demonstrated 67-fold concentration of tubercle bacilli in raw sludge as compared to that in the influent wastewater. These studies

Table 15-3. Removal of pathogens by primary treatment

Pathogen	Reported removal efficiency (%)
Salmonella	15[a]
Mycobacterium	48 to 57
Amoebic cysts	No reduction in 3 hours
Helminth ova	72 to 98
Virus	3 to extensive removal

a. Based on frequency of isolation

would indicate that bacterial pathogens are ineffectively removed from wastewater by primary treatment and, furthermore, the process produces sludges which constitute a hazard without further treatment.

Removal of amoebic cysts by primary treatment has not been extensively studied. Cram (1943) observed that three hours settling in laboratory units had little effect on the density of *E. histolytica* cysts in the supernatant. Eggs of parasitic worms were removed more effectively. Cram's work showed that some hookworm eggs still remained in the upper 1/3 of a laboratory settling basin after 2½ hours sedimentation. *Ascaris* ova, on the other hand, appeared to settle within 15 minutes with the eggs concentrated in the sludge. *Taenia saginata* ova have been reportedly removed to the extent of 98 percent within two hours (Newton *et al.*, 1949). Others have, on the other hand, indicated removals as low as 72 percent during sedimentation (Greenberg and Dean, 1958). It may be concluded that primary sedimentation for 2½ hours or more cannot be depended upon to produce effluents free of parasitic worm ova or amoebic cysts. Additionally, primary sludges may contain significant quantities of helminth ova (Aiba and Sudo, 1965).

The majority of the studies involving the removal of viruses by primary treatment would indicate that few viruses are removed during this operation. Poliovirus 1 seeded into raw wastewater was removed only to the extent of three percent following three hours of settling (Clarke *et al.*, 1961). In another study isolations of virus from primary effluent were more frequent compared to isolations in the primary influent (Mack *et al.*, 1962). On the other hand, Bush and Isherwood (1966) suggested that the survival of mice inoculated with primary effluent indicated extensive removal in the primary clarifier since large quantities of virus were known to be present in the influent. Laboratory studies where wastewater has been seeded with virus, such as that of Clarke *et al.* (1961), may not reflect removal of viruses that would be associated with sewage solids in natural systems. Many studies of field size units have involved filtering out solids from influent samples prior to assaying and would, therefore, not reflect virus particles associated with wastewater solids. Lund's (1969) work demonstrated conclusively that many virus particles are associated with wastewater solids. Indeed, the increase in virus seen in a primary settling tank, as in the study cited above, may reflect the release of virus from raw sludge. It may well be then that removal of virus in primary treatment has been underestimated.

Secondary Treatment

Biological treatment appears to be quite efficient in removing wastewater pathogens but does not produce an effluent which is pathogen

Table 15-4. Removal of pathogens by secondary treatment

| Pathogen group | Reported removal efficiency | |
	Activated sludge	Trickling filters
	%	%
Salmonella	96 to 99	84 to 99.9
Mycobacterium	Slight to 87	66 to 99
Amoebic cysts	No apparent removal	11 to 99.9
Helminth ova	No apparent removal	62 to 76
Virus	76 to 99	0 to 84

free (Table 15-4). Beard (1938) reported that *S. typhosa* was reduced
in density by 96 percent in six hours and 99 percent in eight hours
aeration in activated sludge units. When sterile sewage was inoculated
with *Salmonella* and aerated an increase in density was noted indicating that biological action and not aeration *per se* was responsible
for the reductions seen in normal waste treatment (Greenberg and
Beard, 1938). *M. tuberculosum* was affected little by aeration for 24
hours (Pramer *et al.*, 1950). Others have reported similar failure of
the activated sludge treatment to completely remove tubercle bacilli
even when the aerobic bacterial content had been reduced to 0.2
percent of its original numbers (Jensen and Jensen, 1942). Heukelekian and Albanese (1956) observed an 87 percent reduction in tubercle bacilli following six hours aeration in activated sludge units.
Increasing the aeration period to 24 hours effected only another one
percent removal. The bacilli were rapidly transferred to the sludge
phase apparently by adsorption to the settling particles resulting in a
sludge tubercle bacilli concentration at the end of six hours that was
13 times greater than the supernatant liquor. Therefore, the sludge
should also be considered a potential hazard and could infect soil with
tubercle bacilli if applied to land without further treatment.

Trickling filters were found to reduce the concentration of paratyphoid organisms by 84 to 99 percent (Kabler, 1959). Low rate
trickling filters were apparently capable of removing up to 99.9 percent of *S. typhosa* while a 95 percent reduction was accomplished
even at loadings of 12 mgad (Lund *et al.*, 1969). A 99 percent
reduction in *M. tuberculosum* by trickling filters has also been observed (Pramer *et al.*, 1950). On the other hand, only a 66 percent
reduction has been noted (Heukelekian and Albanese, 1956). It
should be pointed out that the removal in activated sludge was higher
by more than 20 percent than in trickling filters in this same study.
Activated sludge treatment has no apparent effect on *E. histolytica*
cysts, even when aeration was extended to 48 hours (Cram, 1943). It
should be recalled that primary sedimentation also seemingly produces no reduction in cyst numbers so that cyst densities in the
effluents of activated sludge plants may change little from those in the

influent. Removal varied from 88 to 99.9 percent in laboratory scale trickling filter plants in one study and another full scale study has reported 11 to 50 percent reduction in cyst densities in wastewater (Cram, 1943; and Kott and Kott, 1967).

Ova of intestinal parasites are apparently not affected by the activated sludge process (Cram, 1943; and Newton *et al.*, 1949); and, in fact, the literature indicates that activated sludge mixed liquor provides an excellent hatching medium for the eggs (Kabler, 1959). Trickling filters, on the other hand, reduced ova concentrations 62 to 76 percent but may produce live larvae in the effluent when the filters slough off surface growth (Newton *et al.*, 1949). In general, activated sludge appears to be ineffective in removal of both cysts and ova; and, while trickling filters are somewhat more efficient, they still pass significant portions of the incoming pathogens out the effluent. Secondary settling will not effect much further reduction of cysts; and, therefore, the final effluent will contain pathogens (Kott and Kott, 1967). Final clarifiers could be expected to bring about similar removals of parasitic worm ova as observed in primary sedimentation, *i.e.*, 70 to 90 percent.

Laboratory activated sludge units seeded with virus have shown 96 to 99 percent removal of Coxsackie A9 virus and lesser efficiency with Poliovirus 1 (Clarke *et al.*, 1961). Since many virus particles are apparently naturally bound to solids, studies of activated sludge systems seeded with virus may not be representative of "real wosld" situations. Lund *et al.* (1969) estimated that 95 to 99 percent of viruses were removed by activated sludge on the basis of frequency of isolations in the influent and effluent. Studies of full scale wastewater treatment following community-wide administration of oral polio vaccines showed 76 to 90 percent removal of virus by activated sludge (England *et al.*, 1967). Since swab samples for naturally occurring viruses were positive for 90 of 93 activated sludge effluent samples, one may conclude that viruses are generally present in the effluent.

Theios *et al.* (1967) concluded that activated sludge was more efficient in removing virus than trickling filters based on studies of full scale plants during a polio vaccine campaign. In another study, the frequency of isolations in the influent and effluent of trickling filters has been reported to be approximately equal (Kelly and Sanderson, 1959). Shuval (1969) found trickling filter efficiency to be 0 to 84 percent in removing viruses. Trickling filters cannot be depended upon to produce a significant reduction in viruses.

Anaerobic Digestion of Sludges
Large quantities of pathogenic bacteria, helminth ova, and viruses can be found in sludges from primary and secondary clarifiers. Smaller

quantities of amoebic cysts may also occur. These raw sludges would constitute a hazard if disposed of on land without further treatment. Anaerobic digestion at 30 to 35°C accomplishes a considerable reduction in the organic content of the sludge and may result in destruction of pathogens. *S. typhosa* survived to the extent of 0.3 to 17 percent after only 12 hours in batch digestion studies (McKinney *et al.*, 1958). Use of continuously fed digesters demonstrated reductions of 84 to 92 percent for 6 and 20 days digestion, respectively.

Mycobacteria may survive a digestion period of more than 35 days in laboratory units and were reduced from 9700 to 3000 per ml in field scale units (Heukelekian and Albanese, 1956). No appreciable decrease in numbers occurred in the dried digested sludge even after 25 days drying. Others have observed a 90 percent reduction in tubercle bacilli during digestion (Pramer *et al.*, 1950). Reports of survival of tubercle bacilli in dried sludges exposed to natural conditions indicate survival times of from 6½ months to two years (Jensen and Jensen, 1942; and Müller, 1959).

The data reviewed by Chang (1965) on survival of helminth ova in digesters indicated that at least one month detention is necessary for their destruction. *Ascaris* ova are not affected by three months digestion and 10 percent remain viable even after six months (Cram, 1943). Cysts, though probably not present in sludge in large quantities, are readily destroyed in 10 days at 30°C. Polio virus has been isolated from digester sludge despite exposure to 50°C for up to 50 to 60 days. No virus was isolated from digested sludge in another study where only two samples were examined (Kelly and Sanderson, 1959). When sludge samples from a digester seeded with a swine virus were fed to germ free piglets, no indication of piglet infection was observed for all samples taken after the fourth day of digestion at 34.5°C (Meyer *et al.*, 1971). Coxsackie B5 survived thermophilic anaerobic digestion for 30 days while bacteriophage survived mesophilic digestion for four months (Grigoryeva *et al.*, 1969). It is apparent that some viruses are capable of withstanding sludge digestion for long periods while others are not. Determination of the range of survival of viruses representative of each of the major virus groups during digestion is required before potential hazards arising from application of liquid and dried digested sludges on land can be fully assessed.

Disinfection of Wastewater
The disinfection of wastewater is perhaps one of the most thoroughly studied areas with respect to the reduction of numbers of pathogenic organisms by waste treatment processes. This is as it should be, since final effluent disinfection is the last line of defense before the wastewater and the pathogens it might contain are placed in the environment. Unfortunately, much of the research has been ill-defined with

little appreciation of the fact that a disinfectant may react with components of the system other than the pathogens; and, thus, change its potency for pathogen destruction. With chlorine, the most commonly used wastewater disinfectant in the United States, the initial dosage, the pH value, contact time, temperature, quantity of nitrogenous compounds present, and their nature, *i.e.,* whether they are organic or inorganic, should be stated in order to interpret results of chlorination experiments; all these factors will have impact on the disinfecting capability of chlorine. Since much of this information is not available in many of the studies to be reviewed here, only general statements of relative resistance will be given.

Kabler (1951) found that resistance of *E. coli* and *Pseudomonas aeruginosa* to free chlorine at neutral pH values was approximately the same but less than that for *S. typhosa* and *Shigella dysenteriae.* Resistance to combined chlorine was comparable between these organisms but was considerably greater than that found for free chlorine. Survival with 0.3 mg/l of free chlorine was negligible while under the same conditions the test organisms were able to completely survive contact with 0.3 mg/l of combined chlorine. A reduction in temperature from the 20 to 25°C range down to 2 to 6°C resulted in a further loss of bactericidal action of combined chlorine. *Mycobacteria* have layers of lipids and mycolic acids in their cell walls which cause a higher degree of chlorine resistance in this group of bacteria (Grabow *et al.,* 1969). A review of over a dozen different wastewater disinfection studies led Greenberg (1957) to conclude that a combination of biological purification and effluent chlorination with a chlorine dosage of 20 mg/l with a two to three hour contact time or a chlorine residual of at least 1 mg/l following a one hour contact was necessary to destory tubercle bacilli. Chlorine dosages up to 340 mg/l and two hour contact times have been found necessary to destroy *Mycobacteria* in other studies (Musehold, 1900). Higher chlorine residuals and longer contact times are thus required to inactivate tuberculosis organisms in comparison to other bacterial pathogens.

Cysts are apparently the most chlorine resistant waterborne pathogens. When the cysticidal properties of 2 mg/l each of free, combined inorganic, and combined organic chlorine residuals were compared in one study, it was observed that a 10 minute and 40 minute contact time was necessary for a 99.9 percent kill for the first two categories of compounds while organic chloramines failed to destroy more than 50 percent of the cysts even after 100 minutes of contact (Stringer and Kruse, 1970). Since wastewater effluents may contain organic and inorganic nitrogenous compounds, breakpoint effluent chlorination may be required in order to destroy cysts present in secondary effluents.

The reported response of viruses to chlorine varies widely depend-

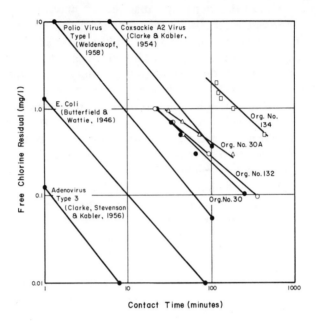

Figure 15-1. Free chlorine residuals and contact times necessary for 99.9 percent kill for Isolates No. 134, No. 30A, No. 132 and No. 30 as well as for organisms compiled by Berg (1966)

ing on the condition used in a given study and the type of virus examined. Poliovirus 1 and Coxsackie A2 (Figure 15-1) are much more resistant to chlorine than coliforms while adenovirus 3 is apparently more sensitive. The figure also illustrates the resistance of three organisms isolated at the University of Illinois from chlorinated wastewater. Isolate No. 30 is a yeast and Isolate Nos. 132 and 134 are acid-fast bacilli. The chlorine resistance of these vegetative organisms places them in the range regarded as necessary for an indicator of the chlorine resistance of viruses. Infectious hepatitis virus is able to survive 30 minutes contact time with 1 mg/l total residual chlorine in fecal suspensions if no other treatment is provided.

Liu *et al.* (1971) studied the chlorine resistance of 20 human enteric viruses seeded in Potomac River water. The least chlorine resistant virus, Reovirus 1, required only 2.7 minutes contact with 0.5 mg/l of free chlorine for 99.99 percent inactivation. Coxsackie A5 and Echovirus 12 required 53.5 and 60 minutes contact, respectively, to reach the same level of inactivation under these conditions. Combined chlorine has very little viricidal capability (Kruse *et al.*, 1970). It is evident that the resistance of viruses to chlorine is quite variable. Since more than 80 viruses have not been subjected to detailed studies of their resistance, the disinfection conditions necessary to kill all viruses in wastewater effluents is still an open question. It would appear that as with cysts, a free chlorine residual at a contact time of at least ½ hour is necessary to destroy many of the viruses.

Pathogens Applied to Soil

Table 15-5 is an attempt to summarize the data on the removal of pathogens in wastewater. Where definitive data do not exist for removal efficiency at a particular treatment step, values have been assumed based on any available information. Removal percentages assumed are given in parentheses. A uniform disinfection efficiency of 99.9 percent has been assumed. If the conditions necessary to destroy the more chlorine resistant pathogens were applied to wastewater, kills of relatively sensitive organisms such as *Salmonella,* greater than 99.9 percent would be obtained, thus further reducing the quantity of some pathogens. However, since the survival time of the remaining organisms may be quite long in soil, continuous application of wastewater onto soil could result in an accumulation of pathogens. An equilibrium value could be reached where die-off and removal through percolation and runoff are balanced by the daily input of new pathogens. The longer the survival time in soil the greater the equilibrium level. *S. typhosa* reportedly survive up to 85 days in soil but with soils which have poor moisture retaining power, survival in periods of drought may be as brief as two days (Beard, 1938; and Mallmann and Litsky, 1951). With continuous application of wastewater soils may not have sufficient opportunity to dry out; and, therefore, survival of *Salmonella* could be prolonged. *Mycobacteria* can survive dry conditions in soil for more than 150 days and survival times as long as 15 months have been reported (Greenberg and Kupka, 1957). While protozoan cysts are sensitive to dessication, *Ascaris* and *Ancylostoma* ova remain viable for long periods and have withstood conditions where the moisture content of soil was less than six percent and temperatures above 40°C for 60 to 80 days (Cram, 1943). Viable *Ascaris* eggs have been recovered up to 170 days under more favorable conditions. Little definitive information on the survival of virus in soil exists, but one could expect it to be of the same order of magnitude as survival in wastewater where persistence as long as 100 days has been reported (Akin *et al.,* 1971).

If one accepts the figures given in Table 15-5 as reasonably accurate estimates of the possible quantities of pathogens that may be

Table 15-5. Estimated wastewater pathogens applied to soil

| Pathogen | Raw wastewater | Number of organisms per million gallons | | Disinfection[a] | Organisms applied per acre per day[b] |
		Primary effluent	Secondary effluent		
Salmonella	2×10^{10}	1×10^{10} (50%)[c]	5×10^8 (95%)	5×10^5	3.9×10^3
Mycobacterium	2×10^8	1×10^8 (50%)	1.5×10^7 (85%)	1.5×10^4	1.2×10^2
E. histolytica	1.5×10^7	1.3×10^7 (10%)	1.2×10^7 (10%)	1.2×10^4	9.3×10^1
Helminth ova	2.5×10^8	2.5×10^7 (90%)	5×10^6 (80%)	5×10^3	3.9×10^1
Virus	4×10^{10}	2×10^{10} (50%)	2×10^9 (90%)	2×10^6	1.6×10^4

a. Conditions sufficient to yield a 99.9% kill
b. Applied at a rate of 2 inches per week
c. Estimated pathogen percentage removal efficiency of the treatment

applied to land from chlorinated effluents, then one might conclude that considerable numbers of pathogens could be placed in the environment. The density of organisms on land will be even greater if they accumulate in the soil. Any degree of treatment less than secondary treatment in combination with free residual effluent disinfection will result in greater quantities of pathogens being applied to soil. If, for example, the wastewater is not chlorinated the quantities of pathogens applied will be three logs greater. Yet are these quantities sufficient to result in much danger of disease transmission? The density of pathogens with the application of chlorinated secondary effluent for any one of the pathogens cited would not be greater than one viable pathogen per four square feet per day. At the other extreme, the total pathogen load for unchlorinated secondary effluent is approximately 460 per square foot per day.

Public Health Hazards

Several studies have attempted to assess the hazards involved in the application of wastewater on land and provide interesting comparisons to the figures in Table 15-5. Basically, the studies have been concerned with (1) hazards from aerosols in spray irrigating the wastewater on land, (2) contamination of edible crops, and (3) contamination of water from runoff and percolation.

Aerosol generation from spray irrigation could produce particles of a size which would either pass into the lungs or pass from the bronchi to the pharynx and into the intestine (Sorber and Guter, 1972). Infections such as Salmonellosis could therefore result from such exposure. However, enteric bacteria such as *Salmonella* are apparently not long lived as unprotected aerosols. Tubercle bacilli are resistant to drying and, therefore, should survive in the atmosphere as aerosols for extended periods. Greenberg and Kupka (1957) felt the use of sewage sprays containing *Mycobacteria* to be especially dangerous. Inhalation would place the bacilli in the location where they can do the most damage as causative agents of pulmonary tuberculosis. Viability of airborne virus is relatively long. For example, in one study the majority of polio virus aerosols persisted for more than 23 hours when the relative humidity was high (Walker, 1970). Reports of disease incidences resulting from contact with aerosols from spray irrigation have not appeared in the literature but this area should warrant further study.

Crop contamination research has mainly focused on vegetables which normally are eaten raw such as tomatoes, radishes, etc. Other studies have dealt with irrigation of pasture land for grazing of livestock. When tomatoes were field sprayed with feces or wastewater containing *Salmonella* and *Shigella,* survival of these organisms did not exceed seven days (Rudolfs *et al.,* 1951). However, a radish patch to which tubercle bacilli contaminated wastewater sludge had been applied yielded viable bacilli after three months exposure to the elements (Musehold, 1900). Rudolfs' (1951) statement that cessation of application of fecally contaminated fertilizer one month before harvesting offers a margin of safety against bacterial disease would not seem to apply to *M. tuberculosum. E. hystolytica* cysts are quite sensitive to dessication and do not survive longer than three days of dry weather when applied to crops such as lettuce and tomatoes (Rudolfs *et al.,* 1951). Immature *Ascaris* ova were not found to survive field conditions longer than 35 days (Rudolfs *et al.,* 1951). Rudolfs noted that exposure of immature ova to the prevailing environmental conditions retarded their development into motile embryos. It must be pointed out, however, that studies of Cram (1943) and others (Kabler, 1959) have shown that the secondary waste treatment environment provides an excellent medium for development of ova. It is likely, therefore, that mature rather than immature ova would be present in large quantities in the effluent. If this is the case, Rudolfs' work may have underestimated the ability of *Ascaris* ova to survive and mature under field conditions. In general, there appears to be a danger of pathogen contamination of vegetables to be eaten raw if wastewater is applied to fields within two to three months of harvesting. If this is the case, it could limit its usefulness for crops such as lettuce and radishes which have short growing seasons.

Irrigation of fields for forage crops has produced interesting results which could eliminate some of the concern expressed about contamination of vegetables. Grass sprayed with 4×10^6 tubercle bacilli per square foot was fed to guinea pigs with no apparent effects (Greenberg and Kupka, 1957). Heavier inoculations, however, resulted in deaths in both guinea pigs and bovine test animals. The predicted values for tubercle bacilli applied to land in unchlorinated effluents obtained from the data of Table 15-5 (*i.e.,* 2.7×10^0 bacilli per square foot) would indicate that the daily pathogen load would be at least six orders of magnitude below the levels which had no effect on guinea pigs. The danger to man and animals from ingestion of tubercle bacilli from crops irrigated with wastewater would appear to be slight.

The movement of bacterial and viral pathogens in percolation and runoff has been extensively reviewed in the literature (Krone, 1968; Krone *et al.,* 1958; and Romero, 1970). Generalizations are difficult but it appears that virus and bacteria movement in soils is related directly to the hydraulic infiltration rate and inversely with media particle diameters. Factors influencing bacterial and viral inactivation in soil such as oxygen tension, temperature, and the presence of competing organisms and antimicrobial agents will also be determining variables. Other factors which have an influence on adsorption phenomena in soils such as pH value, multivalent cation concentration, and clay content of the soil will influence removal of pathogens, particularly virus, in soils. The majority of the studies reviewed indicate that the upper layers of soil are most efficient in removing bacteria. At Lodi, California, coliform levels were observed to decrease to below drinking water standards within seven feet of the surface (Romero, 1970). Other research demonstrates that 92 to 97 percent of applied coliforms were retained in the uppermost one cm of agricultural soil. Even in the coarse gravel-sand used at Santee, California, most applied bacteria did not travel more than 200 feet. Cram (1943) reported *Ascaris* eggs would pass a 12 inch layer of sand but were removed by 24 inches as were hookworm ova and *E. histolytica* cysts. Drewry and Eliassen (1968) studied removal of viruses in a variety of soil lysimeters and concluded that no column studied was saturated with virus over more than two cm. Up to five percent of the applied virus passed the columns but generally removals were quite high, particularly in the upper layers. Virus seeded into the influent of the Santee percolation beds could not be recovered from samples concentrated by swabs located in an observation well 200 feet from the influent application site (Akin *et al.*, 1971). It is likely, therefore, that pathogens do not travel to any great extent in soils and are removed principally in the upper layers. Even where organisms do travel up to 50 feet from the point of entry into the soil, "soil defense" mechanisms such as antibiotic activity and competition will begin to act and cause increased die-off resulting in a retreat of the bacterial front (Romero, 1970).

It should be noted that pathogens removed in the upper layers of soil will be concentrated near the soil area where crops will be grown. Pathogens could directly pass to crops such as lettuce or beets from soil contamination or be carried to above ground crops by flies or dust. The dust-borne epidemic of Salmonellosis in Israel indicates that this is not outside the realm of possibility. Fractures or channels in underlying geological formations will also affect pathogen movement in soil. Vogt (1961) reported a waterborne epidemic of infectious hepatitis which followed limestone fractures from a septic tank to individual wells considerable distances away from the source. Laboratory and field studies cannot be completely relied upon as to distance of travel since small quantities of pathogens may escape removal, particularly in fractured geological formations. Epidemiological evidence of bacteria and viruses traveling considerable distances to water supplies is discomfiting, particularly since levels of pathogens sufficient to result in infection may not be detectable in dilute solution with presently available techniques.

Summary and Conclusions

This paper has presented a good deal of data couched in terms of possible or potential hazards. How real are the hazards in terms of the realities of actual cases of disease resulting from wastewater application on soil? The epidemiological evidence suggests that few disease incidences have been related to this practice. Krone (1968) reviewed an incident involving sewage contamination of fruits and vegetables on a farm in 1919 which resulted in eight cases of typhoid fever. A possible 2500 cases of gastroenteritis due to *Shigella* and *Salmonella* occurred in California in 1965 under highly unusual circumstances (Browning and Mankin, 1966). Wastewater applied to a pasture traveled overland to a gopher hole and then into a poorly protected municipal water supply well. The chances of such an event repeating itself are highly unlikely. The literature is quite unusual in the paucity of information available on irrigation-caused epidemics. This may well reflect an absence of a problem despite other evidence indicating that significant quantities of pathogens are placed on soil by this practice. On the other hand, it may only reflect prejudices which regard only significant outbreaks of disease to be worthy of investigation. Epidemiological tools are insensitive for isolated or sporadic small scale outbreaks. Resulting sporadic infection may not result in actual clinical symptoms but could create foci for disease dissemination by other modes of transmission. While the potential for low-level transmission of disease is speculative, it is a possibility worthy of investigation. Until such time as the danger of sporadic disease transmission can be ruled out, a high degree of treatment of applied wastewater including free residual chlorination would seem to be indicated. Geological conditions underlying soil to which wastewater is applied should not contain channels or fractures which may permit pathogens to move long distances. More than one month, preferably more than two months, should be allowed between the last application of wastewater and harvesting edible crops. In this way both actual hazards of disease transmission and public apprehension may be reduced.

Literature Cited

Aiba, S., and R. Sudo. 1965. Discussion of paper by H. Liebman, in *Adv. in Water Poll. Res.*, 282, Vol. 2, Pergamon Press, London.

Akin, E. W., W. H. Benton, and W. F. Hill, Jr. 1971. Enteric viruses in ground and surface water: a review of their occurrence and survival, *13th Water Quality Conf.*, 59, University of Illinois.

Beard, P. J. 1938. The survival of typhoid in nature, *Jour. Amer. Water Works Assn.*, 30:124.

Berg, G. 1966. Virus transmission by the water vehicle, III, Removal of viruses by water treatment procedures, *Health Lab. Sci.*, 3:170.

Bloom, H. H., W. N. Mack, and W. L. Mallmann. 1958. Enteric viruses and *Salmonellae* isolations, II, Media comparison for *Salmonellae*, *Sew. and Indust. Wastes*, 30:1455.

Browning, G. E. and J. O. Mankin. 1966. Gastroenteritis epidemic owing to sewage contamination of public water supply, *Jour. Amer. Water Works Assn.*, 58:1465.

Bush, A. F. and J. D. Isherwood. 1966. Virus removal in sewage treatment, *Jour. San. Engr. Div., Amer. Soc. Civil Engr.*, 92:99.

Chang, S. L. 1965. Discussion of paper by H. Liebman, in *Adv. in Water Poll. Res.*, 279, Vol. 2, Pergamon Press, London.

Chang, S. L. and P. W. Kabler. 1956. Detection of cysts of *Endamoeba histolytica* in tap water by use of membrane filter, *Amer. Jour. Hygiene*.

Clarke, N. A., G. Berg, P. W. Kabler, and S. L. Chang. 1964. Human enteric viruses in water: source, survival and removability. *Adv. in Water Poll. Res.*, 523, Vol. 2, Pergamon Press, London.

Clarke, N. A., R. E. Stevenson, S. L. Chang, and P. W. Kabler. 1961. Removal of enteric viruses from sewage by activated sludge treatment, *Amer. Jour. Pub. Health*, 58:1118.

Cleere, R. L. 1960. Resume of swimming pool granuloma. *Sanitation*, 23:105.

Cram, E. B. 1943. The effect of various treatment processes on the survival of *helminth* ova and protozoan cysts in sewage, *Sew. Works Jour.*, 15:1119.

Dolin, R., N. R. Blacklow, H. Dupont, S. Formal, R. F. Buscho, J. A. Kasel, R. P. Chames, R. Hornick, and R. M. Chanock. 1971. Transmission of acute non-bacterial gastroenteritis to volunteers by oral administration of stool filtrates, *Jour. Infectious Diseases*, 123:307.

Drewry, W. A. and R. Eliassen. 1968. Virus movement in ground water, *Jour. Water Poll. Control Fed.*, 40:R257.

England, B., R. E. Leach, B. Adame, and R. Shiosaki. 1967. Virologic assessment of sewage treatment at Santee, California, in *Transmission of Viruses by the Water Route*, G. Berg, ed., 401, Interscience, New York.

Gordon, I., M. S. Ingraham, and R. F. Korns. 1947. Transmission of epidemic gastroenteritis to human volunteers by oral administration of fecal filtrates, *Jour. Exper. Med.*, 86:409.

Grabow, W. O. K. 1968. The virology of waste water treatment, *Water Res.*, 2:675.

Grabow, W. O. K., N. A. Grabow, and J. S. Burger. 1969. The bactericidal effect of lime flocculation/flotation as a primary unit process in a multiple system for the advanced purification of sewage works effluent, *Water Res.*, 3:943.

Green, C. E. and P. J. Beard. 1938. Survival of *E. typhi* in sewage treatment plant processes, *Amer. Jour. Pub. Health*, 28:762.

Greenberg, A. E. and B. H. Dean. 1958. The beef tapeworm, measly beef, and sewage — a review, *Sew. and Indust. Wastes*, 30:262.

Greenberg, A. E. and E. Kupka. 1957. Tuberculosis transmission by wastewaters — a review, *Sew. and Indust. Wastes*, 29:524.

Greenberg, A. E. and H. J. Ongerth. 1966. Salmonellosis in Riverside, California, *Jour. Amer. Water Works Assn.*, 58:1145.

Grigoryeva, L. V., G. I. Korchak, and T. V. Bey. 1969. Survival of bacteria and viruses in sewage sludges, *Mikrobiol. Zh.*, 31:659.

Heukelekian, H. and M. Albanese. 1956. Enumeration and survival of human tubercle bacilli in polluted waters, II, Effect of sewage treatment and natural purification, *Sew. and Indust. Wastes*, 28:1094.

Heukelekian, H. and H. B. Schulhoff. 1935. Studies on the survival of *B. typhosus* in surface waters and sewage, *N. J. Agric. Expt. Sta. Bull.*, 589.

Jensen, K. A. and K. E. Jensen. 1942. Occurrence of tubercle bacilli in sewage and experiments on sterilization of tubercle bacilli-containing sewage with chlorine, *Acta Tuberc. Scandinavica*, 16:217.

Kabler, P. K. 1959. Removal of pathogenic microorganisms by sewage treatment processes, *Sew. and Indust. Wastes*, 31:1373.

Kabler, P. W. 1951. Relative resistance of coliform organisms and enteric pathogens in the disinfection of water with chlorine, *Jour. Amer. Water Works Assoc.*, 43:553.

Kelly, S. M., M. E. Clark, and M. B. Coleman. 1955. Demonstration of infectious agents in sewage, *Amer. Jour. Pub. Health*, 45:1438.

Kelly, S. M. and W. W. Sanderson. 1960. The density of enteroviruses in sewage, *Jour. Water Poll. Control Fed.*, 32:1269.

Kelly, S. and W. W. Sanderson. 1959. The effect of sewage treatment on viruses, *Sew. and Indust. Wastes*, 31:683.

Komiya, Y. and H. Kutsumi. 1965. Discussion of paper by H. Liebman, in *Adv. in Water Poll. Res.*, 276, Vol. 2, Pergamon Press, London.

Kott, H. and Y. Kott. 1967. Detectability and viability of *Endamoeba histolytica* cysts in sewage effluents, *Water and Sew. Works*, 114:117.

Kroger, E. and G. Trettin. 1950. Abwasseruntersuchung auf tuberkelbakterien, *Zentralbl. f. Bakt. Abt. I. Orig.*, 157:851.

Krone, R. B. July 30, 1968. The movement of disease producing organisms through soil, presented at the Symp. on the Use of Municipal Sewage Effluent for Irrigation, Louisiana Poly. Instit., Ruston, La.

Krone, R. B., G. T. Orlob and C. Hodkinson. 1958. Movement of coliform bacteria through porous media, *Sew. and Indust. Wastes*, 30:1.

Kruse, C. W., Y. C. Hsu, A. C. Griffiths, and R. Stringer. 1970. Halogen action of bacteria, viruses and protozoa, *Proc. National Specialty Conf. on Disinfection*, 113, Amer. Soc. Civil Engr., New York.

Laird, A. T., G. L. Kite, and D. A. Stewart. 1913-1914. The presence of tubercle bacilli in the feces, *Jour. Med. Res.*, 24:31.

Liebman, H. 1965. Parasites in sewage and the possibilities of their extinction, *Adv. in Water Poll. Res.*, Vol. 2, 269, Pergamon Press, London.

Liu, O. C., H. R. Seraichekas, E. W. Akin, D. A. Brashear, E. L. Katy, and W. F. Hill, Jr. 1971. Relative resistance of 20 human enteric viruses to free chlorine in Potomac water, *13th Water Qual. Conf.*, University of Illinois.

Lund, E. 1970. Observations on the virus binding capacity of sludge, presented at 5th International Conf. on Water Poll. Res., San Francisco, Calif.

Lund, E., C. E. Hedstrom, and N. Jantzen. 1969. Occurrence of enteric viruses in wastewater after activated sludge treatment, *Jour. Water Poll. Control Fed.*, 41:169.

Mack, W. N., J. R. Frey, B. J. Riegle, and W. L. Mallmann. 1962. Enterovirus removal by activated sludge treatment, *Jour. Water Poll. Control Fed.*, 34:1133.

Mallmann, W. L. and W. Litsky. 1951. Survival of selected enteric organisms in various types of soil, *Amer. Jour. Pub. Health*, 41:38.

Mannsfeld, M. 1937. Untersuchungen über die resistenz der tuberkelbazillen im abwasser., *Acta Soc. Biol. Latviae*, 7:153.

McKinney, R. E., H. E. Langely, and H. D. Tomlinson. 1958. Survival of *Salmonella typhosa* during anaerobic digestion, *Sew. and Indust. Wastes*, 30:1469.

Meyer, R. C., F. C. Hinds, H. R. Isaacson, and T. D. Hinesly. 1971. Porcine enterovirus survival and anaerobic sludge digestion, *Proc. Intl. Symp. on Livestock Wastes*, 183, Amer. Soc. Agric. Engr., St. Joseph, Michigan.

Mosley, J. W. 1965. Transmission of viral diseases by drinking water, *Transmission of Viruses by the Water Route*, G. Berg, ed., Interscience, New York.

Müller, G. 1959. Tuberkelbakterien im schlam mechanisch-biologisch arbeitender abwasserreinigungsanlagen, *Städtehyg.*, 5:46.

Musehold, P. 1900. Uber die widerstand fähigkeit der mit dem lungenauswerfherausbeforderten tuberkelbazillen im abwassern, im flusswasser und im kultiverten boden, *Arbeiten a.d. Kaiserlichen Gesundheitant*, 17:56.

Neefe, J. R., J. B. Baby, J. G. Reinhold, and J. Stokes, Jr. 1947. Inactivations of the virus of infectious hepatitis in water, *Amer. Jour. Pub. Health*, 37:365.

Newton, W. L., H. J. Bennett, and W. B. Figgat. 1949. Observations on the effects of various sewage treatment processes upon the eggs of *Taenia saginata*, *Amer. Jour. Hygiene*, 49:166.

Noble, E. R. and G. A. Noble. 1964. *Parasitology: The Biology of Animal Parasites*, 2nd ed., Lea and Febiger, Philadelphia.

Northington, C. W., S. L. Chang, and L. T. McCabe. 1970. Health aspects of wastewater reuse, in *Water Quality Improvement by Physical and Chemical Processes*, E. F. Gloyna and W. W. Eckenfelder, eds., University of Texas Press.

Pramer, D., H. Heukelekian, and R. A. Rago zkie. 1950. Survival of tubercle bacilli in various sewage treatment processes, I, Development of a method for the quantitative recovery of *Mycobacteria* from sewage, *Pub. Health Reports*, 65:851.

Rhines, C. 1935. The longevity of tubercle bacilli in sewage and stream water, *Amer. Rev. Tuberc.*, 31:493.

Rochaix, A. 1930. Experiments on the persistence and disappearance of pathogenic bacteria in sewage, *Ann. D'Hyg.*, 8:669.

Romero, J. C. 1970. The movement of bacteria and viruses through porous media, *Ground Water*, 8:37.

Rudolfs, W., L. L. Falk, and R. A. Ragotzkie. 1951. Contamination of vegetables grown in polluted soil, I, Bacterial contamination, *Sew. Works Jour.*, 23:253.

Rudolfs, W., L. L. Falk, and R. A. Ragotzkie. 1951. Contamination of vegetables grown in polluted soil, II, Field and laboratory studies on *Endamoeba* cysts, *Sew. Works Jour.*, 23:478.

Rudolfs, W., L. L. Falk, and R. A. Ragotzkie. 1951. Contamination of vegetables grown in polluted soil, III, Field studies on *Ascaris* eggs, *Sew. Works Jour.*, 23:656.

Rudolfs, W., L. L. Falk, and R. A. Ragotzkie. 1950. Literature on the occurrence and survival of enteric, pathogenic, and relative organisms in soil, water, sewage, and sludges, and on vegetation, I, Bacterial and virus diseases, *Sew. and Indust. Wastes*, 22:1261.

Salle, A. J. 1967. *Fundamental Principles of Bacteriology,* 6th ed., McGraw-Hill, New York, N. Y.

Seligman, R., and R. Reitler. 1965. Enteropathogens in water with low *Esch. coli* titer, *Jour. Amer. Water Works Assn.*, 57:1572.

Shuval, H. I. 1969. Detection and control of enteroviruses in the water environment, in *Developments in Water Qual. Res.*, H. I. Shuval, ed., Ann Arbor-Humphreys, Ann Arbor.

Sorber, C. A. and K. J. Guter. 1972. Health and hygiene aspects of spray irrigation, in *Wastewater Management by Disposal on the Land*, S. C. Reed, Coordinator, Cold Regions Res. and Engr. Lab., Corps of Engineers, U.S. Army, Hanover, N. H.

Stringer, R. and C. W. Kruse. 1970. Amoebic cysticidal properties of halogens in water, *Proc. National Specialty Conf. on Disinfection*, 319, Amer. Soc. Civil Engr., New York, N. Y.

Theios, E. P., J. G. Morris, M. J. Rosenbaum, and A. G. Baker. 1967. Effect of sewage treatment on recovery of polio virus following mass oral immunization, *Amer. Jour. Pub. Health*, 57:295.

Vogt, J. E. 1961. Infectious hepatitis outbreak in Posen, Michigan, *Proc. 1961 Symp. on Groundwater Contamination*, 87, USPHS Tech. Rept. W61-5.

Walker, B. 1970. Viruses respond to environmental exposure, *Jour. Environ. Health*, 32.

Wang, W. L. L., S. G. Dunlop, and R. G. Deboer. 1956. The survival of shigella in sewage, I, An effect of sewage and fecal suspensions on *Shigella flexneri, Appl. Micro.*, 4:34.

Weibel, S. R., F. R. Dixon, R. B. Weidner, and L. J. McCabe. 1964. Waterborne disease outbreaks 1946-60, *Jour. Amer. Water Works Assn.*, 56:947.

Wilson and Rosenberger. 1909. The duration of the actively infectious stage of tuberculosis, *Jour. Amer. Med. Assn.*, 7:449.

Wilson, W. J., and E. M. Blair. 1931. Further experience of the bismuth sulfite media in the isolation of *Bacillus typhosus* and *B. paratyphosus* B from feces, sewage, and water, *Jour. Hygiene*, 31:138.

V / VEGETATION RESPONSES

16
Vegetation Responses to Irrigation with Treated Municipal Wastewater

William E. Sopper and Louis T. Kardos*

Many water pollution problems have been created and worsened by the disposal of treated municipal wastewater into streams, lakes, and oceans. There are currently about 16,000 sewage treatment plants in the United States discharging more than 26 billion gallons of effluent daily. This is only a beginning. As environmental quality pressures mount, more plants will have to be built to meet new stringent water quality standards. This move from dispersed simple wastewater treatment by many individual septic tanks to collection and concentration of wastewater for treatment at a single plant provides only a partial solution to water pollution problems. Advanced secondary treatment eliminates the health hazard associated with untreated wastes and most of the organic matter is decomposed into its inorganic components. However, it is the concentrated discharge of these mineral-enriched effluents into a balanced aquatic environment which causes ecological chaos and disrupts the natural recycling process.

Chemical Composition of Municipal Sewage Effluent

The chemical composition of municipal effluent is illustrated in Table 16-1 based upon samples collected during 1971 from the University treatment plant. This plant services both the University and the borough of State College. Treatment consists of both primary and secondary treatment. Secondary treatment includes standard and high-rate trickling filters and a modified activated sludge process followed by final settling. Weekly variations in concentration of con-

*School of Forest Resources and Department of Agronomy, The Pennsylvania State University

Table 16-1. Chemical composition of sewage effluent applied during 1971

Constituent	Range Minimum	Maximum	Average	Total amount applied[a]
	mg/l	mg/l	mg/l	lbs/acre
pH	7.4	8.9	8.1	—
MBAS[b]	0.03	0.88	0.37	5
Nitrate-N	2.6	17.5	8.6	128
Organic-N	0.0	7.0	2.4	36
NH_4-N	0.0	5.0	0.9	13
Phosphorus	0.250	4.750	2.651	39
Calcium	23.1	27.8	25.2	375
Magnesium	9.1	15.1	12.9	192
Sodium	18.8	35.9	28.1	419
Boron	0.14	0.27	0.21	3
Manganese	0.01	0.04	0.02	0.2

a. Amount applied on areas which received two inches of effluent per week.
b. Methylene blue active substance (detergent residue) values are for 1970, constituent not included in analyses in 1971.

stituents are shown by the range between maximum and minimum values. The total amount of each constituent applied per acre per year at the two-inch-per-week rate is also given in Table 16-1.

The fertilizer value of these wastewaters is readily evident. The amount of N-P-K applied through spray irrigation of effluent in forested areas at the rate of two inches per week during the past nine years is given in Table 16-2. The average annual applications provided commercial fertilizer constituents equivalent to approximately 208 pounds of nitrogen, 200 pounds of phosphate (P_2O_5), and 227 pounds of potash (K_2O). This would be equal to applying about 2000 lbs of a 10-10-11 fertilizer annually.

The Penn State Wastewater Renovation and Conservation Project

Treated municipal sewage effluent has been spray-irrigated on cropland and in forest stands for a ten-year (1963-72) period. Effluent has been applied in various amounts ranging from one inch per week to six inches per week and over various lengths of time ranging from as little as 16 weeks during the growing season on cropland to the entire 52 weeks in forests. Rates of application have varied from 0.25 to 0.64 inch per hour.

Types of crops irrigated with effluent were wheat, oats, corn, alfalfa, red clover, and reed canarygrass. Forested areas irrigated consisted of a mixed hardwood forest, a red pine plantation (*Pinus resi-*

Table 16-2. Amount of N-P-K applied annually in forested areas through spray irrigation of effluent

Year	Total effluent applied[a]	N	P	K
	inches	lbs/a	lbs/a	lbs/a
1963[b]	46	119	54	127
1964	66	256	116	234
1965	62	139	122	199
1966	62	170	129	238
1967	56	157	98	176
1968	62	351	119	261
1969	56	275	66	175
1970	54	217	43	120
1971	58	184	40	174
Mean	58	208	87	189

a. Applied two inches per week.
b. First year irrigation started June 18, 1963 and therefore values only represent a partial year.

nosa Ait.), and a sparse white spruce (*Picea glauca* Muench Voss.) plantation established on an abandoned old field. Detailed descriptions of these areas have been previously reported by Sopper (1971).

Crop Responses

Yields
The sequence of annual crop rotation is given in Table 16-3. During the initial years of the project a variety of crops were tested. Since 1968 the two primary crops used have been silage corn and reed canarygrass. As will be discussed later these two crops appear to be the most efficient in terms of the utilization of the crop to remove nutrients applied to a site in the effluent.

Average crop yields obtained from 1963 to 1970 are given in Table 16-4. During this eight-year period the crop areas irrigated with two inches of effluent weekly received a total of 392 inches of wastewater equivalent to applying 10,000 pounds of a 13-6-15 commercial fertilizer. The control area was fertilized with commercial fertilizer ranging from 200 pounds of 0-20-20 per acre for oats to 1000 pounds of 10-10-10 on corn. Effluent irrigation at two inches per week resulted in annual yield increases ranging from −8 to 346 percent for corn grain, 5 to 130 percent for corn silage, 85 to 191 percent for red clover, and 79 to 139 percent for alfalfa. Yield differences between

Table 16-3. Annual crop sequence

Area	1963	1964	1965	1966	1967	1968-72
1	corn[a]	oats	alfalfa	alfalfa	alfalfa	corn
2	wheat	red clover	corn	corn	corn	corn
3	red clover	corn	oats	alfalfa	alfalfa	corn
4	wheat	red clover	corn	corn	corn	corn
5	corn	oats	alfalfa	alfalfa	alfalfa	corn
6	red clover	corn	oats	alfalfa	alfalfa	corn
7	alfalfa	corn	oats	alfalfa	alfalfa	corn

a. Includes one-inch and two-inch per week irrigated plots and a control plot.

Table 16-4. Average annual crop yields at various levels of application of sewage effluent[a]

	0 inch/week	1 inch/week	2 inches/week
1963			
Wheat (bushels/acre)	48	45	54
Corn (bushels/acre)	75	105	106
Alfalfa (tons/acre)	2.18	3.73	5.12
Red clover (tons/acre)	2.48	4.90	4.59
1964			
Red clover (tons/acre)	1.76	5.30	5.12
Corn (bushels/acre)	81	121	116
Corn stover (tons/acre)	3.83	7.29	8.48
Oats (bushels/acre)	82	124	97
1965			
Alfalfa (tons/acre)	2.27	4.67	5.42
Corn (bushels/acre)	63	114	111
Corn silage (tons/acre)	3.11	3.93	4.32
Oats grain (bushels/acre)	45	80	73
Oats straw (tons/acre)	1.62	2.90	2.63
Reed canarygrass (tons/acre)	–	–	6.13
1966			
Alfalfa (tons/acre)	1.95	3.86	4.38
Corn (bushels/acre)	33	98	115
Corn silage (tons/acre)	2.47	4.45	5.68
Reed canarygrass (tons/acre)	–	–	4.32
1967			
Corn Pa. 444			
19-inch row (bushels/acre)	98	101	122
38-inch row (bushels/acre)	92	83	84
Corn Pa. 602-A			
19-inch row (bushels/acre)	122	121	114
Corn silage Pa. 602-A			
19-inch row (tons/acre)	4.43	4.47	4.67
Alfalfa (tons/acre)	2.43	3.77	4.36
Reed canarygrass (tons/acre)	–	–	7.03
1968			
Reed canarygrass (tons/acre)	–	–	5.09
1969			
Corn Silage			
Pa. 602-A (tons/acre)	5.19	5.77	5.49
Pa. 890-S (tons/acre)	6.90	6.66	7.27
Reed canarygrass (tons/acre)	–	–	5.18
1970			
Corn Silage			
Pa. 602-A (tons/acre)	4.35	6.44	6.00
Pa. 890-S (tons/acre)	5.20	4.97	5.58
Reed canarygrass (tons/acre)	–	–	5.53

a. Part of table obtained from Kardos (1971); yields in tons per acre reported on a dry weight basis; corn grain yields are expressed on the basis of 56 pounds per bushel at 15.5 percent moisture content.

Table 16-5. Average nutrient composition of two varieties of corn silage receiving various levels of effluent during 1970

	Variety and amount of effluent applied per week					
	Corn silage. Pa. 890-S			Corn silage. Pa. 602-A		
Nutrient	0	1	2	0	1	2
	%	%	%	%	%	%
Nitrogen	1.18	1.24	1.32	1.34	1.36	1.34
Phosphorus	0.22	0.29	0.31	0.21	0.28	0.35
Potassium	1.00	0.98	1.02	1.04	1.10	1.07
Calcium	0.39	0.28	0.25	0.48	0.32	0.23
Magnesium	0.16	0.22	0.22	0.16	0.21	0.19
Chloride	0.21	0.36	0.34	0.19	0.36	0.39
	µg/g	µg/g	µg/g	µg/g	µg/g	µg/g
Sodium	14	171	176	12	167	201
Boron	6	8	8	7	7	7

the effluent-irrigated and control plots were greatly influenced by growing season precipitation. During the years, 1963 to 1966, when growing season (May 1 to September 30) precipitation was five to eight inches below normal, yields on the irrigated areas were significantly greater than on the control areas, but usually differences between the one-inch- and two-inch-per-week applications were not enough to be significant. In 1967 and 1969, when growing season precipitation was slightly above normal, yield differences were not significant. In 1970, with growing season precipitation again below normal (1.55 inches), yield differences between the control and irrigated areas were again significant but the two levels of irrigation were not.

Nutrient Composition
Under the "living filter" concept the higher plants growing on the soil are an integral part of the system and assist the microbiological and physio-chemical activities occurring within the soil to renovate the sewage effluent through removal and utilization of the nutrients applied. The average nutrient composition of the corn silage and reed canarygrass harvested during 1970 is given in Tables 16-5 and 16-6. The crops harvested from the two-inch-per-week irrigated areas are usually higher in nitrogen and phosphorus than the control crops. As indicated in Table 16-5 the differences are not large. This is partially due to the fact that the control area receives a normal application of commercial fertilizer each year. For instance, the silage corn control area has received 600 to 1000 pounds of a 10-10-10 fertilizer per acre annually.

Table 16-6. Average nutrient composition of reed canarygrass irrigated with two inches of effluent during 1970

Nutrient	First cut	Second cut	Third cut	Weighted average
	%	%	%	%
Nitrogen	4.06	3.44	3.34	3.69
Phosphorus	0.44	0.51	0.64	0.50
Potassium	2.50	2.26	1.63	2.23
Calcium	0.39	0.40	0.42	0.40
Magnesium	0.36	0.40	0.32	0.36
Chloride	1.50	1.64	0.94	1.57
	μg/g	μg/g	μg/g	μg/g
Sodium	331	329	228	309
Boron	8	8	8	8

Table 16-7. Quantities of nutrients removed by reed canarygrass irrigated with two inches of effluent during 1970

Nutrient	First cut	Second cut	Third cut	Total
		pounds per acre		
Nitrogen	196.5	134.2	77.5	408.2
Phosphorus	21.3	19.9	14.8	56.0
Potassium	121.0	88.1	37.8	246.9
Calcium	18.9	15.6	9.7	44.2
Magnesium	17.4	15.6	7.4	40.4
Chloride	72.6	64.0	21.8	158.4
Sodium	1.6	1.3	0.5	3.4
Boron	0.04	0.03	0.02	0.09

Nutrients Removed By Crop Harvest

The contribution of the higher plants as renovators of the wastewater is readily evident from Tables 16-7 and 16-8 where the quantities of nutrients, expressed in pounds per acre, removed in the 1970 crop harvest are given. These data indicate that the vegetative cover can contribute substantially to the durability of a "living filter" system particularly where a crop is harvested and utilized. At the two-inch-per-week level of effluent irrigation the two corn varieties removed 148 and 160 pounds of nitrogen and 35 and 43 pounds of phosphorus. Reed canarygrass, which is a perennial grass, was even more efficient in that it removed 408 pounds of nitrogen and 56 pounds of phosphorus. The difference is primarily due to the fact that the grass is already established and actively growing in early spring even before the corn is planted.

The amounts of nutrients removed annually vary with the amount of wastewater applied, amount of rainfall, length of the growing season, and the number of cuttings of the reed canarygrass. The annual variation in the amounts of nitrogen and phosphorus removed by the two types of crops (annual row crop vs. perennial grass) is shown in Figures 16-1 and 16-2.

The efficiency of crops as renovating agents can be assessed by computing a "removal efficiency" expressed as the ratio of the weight of the nutrient removed in the harvested crop to the weight of the same nutrient applied in the wastewater. Renovation efficiencies for the silage corn and the reed canarygrass crops harvested in 1970 are given in Table 16-9. At the one-inch-per-week level of application of wastewater, the two varieties of corn silage removed nutrients equivalent to 242 and 334 percent of the total applied nitrogen, 190 and 230 percent of the applied phosphorus, and 195 and 280 percent of the applied potassium. At the two-inch-per-week level, both varieties

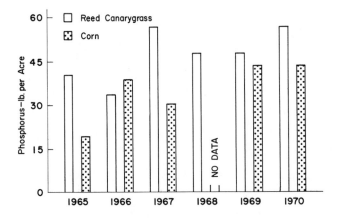

Figure 16-1. Amounts of phosphorus removed in the harvest of corn and reed canary-grass crops during the period 1965 to 1970

of corn silage removed more than 100 percent of the applied nitrogen, phosphorus, and potassium.

During 1970 the reed canarygrass removed only 75 percent of the applied nitrogen, and 63 percent of the applied phosphorus. These are not typical annual values for the 1965-70 period. During the period 1965 to 1969 only sewage effluent was applied. In 1970 irrigation applications included a combination of sewage effluent and injected liquid digested sludge. During the period 1965-69, 1581

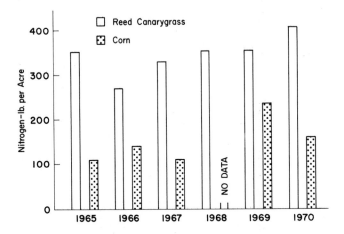

Figure 16-2. Amount of nitrogen removed in the harvest of corn and reed canarygrass crops during the period 1965 to 1970.

Table 16-8. Quantities of nutrients removed by two varieties of corn silage receiving various levels of effluent during 1970

Nutrient	Variety and amount of effluent applied per week					
	Corn silage, Pa. 890-S			Corn silage, Pa. 602-A		
	0	1	2	0	1	2
	pounds per acre			pounds per acre		
Nitrogen	129.4	126.1	148.4	117.5	174.4	160.6
Phosphorus	24.3	29.4	34.7	18.6	35.6	42.8
Potassium	105.6	95.7	113.1	91.6	137.1	129.3
Calcium	41.2	27.4	28.5	39.9	41.4	27.0
Magnesium	16.3	21.5	23.7	14.1	27.6	23.2
Chloride	21.6	35.2	37.2	17.1	44.6	46.4
Sodium	0.14	1.66	1.90	0.11	2.13	2.39
Boron	0.06	0.08	0.08	0.06	0.10	0.09

Table 16-9. Renovation efficiency of the silage corn and reed canarygrass crops harvested in 1970

	Variety and amount of effluent applied						
Nutrient	Corn silage, Pa. 890-S		Corn silage, Pa. 602-A		Reed canarygrass	
	1	2	1	2		2
	%	%	%	%		%
Nitrogen	242	134	334	145		75
Phosphorus	190	116	230	143		63
Potassium	195	114	280	130		117
Calcium	25	16	38	15		9
Magnesium	41	28	53	27		19
Chloride	20	11	26	14		20
Sodium	1	1	2	1		1
Boron	8	4	10	4		2

pounds of nitrogen were applied and the harvested reed canarygrass removed 1663 pounds, equivalent to a 105 percent renovation efficiency. In 1970, an additional 546 pounds of nitrogen were applied making the total 2127 pounds applied in 536 inches of wastewater. Since only 408 pounds were removed by crop harvesting the overall six-year period renovation efficiency was lowered to 97.5 percent.

During the same period, 797 pounds of phosphorus were applied in the wastewater and 279 pounds removed in crop harvesting resulting in an overall renovation efficiency of 35 percent. Annual renovation efficiencies have varied from 24 to 63 percent for reed canarygrass irrigated at the two-inch-per-week level. For corn silage it has varied from 39 to 230 percent for the one-inch-per-week level and from 21 to 143 percent for the two-inch-per-week level. Hence, it is obvious that some process other than utilization by the vegetative cover must be used to assure the removal of this key eutrophic nutrient. This additional renovation and removal of phosphorus is usually accomplished by way of the large fixing capacity of most agricultural soils for phosphorus. At the Penn State sites, the Hublersburg soils, which range in texture from a silt loam to a silty clay loam, have persistently and effectively removed the phosphorus.

The fates of phosphorus and nitrogen on the reed canarygrass area irrigated with municipal wastewater at two inches per week since 1965 are shown in Table 16-10. After six years of applying chlorinated effluent, 797 pounds of phosphorus and 2127 pounds of nitrogen had been applied to each acre in 536 inches of effluent. Harvested crops removed 279 pounds of phosphorus, the equivalent of 35 percent of the amount added. Since the concentration of phosphorus in the percolate at the four-foot soil depth was only 0.05 mg/l and was no greater than that in an unirrigated adjacent forest area, the net percolation losses of phosphorus from the wastewater treated areas were assumed to be proportional only to the excess percolation induced by the added wastewater. Further, since precipitation always exceeds potential evapotranspiration on an annual basis, the wastewater was assumed to be totally recharged. On the basis of these assumptions, the net percolation loss of phosphorus from the waste-

Table 16-10. Phosphorus and nitrogen balances for reed canarygrass irrigated with effluent at two inches per week during the period 1965 to 1970

Period	Amount applied		Removed		Retained
	Wastewater	Nutrient	By crop	By leaching	By soil
	inches	lbs/acre	lbs/acre	lbs/acre	lbs/acre
1965-70	536	797(P)	279(P)	6.4(P)	512(P)
		2127(N)	2073(N)	452(N)	−398(N)

water-irrigated areas was calculated to be 6.4 pounds per acre during the six-year period, or only 0.8 percent of the amount applied. Thus the soil with its strong adsorptive capacity for phosphorus, together with the crop harvests, has persistently removed 99.2 percent of the added phosphorus.

Nitrogen removals by the soil and crop system have also been equally efficient. Over the six-year period 2127 pounds of nitrogen were added to each acre. Protein removed in the harvested reed canarygrass was equivalent to 2073 pounds of nitrogen per acre. Kjeldahl nitrogen content of the upper foot of soil was approximately 5000 pounds per acre. Average concentration of nitrate-N in the percolate at the four-foot soil depth during the six-year period was 3.5 mg/l in the effluent-irrigated areas and 0.2 mg/l in the control areas. On the basis of the same assumptions used above, the excess percolate from the 536 inches of wastewater applied per acre would have carried a total of 452 pounds of nitrogen into the groundwater. This quantity is 398 pounds in excess of the 54 pounds per acre difference between the amount of nitrogen added in the wastewater and the amount removed in the harvested crops and could easily have been derived from the large amounts of native soil nitrogen. Thus the reed canarygrass was effective in removing 97.5 percent of the added nitrogen.

Forest Responses

Red Pine

Experimental plots were established in a red pine plantation in 1963. These plots have been irrigated with sewage effluent during the past 10 years at rates of one inch and two inches per week during the growing season (April to November). The plantation was established in 1939 with the trees planted at a spacing of eight by eight feet. In 1963 the average tree diameter at breast height was 6.8 inches and average height was 35 feet.

Diameter and height growth measurements were made annually on sample trees selected at random on each irrigated plot and on adjacent control areas. Average annual height growth for the period 1963 to 1970 is given in Table 16-11. Irrigation with sewage effluent at both rates produced slight increases in height growth during the first two years. This slight increase in height growth has been maintained on the plot receiving one inch per week. However, on the plot receiving two inches per week, height growth continually decreased

Table 16-11. Average annual terminal height growth of red pine irrigated with sewage effluent

Treatment	Average annual height growth
	feet
Irrigated – 1 inch per week (1963-70)	1.8
Control	1.4
Irrigated – 2 inches per week (1963-68)	1.6
Control	1.7

up to 1968 when high winds during a wet snowfall completely felled every tree on the plot.

Diameter growth was computed from annual circumference measurements with dendrometer bands. In addition increment cores were taken in 1972 from sample trees in all areas. The actual measurements of average radius growth taken from the increment cores indicate that the previous diameter growth data reported (Sopper, 1971) which were based upon dendrometer band measurements of tree circumferences were incorrect. Average annual diameter growth based on increment core measurements is given in Table 16-12. Irrigation at the one-inch-per-week level increased the average annual diameter growth (1963-68). In addition, during the sixth year (1968) of irrigation the needles of the pines being irrigated at the higher rate began to turn yellow. Boron toxicity was suspected since other investigators (Stone and Baird, 1956) have previously reported that applications of 1.1 pounds of boron per acre were sufficient to induce toxicity symptoms. Approximately four pounds of boron per acre are applied annually in the sewage effluent. However, foliar analyses indicated that there was no significant difference between boron concentrations of the needles of trees on the irrigated (33 micrograms per gram) and control (23 micrograms per gram) trees.

White Spruce

Two experimental plots were established in a sparse white spruce plantation on an abandoned old field area. The trees in 1963 ranged from three to eight feet in height. One plot has been irrigated with sewage effluent during the past 10 years at the rate of two inches per week, while the second plot has been maintained as a control. Height growth measurements have been made annually. In 1972, all tree diameters were measured and increment cores taken to determine the average annual diameter growth.

Total height of the trees was measured in August 1972. Average height of the trees on the irrigated plot was 20 feet and ranged from

Table **16-12.** Average annual diameter growth of red pine irrigated with sewage effluent

Treatment	Average annual diameter growth
	inches
Irrigated — 1 inch per week (1963-72)	0.17
Control	0.06
Irrigated — 2 inches per week (1963-68)	0.06
Control	0.07

12 to 25 feet. The average height of the trees on the control plot was nine feet and ranged from 8 to 15 feet. Over the 10-year period average annual height growth was 18 inches on the irrigated areas and five inches on the control areas, representing a 360 percent increase as a result of sewage effluent irrigation.

Average diameter of trees on the irrigated plot was 3.7 inches, on the control plot it was 1.1 inches. Measurements taken from increment cores indicated that the average annual growth on the irrigated trees was 0.40 inch and on the control trees 0.18 inch, representing a 122 percent increase.

Old Field Herbaceous Vegetation

The predominant ground cover on the old field area of the spruce plantation was poverty grass (*Danthonia spicata* Beauv.), goldenrod (*Solidago spp.* Ait.), and dewberry (*Rubus flagellaris* Willd.).

Permanent transect plots were established in 1964 and measured annually to determine the effects of sewage effluent irrigation on the herbaceous ground cover in terms of species composition, height growth, dry matter production and percentage areal cover.

Average annual dry matter production during the 10-year period was 5457 pounds per acre on the irrigated plot and 1810 pounds per acre on the control plot (Table 16-13). This represents an average annual increase of 201 percent. Annual increases ranged from 100 to 350 percent.

Species composition of the ground vegetation has changed considerably during the 10 years as a result of sewage effluent irrigation. Several species which were predominant prior to wastewater irrigation have been drastically reduced in number or have disappeared completely. For instance, goldenrod (*Solidago spp.*) which had 155,090 stems per acre in 1963 was reduced to 13,612 stems per acre by 1972. White aster (*Aster pilosus*) which had 122,970 stems per acre in 1963 was not present on the site in 1972. The predominant species on the irrigated plot was clearweed (*Pilea pumila* L.) which

Table 16-13. Average annual dry matter production of herbaceous vegetation in the oil field area

Year	Irrigated plot	Control plot
	lbs/acre	lbs/acre
1963	3381	1470
1964	7607	1763
1965	5672	1675
1966	6417	1435
1967	4075	2010
1968	6044	1550
1969	5909	2015
1970	5505	1605
1971	–	–
1972	5007	2770
Mean	5457	1810

covered more than 75 percent of the plot with approximately 19 million stems per acre. This species is typical of shaded moist sites.

Species composition changes are illustrated in Table 16-14 based on measurements made in 1972. The control plot is representative of preirrigation vegetation conditions.

The average height of the tallest plant species on the irrigated plot was 5.3 feet in comparison to 1.8 feet on the control plot. While the irrigated plot had a complete dense vegetative cover approximately 10 percent of the control was barren of vegetation.

Table 16-14. Predominate herbaceous vegetation species on the irrigated and control plots of the white spruce area in 1972

Species	Irrigated plot		Control plot	
	Percent cover	Average height	Percent cover	Average height
	%	feet	%	feet
Goldenrod (*Solidago juncea*)	<1	2.8	5	1.8
Aster (*Aster spp.*)	0	–	5	1.1
Dewberry (*Rubus flagellaris*)	0	–	40	0.8
Strawberry (*Fragaria vesca*)	<5	0.9	10	0.5
Poverty grass (*Danthonia spicata*)	0	–	20	0.3
Everlasting (*Antennaria spicata*)	0	–	5	0.1
Goldenrod (*S. rugosa, S. graminifolia, S. juncea*)	<5	5.3	0	–
Milkweed (*Asclepias rubra*)	<5	5.1	0	–
Indian hemp (*Apocynum cannabinum*)	<5	3.3	0	–
Night shade (*Solanum dulcamara*)	10	2.3	0	–
Clearweed (*Pilea pumila*)	75	1.5	0	–

Coniferous Tree Seedling Growth Responses

In 1965 eight coniferous tree species were planted in an old field area to determine which species might be best suited for sites to be used as disposal areas for sewage effluent. One- and two-year-old seedlings of European larch (*Larix decidua*), Japanese larch (*Larix leptolepis*), white pine (*Pinus strobus*), red pine, white spruce, pitch pine (*Pinus rigida*), Austrian pine (*Pinus nigra*), and Norway spruce (*Picea abies*) were planted in a randomized block design with three blocks irrigated with two inches of sewage effluent per week and three blocks maintained as a control. Each block contained 10 trees of each species or a total of 80 trees per block. Average first-year survival on the irrigated plots was 88 percent and on the control plots, 52 percent. At the termination of the study in 1970 survival percentage on the irrigated plots was still 88 percent, whereas the survival percentage on the control plots had decreased to 41 percent. The total height growth of surviving tree seedlings as of 1970 is given in Table 16-15.

Results indicate that European and Japanese larch and white pine had the greatest growth response to sewage effluent irrigation

Hardwood Species Growth Responses

Mixed hardwood forests, consisting primarily of oak species, have been irrigated with sewage effluent at rates ranging from one inch to four inches per week and for periods ranging from the growing season (28 weeks) to the entire year (52 weeks). Principal species are white oak (*Quercus alba* L.), chestnut oak (*Q. prinus* L.), black oak (*Q. velutina* L.), red oak (*Q. rubra* L.), scarlet oak (*Q. coccinea* Muench.), red maple (*Acer rubrum*), and hickory (*Carya spp.*).

Average annual diameter growth in various treatment areas from increment core measurements in 1972 is given in Table 16-16. One-inch-per-week applications produced only slight increases in diameter

Table 16-15. Total height growth of surviving tree seedlings during the period 1965 to 1970

Species	Irrigated plots		Control plots	
	Survival	Height	Survival	Height
	%	feet	%	feet
European larch	23	8.7	0	—
Japanese larch	17	8.4	0	—
White pine	70	6.3	17	2.6
Red pine	40	5.4	20	2.0
White spruce	30	4.3	3	2.8
Pitch pine	3	3.8	3	1.4
Austrian pine	13	3.6	13	2.1
Norway spruce	47	3.6	7	1.6

Table 16-16. Average annual diameter growth in hardwood forests irrigated with sewage effluent

Weekly irrigation amount	Average diameter growth Control	Irrigated
inches	inch	inch
1[a]	0.16	0.18
2[b]	0.13	0.22
4[c]	0.15	0.21

a. Irrigated with one inch of sewage effluent weekly during growing season from 1963 to 1972.
b. Irrigated with two inches of sewage effluent weekly during the entire year from 1965 to 1972.
c. Irrigated with four inches of sewage effluent weekly during the growing season only from 1964 to 1967; during the dormant season only from 1968 to 1971; and with two inches of effluent weekly during the growing season in 1972.

growth on the older trees (50-70 yrs.); however, the two- and four-inch-per-week levels in a younger stand (30-50 yrs.) resulted in 69 and 40 percent increases, respectively. These values pertain primarily to the oak species. Some of the other hardwood species present on the plots have responded to a greater extent. For instance, increment core measurements made on young red maple and sugar maple (*A. saccharum*), indicate that the average annual diameter growth during the past 10 years has been 0.43 inch on the trees irrigated with one inch of effluent per week in comparison to 0.10 inch on control trees, a 330 percent increase in average annual diameter growth. Similarly, increment core measurements made on aspen (*Populus tremuloides*) irrigated with two inches of effluent weekly during the growing season indicated that the irrigated trees had an average annual diameter growth of 0.47 inch in comparison to 0.24 inch for unirrigated trees, a 96 percent increase in growth. Saplings which averaged 0.65 inch in diameter in 1963 increased in diameter to an average of 5.3 inches on the irrigated areas in comparison to 3.1 inches on the control areas.

Tree Seedling Reproduction
Mil-acre plots were established in 1964 in the hardwood forest irrigated with one inch of effluent weekly. These plots have been measured annually to determine the effect of wastewater irrigation on tree seedling reproduction and growth of herbaceous vegetation. Measurements made in 1972 after 10 years of sewage effluent irrigation indicate a drastic reduction in the number of tree seedlings present in the irrigated area. The initial survey in 1964 indicated about 15,800 tree seedlings per acre in the control area with a slight reduction to 13,600 in 1972. However, in 1964 (the second year of irrigation)

there were 14,500 tree seedlings per acre present in the irrigated area and only 1,830 in 1972. No conclusive evidence is yet available to explain these results. These results may be partially due to the fact that effluent irrigation stimulates leaf growth which produces a more dense canopy and reduces light intensity at the forest floor. Average light intensity under the canopy in the irrigated area was less than 50 percent of that under the control plot canopy.

A similar reduction was also found in the number of herbaceous plants in the irrigated area. The initial survey in 1964 indicated about 86,333 stems per acre, whereas in 1972 there were only 14,800 stems per acre. On the control area, the 1964 survey indicated 63,170 stems per acre in comparison to 25,000 stems per acre in 1972.

Mortality

In 1972 a survey was made in the irrigated and control forested areas at the Gamelands site to determine the effect of eight years of sewage effluent irrigation on mortality. Mortality was defined as all standing dead trees. The irrigated plot received four inches of sewage effluent weekly during the growing season only from 1964 to 1967; during the dormant season only from 1968 to 1971; and two inches of effluent weekly during the growing season in 1972. The results of the survey are given in Table 16-17. Results indicated that there was no difference in mortality between the irrigated and control areas. There was, however, a large difference in the number of living trees per acre, particularly in the two-inch diameter class. Unirrigated forest areas averaged 290 trees per acre in the two-inch diameter class compared to only 70 trees per acre in the irrigated forest areas.

Although many of these young saplings are lost through natural suppression, a considerable number are lost in the irrigated areas

Table 16-17. Population and mortality in forested stands in control plots and plots irrigated with sewage effluent for eight years

Diameter class	Living trees		Mortality	
	Irrigated	Control	Irrigated	Control
inches	stems per acre		stems per acre	
2	70	290	55	42
4	100	110	27	32
6	40	80	20	5
8	60	80	2.5	2.5
10	40	50	–	5
12	30	25	–	–
14	2	7	–	–
16	5	–	–	–
Total	347	642	104.5	106.5

through ice breakage during winter irrigation. The 1972 survey results indicated that approximately 52 stems per acre showed visible ice damage in the irrigated areas in comparison to 7.5 stems per acre in the control areas. Seventy-five percent of these trees were in the two-inch diameter class and the remainder in the four-inch diameter class. The species most susceptible to ice damage was red maple. A reasonable amount of ice damage must be expected if disposal systems are to operate throughout the year. In northern latitudes where the temperatures drop below freezing, the system must rely more on the adsorptive capacity of the soil and less on the microbial activity and vegetation for renovation of the wastewater. During the winter period, forested areas provide better infiltration conditions. They also provide larger phosphorus-adsorptive capacity due to the acid conditions associated with forest soils. Ice damage can be minimized through the proper design of the spray-irrigation system and the use of low-trajectory rotating sprinklers (Parizek *et al.,* 1967; Myers, 1973).

A comparison of the results of the 1972 survey made in the effluent-irrigated forest areas with the results of forest surveys (Melton, 1972) of several mixed hardwood stands on a variety of sites in central Pennsylvania indicates that 10 years of effluent irrigation have produced no great differences. The average number of living trees, five inches in diameter and greater, in the effluent-irrigated forests was 177 stems per acre in comparison to an average of 155 stems per acre in several natural mixed hardwood stands. Mortality of trees, five inches in diameter and greater, in the effluent-irrigated forests was 22.5 stems per acre in comparison to an average 21 stems per acre in several natural mixed hardwood stands.

Annual Nutrient Balance

Foliar samples were collected annually up to 1967 from the hardwoods, red pine, white spruce, and herbaceous vegetation to determine the extent of utilization of the nutrient elements applied in the sewage effluent. The nutrient element contents of the vegetation foliage based on samples collected in August 1967 are given in Table 16-18. Average concentrations of N, B, P, Mg, Cu, and Na were almost consistently higher on the irrigated plots than on the control plots. Conversely, average concentrations of K, Mn, Al, and Zn were generally lower on the irrigated plots. Concentrations of Ca and Fe were highly variable and indicated no distinct trends. It is therefore obvious that the forest vegetation is contributing to the renovation of the percolating effluent; however, its order of magnitude is difficult to estimate because the annual storage of nutrients in the woody tissue and the extent of recycling of nutrients in the forest litter are ex-

Table 16-18. Average chemical content of the tree foliage and herbaceous vegetation from samples collected in 1967

Plot	N	P	K	Ca	Mg	Mn	Fe	Cu	B	Al	Zn	Na
	Percent of dry weight					µg/g						
Hardwoods 1-inch												
Irrigated	2.45	0.22	0.86	1.00	0.14	1500	88	8	81	68	26	15
Control	2.20	0.18	0.87	0.99	0.08	1845	80	7	49	66	27	16
Hardwoods 2-inch												
Irrigated	2.97	0.29	0.93	0.77	0.19	1830	81	7	117	50	33	13
Control	2.20	0.18	1.13	1.01	0.09	2725	83	8	65	80	25	16
Red pine 1-inch												
Irrigated	1.62	0.17	0.58	0.19	0.09	942	41	4	28	142	33	44
Control	1.15	0.16	0.53	0.29	0.09	1103	53	4	19	496	45	8
Red pine 2-inch												
Irrigated	2.17	0.13	0.52	0.26	0.10	947	58	4	33	97	32	114
Control	1.33	0.15	0.61	0.24	0.08	925	54	3	23	394	40	11
White spruce 2-inch												
Irrigated	2.19	0.29	0.67	0.84	0.12	517	90	6	38	87	35	117
Control	1.48	0.19	0.71	0.93	0.13	834	57	5	26	100	95	10
Old field vegetation 2-inch												
Irrigated	3.28	0.45	2.34	1.23	0.44	235	379	19	39	825	94	473
Control	1.30	0.16	1.19	1.09	0.13	642	400	13	35	958	95	28

tremely difficult to measure. Although considerable amounts of nutrients may be taken up by trees during the growing season, many of these nutrients are redeposited annually in leaf and needle litter rather than being hauled away as in the case of harvested agronomic crops. Tree leaves are by far the largest single source of forest soil organic matter, and their annual contribution of mineral elements to the soil greatly exceeds that of all other tree parts combined.

A comparison between the annual uptake of nutrients by an agronomic crop (silage corn) and a hardwood forest is given in Table 16-19. It is obvious that trees are not as efficient renovating agents as agronomic crops. Whereas harvesting a corn silage crop removes 145 percent of the nitrogen applied in the sewage effluent, the trees only remove 39 percent most of which is returned to the soil by leaf fall. Similarly only 19 percent of the phosphorus applied in the sewage effluent is taken up by trees in comparison to 143 percent by the corn silage crop.

Problems of Forest Irrigation

Three potential problems that may be encountered with effluent irrigation in forested areas are (1) ice damage, (2) windthrow, and (3) bark damage by sprinkler spray. The ice breakage problem has already been discussed. Bark damage by sprinkler spray can be avoided if sprinkler nozzle pressures are operated at or less than 55 p.s.i. Nozzle pressures for the solid set system used in the forests on the Penn State project are approximately 50 p.s.i. Little tree damage has been observed even on small trees within a two-foot radius of the sprinkler head.

Windthrow of individual trees and large numbers of trees (the one-acre red pine plot irrigated with two inches of effluent weekly)

Table 16-19. Annual uptake of nutrients by a silage corn crop and a hardwood forest irrigated with two inches of effluent weekly during 1970

Nutrient	Corn silage Pa. 602-A	Renovation efficiency[a]	Hardwood forest[b]	Renovation efficiency
	lbs/acre	%	lbs/acre	%
N	161	145	84	39
P	42	143	8	19
K	129	130	26	22
Ca	27	15	22	9
Mg	23	27	5	4

a. Percentage of the element applied in the sewage effluent that is utilized and removed by the vegetation.
b. Calculations based on an average annual leaf fall of 2825 pounds of dry matter per acre (Lutz and Chandler, 1946).

has been the greatest problem. Weekly irrigation of sewage effluent at rates of one and two inches per week keeps the soil moisture status near field capacity and hence encourages the development of shallow tree root systems. In November of 1968, following a weekly application of two inches of sewage effluent, a heavy snowfall accompanied by strong winds resulted in the complete blow down of the one-acre plot. Since then several individual trees have also been windthrown in the mixed hardwood forests. Most of these trees have been adjacent to natural forest openings, agricultural fields, or power line rights-of-way. It appears that this problem could be minimized if an unirrigated buffer zone 50 to 100 feet wide were left on the windward side of any irrigated forest area. This buffer zone would provide a wind break against prevailing winds.

Conclusions

Sewage effluent irrigation during the past 10 years on cropland and in forestland has, for the most part, produced beneficial vegetation responses. Crop yields and tree growth were significantly increased. In addition the value of the vegetation as a renovating agent has been demonstrated to be a vital part of the system. For year-around operations a combination of cropland and forestland will provide the greatest flexibility in operating a system using the "living filter" concept.

Acknowledgments
Research reported here is part of the program of the Waste Water Renovation and Conservation Project of the Institute for Research on Land and Water Resources, and Hatch Projects No. 1481 and 1809 of the Agricultural Experiment Station, The Pennsylvania State University, University Park, Pennsylvania. Portions of this research were supported by funds from Demonstration Project Grant WPD 95-01 received initially from the Division of Water Supply and Pollution Control of the Department of Health, Education, and Welfare and subsequently from the Federal Water Pollution Control Administration, Department of the Interior. Partial support was also provided by the Office of Water Resources Research, USDI, as authorized under the Water Resources Research Act of 1964, Public Law 88-379 and by the Pinchot Institute for Environmental Forestry Research, Forest Service, USDA.

Literature Cited

Kardos, L. T. 1971. Recycling sewage effluent through the soil and its associated biosystems, *Proc. Int. Symp. on Ident. and Measurement of Environmental Pollutants*, pp. 119-123, Ottawa, Ontario, Canada.

Lutz, H. J. and R. E. Chandler. 1946. *Forest Soils.* John Wiley and Sons, Inc. New York, 514 pp.

Melton, R. E. 1972. Personal communication.

Myers, E. A. 1973. Sprinkler irrigation systems: design and operation criteria. *Recycling Treated Municipal Wastewater and Sludge through Forest and Cropland.* The Pennsylvania State University Press, University Park, Pa.

Parizek, R. R., L. T. Kardos, W. E. Sopper, E. A. Myers, D. E. Davis, M. A. Farrell, and J. B. Nesbitt. 1967. Waste water renovation and conservation. Penn State Studies No. 23, 71 pp.

Sopper, W. E. 1971. Effects of trees and forests in neutralizing waste. In *Trees and Forests in an Urbanizing Environment.* Coop. Ext. Service, Univ. of Massachusetts, pp. 43-57.

Stone, E. L. and G. Baird. 1956. Boron level and boron toxicity in red and white pine. *Journ. of Forestry* 54:11-12.

17
Anatomical and Physical Properties of Red Oak and Red Pine Irrigated with Municipal Wastewater

W. K. Murphey, R. L. Brisbin, W. J. Young, and B. E. Cutter*

The amelioration of the mineral content of treated sewage effluent by the forest has been demonstrated (Sopper, 1971). The utility of the forest as a receptor for this effluent could be increased if beneficial tree response occurred. This forest could become an important fiber source if the irrigation resulted in increased growth, more uniform fibers, or fibers which had attributes sought by the papermakers. Primarily, the papermaker would like to have long, thin-walled cells with which to work. With this in mind, two studies were established in which the individual cells produced by effluent-irrigated trees were measured.

Red pine (*Pinus resinosa* Ait.) plantations were irrigated, beginning in 1963, (Table 17-1) with effluent throughout the growing season at rates of one and two inches per week from spraying heads 42 feet above the forest floor. Another two-inch application, beginning in 1964, utilized spraying heads on five-foot risers. Specific gravity, mean annual increment and tracheid dimensions were measured from the growth rings developed throughout the period of irrigation and compared to those of nonirrigated wood grown during the same time or wood grown during a similar period immediately prior to irrigation.

Red oak (*Quercus rubra* L.) trees irrigated throughout the year beginning in 1965, at a rate of two inches per week were sampled to determine if irrigation altered the anatomy of these trees. Comparisons were made with wood in the same trees laid down prior to irrigation.

Procedure

Selection of Sample Trees

Red Pine Study. Eight red pine trees were randomly selected in 1966 from one-acre plantation plots irrigated with one inch or two inches

*School of Forest Resources, The Pennsylvania State University

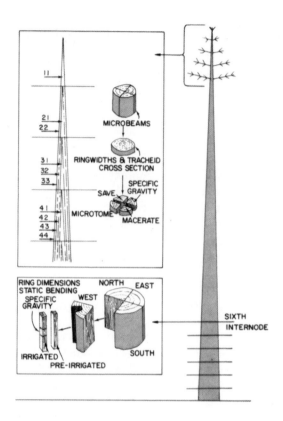

Figure 17-1. Sampling pattern of red pine 28 years old at the time of harvest

per week of municipal wastewater. Control trees were obtained from adjacent untreated plots. Each tree was divided as shown in Figure 17-1. The crown wood and stem wood were treated as separate populations. Mechanical properties of the wood were measured using American Society for Testing Material Standards (Murphey and Brisbin, 1970).

Red Oak Study. At the end of the fifth growing season after initiation of treatment, six dominant or codominant red oak trees were randomly chosen from the natural stand irrigated at a rate of two inches per week throughout the year. Also, six control trees were cut from an adjacent nonirrigated area. Treated trees ranged in age from 30 to 58 years. The felled trees were cut at 4, 10, 20, 30, and 40 foot heights. Discs were removed and the north face marked for ori-

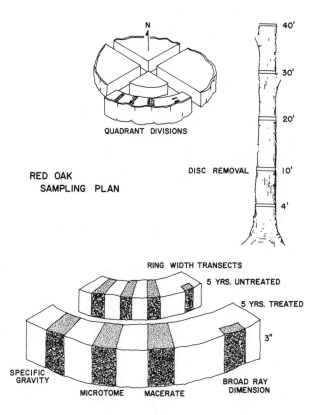

Figure 17-2. Sampling pattern of red oak trees

entation. Material was stored at 0°F until sectioned as shown in Figure 17-2.

Cell Dimensions

The same procedure was utilized for all of the fiber measurements. Cell lengths were measured from macerated samples removed from each growth ring. Splinters were cooked at 135°C for 35 minutes in a solution of triethylene glycol and paratoluene sulfonic acid (Burkhart, 1966). After maceration, complete fiber separation was accomplished by shaking the sample in a container with distilled water and glass beads. The individual fibers were washed thoroughly then randomly retrieved and mounted in a glycerin jel on glass slides. A micro-projector was used to project each slide on a screen using

Technical Association of Pulp and Paper Industries (TAPPI) T232-SU68, except that each fiber was measured. Twenty-five tracheids were sampled for each growth ring position.

Cross Sections
Cell cross sections and cell wall thickness measurements were made from microtome sections prepared by dehydrating the designated block by passing it through increasing concentrations of absolute alcohol, prior to embedding in celloidin and sectioning. Sections 10-micrometers thick were cut, and celloidin removed by washing with ether. The sections were then stained with safranin and fast green and mounted. A compound microscope equipped with a filar micrometer was used to obtain the 25 measurements made for each growth ring and cell element investigated for each quadrant.

Ring Width Measurements
Individual ring widths were measured on green discs using a De Rouen Dendrochronograph. Two measurements at right angles to each other were made across the diameter of each disc, resulting in four ring width measurements for each disc. Data reported are the mean annual increment values.

Specific Gravity Determination
The specific gravity or density of each growth ring was determined by using one or two of the several techniques available. The maximum moisture content procedure (Smith, 1954) or the standard pycnometric procedure was used for the small material obtained from some of the growth rings, particularly the red pine material. The wider growth rings found in the red oak were measured using the ovendry weight-ovendry volume by water immersion technique. Thirty-two observations were made for each mean red pine density value. One hundred and twenty measurements were represented in each mean calculated in the red oak study.

Abnormal Wood
The procedures outlined above were to insure that no abnormal wood (compression or juvenile wood in red pine or tension wood in red oak) existed in the samples. Static bending tests, specific gravity determinations and shrinkage values support the contention that no abnormal wood existed in any of the material sampled.

Control Material
In both the red pine and red oak studies specific gravity determinations of the wood grown during the period prior to irrigation indicated

that the mean densities of the trees grown on the treated and un-treated areas were not the same. Since this control period density was not comparable for differences existing prior to treatment for trees located in designated plots, data from control trees were not used. The material that was then used as a control was that wood grown prior to treatment in each of the treated trees. Thus, all data are within tree comparisons. The exception, of course, is the crown wood data where comparisons had to be made between material obtained from treated and untreated red pine trees.

Results

Each variable measured was subjected to analysis of variance. If a difference existed between treatments at the $P \geq 0.05$ level, Duncan's Modified (Bayesian) least significant difference test (1965) was conducted. The results are shown in the following Tables.

Red pine crown wood response to one-inch irrigation is the most striking (Table 17-1). Although the plot O1 specific gravity is significantly less than all others except plot O2, the ring width and tracheid length are significantly greater than any of those of any other treatment. Tracheid diameters are comparable to those developed in the two-inch overhead irrigation treatment plot while cell wall thickness is comparable to the two-inch control.

Density is definitely affected by the irrigation with the municipal wastewater. Also notable is the median position of the specific gravity of the plot receiving two inches per week on the undergrowth. Perhaps this is a development associated with the relatively high mineral content of the irrigation water placed on the forest floor rather than on the canopy.

The red pine stem wood means are listed in Table 17-2. Comparisons are made only between irrigation and pre-irrigation stem wood within plots. Growth rate and tracheid length prior to irrigation did not differ from those during irrigation. Specific gravity for O1 and U2 plots increased due to irrigation. The O2 plot receiving 2 inches per week had significantly lower specific gravity. Generally tracheid diameter increased and cell wall thickness decreased when the red pine was irrigated. Differences were statistically significant except for the tracheids from the red pine receiving 1 inch per week and the latewood of the trees from the U2 plot.

The red oak data shown in Table 17-3 demonstrated the more complex anatomy of this ring-porous species. Those average percent change values listed are those where differences existed at the

Table 17-1. Physical and anatomical properties of red pine crown wood. Treatment mean separation at the P ≥ 0.05 level by Duncan's new multiple range test

Specific gravity[1]		Specific gravity[2]		Ring width		Tracheid length		Tracheid diameter		Cell wall thickness	
Plot[3]	Mean[4]	Plot	Mean	Plot	Mean	Plot	Mean	Plot	Mean	Plot	Mean
					mm		mm		μm		μm
O1	0.335[a]	O1	0.333[a]	C1	3.40	C2	1.51[a]	C1	18.62[a]	O2	1.64[a]
O2	0.338[a]	O2	0.334[a]	C2	4.05	O2	1.51[a]	U2	18.91[a]	U2	1.68[ab]
U2	0.353	U2	0.351	U2	4.49[a]	C1	1.53[a]	C2	19.00[a]	C1	1.70[ab]
C1	0.369[b]	C1	0.361	O2	4.56[a]	U2	1.54[a]	O2	19.62[ab]	C2	1.75[bc]
C2	0.378[b]	C2	0.377	O1	4.83	O1	1.63	O1	20.61[b]	O1	1.77[c]

1. Computed by the maximum moisture content method.
2. Computed by the pycnometric method.
3. Plot O1 – 1 in. irrigated (overhead); plot O2 – 2 in. irrigated (overhead); plot U2 – 2 in. irrigated (under canopy); plot C1 – 1 in. control; plot C2 – 2 in. control.
4. Any two means marked with the same superscript letter are not significantly different.

Table 17-2. Physical and anatomical properties of red pine stem-formed wood grown on irrigated plots

Plot	Period	Specific gravity	Mean annual increment[1]	Tracheid length	Tracheid diameter Earlywood	Tracheid diameter Latewood	Cell wall thickness Earlywood	Cell wall thickness Latewood
				mm	μm	μm	μm	μm
O1	Prior to irrigation[2]	0.401	2.81a	2.93a	38.00a	34.41a	2.37a	6.12
O1	Irrigated[3]	0.408	2.99a	2.63a	38.81a	34.82a	2.35a	5.79
O2	Prior to irrigation	0.379	2.81b	3.07b	37.36	33.73	2.00	5.10
O2	Irrigated	0.367	2.50b	2.84b	38.20	34.79	1.91	4.48
U2	Prior to irrigation	0.387	2.40	3.02c	37.62	34.00b	1.83	5.00
U2	Irrigated	0.408	1.74	3.14c	38.84	34.82b	1.77	4.64

1. Control plot mean annual increment during the treatment period was: C1 = 2.37 mm, C2 = 2.95; neither value is significantly different at the $P \geq 0.05$ level from corresponding treated plot. Prior to irrigation, control plot growth was C1 = 2.89 mm and C2 = 3.59 mm. The C2 plot grew at a significantly greater rate than all other plots prior to irrigation.
2. Growth rings 5, 6, 7, and 8 from bark.
3. Growth rings 1 and 2 from bark.

Table 17-3. Response of red oak to irrigation by municipal wastewater and the treatment effect on anatomical properties

Variables	Before treatment	During treatment	Average change*
			%
EW[a] vessel segment length (mm)	0.339	0.441	+30
EW vessel segment diameter (mm)	0.255	0.242	−5
EW vessel cell wall thickness (μm)	7.44	8.42	+13
LW[b] vessel segment length (mm)	0.472	0.504	+7
LW vessel segment diameter (mm)	0.079	0.076	+4
LW vessel cell wall thickness (μm)	8.49	9.05	+7
Fiber length (mm)	1.360	1.427	+5
Fiber diameter (μm)	13.83	14.11	−
Fiber cell wall thickness (μm)	4.92	4.92	−
Broad ray number	17.04	21.02	−24
Broad ray height (mm)	7.16	7.56	+6
Broad ray width (mm)	0.377	0.369	−
Growth ring width (mm)	2.55	4.18	+63
Specific gravity (O. D. volume)	0.634	0.664	+5
Percent EW	44.9	25.2	−44
Percent LW	55.1	74.8	+36

*Percentage shown is significant at $P \geqslant 0.05$ level.
a. EW = earlywood
b. LW = latewood

$P \geqslant 0.05$ level. Statistically significant changes in anatomy occurred in all but two of the variables measured — fiber cell wall thickness and broad ray width. Percent change was calculated by using the before-treatment mean as the base. From it the during-treatment value was subtracted. The resulting value was divided by the base value and the answer multiplied by 100 to arrive at the percentage. Significance was obtained by analysis of variance and Duncan's test on the mean values.

Discussion

A review (Sopper, 1971) of applications of municipal and industrial wastewater on forest and crop lands is indicative of the lack of regard for the response and possible utility of trees receiving such irrigation. Little work has been done regarding the effects of combined fertilizer and irrigation treatments on forest trees. Smith *et al.* (1972) in a study of six-year-old slash pine found irrigation plus fertilization increased the growth rate with no effect on the specific gravity. In our study the red pine crown wood response to irrigation by the mineral rich effluent was an increase in growth rate with significant decrease in specific gravity. Zahner (1962) examined five-year-old loblolly pine grown under two soil moisture regimes. Trees grown in drought conditions had a higher percentage of summerwood and reduced growth when compared to those trees growing on near field capacity soil. Zobel, Kellison and Kirk (1972) examined wood properties of the crown wood and juvenile wood and compared them to 25-year-old loblolly and slash pines. They found crown wood of mature trees low in specific gravity compared to that of the stem wood. Tracheid dimensions were also less than mature stem wood but tracheid length was greater than juvenile wood. Brunden (1964) states crown wood and stem wood are separate populations. This study confirms that properties of red pine crown and stem wood must be considered separately. Thus no combining of data would be in order. Tracheids are altered favorably if paper pulp is the intended use of the wood. Paper properties related to fiber-to-fiber bonding are improved because the lower density, thinner-walled tracheids conform better in a paper sheet.

The red pine stem wood response to irrigation by municipal wastewater was an increase in density with no change in ring width, except in those trees irrigated from five-foot risers, or tracheid length. Again the literature related to irrigation plus fertilization is sparse. Most of that which is available concerns non-porous species. Howe (1968) attributed an increase in specific gravity to irrigation of ponderosa pine. Larson (1957, 1963) and Van Buijtenen (1958) state specific gravity increased due to heavy summer precipitation but decreased if heavy spring precipitation occurred. Application of fertilizers resulted in the decrease of specific gravity (Williams and Hamilton, 1961; Siddiqui, Gladstone and Marton, 1972; Zobel et al., 1961). Specific gravity increased in two treatments (O1 and U2) and decreased in the third (O2). This overhead two-inch plot was reported to have been dying and infrared pictures of the area indicated these trees were not normal. The plot was blown down the winter following sampling. Posey (1964) reported tracheid length was reduced five to ten percent in fertilized loblolly pine while tangential tracheid diameter was unaffected. Cell wall thickness was reduced in the fertilization studies. Zobel et al. (1961) found no differences in tracheid length as a result of fertilization. The one-inch per week rate did not affect tracheid diameter or earlywood tracheid wall thickness. Latewood tracheid thickness was reduced. Those trees receiving two inches per week developed wider tracheids with reduced cell wall thickness. Tracheid length was unchanged in trees irrigated at both levels in this study. Tracheid diameters ranged from unchanged in the one-inch application to an increase of six percent in latewood tracheids in trees from the U2 plot.

There is much less literature concerning irrigation and fertilizer effects on ring-porous wood than on non-porous wood. Broadfoot (1964) found radial growth increased significantly in several hardwoods when irrigated. Mitchell (1972) reported similar response to nitrogen for several species of hardwoods and from his study concluded, where valid comparisons could be made, there was a trend toward increasing specific gravity with increasing growth rate. Saucier and Ike (1972) state specific gravity and fiber length of young sycamore are positively correlated with rate of growth. Stand thinning rather than nitrogen accounted for growth in their study. They also concluded the proportional values of fibers, vessels and rays were unaffected by growth rate. Aspen response to irrigation and fertilization reported by Einsphar, Benson and Harder (1972) was considerable. A 140 percent increase in volume occurred in trees in the fertilizer plus water treatment series when compared to the untreated control. Specific gravity was significantly lower. Tissue composition remained the same while fiber length was greater in trees grown in irrigated plots and this increase in fiber length was related to total height of trees. In our study tissue composition did change; however, no statistical relationship existed between any dependent variable when height was the independent variable.

Positive changes occurred in the red oaks due to irrigation with effluent. The five percent reduction in earlywood vessel segment diameter may reduce a problem associated with pulps from ring-porous woods. These large barrel-shaped elements are causes of "picking"; the lifting of the surface of paper during printing. The smaller, longer cell may be less likely to pick. Unlike the sycamore (Saucier and Ike, 1972), a change in tissue composition did occur in the red oaks. An increase in the number and height of broad rays resulted in an increase in the amount of wood volume occupied by the broad rays from nine percent in the untreated xylem to 11.5 percent of the wood laid down during irrigation. The increase in number and height of broad rays would cause an increase in the percentage of "fines" in a pulp mix. Increase in specific gravity and particularly the change in the amount of latewood from about one-half to three-quarters of the growth provide more mass of fibers per unit volume. Coupled with the growth rate change, irrigation with municipal wastewater results in the development of more fiber per treated tree. The increase in fiber and vessel segment length also increased the utility of this wood for pulp. Wangaard and Williams (1970) have shown a relationship exists between fiber length and tear strength for known paper sheet densities and fiber strength. The longer the fiber the stronger the paper for a given fiber strength below a critical sheet density.

Table 17-4. Red pine crown wood fiber length to cell wall thickness ratio values

Plot	Fiber length	Cell wall thickness	Ratio L/T
	mm	μm	
O1	1.63	1.77	920.9
O2	1.51	1.64	920.7
C1	1.53	1.70	900.0
C2	1.51	1.75	862.9
U2	1.54	1.68	916.7

Horn (1972) shows a curvilinear relationship exists between burst strength and a ratio between fiber length (L) and cell wall thickness (T) for twelve western softwoods. Although these data are not directly applicable, the probability that a similar relationship exists with the red pine tracheid and red oak fibers and vessel segments is good. Tables 17-4, 17-5 and 17-6 show L/T data for this study. The changes in the L/T value are not large. Changes in the L/T ratio of red pine tracheids similar to those shown by Horn (1972) would result in a five to eight percent increase in burst strength of paper. Also, tracheids from those plots where a significant reduction in cell wall thickness took place should conform better in the paper sheet. In the red pine, differences in L/T between plots prior to irrigation are indicative of the problem confronting us when making inferences from the data. These trees on the various plots were not similar prior to irrigation thus all inferences must be made within a plot.

One other attribute developed by the xylem grown during irrigation by municipal wastewater is a reduction in the variability about the mean for most cell dimensions measured. Figure 17-3 shows frequency diagrams for the red oak study data. Megraw and Nearn (1972) in a study of fertilized Douglas fir stated a reduction in range of within-ring densities should contribute favorably to pulp characteristics.

Table 17-5. Red pine stem wood fiber length to cell wall thickness ratio values

Plot	Period	Fiber length	Cell wall thickness		Ratio L/T	
			Early-wood	Late-wood	Early-wood	Late-wood
		mm	μm	μm		
O1	Prior to irrigation	2.93	2.37	6.12	1236.3	478.8
O1	Irrigated	2.63	2.35	5.79	1119.1	454.2
O2	Prior to irrigation	3.07	2.00	5.10	1535.0	601.9
O2	Irrigated	2.84	1.91	4.48	1486.9	633.9
U2	Prior to irrigation	3.02	1.90	4.85	1589.4	622.6
U2	Irrigated	3.14	1.77	4.64	1774.0	676.7

Table 17-6. Red oak fiber length to cell wall thickness ratio values

Period	Vessels						Fibers		
	Earlywood			Latewood					
	Length	Cell wall thickness	L/T	Length	Cell wall thickness	L/T	Length	Cell wall thickness	L/T
	mm	μm		mm	μm		mm	μm	
Prior to irrigation	0.34	7.4	45.9	0.47	8.5	55.3	1.36	4.9	277.6
Irrigated	0.44	8.4	52.4	0.50	9.1	54.9	1.43	4.9	291.8

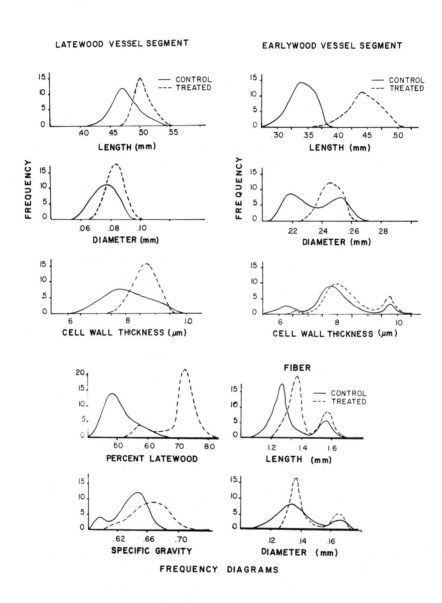

Figure 17-3. Frequency diagrams for anatomical and physical properties of red oak

Conclusions

The technique of using the forest to ameliorate treated sewage plant effluent while recharging the groundwater can alter the properties of the wood being produced. Primarily this study was concerned with the utility of wood grown in such a forest for pulp wood. The anatomy of two species studied responded in a similar manner as that reported in the related but not comparable literature. The morphology of the pulp fiber is important in the strength and conformity of the paper sheet and, therefore, the utility of the pulp. Alteration of the dimensions of the pulp fibers by the wastewater were such as to enhance their use as a raw material for paper. The lack of a separate control area did restrict the findings; however, the following conclusions may be made:

1. The response to irrigation by two inches of municipal wastewater weekly by red pine crown wood was a lower specific gravity, greater ring width, and no change in tracheid length. The red pine irrigated at one-inch per week had longer tracheids, and larger, thicker cell walls than the red pine irrigated with two inches or the red pine receiving no irrigation.

2. Specific gravity of stem wood of red pine increased in two treatments (O1 and U2) and decreased in the third (O2). Tracheid length and ring width were unaffected. Increases in earlywood and latewood tracheid diameters occurred in the trees receiving the four-year, two-inch per week applications and in the latewood tracheid diameter of the three-year, two-inch per week plot. Latewood tracheid cell wall thickness decreased as a result of irrigation by municipal wastewater.

3. Red oak responded favorably to irrigation at the two-inch per week rate. Specific gravity, percent latewood, and cell dimension changes are considered plus factors in the utility of the material for wood pulp.

The results of these experiments indicate that a one-inch spray enhanced the fiber properties of red pine. A two-inch application of the effluent was beneficial if red oak is to be used as a pulp species.

4. If similar projects are to be considered, the multiple relationships of crop response, wastewater ,amelioration and other facets demonstrated by this entire study should consider effects on forest products, particularly as a wood pulp source in the initial planning. This would permit more inferences regarding the xylem of those trees studied.

Literature Cited

Broadfoot, W. M. 1964. Hardwoods respond to irrigation, *Jour. Forestry* 62:579.

Brunden, M. N. 1964. Specific gravity and fiber length in crown-formed and stem-formed wood, *Forest Prod. Jour.* 14(1):13-17.

Burkhart, L. F. 1966. New technique for maceration of woody tissue, *Forest Prod. Jour.* 16(7):52.

Duncan, D. B. 1965. A Bayesian approach to multiple comparisons, *Technometrics* 7:171-222.

Einsphar, D. W., M. K. Benson, and M. L. Harder. 1972. Influence of irrigation and fertilization on growth and wood properties of quaking aspen, *Proc. of the Symp. on the Effect of Growth Acceleration on the Properties of Wood,* U.S. Dept. Agric. Forest Service, Forest Products Lab., Madison, Wisconsin.

Horn, R. A. 1972. Fiber morphology considerations in paper properties. *Proc. of the Symp. on the Effect of Growth Acceleration on the Properties of Wood,* U.S. Dept. of Agric. Forest Service, Forest Products Lab., Madison, Wisconsin.

Howe, J. P. 1968. Influence of irrigation on ponderosa pine. *Forest Prod. Jour.* 18(1):84-93.

Larson, P. R. 1957. Effect of environment on the percentage of summerwood and specific gravity of slash pine, Yale Univ. School Forestry Bull. No. 63.

Larson, P. R. 1963. The indirect effect of drought on tracheid diameter in red pine, *Forest Sci.* 9(1):18-27.

Megraw, R. A. and W. T. Nearn. 1972. Detailed DBH density profiles of several trees from Douglas-fir fertilizer/thinning plots, *Proc. of the Symp. on the Effect of Growth Acceleration on the Properties of Wood,* U.S. Dept. Agric. Forest Service, Forest Products Lab., Madison, Wisconsin.

Mitchell, H. L. 1972. Effect of fertilizer on the growth rate and certain wood quality characteristics of sawlog red oak, yellow-poplar, and white ash, *Proc. of the Symp. on the Effect of Growth Acceleration on the Properties of Wood,* U.S. Dept. Agric. Forest Service, Forest Products Lab., Madison, Wisconsin.

Murphey, W. K. and R. L. Brisbin. 1970. Influence of sewage plant effluent irrigation on crown wood and stem wood of red pine, *Pa. Agric. Expt. Sta. Bull.* 772.

Posey, C. E. 1964. The effects of fertilization upon wood properties of loblolly pine, (*Pinus taeda* L.), North Carolina State College School of Forestry, Tech. Report No. 22, 62pp.

Saucier, J. R. and A. F. Ike. 1972. Response in growth and wood properties of American sycamore to fertilization and thinning, *Proc. of the Symp. on the Effect of Growth Acceleration on the Properties of Wood,* U.S. Dept. Agric. Forest Service, Forest Products Lab., Madison, Wisconsin.

Siddiqui, K. M., W. T. Gladstone and R. Marton. 1972. Influence of fertilization on wood and pulp properties of Douglas-fir, *Proc. of the Symp. on the Effect of Growth Acceleration on the Properties of Wood,* U.S. Dept. Agric. Forest Service, Forest Products Lab., Madison, Wisconsin.

Smith, D. M. 1954. Maximum moisture content method for determining specific gravity of small wood samples, U.S. Dept. Agric. Forest Service, Forest Prod. Lab. Report No. 2014.

Smith, D., H. Wahlgren, and G. W. Bengtson. 1972. Effect of irrigation and fertilization on wood quality of young slash pine, *Proc. of the Symp. on the Effect of Growth Acceleration on the Properties of Wood,* U.S. Dept. Agric. Forest Service, Forest Products Lab., Madison, Wisconsin.

Sopper, W. E. 1971. Effects of trees and forests in neutralizing waste, *Trees and Forests in an Urbanizing Environment,* Univ. of Mass. Cooperative Ext. Service.

Van Buijtenen, J. P. 1958. Experimental control of environmental factors and their effect on some aspects of wood anatomy in loblolly pine, *TAPPI* 41(4):175-178.

Wangaard, F. F., and D. L. Williams. 1970. Fiber length and fiber strength in relation to tearing resistance of hardwood pulps. *TAPPI* 53(11):2153-2154.

Williams, R. E. and J. R. Hamilton. 1961. The effect of fertilization on four wood properties of slash pine, *Jour. Forestry* 59(9):662-665.

Zahner, R. 1962. Terminal growth and wood formation by juvenile loblolly pine under two soil moisture regimes. *Forest Sci.* 8(4):345-352.

Zobel, B. J., J. F. Goggans, T. E. Maki, and F. Hensen. 1961. Some effects of fertilizers on wood properties of loblolly pine, *TAPPI* 44(3):186-192.

Zobel, B. J., R. C. Kellison, and D. G. Kirk. 1972. Wood properties of young loblolly and slash pine, *Proc. of the Symp. on the Effect of Growth Acceleration on the Properties of Wood,* U.S. Dept. Agric. Forest Service, Forest Products Lab., Madison, Wisconsin.

Discussion

Mace: Did you conduct tests relative to the strength properties?

Cutter: Yes. We did.

Mace: Was it positive or negative for red oak?

Cutter: For red oak it was negative. The modulus of elasticity and modulus of rupture were decreased. We conducted strength properties on both the red pine and the red oak. In the red oak, the specific gravity was increased. You might expect strength to increase also but it did not. It was decreased as a result of the irrigation with sewage effluent.

18
Effects of Spray Irrigation of Forests with Chlorinated Sewage Effluent on Deer and Rabbits

Gene W. Wood, D. W. Simpson and R. L. Dressler*

That chlorinated sewage effluent can be renovated and recycled to the groundwater table by spray irrigation on agronomic and forest lands appears to have been well documented. Three important gains from this wastewater disposal method are recognized: (1) conservation of the water resource, (2) elimination of a stream pollution source, and (3) increased crop production on the irrigation sites.

While the water, soil, and floral response to wastewater irrigation have been intensively studied, very little attention has been paid to faunal response. The latter will be of tremendous importance in environmental impact statements presented to the public where this treatment system might be deployed. If there is a general belief among the public that this type of land treatment is deleterious to wild birds and mammals, there is small chance that it will be instituted on a large scale. This is primarily true, of course, where the system would be deployed on publicly owned land. In fact, the institution of the current studies of faunal response to wastewater irrigation was a result of just such sentiment regarding the use of Pennsylvania State Game Lands 176 for expansion of the Penn State Wastewater Renovation Facility.

Objectives

The first efforts in evaluating the effects of sewage effluent irrigation on wild animals have been directed toward the principal game species on the treatment areas. The cottontail rabbit (*Sylvalagus floridanus*)

*School of Forest Resources, The Pennsylvania State University and the white-tailed deer (*Odocoileus virginianus*) are rated as high priority species by hunters using State Game Lands 176. The first objective was to determine changes in the nutritive value of rabbit and deer foods that were caused by the irrigation treatment. The second objective was to determine the effects of the treatment on deer feeding behavior. That is, do the deer feed on treated sites as readily as untreated sites? Thirdly, it was important to determine whether or not rabbits could reproduce and survive if they were restricted to treatment sites.

Procedures

Changes in nutritive values of foods were evaluated by simultaneously collecting samples of plant parts of species known to be used as a food source by rabbits and/or deer at various times of the year. These samples were then dried at 65°C for 72 hours, ground in a Wiley mill, and subsequently analyzed for crude protein, phosphorus, potassium, calcium, and magnesium. Crude protein determinations were by macro-Kjeldahl methods; P by the vanadomolydophosphoric acid method and K, Ca, and Mg by atomic absorption spectrophotometry.

Digestion trials of a standard lab ration for rabbits and of alfalfa hay were run using adult female wild rabbits. These foods were used as standards for comparison of trials using reed canarygrass from both treated and untreated sites. The digestion coefficients (DC) were calculated by the equation

$$DC = \frac{\text{wt. of material ingested} - \text{wt. of material in feces}}{\text{wt. of material ingested}}.$$

Deer feeding behavior studies are being done using the lead deer technique which was developed at Penn State some 10 years ago.

Three animals, one two-year-old male, a yearling male, and a yearling female, have been and are continuing to be used as study animals. Each animal is transported to the study area two to three times each week and observed for a 90-minute period. The study area is 10.2 acres in size. Five acres receive two inches of chlorinated sewage effluent during an eight-hour period each week. An adjacent 5.2 acres serve as the control. The plants that the animals are observed utilizing as food, the time (in seconds) spent feeding on each of these plants, and the time spent on treated and untreated sites are recorded by the observer. Preference for foods by individual species and foods in general on variously treated sites are calculated by the following equation:

$$\text{Preference} = \frac{\dfrac{\text{Food biomass on site X}}{\text{Food biomass on total study area}}}{\dfrac{\text{Time spent feeding on site X}}{\text{Total time spent feeding}}}$$

Cottontail rabbit reproduction and survival studies on animals restricted to treatment sites receiving two inches of effluent during a 16-hour period each week have been carried on since May, 1971. The study method has been to construct four 4-acre rabbit enclosures, two of which are treated and two untreated. The animals in each of these enclosures are periodically trapped, marked for identification, examined for nutritional condition, and released. Trapping has been done using the Mosby-type box trap with a trap density of ten per acre.

Results and Discussion

Tables 18-1, 18-2, and 18-3 list a total of 32 plant species which were analyzed for total nutrient concentrations. In general, the crude protein, P, K, and Mg concentrations were higher on irrigated sites than adjacent control sites. The opposite was true for Ca. In all but four cases Ca concentrations were apparently lowered by the irrigation treatment.

It will be noted that the greatest differences in nutrient concentrations between treated and untreated sites occur among the plants sampled in the summer and the smallest differences between those sampled in the winter. This is not surprising since summer foods of wild herbivores are primarily composed of perennial and annual herbs, deciduous foliage, and unhardened current woody growth. These all have high proportions of active meristematic tissue, already high in nutrient concentrations, and presumably serving as a deposition site during luxury consumption of available nutrients. Although the differences between areas are not as pronounced during the fall and winter, there still appear to be real differences for many nutrients. That is, concentrations are still higher in winter although to a lesser extent than in summer.

Table 18-4 presents the results of several digestion trials on rabbit foods. As previously mentioned a standard lab ration for rabbits and alfalfa hay were run as references.

Table 18-1. Percentage concentrations of nutrients in forages collected in pole-sized mixed-oak stands irrigated with two inches of sewage effluent per week (T) and on adjacent untreated sites (U)

Species	Plant Part	Treat-ment	Month of Collection	Crude Protein	P	K	Ca	Mg
White oak	leaves	T	July	22.8	0.268	0.843	1.29	0.332
(*Quercus alba*)		U		16.9	0.220	0.790	1.85	0.195
Flowering dogwood	leaves &	T	July	21.6	0.414	1.658	3.55	0.721
(*Cornus florida*)	twigs	U		12.9	0.208	0.902	3.91	0.422
Red oak	leaves	T	July	16.2	0.227	0.694	0.63	0.220
(*Q. rubra*)		U		14.6	0.174	0.673	1.24	0.142
Chestnut	leaves	T	July	20.2	0.300	0.976	1.06	0.510
(*Castanea dentata*)		U		17.2	0.215	1.007	1.24	0.329
Sassafras	leaves &	T	July	32.2	0.541	2.824	0.89	0.285
(*Sassafras albidum*)	twigs	U		19.7	0.274	2.569	1.32	0.229
Bracken fern	fronds	T	July	29.4	0.808	5.421	0.53	0.376
(*Pteridium aquilinum*)		U		14.5	0.203	3.296	0.64	0.283
Whorled loosestrife	leaves &	T	July	25.9	0.573	4.820	0.77	0.340
(*Lysimachia quadrifolia*)	stems	U		16.1	0.237	3.562	0.73	0.220
Huckleberry	leaves &	T	July	14.0	0.188	0.705	0.87	0.311
(*Gaylussacia* sp.)	twigs	U		12.0	0.157	0.787	0.97	0.209
	twigs	T	Sept.	12.3	0.119	0.479	1.21	0.353
		U		12.4	0.101	0.565	1.48	0.191

Table 18-1. (continued)

Species	Plant Part	Treatment	Month of Collection	Crude Protein	P	K	Ca	Mg
Black cherry (Prunus serotina)	leaves & twigs	T	July	24.8	0.323	1.383	1.66	0.546
		U		17.3	0.336	1.973	1.82	0.455
		T	Sept.	19.6	0.195	0.444	1.32	0.400
		U		16.0	0.233	0.831	1.83	0.303
Red maple (Acer rubrum)	leaves & twigs	T	July	20.4	0.444	1.105	1.43	0.511
		U		11.9	0.191	0.748	1.20	0.233
		T	Sept.	17.5	0.389	0.539	1.39	0.408
		U		11.4	0.124	0.308	1.22	0.199
Teaberry (Gaultheria procumbens)	leaves & stems	T	July	11.8	0.224	0.819	1.20	0.372
		U		9.0	0.128	0.718	1.95	0.274
		T	Sept.	11.3	0.134	0.317	1.23	0.407
		U		9.4	0.085	0.277	1.89	0.279
Pokeberry (Phytolacca americana)	leaves & stems	T	July	40.2	0.552	9.383	0.76	1.105
		T	Sept.	32.4	0.451	4.159	0.94	1.439

Table 18-2. Percentage concentrations of nutrients in forages collected in aspen-white pine stands treated with two inches of sewage effluent per week (T) and on adjacent untreated sites (U) in October 1971

Species	Plant Part	Treatment	Crude Protein	P	K	Ca	Mg
Striped pipsissewa	leaves &	T	16.6	0.256	0.386	0.938	0.217
(*Chimaphila maculata*)	stems	U	14.7	0.267	0.558	0.933	0.137
Pipsissewa	leaves &	T	12.3	0.218	0.125	1.435	0.221
(*C. cisatlantica*)	stems	U	10.2	0.206	0.379	1.300	0.175
Partridgeberry	leaves &	T	13.8	0.165	0.892	0.651	0.472
(*Mitchella repens*)	stems	U	9.6	0.234	0.774	1.523	0.428
Ground cedar	leaves &	T	9.7	0.143	1.142	0.209	0.115
(*Lycopodium tristachyum*)	stems	U	7.0	0.101	1.017	0.234	0.170
Sheep sorrel	leaves	T	19.0	0.767	2.175	0.650	0.325
(*Rumex acetosella*)		U	15.6	0.254	1.878	0.654	0.200
Strawberry	leaves &	T	15.7	0.601	1.278	1.505	0.305
(*Fragaria* sp.)	stems	U	11.0	0.408	0.521	1.680	0.237
Goldenrod	leaves	T	14.3	0.366	2.500	1.160	0.258
(*Solidago* sp.)		U	9.4	0.153	1.278	1.209	0.153
Yellow mustard	leaves	T	17.6	0.509	4.454	1.063	0.273
(*Brassica rapa*)		U	15.3	0.431	4.673	1.141	0.181
Plantain	leaves	T	12.1	0.414	2.825	2.111	0.251
(*Plantago lanceolata*)		U	10.2	0.449	2.595	2.009	0.132
Broadleaf plantain	leaves	T	15.8	0.365	2.072	1.935	0.427
(*P. major*)		U	10.3	0.260	0.849	1.558	0.356
	seed heads	T	13.9	0.543	2.500	0.742	0.239
		U	6.1	0.267	1.266	1.231	0.158

Table 18-2. (continued)

Species	Plant Part	Treatment	Crude Protein	P	K	Ca	Mg
Birdsfoot trefoil	leaves &	T	24.6	0.340	1.327	1.055	0.183
(*Lotus corniculatus*)	stems	U	21.0	0.203	0.514	1.644	0.247
White clover	leaves &	T	26.3	0.395	2.877	1.097	0.315
(*Trifolium repens*)	stems	U	25.4	0.356	1.780	1.163	0.225
Wood sorrel	leaves &	T	16.2	0.755	1.928	1.031	0.349
(*Oxalis* sp.)	stems	U	11.4	0.815	1.761	1.624	0.288
Virginia creeper	leaves &	T	12.7	0.404	0.929	2.633	0.350
(*Parthenocissus quinquefolia*)	stems	U	9.0	0.266	0.682	2.370	0.391
Bigtooth aspen	leaves	T	14.7	0.267	0.308	1.486	0.276
(*Populus grandidentata*)		U	9.4	0.152	0.285	1.557	0.225
Gray dogwood	leaves	T	11.5	0.263	0.514	2.128	0.371
(*Cornus racemosa*)		U	8.9	0.287	0.324	2.229	0.293
Red maple	leaves	T	12.4	0.267	0.316	1.177	0.276
(*Acer rubrum*)	leaves	U	10.3	0.218	0.641	1.072	0.179

Table 18-3. Percentage concentrations of nutrients in forages collected in aspen-white pine stands treated with two inches of sewage effluent per week (T) and on adjacent untreated sites (U) in February 1972

Species	Plant Part	Treatment	Crude Protein	P	K	Ca	Mg
Quaking aspen	bark	T	8.6	0.187	0.652	1.699	0.134
(*Populus tremuloides*)		U	6.3	0.131	0.571	1.886	0.104
	browse[a]	T	9.1	0.207	0.575	1.677	0.176
		U	9.1	0.202	0.601	1.515	0.143
Bigtooth aspen	bark	T	7.3	0.167	0.583	2.038	0.147
(*P. grandidentata*)		U	6.9	0.138	0.515	1.702	0.103
	browse	T	10.2	0.232	0.682	1.489	0.154
		U	7.5	0.191	0.467	1.518	0.167
Red maple	bark	T	8.1	0.124	0.360	1.420	0.054
(*Acer rubrum*)		U	6.7	0.137	0.337	0.936	0.076
	browse	T	9.8	0.178	0.497	1.195	0.099
		U	7.3	0.156	0.373	1.768	0.090
Staghorn sumac	bark	T	10.1	0.201	1.317	0.859	0.114
(*Rhus typhina*)		U	8.7	0.154	1.424	0.827	0.110
Blackberry	stems	T	6.5	0.139	0.269	0.489	0.106
(*Rubus allegheniensis*)		U	5.3	0.125	0.332	0.608	0.084
	twigs[b]	T	10.7	0.169	0.349	0.679	0.161
		U	8.4	0.142	0.516	0.794	0.169

a. Terminal two inches of twig growth.
b. Terminal eight inches of twig growth.

Table 18-4. Digestion coefficients for dry matter and crude protein in cottontail rabbits

Forage	No. of Rabbits	Dry Matter	Crude Protein
Lab ration	10	0.645 ± 0.013	0.697 ± 0.027
Alfalfa hay	7	0.496 ± 0.016	0.695 ± 0.026
Reed canarygrass			
Irrigated	5	0.330 ± 0.033	0.730 ± 0.053
Control	3	0.352 ± 0.023	0.622 ± 0.088

Obviously reed canarygrass is not as good a food as either of the other two from the standpoint of dry matter digestibility. On the other hand, the crude protein concentration is quite adequate and the plant is used as a food source to some extent in agricultural areas. Analysis of the effects of irrigation on its digestibility shows that treatment resulted in no significant changes in percentage of digestible dry matter or crude protein.

Studies of white-tailed deer feeding behavior in relation to the irrigation treatment indicate that the animals use treated sites at least as readily as untreated sites. Table 18-5 lists the preference indices based on available food biomass from May 1 to June 15 and relative sizes of study sites. When all three test animals are averaged there appears to be a definite preference for the treated site. This is probably a spurious relationship, however, due to the tendency of the two yearling animals to feed near the unloading area, which happened to be adjacent to the treated site. These animals did very little investigating of alternate feeding areas and fed only sporadically during testing periods. The two-year-old buck, however, explored and fed readily on all sites. If anything the two-year-old showed a preference for the transition zone between the treated and untreated sites. This is a normal and somewhat predictable deer-use response to spatial changes in habitat. That is, the edges receive proportionately greater use. Beyond the "edge effect" response the treated site was used at about the same level as was the untreated.

Table 18-5. Indices of site preference by semi-free ranging white-tailed deer

	Irrigated	Transition	Non-irrigated
	Index based on relative site size		
All test animals	1.33	0.85	0.59
2-yr-old male	0.94	1.32	0.92
	Index based on relative amounts of food		
All test animals	1.46	[a]	0.63
2-yr-old male	1.03	[a]	0.93

a. The transition zone was not recognized in the biomass sampling.

No lead deer work has been done during the winter period. Studies of site use by wild deer have been conducted, however, using snow track and bed counts. Our observations indicate that the deer readily use irrigated sites during this period of the year for feeding and especially for resting. Numerous beds have been frequently observed in close proximity to the delivery sprinklers. There is some reason to believe that the animals may use the area during actual irrigation periods because of warmer ambient temperatures on the site during the spraying of the effluent which is about 75°F when it leaves the sprinkler.

After a year and a half of studying two populations of rabbits confined to treatment sites and two populations on untreated sites, but similar habitat, we are still unable to get a measure of the influence of irrigation on rabbit reproduction. During the first year of study we were only able to state that there was at least some reproduction in all study populations. This was only because we caught at least one juvenile animal in each area during the trapping period. Since we started with uneven populations at the beginning of the study period in the spring of 1971, total population estimates in the following fall could give no clue as to what natural increases or decreases in the populations had occurred. In an attempt to remedy this situation we adjusted all study populations to six adult animals (2 males, 4 females) in the spring of 1972. Our summer trapping success in 1972 has been similar to that of 1971 allowing only the determination that we have some reproduction in all four populations. Based on our past experience we should be able to get good trapping success in October and November. At that time we should at least be able to determine any net changes in the populations.

Again due to the extreme difficulty of capturing rabbits during the late spring and summer months we have no measure of the influence of the irrigation treatment on rabbit survival during this time. We do have a good measure of winter survival, however. Table 18-6 presents the population estimates of the study areas based on the assumption of total population capture for fall 1971 and late winter 1972.

Although the percentage survival was higher on non-irrigated sites (80 percent) than on irrigated sites (70 percent), the irrigated sites started with a 30 percent greater density and ended with one still higher by 11 percent. In addition, the animals on treated sites were superior to those on untreated sites with respect to nutritional condition. The former were all healthy specimens at the end of the winter while the latter were as much as a third lighter in weight and showed obvious signs of emaciation. This phenomenon can be explained by several observations. First, it has already been pointed out that the nutritional quality of the foods available on irrigated sites was higher

Table 18-6. Minimum winter survival on irrigated and non-irrigated sites based on total population capture in the fall of 1971, and number of recaptures in late winter of 1972

| | Number Marked Fall 1972 | | | Recaptured Late Winter 1972 | | |
	Males	Females	Total	Males	Females	Total
Irrigated site 1	3	6	9	3	4	7
Irrigated site 2	2	2	4	2	0	2
Non-irrigated site 1	2	3	5	2	1	3
Non-irrigated site 2	1	4	5	1	4	5

than that on non-irrigated sites. Secondly, there was more food available on treated sites during the winter due to the pulling down of sapling trees by the ice formation resulting from the spray irrigation. Thirdly, the ice mounds are laced with crevices and caves which offer and are heavily used by the rabbits for cover.

Conclusions

The spray irrigation of chlorinated sewage effluent at the rate of two inches per week appears to have a favorable influence on the nutritive value of rabbit and deer forages. Generally the crude protein, P, K, and Mg can be expected to be raised in these forages while the Ca is lowered. Reed canarygrass, the only forage tested for changes in digestibility due to treatment, showed no significant response with respect to digestible dry matter and protein.

Studies using the lead deer technique to determine preference for or avoidance of irrigated sites and forage from these sites indicate that the deer use treated sites at least as readily as untreated sites. During the winter period wild deer do not avoid the area but appear to use it quite readily for resting and feeding.

At this time we have no conclusive evidence of the effects of spray irrigation on rabbit reproduction. We do know that the winter carrying capacity of treated sites exceeds that of untreated sites presumably due to higher levels of available nutrition and improved cover conditions.

Discussion

Unknown: Do you feel that the increase in the numbers of mosquitos and biting flies will at some time be a limiting factor as far as the wildlife is concerned in these areas that are under irrigation?

Wood: We don't have any good information to indicate that we do have increases in arthropod populations. We have only started collecting numerical data on this during the past year and this has been in relation to all of our studies. If this kind of thing is happening then we suspect that there might be a problem because the animal may avoid the area because of the insect nuisance there. We've seen this in other areas. In some of our clearcut areas where we have deer fenced in and we're looking at the animals' response to habitat changes and plant succession it was found that in the summer time the animals usually are in very poor condition. It's just the reverse of what is expected because of the fly populations in the clearcut areas. It's my belief that the animals are constantly running trying to brush off the flies in the brush.

Unknown: How about the incidence of disease caused by the flies?

Wood: We have initiated studies on this with a grant from the Office of Water Resources Research. We take three blood samples a year from these deer. They are compared with two other sets of penned deer from which we take blood samples. Then we also have rabbits which are out in enclosures in the woods from which we are taking blood samples to determine if we have a difference in the appearance of arbor viruses in these animals. We also are monitoring fecal samples every three days from the three animals that are used in the field and the three penned animals. Coliform counts are run on these and the coliform bacteria serotyped to see if we are getting correlations between serotypes of *E. coli* in the effluent being sprayed on the site and those occurring in the animal.

Unknown: Do you feel that these data are realistic if these animals are fed on artificial food and are not really wild animals?

Wood: This has always been a criticism of lead deer studies and there have been many modifications made of this. But from a standpoint of whether the animal prefers or avoids a particular area or a particular type of food we believe that the observations are quite good. From the standpoint of the amount of species preference when you're trying to get the exact food habits of the animals this may become limited. However, there have been some studies in the southwest in Arizona that have shown that animals raised in pens and taken out onto the range — that those animals were eating the same forages that wild deer that had never seen a pen were using.

Unknown: Do you know of any data that would indicate the response of cattle to pastures that have been irrigated with sewage effluent?

Wood: I'm sorry, I don't.

VII / SYSTEMS DESIGN, OPERATION, AND ECONOMICS

19
Sprinkler Irrigation Systems: Design and Operation Criteria

Earl A. Myers*

Wastewater must be applied uniformly over the land surface at the proper rate in inches per hour and the appropriate amount in inches per week, if adequate renovation is to be expected. Two areas which greatly affect this judicious application are proper design and diligent management.

This chapter first lists the variables involved in the design of an irrigation distribution system, then discusses a number of factors which affect the choice of specific value for each variable, and concludes with comments concerning the various and sundry management decisions that must be made when operating the system.

Design Variables

In the design of a solid-set irrigation system for any wastewater facility, five variables must be considered. These are daily flow from the facility, weekly loading depth on the land area, hourly application rate, sprinkler spacing, and nozzle operating pressure. Each of these variables can be considered to be independent, however, they are also strongly interrelated.

The daily flow from the facility in combination with the weekly loading depth determines the overall size of the irrigation distribution system. The loading depth usually is expressed in inches of waste-

*Department of Agricultural Engineering, The Pennsylvania State University

water applied each week over the entire disposal area. For a plant outflow of 0.5 mgd (million gallons per day), 64.5 acres are required if the loading depth per week is two inches, whereas, if the loading depth is only one inch per week, 129 acres will be needed. The 0.5 mgd, two-inch per week, and 64.5-acre statistics essentially describe Penn State's arrangement at the present time.

The application rate, expressed in inches per hour, in conjunction with the loading depth per week establishes the number of irrigation periods per day or per week. Thus, for a two-inch per week loading depth if the application rate is ¼ inch per hour, each irrigation period would be eight hours and there could be three irrigation periods per day or 21 periods per week. When using an application rate of ⅙ inch per hour each irrigation period would be 12 hours and there could be only two periods per day or 14 periods per week.

To apply the 0.5 mgd of effluent at the rate of ¼ inch per hour required 21 periods in each of which approximately 3.1 acres were irrigated. After the application rate was changed to ⅙ inch per hour, 14 periods were required in each of which approximately 4.6 acres were irrigated.

The sprinkler spacing, in conjunction with the rate of application, establishes the number of gallons per minute (gpm) each sprinkler must emit, whereas the sprinkler spacing and the acres per period establish the number of sprinklers which should operate at any one time. For example, consider the ¼ inch per hour application rate which requires a 3.1-acre area. If a 60 by 80 foot spacing is chosen, 28 sprinklers are needed and each sprinkler should emit 12.5 gpm. Had a 40 by 60 foot or 80 by 100 foot spacing been chosen, 56 or 17 sprinklers would have been required and 6.3 or 21 gpm would be needed. Penn State's system has used all of these arrangements and many more.

The fifth variable is the operating pressure at the sprinkler nozzle. This pressure, in conjunction with the required gallons per minute of the sprinkler, determines the diameter of nozzle hole which is needed. Forty pounds of pressure per square inch (psi) are required to force 6.3 gpm through a ³/₁₆ inch nozzle, whereas 55 psi are needed for 12.5 gpm through a ¼ inch nozzle. Nozzle diameters used on the Penn State project ranged from ³/₃₂ to ⁵/₁₆ inch, while pressures ranged from 35 to 65 psi.

Figure 19-1 lists the design statistics for a typical solid-set irrigation system for a town of 5,000 people. Once a specific figure has been chosen for each of the five variables, much of the remaining design becomes mere arithmetic. The primary engineering involved is in the choice of the proper value for each of the variables.

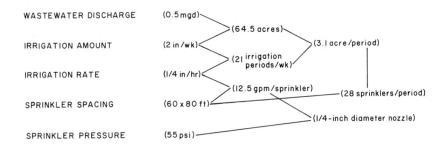

Figure 19-1. Typical solid-set irrigation system design statistics for a town of 5,000 people

Factors Affecting Variables

Wastewater Discharge

The design example just described considers only wastewater quantity, which is satisfactory for many municipalities. The quality of the wastewater, however, in most situations must also be considered. Irrigation installations using Penn State's "Living Filter" concept should be utilized only where the wastewater contains pollutants of such type and concentration that they can be removed by the soil-crop complex. That is, only certain pollutants can be removed appropriately by the absorptive, biological, chemical, and physical reactions within this biosphere. Other pollutants can completely destroy this living filter, thus producing additional pollution rather than renovation. Wastewaters containing high concentrations of heavy metals, chlorides, toxic constituents, etc. will probably require special pre-treatment before land distribution.

Irrigation Amount

The choice of weekly loading depth depends upon the renovation and hydrologic capabilities of the site relative to the quality of the liquid wastes applied and the water quality constraints imposed by the regulatory agency. Most of the work at Penn State was with an application amount of 100 inches per year applied at two inches per week. The material applied was secondary treated and chlorinated domestic municipal effluent from the University and from the Borough of State College.

The renovation capacity of a site depends upon such factors as the soil and the crop to be grown, whereas the degree of renovation required depends upon the pollutants in the wastewater and the proposed use of the renovated liquid; both must be considered in selecting the irrigation amount.

Corn and reed canarygrass can remove larger amounts of nitrogen than legumes or trees. The removal of crops also permits larger amounts of application. The deeper the soil and the finer the texture the greater the amounts of phosphorus one can apply because of the greater total chemical fixation capacity. A two-foot depth of soil may be adequate since 90 percent or more of the crop roots are in this layer. In sandy soils the amount per application period may need to be decreased so that the nutrients are not carried below the plant root zone before they can be used. Soil profiles with controlled shallow water tables which reach up into the biologically active zone may remove substantial amounts of nitrogen by denitrification. On such a site, removal of a harvested crop may not be necessary to obtain adequate nitrogen removal.

The amount of application may have to be decreased when the irrigation site is over a domestic water supply aquifer rather than an aquifer which would be used for agricultural irrigation or some other less demanding use. The amount of application at any location must not produce a water table sufficiently higher to cause direct runoff of untreated water.

The hydrologic capabilities of a site must be considered independently from the site's renovation ability. While sandy surface soils will permit infiltration of high rates of application, the amount one should apply may be controlled by underlying tighter layers. Some soils can appropriately be drained to receive high loadings of liquid wastes while others cannot. Fine textured soils covered with thick stands of vigorously growing hay crops can accept large amounts of water during the summer months, but may produce excessive runoff in early spring or late fall at these loadings.

Since the amount of wastewater applied affects the quantity and quality of water that will leave the watershed, one needs to consider the final disposition of the treated water when choosing the irrigation amount. Final disposition includes potential reuse, as well as the rate and quality of discharge.

Reuse of renovated water usually is governed by economics and by local legal limits. Potential reusers include industrial, domestic, and agricultural. The renovation requirements for certain industrial uses, cooling for example, may not be as high as for domestic uses, therefore, a greater amount can be applied per week or per year. Under certain terrain and soil conditions it may be possible to treat the effluent in the surface soil and then permit it to resurface at a lower elevation. After it has returned to the surface it may be used directly or it may be stored behind large dams for future use. These reservoirs may also function as recreational areas. Thus, certain reuses permit greater application amounts.

The quantity of water recharged often is considered equal to the amount distributed minus such losses as evapotranspiration associated with plant growth and as direct evaporation from the sprinklers. This, however, assumes that the water actually infiltrates through the soil surface and percolates to the groundwater reservoir. In many instances on Pennsylvania hillsides covered with permeable topsoils but slowly permeable subsoils this is not necessarily true. During the spring thaw and other naturally wet periods, extensive amounts of water may become interflow or may not infiltrate at all. Thus, it is imperative that the design and operation of the system is such that the application amount is controlled to assure adequate renovation for the desired reuse.

Additional factors pertaining to the hydrologic regime of irrigated liquid wastes have been described by Parizek and Myers (1968).

Irrigation Rate
An application rate of ¼ inch per hour was used for most of Penn State's systems during the first five years, whereas most of the present systems have been converted to ⅙ inch per hour. This lower application rate is preferable since often irrigation must be continued during and after heavy rains, when the crops are very young, in early spring and in late fall, and when the soil is near or at field capacity.

There is also a labor advantage with the ⅙ inch per hour rate. When a manual system is used, a two-inch application requires a valve turn every eight hours with a ¼ inch per hour rate and only every 12 hours with a ⅙ inch per hour rate. The valves were turned at 8 A.M., 4 P.M., and midnight with the ¼ inch per hour arrangement, whereas they are now turned only at 8 A.M. and 8 P.M. This new arrangement obviously is preferred by the personnel turning valves.

Sandy loam soils are somewhat poorer in inherent nutrients and more droughty than ideal for regular agricultural purposes. Since the nutrients and water are supplied by the effluent, however, these soils are excellent for final distribution of most wastewaters. They also permit higher rates of application than finer textured soils and this provides more flexibility in the choice of irrigation system type.

Additional factors which affect the rate of application include: soil structure and permeability, soil cover crop and management procedures, surface topography, and climatic conditions.

Soils having good structure and aggregates which are stable permit higher rates of application, as do highly permeable soils which have rapid and continuing internal drainage. Thick hay and grass cover crops permit a higher application rate than does a bare soil. Good management provides proper crops and cropping procedures which help maintain good soil structure and permeability. Steep surface topography and low temperatures require reduced rates of application to decrease chances of overland flow and runoff.

Sprinkler Spacing and Pressure

The choice of spacing between sprinklers is associated closely with both the application rate and the amount of pressure at the nozzle. The primary factor which affects the choice of spacing is the vegetative cover — open field crops or forests. An 80 by 100 foot spacing is preferred for open fields and a 60 by 80 foot spacing is recommended for wooded areas. These spacings seem to give the best relationship between good distribution and reasonable costs.

Rectangular, square, or triangular sprinkler patterns may be used with solid-set distribution systems. Ordinarily some type of triangular (or staggered rectangular) pattern permits the maximum spacing between lateral lines which reduces installation costs. In order to insure reasonable uniformity of application depth over the area, the maximum spacing between sprinklers should not exceed 75 percent of the effective sprinkler distribution diameter.

The frequency and intensity of wind affect the spacing of sprinklers, the uniformity of application, and the preference of nozzle pressure and size. As the spacing is increased, the height of the spray stream must be increased according to the laws of projectile motion. As the top of the spray stream arc becomes higher, the wind has a greater effect on the distribution pattern. Thus, windbreaks and border strips often become an integral part of the irrigation distribution system design and must be considered in the economic analysis.

The nozzle pressure and diameter are chosen such that the appropriate rate of wastewater can be distributed uniformly over the specified area. For a specific hole size if the pressure is too high, the water will mist and drift extensively. If the pressure is too low, the emitting stream will not be adequately broken and poor distribution again will result. The best advice is to follow the manufacturers' recommendations of nozzle pressure-diameter combinations.

While the above discussion of application rate, sprinkler spacing, and nozzle operating pressure is appropriate for the design of a solid-set irrigation system, it is not appropriate for the designs of other irrigation systems like the center pivot, the giant gun, the traveling gun, and various other self-propelled or hand moved systems. In open fields one of these systems may be just as appropriate as the solid-set system and often may be more economical. In most of central Pennsylvania, however, the geology, topography, and tree cover encourage the use of solid-set systems.

Additional Factors

The physical features of the land, in addition to affecting the sprinkler system variables, also affect the design and cost of the entire system. The total head requirement for the system is directly dependent upon the difference in elevation between the pumping plant and the distribution areas, the friction loss in the transmission and distribution lines, and the pressure requirements of the sprinkler heads.

Design for a rough, undulating terrain, of course, is more complicated than for a gentle sloping area because of static head changes, and more importantly, the need for draining all lines during periods of freezing conditions. The rougher the terrain the more difficult this becomes. In areas with complex slopes the laterals may need to be placed on supports to provide the uniform grade required for rapid drainage. The number of drain locations should be kept to a minimum to reduce labor and to permit more efficient management.

The configuration of the distribution area frequently is determined by the availability of land. Inefficient distribution system arrangements involving greater costs often are required due to unavailability of large, concentrated, gently sloping areas having appropriate soil and geological conditions.

Farmers ordinarily irrigate the best soils or fields on their farms. The same should be true for canneries, industries, and municipalities when irrigating their effluents. Unfortunately, too many make the sad choice of acquiring the cheapest land available which often is too wet, is too steep, or has insufficient soil depth to provide adequate renovation.

In the choice of materials, one should remember that dissolved chemicals in the effluent may cause corrosion or electro-chemical deterioration. This deterioration may occur for 12 months each year when irrigating liquid wastes, compared to one to two months for typical agricultural irrigation. The chemical strength of the wastes, especially animal and certain cannery or industrial wastes, may be many times that of typical agricultural irrigation water.

Laws and regulations concerning liquid wastes frequently restrict design flexibility. The departments of public health in many states do not permit sewage effluent irrigation of crops used for human consumption; with this most people agree. Some also do not permit the irrigation of golf courses. Since regulatory requirements differ from state to state it is essential to find out what their design "suggestions" are as early as possible because they can greatly influence a systems design.

Some regulatory agencies arbitrarily "suggest" maximum sprinkler diameters of coverage or minimum specific borders beyond ordinary sprinkler wetting diameters. Unfortunately these suggestions too often become required criteria on a check list, rather than the beginning points for design consideration.

Management Decisions

Management of the system will be the deciding factor between success and failure for many wastewater renovation facilities using the living filter approach. Adequate size and flexibility frequently are designed into the system, especially with the aid of state and federal money. Unfortunately, in the hope of saving operational money, systems too often are poorly managed.

Many new concepts and often completely new orientations are required when managing irrigation systems for liquid waste disposal. Whereas farmers now ordinarily manage for crop requirements, in liquid waste irrigation one needs to manage for adequate renovation, and the crop must be secondary. This indicates that usually the municipality or company producing the liquid waste should own the land and not the farmer. No matter how conscientious a farmer is, it will be difficult to convince him to irrigate a crop which already has received twice as much rain as necessary. In wastewater disposal management one applies maximum amounts of water to the land, not minimum amounts. Most of the research and experience with irrigation to date, however, has been with minimum amounts.

Monitoring of the effluent which leaves the renovation area is an essential part of system management. Both surface and subsurface water discharge should be monitored in each dominant direction of water egress. Monitoring facilities usually assay only the quality of the discharge from the renovation area. Under proper management, however, quantity also should be considered.

Costs always play a major role in management decisions, especially in determining the amount of original capital outlay relative to the amount that will be required for labor to operate the system. Sewage effluent irrigation systems may be designed to operate from six to twelve months per year and for seven days a week. With that many hours of operation, hand moved systems usually can not be justified. But, can a city afford to pay $2,000 to $4,000 per acre for a buried distribution system?

Traveler or center pivot irrigation systems may be used to reduce the capital costs. These types of distribution equipment may be secured for $150 to $500 per acre. The center pivot type systems have both capital and labor-saving advantages if the topography, field size and shape, lack of trees and streams, etc. are conducive to their use. Traveler systems are not flexible under adverse field conditions and require more labor and may cause wind drift nuisance.

As one compares the management decisions between agricultural and liquid waste irrigation, he should ponder seriously the following facts. In agricultural irrigation an individual farmer usually buys the system; he operates this system with a wealth of background and ingenuity; he works with his own equipment; he irrigates his best land; he decides when to irrigate and when not, what crops and soils to irrigate, and how much; and he makes all of his own decisions and legally has the right to do so.

In liquid waste irrigation top level personnel of a municipality, a company, or a corporation usually are responsible for the management policy, however, someone far down the chain of command frequently makes the day to day operational decisions. Management policy generally provides for meeting federal or state agency regulations. The employee making the specific system operational decisions, however, all too often is not aware of the requirements which must be met or of the consequences of improper choices.

When one chooses to irrigate year-round in areas where temperatures drop appreciably below zero there are many additional management decisions that must be made. In addition to the management of the sprinkler disposal system one must assure that no pollution results from irrigation on frozen soil. Pumping, pipe system, and sprinkler head problems associated with irrigation during times of below-freezing temperatures have been previously reported by Myers (1966).

Management is the key to irrigation of effluent becoming a significant tool for the conservation of nutrients and renovated water, and for the elimination of much pollution in our present water bodies. Proper management of the crops and of the irrigation rates and amounts can produce the biological balance required. When astute management of soils is added to the above, adequate hydrological balance can also be attained.

Acknowledgments
Research reported here is part of the program of the Waste Water Renovation and Conservation Project of the Institute for Research on Land and Water Resources, and Hatch Projects No. 1481 and 1809 of the Agricultural Experiment Station, The Pennsylvania State University, University Park, Pennsylvania. Portions of this research were supported by funds from Demonstration Project Grant WPD 95-01 received initially from the Division of Water Supply and Pollution

Control of the Department of Health, Education, and Welfare and subsequently from the Federal Water Pollution Control Administration, Department of the Interior. Partial support was also provided by the Office of Water Resources Research, USDI, as authorized under the Water Resources Research Act of 1964, Public Law 88-379.

Literature Cited

Myers, Earl A. 1966. Engineering problems in year-round distribution of waste water, *Proc. National Symp. on Animal Waste Management,* ASAE Publication No. SP-0366, pp. 38-41.

Parizek, R. R. and Myers, E. A. 1968. Recharge of ground water from renovated sewage effluent by spray irrigation, *Proc. of the Fourth Amer. Water Resources Conf.,* New York, New York, pp. 426-443.

20
Cost of Spray Irrigation for Wastewater Renovation

John B. Nesbitt*

The net cost of effluent disposal by spray irrigation is dependent upon the system required to do a specific job, at a specific location, at a specific time, as well as the procedures adopted for management of the spray field. Since different situations require different designs and management procedures, no general overall cost information can be given. However, if certain basic assumptions are made about design and management a rough cost estimate can be made and that will be done here.

The figures presented are based on work done by Allender (1972). He presented a procedure, supported by many charts and nomographs which can be used as computational aids, which will enable an engineer to make a preliminary design and cost estimate of a wastewater renovation system using spray irrigation. Using the work of Allender (1972), the estimated cost of hypothetical systems carrying flows of one, five, and ten million gallons per day (mgd) will be presented. The figures are based on certain assumptions regarding design and management. These assumptions may or may not fit another specific situation but they will define the basis of the subsequent estimates. They will be discussed under the general areas of pumping system, delivery system, and operation.

Pumping System
It is assumed that the system will be pumping completely treated (secondary treatment) municipal wastewater as this is the type of effluent on which the Penn State study was based. Since wastewater flows will be variable and pumping rates more or less constant I have assumed some sort of equalizing storage will be needed and have chosen a pond designed like an oxidation pond with a forty-day detention time. The detention time was selected on the basis of flow records from several Pennsylvania communities. Other designs which use longer storage or eliminate the storage entirely are possible.

The pumping station is a typical wastewater station, with the usual stand-by pumps, discharging into a force main. Also included is a fine screen (not a microstrainer) before the pump station to reduce clogging of the sprinkler nozzles.

*Department of Civil Engineering, The Pennsylvania State University

Delivery System

The delivery system under discussion includes the transmission pipeline (force main) and the spray field itself with its land, piping, sprinkler heads, and fittings. Costs for a monitoring system are not included.

The estimates include the purchase of land at $140 per acre. As this cost can vary from zero to well over $1,000 an acre, the reader can make the proper adjustment when the final figures are presented. The amount of land required is based on a total application of two inches per week at an application rate of $\frac{1}{6}$ inch per hour. The land is in open fields.

The sprinkler system uses solid set aluminum piping with 140 foot effective distribution diameter sprinkler heads placed in a rectangular spacing of 98 ft. by 70 ft.

The force main is one mile long with a 200 ft. elevation lift. This distance is probably short for many larger installations, but may be quite appropriate for the small system where this process may have its widest application.

Operation

Operation of the system assumes that the municipality must provide its own spray field which is capable of receiving the entire flow. While it is realized this water can be of great benefit to private agricultural lands, it is felt continuous, uninterrupted disposal on these private lands would not be possible. On this basis, sale of effluent to owners adjacent to the transmission pipeline would be a definite possibility. Calculations on the returns available from this sale indicated at best it would be an insignificant fraction of the total cost and it has not been included in these estimates.

The crop for these estimates is reed canarygrass. While the full market potential for this crop has not yet been developed, its use is sufficiently great that a rough estimate of the returns through its sale may be estimated. Alternatively, the cost for its disposal in a sanitary landfill is also estimated.

Estimated System Costs

Now that the basis of design has been established the estimated costs for flows of one, five and ten million gallons per day (mgd) are shown on Table 20-1 in 1967 dollars. The capital cost varies from $439,220 for a one-mgd system to $2,431,280 for a ten-mgd system. Annual cost also shown on Table 20-1 includes amortization of the capital cost in 20 years at six percent interest and ranges from $46,570 to $263,060 for the one- and ten-mgd flows. Labor would be performed by personnel also used for other work and is considered constant in this flow range.

Although the distribution of costs among the various system com-

Table 20-1. Estimated costs for a spray irrigation system (1967 dollars)

Item	Flow (mgd)		
	1	5	10
Capital cost			
Distribution system	$ 66,020	$ 336,700	$ 675,380
Lagoon	123,000	350,000	600,000
Pumping station, screens	84,000	179,000	258,500
One-mile pipeline	71,500	132,000	195,000
Land, survey, site	44,000	219,000	440,000
Engineering and contigencies	50,700	152,100	262,400
Total	$439,220	$1,369,500	$2,431,280
Annual cost			
Amortization (20 yr. @ 6%)	36,750	111,100	197,800
Labor	1,900	1,900	1,900
Power (A), distribution system	2,200	10,800	21,600
Power (B), pump effluent 1 mile and 200 feet in elevation	2,310	11,740	21,260
Maintenance and contingencies	3,410	11,300	20,500
Total	$ 46,570	$ 146,840	$ 263,060

ponents can be determined from Table 20-1, they are presented graphically in Figure 20-1. It can be seen that the capital costs are nearly equally distributed among the system components. Figure 20-1 illustrates the significance of the cost of the transmission pipeline. As this cost would be almost directly proportional to length, it is obvious a longer pipeline would alter the figures considerably.

It is popular these days to present annual wastewater treatment costs in terms of cents per thousand gallons of wastewater treated. Annual cost on this basis is presented in Figure 20-2. The solid line is constructed from the data in Table 20-1. The dashed lines now include estimates of the annual cost for sale or landfill disposal of the reed canarygrass crop.

The cost shown in Figure 20-2 compares favorably with other wastewater treatment costs. With complete treatment cost at 15 cents per thousand gallons for a 15-mgd plant, sprinkler irrigation would add about 50 percent to the total treatment costs. Chemical treatment for phosphorus removal is generally estimated at about five cents per thousand gallons, and tertiary treatment by filtration and activated carbon at 20 cents. Remember, however, that the sprinkler irrigation cost used for comparison is for a one-mile pipeline to the spray field.

Since the cost for wastewater treatment will always revert to the individual homeowner, Figure 20-3 has been prepared to show the cost on this basis. The transformation from Figure 20-2 to Figure 20-3 is based on an average household of 3.5 people at 100 gallons

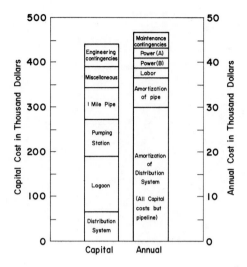

Figure 20-1. Capital and annual cost distribution for a 1-mgd spray system

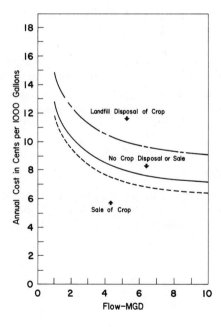

Figure 20-2. Cost of spray irrigation per thousand gallons. Estimated cost includes a 1-mile pipeline plus a 200-foot elevation lift.

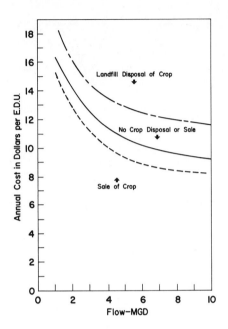

Figure 20-3. Cost of spray irrigation per equivalent dwelling unit (E.D.U.). Estimated cost includes a 1-mile pipeline plus a 200-foot elevation lift.

per capita per day. In comparing costs obtained from this graph with a typical municipal sewer bill, remember that the sewer bill contains costs for both collection and treatment and that the costs presented here consider only a one-mile transmission pipeline.

Literature Cited

Allender, Gerald C. 1972. The cost of a spray irrigation system for the renovation of treated municipal wastewater, Master of Science Thesis, Department of Civil Engineering, The Pennsylvania State University, University Park, Pa.

21
Financing Municipal Wastewater Treatment Facilities, Including Land Utilization Systems

Belford L. Seabrook*

Today, the number of sewered communities in the United States is just over 16,000, serving 68 percent of the nation's population. During the next five-year period, we estimate that about 8,000 of these communities will construct new, upgraded, or expanded wastewater treatment facilities.

This construction is needed primarily to meet established water use goals for the receiving waters. However, a continuing need for pollution abatement facilities will always exist after standards have been achieved to compensate for a growing population, obsolescence, and industrial expansion. Accomplishing this goal will require dedication at all levels of government and will most certainly require the cooperation of industry.

The Environmental Protection Agency is not approaching industry nor anyone else as an adversary. Water pollution is not just an industry problem or a government problem; it is society's problem. The Agency approaches everyone as a partner, convinced that environmental protection is everyone's job and everyone's responsibility. Our waters cannot be cleaned up tomorrow; they cannot be restored easily or without great effort and expense. But the Agency is determined to make a beginning.

From now on "pay-as-you-go" will increasingly be required for insuring against the risks of manipulating nature. This means that provision must be made for the protection and rehabilitation of the environment before, or at the time, these resources are used. The cost of maintaining the environment must be included in the cost of doing business.

General Accounting Office Studies
The General Accounting Office (GAO) submitted reports on the construction grant program to the Congress in November, 1969, and May, 1970. The reports discussed the effectiveness of the program and the awarding of grants to municipalities in cases which benefit industrial users.

*Division of Municipal Waste Water Programs, Environmental Protection Agency

The November, 1969, report pointed out that the suspension of the dollar-limitation clause on grant awards in 1966 provided the initiative for the growing trend toward the treatment of industrial wastes in joint municipal-industrial plants. The report indicated that, should the trend continue, it could result in many of these industry-associated costs for treatment facilities becoming eligible for federal assistance. In other words, the volume and cost of treatment facilities receiving federal financial assistance would increase significantly. In short, the taxpayer would be subsidizing industrial wastewater treatment with no control on the quantity of waste products discharged into the system.

The later GAO report, dated May 8, 1970, called direct attention to the fact that some grants were being awarded for the treatment of industrial wastes only.

Recent Federal Regulations
On July 2, 1970, regulations were promulgated on treatment works design, operation and maintenance, planning requirements, and treatment of industrial wastes in municipal systems. The regulations provide for investment of the anticipated massive amounts of public monies in a more coordinated and effective manner. In addition to responding to criticism from the General Accounting Office, the regulations provide a solid base from which to achieve the Agency's goals of cost-effectiveness in planning, design, and operation of treatment works.

Industrial Waste Cost Recovery Guidelines
Federal guidelines for equitable recovery of costs for industrial waste treatment in municipal systems were issued in October, 1971, to interpret the July 2, 1970, regulation.

A system of "cost recovery" is to be provided by the grantee wherever industrial wastes are to be treated by a facility built with federal aid. A municipality must assess industry's share of the operating and capital cost of the community treatment facility. Under present policy, industry's share will be in proportion to the total costs of waste treatment for operation and maintenance, and in proportion to the grantee's costs for capital costs. Thus, the industry is not required to reimburse the municipality or the federal government for the grant portion which will provide facilities for treatment of industrial wastes. Pretreatment must also be provided by industry for wastes that would otherwise be detrimental to the municipal treatment facility and collection system.

However, the legislation now pending in Congress would require recovery of the grant portion from industrial users. I will discuss this in more detail later.

The guidelines are designed to clarify the general provisions and the criteria of acceptable compliance. The intent of the guidelines is to define the minimum acceptable revenue to be derived from industry for its share of the facility costs. The emphasis is on the necessity for use of average cost pricing for industrial and all other users, based on the contributed loadings in terms of both quality and quantity of wastes. Although EPA will approve any system that satisfies the intent of the regulations, the guidelines will serve to facilitate the determination of compliance with the cost recovery requirements.

The Agency's primary interests with respect to the intent of the regulation are:

1. To implement the Agency's basic principle of imposing the cost of waste treatment directly upon the source of pollution
2. To encourage the use of user charges based upon volume and character of the wastes
3. To promote equity in terms of improved knowledge and acceptance by the system's users of the necessity of paying for waste treatment and control
4. To encourage reduction of waste strength through in-plant control and recycling of by-products
5. To promote local self-sufficiency.

In order for the Agency to determine compliance with an equitable cost recovery system, the grant application must furnish complete information on existing treatment works and the proposed expansion or modification including:

1. General information about industries located and served (or to be served) by the treatment system
2. Treatment works capacity, in terms of hydraulic and BOD loadings
3. Total excess capacity reserved for industrial waste contributors
4. Methods of financing for capital improvements, including amount and amortization schedule
5. Methods for financing the operation and maintenance costs including special costs created by industrial wastes
6. Distribution of the revenues to be collected among classes of users
7. Method of collection of revenues.

This represents the administrative arrangements which were developed to assure equitable allocation of wastewater treatment costs among all users.

A survey is currently being conducted of certain representative, existing wastewater land utilization systems throughout the country to collect facts and experiences for the purpose, among others, of evaluating these facts to form the basis for developing federal guidelines on land application techniques. Hopefully, this information will become available to the public in 1973. With the caveat that the wastewater land application survey report and the federal guidelines can be published in 1973, planning is currently underway to organize and hold the first EPA national symposium on wastewater land utilization techniques, to be held in mid-1973.

Omnibus Clean Water Bills

President Nixon sent a significant number of proposals, representing his water pollution control legislation program, to the Ninety-second Congress during the first session. A number of proposals have also been submitted by various members of Congress. Late in the first session the Senate passed, by an overwhelming vote of 86-0, S. 2770 in lieu of the president's legislative proposals and certain other bills. In the meantime, H.R. 11896 was introduced in the House of Representatives. Hearings were held and the bill was passed by the House March 29, 1972, by a vote of 378 to 14. The versions approved by the Senate and the House provide for a number of substantial changes. Among the most significant are the following:

1. Both versions provide for the application of the best practicable waste treatment technology after June 30, 1974, following examination of all possible alternatives. The administrator is directed in Section 304(d)(2) to publish within nine months after enactment, information on alternative waste treatment techniques and systems available to implement Section 201 of the Act.
2. The Senate bill authorizes a maximum federal share of 70 percent. The House version would authorize a maximum of 75 percent. The Joint Conference Committee (in June '72) adopted the 75 percent maximum and added the provision that there would be no requirement for matching state grants.
3. The House bill would make certain sewage collection systems eligible for federal grants. The Senate bill does not contain this provision. Both versions, however, provide for separation and treatment of storm water.
4. Under the Senate bill, the administrator of EPA is authorized to advance to a municipality up to five percent of the estimated reasonable construction cost of a project, after reviewing the engineering feasibility report, to enable municipalities to complete plans and specifications. Such funds need not be returned in the event no further grants are made on the project. The House bill contains no provisions for such advances.

5. Both the Senate and House versions provide for a charge to be assessed on all users to assure that each class of users pays its share of the cost of operation and maintenance, including replacement of sewage treatment works.
6. Both the House and Senate bills require that municipalities levy charges on all industrial users to recover the portion of the total capital cost covered by both the local share and the federal share, allocable to the industrial load portion of the plant capacity.
7. The Senate bill provides that the federal share recovered from industrial users of federally assisted municipal plants be received by the administrator and deposited in the United States treasury. The House version provides for the recovered funds to stay with the local wastewater treatment management agency to provide for replacements and other plant needs.
8. The Senate bill authorizes a total of $14 billion from fiscal year 1972 through fiscal year 1975 as the federal share of the construction costs of municipal sewage treatment facilities. The House version will make available a total of $20 billion for sewage treatment construction for the same period. The Joint Conference Committee (in June 1972) adopted the House figure of $20 billion.
9. Both bills provide for the development of regional waste treatment management systems.
10. Both bills require that guidelines and regulations be published on pretreatment of industrial wastes prior to discharge to publicly owned systems. This applies to pollutants which interfere with, pass through, or are otherwise incompatible with treatment systems. Provision is also made for monitoring of industrial discharges.

At this point it is not possible to predict the final outcome of the proposed legislation with regard to cost recovery for treatment of industrial wastes. However, it is significant that both bills contain similar provisions for recovery of the grant portion for industrial waste treatment.

The House bill provides that grant funds can not only be utilized for the construction of land application facilities, but such funds can additionally be utilized for site acquisition, including farmland and forest land. The Joint Conference Committee, which is currently considering the pending legislation has yet to resolve this matter.

The reference concerning alternative techniques and systems applies to land treatment and land utilization systems that are an integral part of municipal wastewater facilities. Construction grants can be made to cover the eligible costs under the current program.

The following criteria will be helpful in evaluating wastewater land utilization techniques:

1. Type of wastewater
   (a) Raw sewage. (b) Primary treated sewage. (c) Secondary treated sewage. (d) Liquid digested sludge.
2. End use of wastewater
   (a) Disposal. (b) Agriculture. (c) Industrial reuse. (d) Recharge of aquifer.
3. Esthetic attitudes of community
4. Availability of suitable land
   (a) Ownership. (b) Leasing. (c) Green belts. (d) Highway median strips. (e) Golf courses. (f) Farmland/Ranchland
5. Length of operating experience
6. Social costs, including relocation assistance and eviction costs
7. Institutional restraints
8. Public health factors
9. Build up of mineral and heavy metals in the soil
10. Odor and fly problems
11. Long term problems
    (a) No discharge a fallacy. (b) Run-off. (c) Sources of water supply.

The particular technique and design of a land utilization system for wastewater and liquid digested sludge will depend on the situation and circumstances at each specific project.

VIII / EXAMPLES OF OPERATING AND PROPOSED SYSTEMS

22
Large Wastewater Irrigation Systems: Muskegon County, Michigan and Chicago Metropolitan Region

W. J. Bauer and D. E. Matsche*

The substance of this chapter is directed primarily toward the costs and benefits of large land treatment systems, using the experience with the Muskegon County, Michigan system now under construction and the work done to date on preliminary planning for a system to serve the Chicago metropolitan region. These two projects will be described briefly, then the cost experience and cost estimates for the various components of the system will be analyzed. The division of the costs into functional components is intended to facilitate the use of these figures by others in analyzing, in a preliminary fashion, the cost of a land treatment system in some locality where the relative costs of the components may not be the same as those experienced in the Muskegon County project. For example, the distance from the urbanized area to the irrigation site probably would be relatively more or less in some other project. The selected components for cost analyses are:

1. Collection and transmission.
2. Pretreatment.
3. Irrigation.
4. Drainage.
5. Sludge handling.
6. Return and reuse of treated water.
7. Land acquisition.

In addition to analysis of both the capital and operating costs of these components, potential sources of income from the wastewater irrigation system are evaluated. These are:

1. Agricultural production.
2. Long-term land values.

*Bauer Engineering, Inc.

3. Leasing of space for electric power station.
4. Sale of cooling make-up water.
5. Sale of industrial process water.
6. Leasing of space for solid-waste handling.
7. Recreational uses during nonirrigation seasons.

Muskegon County, Michigan System

This land treatment system is located in parts of Muskegon County, Michigan on sandy soils common to that portion of Michigan lying along Lake Michigan (Figure 22-1). Muskegon County is located approximately opposite Milwaukee, Wisconsin, roughly opposite the midpoint of Lake Michigan. The wastewater management system is physically divided into two parts: a larger portion serving the more heavily urbanized area surrounding Muskegon Lake and Mona Lake; and a smaller portion serving the less urbanized area around White

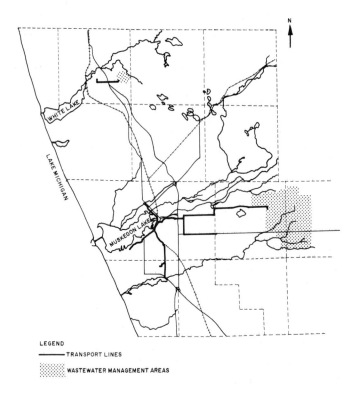

LEGEND

———— TRANSPORT LINES

▓▓▓ WASTEWATER MANAGEMENT AREAS

Figure 22-1. Muskegon Land Treatment Plan

Lake. All of these lakes are large dune-impounded lakes with outlets to Lake Michigan. The purpose of the project is to eliminate the discharge of polluting industrial and domestic discharges into these lakes to enhance the usefulness for recreational purposes, and to eliminate the discharge of polluting materials into Lake Michigan from which the water supply for most of the population of Muskegon County is obtained. The population to be served is estimated to be approximately 160,000 persons when the system is fully developed. The design average flows for the fully developed system are estimated to be about 43 mgd, with a peak capacity of roughly 90 mgd which can be sustained for a relatively long time without adversely affecting the final effluent quality. Of this total design flow, about 40 percent is expected to be industrial and the remainder is expected to be domestic wastewater. Initially, the industrial portion comprises more than half of the total flow, because many of the collecting sewer systems have not been constructed. The largest single industry served is a paper mill with a design average flow of 12 to 16 mgd of wastewater containing waste paper and pulp fibre, plus some waste clay filler.

The larger of the two irrigation sites is an area of about 15 square miles located about 10 miles east of the more heavily urbanized area. It is underlain by medium sand ranging in thickness from a minimum of 20 feet to a typical maximum of 60 feet. There are also areas where the sand thickness is greater than 60 feet. The surficial sand deposits are underlain by an impermeable clay layer which effectively prevents the vertical movement of ground water. Aerated lagoons with a design average residence time of three days are used to provide the biological treatment. The normal procedure to be followed will result in discharging the biologically treated wastewater and associated solids into one of two 850-acre storage lagoons. These storage lagoons provide additional treatment and winter storage of the treated wastewater by being allowed to fluctuate nine feet in depth. A separate eight-acre settling lagoon will be provided for operating flexibility to allow the bypassing of the storage lagoons and permit the direct irrigation of clarified effluent from the aerated lagoon system.

Percolation through the bottom of the storage lagoon is controlled by intercepting ditches around the lagoons from which it can be pumped either back into the storage lagoon, or to the outlet drainage system, or to the irrigation system. Pumping directly to the outlet drainage system is anticipated only during the initial operations of the system, which will occur before all of the irrigation system is ready to operate.

The flow into the major irrigation system would then come from either the storage lagoons or from the ditch which intercepts leakage from the storage lagoons. In either case, it is planned to chlorinate it to provide a desired reduction in coliform count. During the flow in the long open channels leading to the two irrigation pumping stations, the excess chlorine will be dissipated to prevent adverse effects in the soil. The two irrigation pumping stations are each set up in two parts so that a total of four separate irrigation systems may be served. Together these systems utilize about 55 irrigation rigs of the pivot type, each of which irrigates a circular area. These circular areas range in size from about 40 to 160 acres. A total of approximately 6000 acres of land are thus irrigated. The design application of irrigation water is about 7.5 feet per year, or 2.5 million gallons per acre per year. A total of 15,000 million gallons of water are thus planned to be irrigated in the design year, or an average flow of 41.3 mgd. The remainder of the design flow (1.3 mgd) is handled at the smaller site serving the White Lake area. During the irrigation period of roughly 30 weeks per year the average rate of application would be three inches per week. However, maximum rates of four inches per week are anticipated during dry weather.

An extensive underdrainage system is provided in the Muskegon County project, comprised primarily of drainage pipe systems which discharge into drainage ditches. In addition, a smaller portion of the irrigation site is drained by wells. Both pumping wells and observation wells are provided. The purposes of the drainage system are to prevent the saturation of the agricultural soils under the most intense periods of irrigation and precipitation, and also to control the direction of movement of the ground water around the perimeter of the irrigation site. It was required by the Department of Public Health that no outward migration of ground water occur. Consequently, the design provides for a small inward migration of ground water from the surrounding areas into the irrigation site.

Authorization to prepare construction plans and specifications for the Muskegon County system was given in July of 1970; bids were taken in May of 1971; bonds were sold to cover the $16 million local share of the costs in August of 1971; and construction was started in the fall of 1971. Construction continued during the winter of 1971-72 with many of the collection system force mains being completed by August 1972. The land acquisition program began in October of 1971, and by March of 1972 about 85 percent of it had been acquired without the use of condemnation procedures. Clearing of the land began in April of 1972 and construction of the lagoons, major drainage ditches, and other features of the irrigation site were well under way in August of 1972. It is expected that the initial operation of the system will take place early in 1973 with the collection, transmission, pretreatment and storage of a flow of somewhat less than 30 mgd.

Leakage through the bottom of the storage lagoon is expected to be rather large until the sludge builds up a sealing layer over that portion of the bottom which is not lined with clay. Design of the leakage interception system is predicated on the assumption that leakage through the unlined portion will be unimpeded by such sealing. As this leakage will pass through a minimum of 500 feet of sand before being intercepted by the perimeter ditch, and because the sand contains large amounts of iron and other chemicals for the precipitation of phosphate, the leakage water is expected to meet all of the requirements for effluent from treatment plants discharging into Lake Michigan. Therefore, the initial operation of the system could occur without irrigation. The irrigation and drainage system is expected to be completed during 1973, so that full scale operation will take place during 1974.

The capital costs reported here are obtained from the actual bidding for the component construction contracts of this project. The operating costs are estimated from the calculation of energy consumption, labor requirements, and maintenance procedures. The estimate of potential revenues is based upon a forecast of the auxiliary functions which are presently being contemplated at the site, including the construction of a major nuclear power generating station.

Chicago Metropolitan Region

A survey scope report for the U. S. Army Corps of Engineers is being produced by the Chicago District on regional wastewater management plans. The region to be served covers approximately 2500 square miles with a present population of about seven million persons in northern Illinois and northern Indiana. Domestic wastewater, industrial wastewater, discharges from combined sewers, discharge from storm sewers, and runoff from rural watersheds would all be managed in this plan (Fig. 22-2). Alternative treatment technologies, including activated sludge with advanced treatment processes being added on, chemical/physical treatment systems with advanced treatment processes being added on, and biological treatment in lagoons followed by land treatment using irrigation and drainage of agricultural areas are all being considered, both separately and in various combinations. The goal of the study is to produce a comprehensive basis for choosing the course of action to solve the water pollution problems of the Chicago metropolitan region.

The cost estimates presented for this system are based upon a

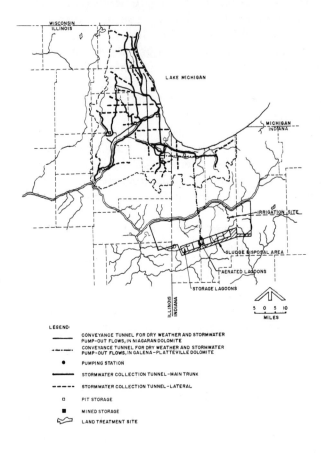

Figure 22-2. Chicago Land Treatment Plan

layout of the physical elements of one of the systems being studied, including several hundred miles of water conductors, 75 square miles of lagoons, and 700 square miles of actual irrigation area. Further details of the layout of the project can be obtained from reports by the chief of engineers issued in March of 1972, together with the Technical Appendix and the Cost Data Annex of those reports.

The operating costs and estimates of potential revenues are calculated on the same basis as those presented for the Muskegon County project. The capital and operating costs are presented without taking credit for any potential revenues from various possible sources of income.

Cost Analyses

Muskegon County Project

Collection and transmission. The costs of the collection and transmission systems for this project are based upon the bids for the following construction contracts:

Contract 10:	66-inch force main, 11 miles	$ 4,502,025
Contract 11:	Smaller force mains	1,230,930
Contract 12:	Smaller force mains	841,309
Contract 13:	Smaller force mains	1,135,400
Contract 15:	Main pumping station, 90 mgd	1,565,000
Contract 16:	Smaller pumping stations (7)	1,163,169
	Total	$10,437,833

It is significant that most of these costs would be incurred regardless of the type of treatment used, as it is necessary to convey the wastewater to the point of treatment. In the case of Muskegon, the alternative treatment plant was located on a site closer to the city, but all of the same pumping stations would have been required. There would have been a shorter main line from the main pumping station out to the site of the treatment plant.

To these costs should be added about two other small pumping stations which were not advertised at the time of the general bidding, plus a proportionate share of the engineering cost. Adding these gives a total of $11,500,000. Spreading this over the rated average capacity of 43 mgd gives a unit capital cost of 27 cents per gpd average capacity. Spreading this over the rated peaking capacity of 90 mgd gives a unit capital cost of 13 cents per gpd.

The operating cost of the collection and transmission system is estimated as follows:

	Cost/Year
Smaller pumping stations, 5 @ 3 mgd avg. flow with a typical head of 60 feet, 50 hp avg. power consumption at $75 per hp-yr	$ 18,000
Service and maintenance labor for preceding	25,000
Intermediate pumping stations, 2 @ 15 mgd flow with typical head of 60 feet, 150 hp avg. power consumption at $75 per hp-yr	22,500
Service and maintenance labor for preceding	20,000

Main pumping station, average of 41 mgd flow with
typical head of 180 feet, 1200 hp avg. power consumption at $75 per hp-yr   90,000

Service and maintenance labor for preceding   30,000

Total $205,500

Dividing by 15,000 million gallons per year pumped, this amounts to
an operating cost of about $14 per million gallons.

Summarizing the collection and transmission cost of the Muskegon
County System we have the following:

Capital cost $11.5 million   27¢ per gpd
Operating cost $ 0.205 million/yr $14 per mg

Pretreatment. The pretreatment of the wastewater prior to the
irrigation involves biological treatment in aerated lagoons, biological
treatment of effluent and digestion of sludge in stabilization lagoons,
and chlorination of the effluent prior to discharge into the irrigation
canals leading to the irrigation pumping stations. The capital costs of
the construction items involved in this portion of the project are as
follows:

Contract 18: (as awarded) $7,044,298
Clay lining   664,000
Soil cement placement   525,000
Cement for soil cement   381,000
Total $8,614,298

This is a cost of 20.6 cents per gpd capacity, exclusive of the sludge
handling equipment.

The sludge handling equipment would consist of a dredge and
pipeline, plus centrifuge to obtain a higher percent solids, plus several
plows to place the sludge into the earth and cover it. The capital cost
of these items is estimated to be $500,000 or 1.2 cents per gpd. The
total capital cost for pretreatment is then 21.8 cents per gpd. Operating cost of the pretreatment system is estimated as follows:

Electric energy consumption of the mixers and blow-
ers, installed capacity of 2000 kw, with an average
load of 1200 kw at $100 per kw-yr. $120,000/yr

Electric energy consumption — lighting, and miscellaneous small motors around the control building
and chlorination buildings.   10,000/yr

Chlorine consumption for chlorinating the treated
effluent prior to irrigation @ 5¢ per lb.   50,000/yr

Sludge processing and pumping costs, 300 hp at $100 per hp-yr.

30,000/yr

Laboratory and treatment process personnel, including personnel for the taking of water quality samples at wells and points of discharge from the system, 10 persons.

150,000/yr

Sludge disposal personnel, including 2 on the dredge, 2 at the centrifuge, and 2 on the plow.

90,000/yr

Total operating cost of pretreatment

$450,000/yr

Summarizing the costs of pretreatment:

Capital cost (including engineering)	$10 million	23¢/gpd
Operating cost	$450,000/yr	$30/mg

These pretreatment costs include the equivalent of secondary treatment of the effluent, and the utilization of the sludge for soil enrichment purposes.

Irrigation. Capital costs of the irrigation system include the following construction contracts:

Contract 1:	Clearing	$1,500,000
Contract 6:	Pressure piping	2,194,615
Contract 8:	Electric power distribution	475,193
Contract 17:	Irrigation pumping stations	500,000
Contract 22:	Pivot irrigation rigs for 6,000 acres	1,500,000
	Sub total	6,169,808
	Total Engineering	600,192
	Total	$6,770,000
	Cost per gpd capacity (avg.)	16¢

Operating cost of the irrigation system may be estimated as follows:

Electric energy consumption, actually consumed over a 7-month period but averaged over the year at the equivalent of 2000 kw @ $100/kw-yr

$200,000

Operating labor, 10 men

150,000

Allowance for replacement of mechanical equipment and other miscellaneous expenses

50,000

Total operating cost

$400,000

Cost per mg

$ 27.00

Drainage system. The capital costs of the drainage system are estimated as follows:

Contract 2:	Agricultural drainage pipe	$ 565,053
Contract 3:	Main drainage pipe	1,970,616
Contract 4:	Highway culvert	84,144
Contract 5:	Main drainage channels	1,104,977
Contract 9:	Well drainage control system	226,332
	Subtotal	$3,951,122
	Engineering allowance	348,878
	Total	$4,300,000
	Cost per gpd	10¢

Operating cost of the drainage system is relatively small, as the pumping stations involved are very low head and the maintenance personnel are the same ones as for the irrigation system. We shall ignore the operating cost of the drainage system, as it is included in the irrigation system for all practical purposes.

Return and reuse of the treated water. In the case of the Muskegon County project, all of this cost is included in the cost of the drainage system as the treated water is simply returned to the waterways and drains naturally, ultimately into Lake Michigan where it becomes available once again as water supply.

Land acquisition. Assembly of the two project sites totaling 10,000 acres required the acquisition of 410 parcels of property including 185 occupied residences. A program of relocation assistance was provided consistent with the requirements of the Federal Uniform Relocation Assistance Act. The costs of the land acquisition program were as follows:

Acquisition of land and structures	$5,000,000
Relocation assistance	1,000,000
Total	$6,000,000
Cost per gpd	14¢

Summary of the Muskegon County Project
The following is a summary of the costs of the Muskegon County project based on 43 mgd.

	Capital Cost ¢ per gpd	Operating Cost $/mg	Number of Employees
Collection and transmission	27	14	5
Pretreatment	23	30	16
Irrigation	16	27	10
Drainage	10	0	0
Return and reuse	0	0	0
Land acquisition	14	0	0
Subtotals	90	71	31

Interest during construction			
and miscellaneous expenses	4	0	0
Totals	94	71	31
General administrative expense	1	11	9
Totals	95	82	40

Chicago Regional Plan

The costs for the Chicago Regional Plan are given in Table 22-1 taken from the Technical Appendix to the report of the Office of the Chief of Engineers, Department of the Army (1972). These costs apply to a system with an average flow rate of 2376 mgd with a peaking factor of 1.75.

Extracting the corresponding costs from Table 22-1, one may construct the following tabular comparison:

Item	Muskegon County	Chicago Region	Ratio
Average flow rate, mgd	43	2376	55
Peaking flow rate, mgd	90	4152	46
Total capital cost, $millions	40	2000	50
Collection and transmission, ¢/gpd	27¢	30¢	1.11
Pretreatment & storage, ¢/gpd	23	11	0.48
Irrigation system, ¢/gpd	16	7	0.58
Drainage system, ¢/gpd	10	8	0.80
Return and reuse system, ¢/gpd	0	12	—
Land acquisition, ¢/gpd	14	13	
Subtotals	90¢	81¢	0.95
Interest during construction			
and miscellaneous expenses, ¢/gpd	4	2	0.715
Subtotals	94¢	83¢	0.89
General administrative expense, ¢/gpd	1	1	0.500
Totals (capital cost)	95¢	84¢	0.890
Operating cost, $/mg	82	106	1.325

The relatively greater collection and transmission costs for the Chicago Regional Plan arise from the 104-mile maximum transmission distance as compared to a maximum distance of about 15 miles for the Muskegon County project. Likewise, the relatively greater pumping head — 1,100 feet versus 230 feet — for the Chicago project largely accounts for the greater operating cost. However, there may be offsetting revenues as discussed in a subsequent section.

The relatively smaller pretreatment and storage costs of the Chicago Regional Plan arise from the much larger lagoons and the resultant great reduction in the volume of earth-moving per million gallons of storage volume.

The irrigation and drainage systems are more economical in the

Table 22-1. Summary of costs for the land treatment alternative for the Chicago metropolitan area[a]

Item	Cost	
Capital cost		
Transmission facilities		
Wastewater tunnel and pipelines	$627,638,000	
Reclaimed water tunnel	257,000,000	
Wastewater pumping station	80,000,000	
Reclaimed water pumping station	22,000,000	
		$ 986,638,000
Land treatment site		
Purchase	291,000,000	
Family relocation	27,000,000	
Clearing and site preparation	36,588,000	
		$ 354,588,000
Irrigation system		
Irrigation pumping station	23,370,000	
Irrigation rigs	58,531,000	
Pressure pipe and appurtenance	60,782,000	
		$ 142,683,000
Drainage system		
Drainage pumping station	2,358,000	
Plastic drainage pipe	16,616,000	
Sewer drainage pipe	172,914,000	
		$ 191,888,000
Aerated lagoon system		
Earthwork	14,300,000	
Slope and roadway construction	4,733,000	
Aerators and mixers	33,877,000	
Inlet, outlet, flow distribution		
and crossing structures	16,766,000	
		$ 69,676,000
Storage lagoon system		
Earthwork	76,560,000	
Slope and roadway construction	17,030,000	
Inlet, outlet & chlorination structures	40,392,000	
		$ 133,982,000
Irrigation and drainage channel system		
Excavation	32,295,000	
Lining	26,879,000	
Crossing, diversion & drop structures	1,253,000	
		$ 60,427,000
Monitoring system		
Observation wells	4,280,000	
		$ 4,280,000
Electrical system	28,340,000	
		$ 28,340,000
Sludge disposal facilities	23,300,000	
		$ 23,300,000

Table 22-1. (continued)

Item	Cost	
Administration and regional lab buildings	3,565,000	
		$ 3,565,000
Subtotal capital costs land treatment system		$2,000,000,000
Operating and maintenance cost Labor (includes 25% overhead)		
Managerial and administration	910,000	
Operating engineers, chemists	2,550,000	
Mechanics, electricians	3,430,000	
Field inspection, maintenance	5,650,000	
Secretarial and janitorial	850,000	
		$ 13,390,000
Power		
Main wastewater pumping station	33,800,000	
Reclaimed water pumping station	7,890,000	
Aerated lagoons	9,235,000	
Irrigation and drainage pumping stations	6,650,000	
Irrigation rigs	1,200,000	
		$ 58,775,000
Chemicals	2,900,000	
		$ 2,900,000
Maintenance and supplies		
Pumping stations	1,150,000	
Aerated lagoons	340,000	
Chlorination facilities	70,000	
Irrigation rigs	1,160,000	
Transmission pipeline and tunnels	885,000	
		$ 3,605,000
Misc. building and site maintenance and supplies (incl. transportation)	1,530,000	
		$ 1,530,000
Sludge disposal	11,200,000	
		$ 11,200,000
Total operating and maintenance cost per year		$ 91,400,000
Present worth for operating and maintenance cost (1975-2025)		$1,255,000,000
Present worth for capital replacement costs (1975-2025)		60,140,000
Total present worth for the land treatment system		$3,315,000,000

a. Department of the Army, Office of the Chief of Engineers. 1972. Regional wastewater management systems for the Chicago Metropolitan Area. Summary Report and Tech. Appendix.

Chicago Regional Plan because of the larger diameter irrigation machines, and because of the thicker aquifer.

The return and reuse system of the Chicago Regional Plan is a significant portion of the cost because of the distance of the farm from the points of reuse.

Sources of Income

There are a number of potential sources of income from operations which can be accommodated at the land treatment site with little, if any, interference with the wastewater renovation operations, plus some that are incidental to the proper management of the system.

Agricultural Production
Crops produced on the farm can significantly reduce operating costs. For example, each acre of irrigated land will treat 2.5 million gallons of water each year. If this acre nets $100 per year in income – not at all impossible with the substantial quantity of water and fertilizer being applied – this is an income of $40 per million gallons of water treated, a significant reduction in net operating cost, representing about 40 percent of it.

Long-term Land Values
Included in the cost of the project is an area of about 200 acres of land for each one mgd average flow. This allows for the irrigated land, the land occupied by lagoons, and the land used for the consumption of the sludge as soil enrichment material. The value of this land over the long term could be very significant, particularly as it is in a large block. For example, assuming that some day in the future there is invented a much less expensive and even more effective method of wastewater treatment and renovation, the land could remain largely open and available for some other use. It would be completely equipped with irrigation and drainage systems, permitting high intensity agricultural use, for example. Assuming this to be the case, the cost recovery at some future date could well be $1000 per acre. This would recover $200,000 per mgd capacity or, roughly, 20 percent of the original cost of the project.

Electric Power Stations
Power generation demands of about four kw per capita are forecast for urban areas prior to the year 2000. Space of these stations appears to be difficult to obtain, as there is a strong desire by most persons not

to live near one. Space provided by the wastewater irrigation farm appears to offer the ideal solution, being near the urban areas, furnishing great isolation from human residential areas, furnishing plenty of make-up water for cooling, and in the large storage lagoons offering a possible heat exchanger facility which otherwise would have to be constructed by the electric utility. Taking the design population of the Chicago region to be 10 million persons, and taking the design average flow rate to be 3000 mgd, the possible installed capacity per mgd of wastewater average flow rate is 40,000 mw/300 mgd = 13 mw/mgd. It is realistic to charge a rental rate of $3 per year per kilowatt of installed capacity — this would be one percent of the capital cost of the facility — which would generate a revenue of roughly $40,000 per year per mgd, or about $110 per million gallons treated. This is seen to more than offset the total operating cost of the wastewater system, and is thus a very important factor in considering the economics of alternative systems. (This rental would be in addition to tax payments to local bodies.)

Sale of Cooling Water

Still another potential revenue comes from the sale of water for making up the water evaporated by cooling processes. Assuming 13 mw per mgd of treatment capacity, and assuming 12 mgd of average annual evaporation per 1000 mw of installed capacity, the amount of water evaporated would be 0.156 mgd/mgd. At a price of $50 per million gallons, this would be a revenue of $7.80 per million gallons treated, say, seven percent of the cost of treatment.

Sale of Industrial Process Water

Some industrial processes such as steel mills and paper mills, could logically be located on the site of the wastewater treatment system to make use of the partially treated water prior to irrigation. Rental space to such industries, and sale of water to them, could also produce a significant revenue. It is not estimated here, as the amount would depend upon the individual circumstances.

Solid-Waste Processing

There is plenty of space in the irrigation farm area to set up a solid-waste processing facility, and to construct land fills with the residual material remaining from such processing. Assuming one ton of solid waste per capita per year, a design population of 10 million persons, and an average flow of 3000 mgd including industrial and storm flows, there would be roughly 10 tons of solid waste per million gallons of water treated. Assuming a revenue of $2 per ton of solid waste processed, this would be a revenue of $20 per million gallons of water treated, or about 20 percent of the operating cost. Again, the amount of potential revenue is significant to the reduction of total costs to the citizen served.

Recreational Uses
During the nonirrigation season, the 6,000-acre Muskegon irrigation area and the 2,000 acres of unused buffer area could potentially be available for various kinds of recreational activities such as snowmobiling, riding, hunting and hiking. The storage lagoon surface area also provides a water habitat for various water fowl and other species. In Michigan, the various wastewater lagoon installations completed to date have significantly augmented the water surface wildlife propagation areas.

The value of land treatment sites as a means of containing urban sprawl and of maintaining agricultural areas is difficult to evaluate with a dollar figure, but many would ascribe significant value to this function.

Summary

The capital and operating costs for the Muskegon County, Michigan project and for the Chicago Regional Wastewater Plan have been presented in a form useful for making comparisons with alternative systems. Auxiliary uses of the land irrigation site are described briefly, and the approximate potential revenues from each estimated. It is obvious that the operating costs of the system could be largely if not entirely offset by using the same land irrigation site for many other purposes in addition to that of renovating the wastewater.

No discussion of the benefits of treating the wastewater to drinking water standards is presented here, as these benefits would be comparable for any other system which would achieve the same end result. It has been assumed that the high standards achievable by the land treatment process will be adopted by society as necessary, and that the most economical means to achieve them will be sought. With the possible incomes from other sources, the operating cost of the land treatment system is obviously very low, probably much lower than any other reasonable system of treatment, even ones with far less effectiveness in renovating the water. It is therefore our conclusion that the use of the land treatment system for large metropolitan areas deserves careful evaluation of those responsible for the planning and engineering of solutions to the present problems of water pollution.

Acknowledgments
The Muskegon County project has been financed in part with federal funds from the Environmental Protection Agency under grant number C261503, and also under grant number 11010 GFS for portions of the project work which are of a research and developmental nature. The contents of this chapter do not necessarily reflect the views and policies of the Environmental Protection Agency, nor does mention of trade names or commercial products constitute endorsement or recommendation for use.

The Chicago regional wastewater study is sponsored by the Chicago District, Corps of Engineers, Department of the Army. The official designation is the Chicago-South End of Lake Michigan Wastewater Management Study.

Discussion

Unknown: Would you explain land acquisition? Is this private large farm land or public land?

Bauer: Yes. In both of these cost estimates we assumed that the land would be acquired from private owners by the agency constructing the system. In the case of Muskegon County, the county is acquiring the land. Most of the land was acquired by direct negotiation. We did have an increase in the cost of the land at Muskegon over the original cost estimates. There are two reasons for the increase. One is, I suppose, that it just was not appraised properly in the first place. An independent land appraiser made an estimate of 2½ million dollars as being the acquisition price of the land, and we put it in our cost estimate as 3.2 million. The land is presently about 85 or 90 percent acquired and projecting on the basis of what has been spent so far, the total acquisition cost is estimated at roughly 5 million at the present time. Now that's 100 percent local cost. It's not shared by the federal and state governments. There is another cost, however, that is shared by the federal government, in fact, it's totally paid by federal funds. There was a law passed during the time the project was getting underway which said if federal money was involved and people were displaced on the land, they were to be compensated. In addition to being compensated for their land, they were to be paid for any other costs they may suffer because of being forced to move, such as additional interest on new mortgages. If they had an old mortgage at a low interest rate and now have to buy a new place and pay a higher interest rate; if they have moving expenses; maybe they couldn't find any property that was suitable without paying a higher price than they got for their old one and that kind of thing. Those payments added up to roughly somewhat less than a million and that's compensated for by the grant from the federal government. So these quoted land costs are the acquisition costs plus the relocation costs.

Davis: For both Chicago and Muskegon how much of this land would be used for farming or forest? You referred to using parts of it for lagoons and for electric plants and so on.

Bauer: Generally about 80 percent of it is used for agriculture and 20 percent of it would be used for the treatment facilities and related access.

Unknown: What kind of authority do you deem sufficient for the boundary area to come in both Illinois and Indiana?

Bauer: That's a subject that's being studied by someone else. The Corps of Engineers has engaged a separate consulting firm to study the jurisdictional and the institutional constraints. There are a number of alternatives. One is a private environmental utility and in that case it could be pretty well funded privately. This private environmental utility would enter into contracts with the various cities from which wastewater would be taken and would enter into contracts with farm operators and into contracts with the power companies that wanted facilities on the site. It would simply provide an environmental function. It would receive and process solid wastes and so forth. That's one very neat way to do it. It would also provide a very large tax base for the area in which the facility would be located. Another way would be to have an authority created that would go across state lines, something like the TVA. There are a number of ways it could be done.

Lyon: What degree of renovation do you expect to get from the irrigation drainage portion of the system?

Bauer: We expect to meet drinking water quality standards, and then beyond that we're very interested in removing as much phosphate as possible. Samples of the soil have been taken in the farm areas to try to make some assessment of its potential for precipitating out the phosphates, and according to the analyses of about 30 samples that have been made so far, in the Chicago region, the calculations show that on the surface of the soil particles is a 10,000 year supply of iron and aluminum for precipitating phosphates. So a very, very high degree of removal of phosphates is expected. The estimated concentration is about .01 milligrams per liter. The logic is based on the fact that this is the background level which is observed in natural streams that are fed by water which is percolating through the soil. It has been assumed natural soils have in the upper horizon a sizable phosphate concentration. They must have, otherwise, the plants wouldn't grow and yet we don't find soluble phosphates leaking down into the ground water and out into the river. Perhaps it is because of the huge surplus of precipitation capacity that exists in that soil. Now more phosphates will be put on the soil. We don't know how much we are going to accelerate the use of this precipitation capacity but after going through our analysis it is possible that the concentration will be down at that 0.01 milligram per liter level.

23
Implementing the Chicago Prairie Plan

Frank L. Kudrna and George T. Kelly*

The Metropolitan Sanitary District of Greater Chicago has been involved in environmental protection since its creation by the Illinois State Legislature over 80 years ago.

Collection, treatment, and recycle of all domestic and industrial waste is a day-to-day responsibility of the Metropolitan Sanitary District. During its long and successful history, the district has researched, investigated, and practiced numerous methods of chemical and biological treatment. The results of this experience have clearly indicated that the ultimate solution to today's problem of environmental destruction must come through an understanding of the environment and its natural purifying cycles. The Sanitary District has developed a program for the recycle and reuse of sewerage solids, the by-products of the water reclamation process. It is a far-reaching, environmentally sound program based on nature and the natural purifying cycles. The Sanitary District calls its concept, "The Prairie Plan."

The first implementation of "The Prairie Plan" is being carried out on over 7,000 acres of land in Fulton County, Illinois. The district is constructing, out of land laid barren by strip mining, an environmentally safe recycle farm with integrated monitoring, quality control provisions, and multiple-use facilities.

In 1967, the Board of Trustees of the Metropolitan Sanitary District formally adopted the environmentally sound policy of "Solids on Land," a concept for the beneficial recycle of sewerage solids, a by-product previously considered a waste material. With the adoption of this policy, the board authorized an extensive program of research and testing to develop a system for implementation of this policy. The resulting engineering reports, demonstration projects, and experimental farms have proven that the solid material removed from the used water, once stabilized, can safely, economically and productively be recycled to rebuild soil and sustain agricultural growth as a fertilizer substitute.

The most significant demonstration project has been a cooperative effort between the Sanitary District and the University of Illinois Agronomy Department under the sponsorship of a federal research

*The Metropolitan Sanitary District of Greater Chicago

grant. This continuing project is being conducted at a test farm at Elwood, Illinois, and is designed to monitor the immediate and long term environmental effect resulting from the use of solids, now called, "liquid fertilizer."

To demonstrate to the residents of communities outside of its jurisdiction boundaries (Cook County) that liquid fertilization is safe and nonobjectionable, the district constructed at least one demonstration project in each of its eight urbanized service basins within and surrounding the Chicago Metropolitan Area. The most significant of these is a working farm at the Hanover Water Reclamation Plant which has, for the past five years, utilized the liquid fertilizer within a successful farming operation. In addition, liquid fertilizer has been applied to park grasslands, has generated topsoil on a landfill in Lake Michigan (Northwestern University), and has generated growth on 37 acres of barren silica sand (Ottawa, Illinois).

The result of the research work and demonstration projects was a clear indication that liquid fertilizer could be safely, economically, and beneficially returned to the soil. Once the small scale programs had proven successful, the Sanitary District developed a concept for the large scale implementation of its recycle program called, the "Prairie Plan."

The Prairie Plan was the methodology for the location and total design development of the 30,000 usable acres of farmland needed for the safe recycle of all wastewater solids generated within the Sanitary District.

Simply stated, the Prairie Plan is a program that utilizes the assimilative capacity of nature for the environmentally sound assimilation of man's by-products. Based on a principle of watershed planning, it utilizes the ground as an immense, natural filter and collection system. Utilizing a single watershed with known physical characteristics as the basis for application, not only do the soil and living plants act as a filter, but there is a natural way to collect all of the filtered runoff at one point for continuous monitoring and water quality control. The result is a flowing stream which is clean, free from silt, and potentially a valuable resource for recreational, commercial, and industrial development.

The Metropolitan Sanitary District, after extensive land investigation, purchased in December of 1970, a parcel of land of approximately 7,000 acres in the northeastern portion of Fulton County located in the upper reaches of the Spoon River Watershed, approximately 200 miles southwest of Chicago.

The land was acquired with the complete knowledge and cooperation of the Fulton County Board of Supervisors. The site, a former strip mine, offered the unique opportunity to not only recycle liquid fertilizer but to reclaim mine spoil, thereby increasing the local tax base.

This site, although a relatively small percent of the entire Spoon River Watershed, is located on the headwaters to several small creek sheds. Its northern boundary follows a natural ridgeline and its eastern boundary is also the upper reaches of the watershed. Its location within the watershed, together with the disruption of existing drainage patterns due to the strip mining operations, has resulted in a site that is basically self-contained in terms of water flow. This condition allows a site plan to be developed around the concept of complete water monitoring and control, assuring environmental quality.

As a first step in the actual site development, an inventory of the physical characteristics of the land was completed. This environmental survey included topographical mapping, boundary mapping, surficial soil mapping, subsurface soil and bedrock investigation, surface drainage investigation and delineation of existing or potential floodplain areas.

The Board of Trustees of the Metropolitan Sanitary District, working in cooperation with the Fulton County Board of Supervisors, in order to assure optimum benefits from the development of its Fulton County project, brought together a Steering Committee to provide input into the land use planning of its property.

The membership of this Steering Committee includes local elected representatives, interested local citizens, agencies and departments of the State of Illinois (Illinois Environmental Protection Agency, Department of Conservation, Department of Business and Economic Development), the Soil Conservation Service, University of Illinois (Agronomy School and Extension Service), representatives of local educational institutions, as well as staff from the Sanitary District.

The goal of this committee has, from the beginning, been optimum use for the greatest public benefit; recognizing that although the land in Fulton County was purchased for the primary purpose of the Solids on Land program, the needs of the local communities could be introduced into the plans with compatible secondary goals of recreation, conservation and natural science education.

The initial land purchase was divided into three zones for planning and development. The land use plan for each of the areas was developed and reviewed under the general direction of the Steering Committee prior to implementation. The result of this action has been a land use policy that reflects the needs of both the citizens of Cook and Fulton Counties.

The primary example of this multiple-use concept has been the leasing of over 700 acres of lake and park land to the citizens of Fulton County by the Metropolitan Sanitary District for the annual

Figure 23-1. Holding basin

fee of $1. This fishing, camping and recreational site has become a well-known and highly utilized county resource.

The first objective of the Sanitary District was to quickly implement a transportation contract and develop temporary holding basins to provide relief for the increasing liquid fertilizer production in the Chicago area. This relief was provided by the construction of the first of three holding basins, a two million cubic-yard basin, costing $586,254. Then a three-year turnkey transportation contract was negotiated involving the shipment of four barge loads of fertilizer daily (7500 wet tons), via the Illinois River, 200 miles to Liverpool, Illinois. There, barge docks and unloading facilities were constructed and the material is pumped approximately ten and a half miles through a pipeline to the completed holding basins (Figure 23-1). The cost of the three-year transportation contract that was required to be operational in 90 days was $17,900,000.

Having solved its immediate problem, the Sanitary District developed farm fields out of the mine spoils and constructed a distribution system consisting of a dredge installed at the holding basins which carried the liquid fertilizer to a distribution header and pump station which then transports it via a series of surface pipelines to mobile water winch vehicles which spray the liquid fertilizer onto the farm fields (Figure 23-2). A total of 810 acres was put back into productive

Figure 23-2. Fertilizer distribution

agricultural utilization by the end of 1972. And by the end of 1973, over 3,000 acres will be in productive agriculture.

To date, the total cost of construction contracts awarded in the Fulton County area is over $22,000,000. At present, the district has under design three additional grading contracts, as well as their distribution piping and pumping facilities.

The overall project cost of the Fulton County operation is at present below the cost of other alternatives. The initial landholdings represent approximately 20 percent of the ultimate land needed for the recycle of all solids generated within the Sanitary District. As additional lands are acquired, a pipeline from the district will be constructed and the unit cost of the Fulton County program will be greatly reduced.

The Sanitary District, with its Prairie Plan program, has developed a way to actually realize the now popularized goals of recycle and reuse. The program has, from its conception, received very favorable local and national press. The district's work continues to be well received at the local level and 3,500 additional acres of land have been acquired as a result of this acceptance.

The slurry pipeline, now being planned, which will transport the liquid fertilizer from Chicago to Fulton County, is being thought of as having a unique multi-use potential of its own. Its location within a rapidly urbanizing region offers the possibility of significant areas of permanent open space, innerconnected with recreational trails, parks and facilities. The pipe is being planned so as to be able to accept inputs along the route from existing and projected urban developments, as well as having the provision for top-off for potential-use areas.

The acquisition and development of 30,000 usable acres of land within the framework of the Prairie Plan offers the possibility for the development of new towns and cities utilizing the open space, clean water and wastes assimilative capacities of the site.

The Prairie Plan, if developed to its full potential, could initiate and provide direction in developing regional parameters for physical economic development, could be the catalyst in the establishment of open-spaced areas, flood control, conservation and recreational space; and provide a new agricultural economic base for soil replenishment. It would become an integrated program for pollution control that would close the loop from user back to resource; converting society's discards into usable forms while maintaining the natural ecological balance.

The overall success of the plan to date has been the direct result of a thorough research and demonstration program and direct cooperative planning with local governments and State regulatory agencies.

The Prairie Plan is a project that is clearly both economically and ecologically sound.

Discussion

Larson: Do plans call for the use of barging transportation system permanently or is a pipeline in the future?

Kudrna: No. The economics are very clear. The pipeline cost is far less than barging. This is an interim measure because of the timetable involved. To get something started when only a portion of the land was available, the barging operation was used. But for long-term use, a pipeline is the most economical transportation method.

Unknown: Is 1 to 1.5% dry weight per year the application rate? The amount mentioned yesterday was 10 to 15 dry tons per acre.

Kudrna: The loading rate of sludge being used has been approved by the Illinois EPA for strip mine land and is a first-year application of 75 dry tons per acre. This will be reduced to 25 tons per acre in a period of five years as the organic content builds up. For undisturbed land that already has an organic content, the application rate begins at 25 tons.

Unknown: Are some cost figures available?

Kudrna: The cost per ton for the initial operation is approximately $70 a ton which is comparable to other processes. However, of that cost per ton, $34 are attributed simply to transportation. That cost is going to be greatly reduced with the pipeline in the long-term solution. Right now, it's either equal to or slightly less than the cost of alternative methods such as heat drying, incineration, Zimpro. However, it will drop when the long-term transportation system is adopted.

24
Spray Irrigation Project, Mt. Sunapee State Park, New Hampshire

Terrence P. Frost, R. E. Towne, and H. J. Turner*

The spray irrigation system in Sunapee State Park, Newbury, New Hampshire, distributes pretreated sewage to mountain slopes forested with mixed hardwoods and scattered conifers interspersed with occasional apple trees indicating orchard or pastureland abandoned a generation or more ago. Conifers tend to dominate the lower part of the slope with the numbers of oaks and birches increasing toward the upper levels. The system was planned and designed around The Pennsylvania State University project (Parizek *et al.*, 1967).

The Sunapee system is unique in size, degree of slope sprayed, seasonal character, relatively poor soils, high groundwater levels, and atypical sewage quality.

Selection of the land application system was based on several timely occurrences in addition to the Pennsylvania studies. The Sunapee State Park sewage disposal system is tributary to Chandler Brook which drains the mountainous ski-slope terrain into Lake Sunapee slightly less than a mile downstream. In 1969 the state legislature by statute upgraded the lake water quality classification from Class B to Class A. In the words of New Hampshire law "there shall be no discharge of any sewage or wastes into waters of this classification." The A classification, therefore, compelled some form of tertiary or advanced waste treatment technique at the State Park to prevent all wastes, treated or otherwise, from entry into Lake Sunapee. Hence, the selection of spray irrigation techniques which we were eager to apply in New Hampshire in anticipation of keeping the nutrients and other wastewater constituents out of the surface waters and away from the groundwater.

The popular demand for reclassification to A was based, primarily on prestigious considerations and fear of phosphorus from sewage sources and the resulting algae nuisances. Mats of water felt (*Vaucheria spp.*), unpleasant to barefooted bathers until controlled by the state, seriously interfered with water-based recreation at the Chandler Cove beaches and shoals. The algae nuisance was attributed in part to the treated, nutrient-bearing sewage entering the lake from the Sunapee Mountain recreational complex.

*Water Supply and Pollution Control Commission, State of New Hampshire

The Sunapee scheme is small. The spray area covers about four acres. The two holding ponds, originally designed as sewage stabilization or oxidation ponds and constructed in 1961 (Figure 24-1), are each about one acre, and located at the foot of the mountain. Influent to these sewage lagoons is by gravity flow in thousand-gallon increments pulled automatically from a siphon tank downstream and in series with the two state park septic tanks. These intermittent siphoned flows provide velocities sufficient to keep the downgrade pipeline clear.

The spray irrigation segment of the Sunapee system is seasonal. Spraying takes place only in the summer for about six weeks between the first of June and mid-July — long enough to draw down the average depth of the two oxidation ponds from six feet to about two feet. Withdrawal of the top two and a half million gallons for spray irrigation renews the ten-month storage volume. Natural runoff is diverted around the storage ponds except during the spray season by plugging one culvert and unplugging another. Prior to land application the stabilization pond effluent was disinfected and discharged annually each spring to the adjacent Chandler Brook during snow melt and subsequent high runoff.

Winter sports enthusiasts, chiefly skiers, enjoy the park in winter from mid-December to mid-March. About 113,000 tickets are sold each winter at Sunapee State Park. Summer tickets sold average nearly 33,000 for each of the last three years, 1969 through 1971. Nearly all of the summer tickets are for rides up the mountain and back by gondola ski lift. The park supervisor advised there are probably as many non-ticket-buying picnickers using the park as there are lift-riders. The park is little-used in late spring and late fall.

Description of the Soils

The soils of the forested spray irrigation plot, according to the United States Soil Conservation Service (Pilgrim, 1972) are typical of those found in the low mountain areas of New England. Granite stones are found both on the surface and within the soil. Natural fertility is quite low and the soils are acid. The area is dominated by well-drained soils with soil depth of more than four feet. Stone piles in the area indicate that the soils were farmed during earlier times.

Four distinct soils (Charlton, Millis, Norwell and Paxton) have been identified on the area. All have developed in loamy glacial till material derived principally from granite and mica schist rocks. Paxton, the dominant soil of the area is characterized as follows:

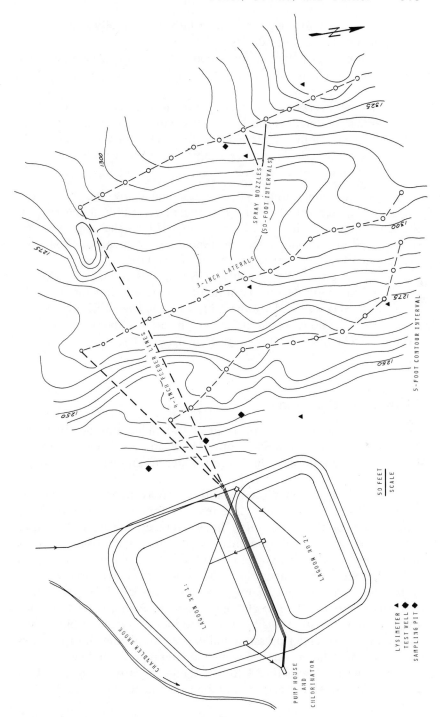

Figure 24-1. Mt. Sunapee State Park spray irrigation system

1. a three-inch forest floor surface layer of partially decomposed pine needles and deciduous leaf material
2. a subsoil layer extending to about 24 inches consisting of dark brown, fine, sandy loam. Water moves at a moderate rate through this layer
3. a distinct hardpan layer occurs at about two feet and extends to depths greater than four feet. This hardpan layer is light olive brown and of fine sandy-loam texture. Vertical water movement is slow through this pan and most water moves laterally down slope on the top of the pan.

Annual soil monitoring is being conducted by the Soil Conservation Service and the New Hampshire Agricultural Experiment Station. Eight soil pits have been established on the area. Pits are opened for soil sampling after the summer spray operation. Soil samples are analyzed for changes in chemical properties.

A comparison of water quality of Sunapee holding pond effluent (spray irrigant) with the quality of holding pond effluents (after secondary treatment) reported by the Corps of Engineers, United States Army, Cold Regions Research and Engineering Laboratory at Hanover, New Hampshire (1972) is given in Table 24-1.

Method of Operation

Oxidation pond effluent chlorinated at five milligrams per liter was sprayed for about six weeks during June and July, 1971 onto the somewhat hilly four-and-a-half acre wooded terrain with slopes of 10 to 15 percent.

Spraying was accomplished via three spray lines, A, B, and C (Figure 24-1) covering about 1.5 acres each for a total coverage of 4.5 acres. Each of the three spray lines averaged fourteen Rain Bird kicker-type spray heads mounted on two-foot high risers. Feeder lines ascending the slope are four-inch diameter aluminum irrigation pipe. Lateral spray lines are three-inch diameter conventional farm-type irrigation pipe. Spray nozzles are spaced 50 feet apart. Laterals range from 600 to 700 feet in length. Piping is held in place by metal fence posts. Initially, when laid loose on cement blocks the pipelines rotated under pressure and caused misalignment of risers as well as chronic uncouplings of main and lateral horizontal pipelines.

Distance from lateral line A to B is about 75 yards. From B to C is about 85 yards. All piping is self-draining to the northernmost holding pond.

Spray nozzles were of three different sizes, one size to each of the

Table 24-1. Comparison of Sunapee holding pond effluent with a typical secondary treatment plant effluent

Constituent	Typical Composition* Range	Sunapee Composition Low	Mean	High
	mg/l		mg/l	
BOD	2-25	12	28	55
SS	3-50	25	83	296
NH_3-N	0-10	0.1	2.0	4.4
NO_2-N	2-13	0.01	0.14	0.95
NO_3-N	7-13	0.16	0.61	1.48
P	4-14	0.7	0.9	1.2
Na	40-100	6.2	17.0	21.2
Cl	40-100	11	23	30
Ca^{++}	1-40	5.8	8.4	14.5
Mg^{++}	1-10	3.45	6.75	11.80
K^+	7-10	5.3	6.8	8.1
LAS	5-10	<0.1	0.2	0.3
pH	6.5-7.5	7.0	7.9	8.5

*Excerpted from Table 3-1, p. 36, *Wastewater Management by Disposal on the Land*, Cold Regions Research and Engineering Laboratory, Hanover, New Hampshire, February 1972.

three lines to compensate for elevation differences between the lines. Circular coverage around each riser was about one hundred feet in diameter. Nozzle pressures ranged from 40 to 60 pounds per square inch. Each line delivered approximately 100 gallons per minute during the fourteen hours it operated once each week. Application rate amounted to 0.14 inch per hour, equivalent to a total weekly application of about two inches.

Spraying was done Tuesday, Wednesday and Thursday. Automatic, sequencing timers started opening a motorized valve at 6:00 A.M. The valve when half-open, energized one of two pumps and the spraying began, continuing until 8:00 P.M.

The system is protected against breaks in couplings or piping by use of a time delay device which will shut off the valve and stop the pump if pressure is not reached within four minutes of starting time. This avoids flooding the pumps and the combination pumphouse and chlorinator room. Both pumps are 15 horsepower, electrically driven with one hundred gallons per minute pumping capacity against a 100-foot head. Pumps were alternated each week.

Configuration of the sprayed terrain is such that most, if not all, of the runoff from the sprayed area will divert back to the stabilization ponds for ultimate reapplication to the irrigation area.

Four forest floor (duff) pan lysimeters constructed as shown in Figure 24-2 were randomly installed within the spray area and two

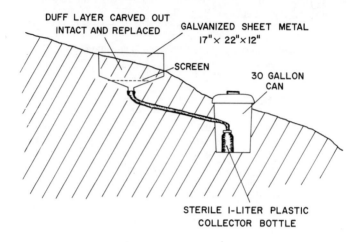

DUFF LAYER CARVED OUT
INTACT AND REPLACED

GALVANIZED SHEET METAL
17" × 22" × 12"

SCREEN

30 GALLON
CAN

STERILE I-LITER PLASTIC
COLLECTOR BOTTLE

Figure 24-2. Diagram of duff pan lysimeter

were placed as controls outside the area, one at a higher and one at a lower elevation than the spray area. Method of placement was to remove the upper four to eight inches of forest floor and soil with as little disturbance as possible, put the duff pan in place, and replace the relatively undisturbed duff layer and soil in the pan. Figure 24-2 also shows the method of sample collection in sterile polyethylene two-liter bottles left in thirty-gallon, friction-top, galvanized, weatherproof cans sunk into the ground down slope of the duff pans. The lysimeters were designed and positioned to collect precipitation and spray liquid so that the volume per unit area could be estimated, and the collected percolate analyzed in the laboratory.

A test pit about three feet wide, seven feet long and five feet deep was dug within the spray area with lysimeter pans staggered along one wall at the one-, two-, three-, and four-foot depths and the pit covered with a hinged four by eight foot sheet of ⅝ inch marine plywood. The pit was later abandoned due to high groundwater and doubt as to ability to collect representative samples.

A standard rain gauge was located under the forest canopy near the top of and within the spray area; a second rain gauge was placed outside the spray area in the open near the holding ponds. Rainfall at the site for three years of record, 1969-1971, averaged 37.6 inches. Rainfall for 30 years of record at the United States Weather Service rain gauge at the Concord, New Hampshire airport, about 30 miles from the spray site, averaged 38.8 inches.

Three well-points were driven along the downstream periphery of the slopes and used as test wells. These three test wells, driven to the point of refusal, average about 11 feet in depth and are used to assay groundwater quality on the downslope periphery of the spray area between the irrigation plot and the holding ponds. In addition seven downstream domestic wells and one public spring were routinely sampled.

Two sampling stations were located on Chandler Brook bracketing the spray area. Comparative water samples from water supply wells, test wells, duff pans, holding pond influent and effluent, and the brook were collected and analyzed weekly for the components listed in the various tables. Sampling continued before, during, and after the spray period.

Results

Preliminary analyses of the data indicate that spray irrigating with pretreated sewage stabilization pond effluent at Sunapee State Park in Newbury, New Hampshire has not resulted in any substantial or discernible alteration in the composition of the groundwater in the test wells, water from the drinking water wells, or downstream surface waters. Quality of the percolate water collected from a lysimeter in the spray irrigated area is given in Table 24-2. For comparison, the quality of the percolate water collected from a lysimeter in the control area is given in Table 24-3. Condensed analytical results from Test Well B are given in Table 24-4. Results, unreported here, were similar for other test wells. Water quality samples collected from Chandler Brook upstream of the project are given in Table 24-5. For comparative purposes, Chandler Brook surface water quality data collected downstream of the project are given in Table 24-6. Groundwater quality in the Herbert Smith family drinking water well is given in Table 24-7. No changes that are positively attributable to the project appear in the water quality data for the Smith water supply. There is a possibility that consistently higher nitrate nitrogen results may, later in the study, be attributed to the spray system. The Smith well is about 800 feet from the spray area and is the private water supply nearest the project. Data were accumulated for four other well supplies and one surface spring. None of these supplies exhibited discernible water quality changes attributable to the spray operation.

The uptake or percentage removal of various constituents in the irrigant by the four to eight inches of forest floor materials in the duff pan lysimeters is shown in Table 24-8.

Table 24-2. Quality of percolate water collected from a lysimeter in the spray irrigated area

Constituent	Time	Number of Samples	Range	Mean
			mg/l	mg/l
PO_4-P	before	12	0.000- 0.090	0.033
	during	5	0.025- 0.072	0.050
	after	15	0.003- 0.174	0.030
pH	before	15	5.5 - 7.7	6.6
	during	5	5.6 - 6.8	6.3
	after	28	5.2 - 7.0	6.2
Alkalinity	before	15	5 -23	13
	during	5	12 -20	17
	after	28	3 -50	15
NO_2-N	before	13	0.000- 0.046	0.014
	during	5	0.002- 0.174	0.075
	after	24	0.010- 1.350	0.291
NO_3-N	before	15	0.052- 2.180	0.860
	during	5	1.17 - 7.17	3.62
	after	28	0.13 -26.20	7.26
Cl^-	before	13	0.5 - 4.8	2.0
	during	5	7.3 -18.5	12.3
	after	22	<1.0 -17.5	<3.0
Ca^{++}	before	14	0.8 - 3.1	2.6
	during	5	5.2 - 9.2	6.8
	after	27	<0.1 -44.2	<14.5
K^+	before	15	0.7 - 4.9	3.6
	during	5	4.9 - 8.2	6.4
	after	28	1.6 -10.0	5.8
LAS	before	12	<0.1 -<0.1	<0.1
	during	4	< 0.1 -<0.1	<0.1
	after	18	< 0.1 -<0.1	<0.1
Mg^{++}	before	14	0.30 - 1.60	0.70
	during	5	0.78 - 1.49	1.12
	after	28	<0.01 - 3.66	1.50
Na	before	15	0.3 - 4.5	1.6
	during	5	0.7 - 7.5	4.2
	after	28	0.6 -11.7	2.1

Table 24-3. Quality of the percolate water collected from a lysimeter in the control area

Constituent	Time	Number of Samples	Range	Mean
			mg/l	mg/l
PO$_4$-P	before	13	0.000- 0.396	.058
	during	1	—	.020
	after	11	0.003- 0.144	.028
pH	before	13	5.1 - 6.7	6.1
	during	1	—	6.1
	after	21	5.3 - 7.4	6.4
Alkalinity	before	14	2 -18	12
	during	1	—	20
	after	20	7 -25	15
NO$_2$-N	before	12	<.001- .013	.067
	during	1	—	.002
	after	20	<.001- .678	.115
NO$_3$-N	before	13	.089- .926	.494
	during	1	—	.556
	after	21	.070- 6.57	1.964
Cl$^-$	before	13	0.4 - 7.0	2.2
	during	1	—	2.0
	after	20	1.0 - 5.1	2.2
Ca^{++}	before	14	0.6 -11.2	2.5
	during	1	—	2.7
	after	24	<0.1 -12.2	3.2
K$^+$	before	14	3.0 - 8.0	4.7
	during	1	—	6.5
	after	24	1.5 -11.0	4.5
LAS	before	12	all <0.1	<0.1
	during	1	—	<0.1
	after	15	<0.1 - 0.2	<0.1
Mg^{++}	before	14	.46 - 3.20	1.01
	during	1	—	0.62
	after	24	.37 - 1.68	0.94
Na	before	14	0.3 - 9.3	1.8
	during	1	—	0.8
	after	24	0.3 - 1.5	0.8

Table 24-4. Water quality of samples collected from Test Well B

Constituent	Time	Number of Samples	Range	Mean
			mg/l	mg/l
PO$_4$-P	before	34	0.000- 0.149	<0.018
	during	7	0.006- 0.017	0.012
	after	30	<0.001- 0.047	<0.012
pH	before	36	6.1 - 8.0	7.2
	during	7	6.4 - 7.5	7.0
	after	46	4.6 - 8.0	7.0
Alkalinity	before	35	30 - 46	38
	during	7	31 - 36	34
	after	46	30 - 45	35
NO$_2$-N	before	33	0.000- 0.163	0.003
	during	7	0.008- 0.019	0.011
	after	40	0.003- 0.167	0.040
NO$_3$-N	before	34	0.011- 1.550	0.191
	during	7	0.051- 0.460	0.218
	after	45	<0.001- 1.110	<0.151
Cl$^-$	before	34	0.5 - 5.5	2.2
	during	7	1.0 - 1.7	1.3
	after	40	1.5 - 5.6	2.8
Ca^{++}	before	37	4.0 - 30.7	10.4
	during	8	7.6 - 12.5	8.5
	after	45	0.2 - 13.8	4.8
K$^+$	before	33	0.7 - 5.1	1.9
	during	8	1.2 - 1.6	1.5
	after	45	0.8 - 3.4	1.5
LAS	before	32	<0.1 - 0.1	<0.06
	during	7	<0.1 -<0.1	<0.1
	after	23	<0.1 -<0.1	- <0.1
Mg^{++}	before	34	0.84 - 5.50	1.63
	during	8	0.86 - 1.11	0.99
	after	45	0.29 - 1.58	0.61
Na	before	33	3.6 - 6.6	4.9
	during	8	1.58 - 4.25	3.71
	after	45	2.4 - 7.3	3.5
MPN		34	<3 <3	<3

Table 24-5. Water quality of samples collected from Chandler Brook upstream of the spray irrigation project

Constituent	Time	Number of Samples	Range	Mean
			mg/l	mg/l
PO$_4$-P	before	18	0.003- 0.032	0.012
	during	7	0.012- 0.162	0.044
	after	27	<0.001- 0.165	0.029
pH	before	20	6.2 - 6.9	6.5
	during	7	6.2 - 7.2	6.8
	after	41	4.6 - 7.2	6.6
Alkalinity	before	20	7 - 20	14
	during	7	18 - 28	23
	after	41	6 - 60	23
NO$_2$-N	before	20	0.002- 0.012	0.005
	during	7	0.001- 0.078	0.014
	after	40	0.001- 0.715	0.039
NO$_3$-N	before	20	0.076- 1.34	0.294
	during	7	0.080- 0.259	0.172
	after	41	<0.010- 2.450	<0.272
Cl$^-$	before	20	4 -175	20
	during	7	10 - 21	15
	after	40	<1.0 -610	<24
Ca^{++}	before	20	3.6 - 19.0	7.74
	during	7	6.8 - 12.8	9.99
	after	41	0.50 - 33.0	7.45
K$^+$	before	20	0.5 - 3.1	0.9
	during	7	0.4 - 1.0	0.8
	after	41	0.4 - 2.8	2.0
LAS	before	17	<0.1 - <0.1	<0.1
	during	6	<0.1 - <0.1	<0.1
	after	20	<0.1 - <0.1	<0.1
Mg^{++}	before	20	0.61 - 1.68	1.01
	during	7	0.14 - 1.73	1.04
	after	41	0.37 - 4.60	0.97
Na	before	20	4.0 -103.0	13.9
	during	7	2.1 - 11.7	8.4
	after	40	3.3 - 27.0	14.2

Table 24-6. Water quality of samples collected from Chandler Brook downstream of the spray irrigation project

Constituent	Time	Number of Samples	Range		Mean
			mg/l		mg/l
PO$_4$-P	before	19	0.002-	0.031	0.012
	during	7	0.001-	0.041	0.019
	after	27	<0.001-	0.054	<0.014
pH	before	20	6.2 -	7.1	6.7
	during	7	6.7 -	7.0	6.8
	after	40	6.1 -	7.3	6.6
Alkalinity	before	20	6 -	22	15
	during	7	9 -	31	23
	after	40	7 -	35	20
NO$_2$-N	before	16	0.004-	0.010	0.007
	during	7	0.001-	0.101	0.019
	after	38	<0.001-	0.825	<0.043
NO$_3$-N	before	20	0.098-	0.467	0.192
	during	7	0.080-	0.348	0.239
	after	38	<0.010-	0.584	0.180
Cl$^-$	before	20	3 -	29	18
	during	7	0 -	39	27
	after	39	0 -	52	21
Ca^{++}	before	20	3.8 -	12.5	8.1
	during	7	9.3 -	15.2	12.8
	after	40	0.7 -	28.6	10.8
K$^+$	before	20	0.5 -	1.8	0.9
	during	7	0.5 -	1.6	1.2
	after	40	0.4 -	2.5	1.2
LAS	before	18	<0.1 -	<0.1	<0.1
	during	6	<0.1 -	<0.1	<0.1
	after	20	<0.1 -	<0.1	<0.1
Mg^{++}	before	20	0.64 -	1.33	1.05
	during	7	0.98 -	2.23	1.66
	after	40	0.38 -	1.95	1.19
Na	before	20	2.9 -	19.4	10.6
	during	6	2.3 -	22.9	12.4
	after	40	1.8 -	25.6	15.1

Table 24-7. Water quality of samples collected from the Herbert Smith well about 800 feet from the spray irrigation project

Constituent	Time	Number of Samples	Range	Mean
			mg/l	mg/l
PO$_4$-P	before	16	0.011- 0.042	0.026
	during	7	0.018- 0.057	0.035
	after	40	<0.001- 0.71	<0.080
pH	before	16	6.0 - 6.8	6.3
	during	8	6.2 - 6.9	6.6
	after	39	6.0 - 6.85	6.4
Alkalinity	before	16	7 - 16	13
	during	8	12 - 24	18
	after	40	2 - 75	17
NO$_2$-N	before	16	0.000- 0.012	0.004
	during	8	0.001- 0.017	0.004
	after	38	0.000- 0.113	0.009
NO$_3$-N	before	16	0.007- 0.096	0.043
	during	8	0.012- 0.184	0.096
	after	39	0.000- 0.57	0.116
Cl$^-$	before	14	0.0 - 20.0	1.8
	during	7	0.0 - 26.8	4.6
	after	38	0.0 - 15.5	1.4
Ca^{++}	before	16	3.4 - 7.0	5.5
	during	8	5.0 - 10.0	6.2
	after	40	0.5 - 12.3	5.3
K$^+$	before	16	0.3 - 3.1	0.8
	during	8	0.3 - 0.5	0.4
	after	40	0.2 - 2.0	0.6
LAS	before	14	0.0 -<0.1	<0.1
	during	6	<0.1 -<0.1	<0.1
	after	20	<0.1 -<0.1	<0.1
Mg^{++}	before	16	0.01 - 6.80	1.65
	during	8	0.48 - 1.00	0.72
	after	40	0.40 - 1.80	0.78
Na	before	16	2.0 - 14.8	3.9
	during	8	0.8 - 4.5	3.0
	after	38	0.9 - 8.3	3.2

Table 24-8. Degree of wastewater reclamation by upper eight inches of forest floor and soil

Constituent		Percentage removal[a]	Average
Nitrite	(N)	47-94	71
Nitrate	(N)	0-46	16
Phosphate	(P)	92-98	95
Potassium	(K^+)	0-32	15
Sodium	(Na^+)	46-92	68
Chloride	(Cl^-)	0-81	34
Magnesium	(Mg^{++})	0-54	24
Detergent	(LAS)	50-100	87
Calcium	(Ca^{++})	0-80	44

a. Values obtained from 4 duff pan lysimeters.

Conclusion

The small, seasonal, atypical sewage spray irrigation system at the Sunapee State Park in Newbury, New Hampshire appears to have worked effectively to date to protect contiguous groundwater and surface waters. Based on experience in New Hampshire and Pennsylvania it is the opinion of the New Hampshire Water Supply and Pollution Control Commission staff that the Sunapee system will probably continue to operate effectively for a long and perhaps indefinite period of time at the present mode of operation.

Literature Cited

Corps of Engineers. 1972. U. S. Army, Cold Regions Research and Engineering Laboratory, *Wastewater Management by Disposal on Land,* Hanover, New Hampshire.

Parizek, R. R., L. T. Kardos, W. E. Sopper, E. A. Myers, D. E. Davis, M. A. Farrell, and J. B. Nesbitt. 1967. Wastewater renovation and conservation, Penn State Studies 23, The Pennsylvania State University, University Park, Penna., 73 pp.

Pilgrim, Sidney. 1972. Personal communication, United States Conservation Service, Durham, New Hampshire.

25
Utilization of Spray Irrigation for Wastewater Disposal in Small Residential Developments

T. C. Williams*

Williams and Works has designed sixteen pond and irrigation waste-water treatment systems for various governmental units in Michigan. Eleven of these are completed, and the other five will be operational in 1974. The first pond and irrigation wastewater system was that for the Village of Cassopolis which was constructed in 1964. The Casso-polis system consisted of a series of ponds, Pond 1 being an anaerobic cell, Pond 2 being a clay-lined facultative pond, Pond 3 and Pond 4 being unsealed seepage ponds which we anticipated would seal up and become facultative ponds. Ponds 3 and 4 were expected to leak but not, in the long run, to be able to handle the total influent hydraulic load, and therefore, we provided a spray irrigation system of about five acres on the tail-end of the system so there would be a way of disposing of any surplus water at the time the ponds sealed. As it turned out, the seepage ponds have been more than enough to handle the total hydraulic loading and in consequence, the spray irrigation system has not been used. It is important to keep the seepage pond areas mowed and to dose them intermittently. So even though this system has been in operation for eight years, we do not have any operating data on the spray irrigation part of the system. In addition to these various pond and irrigation wastewater treatment systems, we have designed, during the past ten years, more than twenty pond systems in which treatment is followed by discharge of the treated wastewater to a nearby water course on a semi-annual basis.

Pond Design

Over the years, the words "lagoon" and "pond" have been used interchangeably. But due to the widespread news coverage given to a western Michigan city when they had odor problems with a sludge lagoon, we have adopted the use of the word "pond" almost exclusively for our purposes. But whether they are lagoons or ponds, one of the following designs has been used for the systems we have developed:

*Williams and Works, Inc.

1. Two facultative ponds designed to operate either in parallel or in series at the discretion of the operator. The operating manuals recommend these ponds should be operated in parallel during the winter and in series during the summer. During the winter, very little biological activity takes place in these ponds and it is important that the organic loading be distributed between the two to minimize odor problems in the spring when biological activity resumes.
2. A series of ponds, consisting of an anaerobic cell followed by at least three facultative cells.
3. Mechanically aerated ponds, followed by holding ponds. These artificially aerated ponds can be either surface aerated with floating aerators or can be aerated with compressed air.

An advantage of using the first type is that facultative ponds require a minimum of operational attention. The treatment is accomplished by natural means using the sun and the wind. Also, there is a heavy algae bloom during the irrigation season and as a consequence, the nitrogen, phosphorus and other organics are, to a large degree, bound up in the algae cells at the time of irrigation. When properly loaded, these ponds are quite nuisance-free. The major disadvantage to this type of design, in Michigan at least, is the result of the climate which limits the possible loading to a maximum of 20 pounds of BOD per acre. This limitation increases the land requirements, of course, to such an extent that in some cases it is not economically feasible to pursue the development. This is the most expensive pond system in terms of capital requirements but it is the least expensive in terms of operating costs.

The second method, the use of an anaerobic cell followed by facultative ponds, is also a natural system. Significant phosphorus and nitrogen reductions are achieved by the growth of different biota in each pond. An added advantage is the fact that less land is required than for facultative pond systems. When they are properly designed and operated, these anaerobic-facultative systems can also be nuisance-free. However, there are instances when it is not possible to control the unit loading on the anaerobic cell and odor problems have resulted. As a part of an EPA-sponsored research project on irrigation of pond effluent at Belding, Michigan, data have been collected for the past five months on the anaerobic-facultative pond system. They show a significant decrease in the phosphorus and nitrogen through the pond system. It has also been noted that while there is an abundance of phosphorus and nitrogen in the last two ponds, there is not always a significant algae bloom. The wastewater to be irrigated from this pond system is much lower in nutrients than that from the activated sludge plant at Penn State. The Belding system is a mature pond system. It has been in operation since 1965 and, incidentally, it does take a significant volume of combined storm and sanitary flow in addition to the strictly sanitary flow from the community.

The third type of design involves the use of artificial aeration and is used most frequently for larger communities because the land requirements are less. The disadvantage is in the additional operating expense necessitated by increased maintenance requirements and the purchase of electricity.

One important consideration in each of the three types of lagoon systems we have designed is the provision for a minimum of five months storage of the wastewater. In our opinion there are three major advantages of this provision:

1. The severe climate in Michigan presents special irrigation problems during the winter. The storage of the wastewater avoids these problems.
2. Operation costs for the treatment portion of the system are substantially reduced as the storage pond can be depended upon to provide a certain portion of the treatment.
3. The storage allows for the development of algae and rotifers. To some extent, a prolific growth of these organisms converts the soluble phosphorus and nitrogen into cells which are of value in the irrigation process. The nutrients are applied to the land in cellular rather than liquid form, and this allows for a slower breakdown and absorption rate.

The selection of the best lagoon design for a particular client should be made on the basis of site availability, economics and operating experience. It is relatively easy to evaluate data pertaining to sites and economics — engineers have been doing that for centuries — but in the area of operating experience, a severe shortage of data is encountered. There is a certain amount of information about the irrigation of effluent from mechanical treatment plants. Unfortunately, however, there are very few systems involving the combination of ponds and irrigation in operation at the present time — and these have been operating for such a short time that there is only a limited amount of data available. At best, theory is guided by opinions.

The following data pertain to the operation and characteristics of   . the pond system at Belding, Michigan, from March 15 through July, 1972:

General characteristics of the influent:
NH_3-nitrogen — 25 ppm
Total phosphorus — 2 to 12 ppm P, about 75% of which is orthophosphate P
pH 7.2, DO 0.0

Pond water quality variations:

Pond 1: NH_3-N – 20 ppm in April, 20-25 ppm in August

	Pond 1		Pond 2		Pond 3		Pond 4		Pond 5	
	Apr.	Aug.	Apr.	Aug.	Apr.	Aug.	Apr.	Aug.	Apr.	Aug.
NH_3-N	20	25	20	5	20	<0.5	20	<0.5	20	<0.5
NO_3-N		<0.6		<0.6		<0.6		<0.25		<0.25
P	5	10	5	5	9	2	9	2	9	2
pH		7.2	varies considerably with photoreproduction							
SS	60 ppm with great variation						20-25			
DO	<0.1 highly variable, max. 25+						highly variable but never 0.0			

With respect to chemical and particulate changes Ponds 1 and 2 are each uniquely different and Ponds 3, 4 and 5 are similar to each other but different from 1 and 2. In general suspended solids (SS) and concentration of living organisms are directly related. Values of pH above 8.3 and dissolved oxygen (DO) above 10 ppm occur together and are products of photosynthesis.

In Pond 1 during March through June decomposition of algae is rapid in the anaerobic deeper waters and phosphorus is released as rapidly as it becomes organic bound in the upper layer. Additional phosphorus is solubilized in May as decay of older detritus becomes significant. In July, Pond 1 "went bad" losing most of its aerated upper water and aerobic populations died and settled out.

In Pond 2 the living populations have their greatest range in photosynthetic activity and population concentration resulting in a more stable total phosphorus concentration and occasional extremely high DO values.

In Ponds 3, 4 and 5 as living populations and concomitant populations of dead and settled organisms increased through March and April, total phosphorus decreased. From mid-May through June, release of phosphorus by decomposition of dead organisms became dominant. DO and pH responded to photosynthesis in all months but were outstandingly volatile in July.

Irrigation Design
The selection of the best land disposal method is only slightly more scientific than the means available for determining the best lagoon system. However, by the end of 1973, we anticipate having better data on the various methods we have utilized. Basically, one or more of the following methods are incorporated into the projects we have designed:

1. Continuously loaded seepage basins.
2. Intermittently loaded seepage basins.

3. Intermittently loaded flood irrigation fields.
4. Portable aluminum pipe systems.
5. Solid set systems in which the pipes are buried.
6. Traveling sprinkler.
7. Center pivot sprinklers.

In selecting the proper land disposal method, consideration must be given to soils, topography, climate, depth to groundwater table, direction of movement of the groundwater table, chemistry of the natural groundwater, proximity of wells tapping the groundwater formation being recharged, and cropping.

In Michigan, it is common practice to chlorinate lagoon effluent before spray irrigation. There is general agreement, however, that chlorination is not necessary in flood irrigation or seepage basin projects except in those instances in which the flood irrigation area is underdrained. The lower power requirements and the avoidance of chlorination costs have combined to make a substantial argument in favor of flood irrigation and seepage methods (1, 2, and 3). However, it is most difficult to achieve uniform distribution of the nutrients over the entire site with these systems. If the concept to be followed involves the reliance upon soil chemistry for nutrient removal, the method of application is not as important. If, however, the Penn State "Living Filter" concept of nutrient removal by cropping is to be utilized, then spray irrigation is the best method.

Tables 25-1 and 25-2 give design data on nine pond and spray irrigation land disposal projects in Michigan. These vary in size from 6,000 to 900,000 gallons per day. Table 25-3 gives the construction cost per capita. In the following table, these costs have been grouped according to the size of the community:

Population Design		Per Capita Cost
Less than 2,000	2 Systems	$212 to $520
2,001–8,000	6 Systems	$ 43 to $170
More than 8,000	1 System	$126

Activated sludge treatment plants in Michigan towns between 3,000 and 12,000 population, for the same time period, varied from $77 to $274 per capita. Generally, in evaluating alternatives, we find that a modified activated sludge treatment plant with chemical precipitation results in the lowest first cost when we take into consideration the land cost for land disposal schemes.

For the past several years in Michigan, grants have totalled 75 percent of all eligible project costs. The State of Michigan provides 25 percent in addition to the 50 percent federal grants available. Since land costs are not grant eligible, land disposal is the "high-priced

Table 25-1. Design data for several spray irrigation systems in Michigan

Project	Design Population (year)	Future Population	Design Flow	Loading in lbs. BOD per day	Total Retention Time	Total Pond Area
			gpd		months	acres
Belding	8,000 (1993)		800,000	1,360	4	51.4
Middleville	2,200	3,200 (1990)	150,000[a]	374	5	22.0
Ottawa Co. Infirmary	63 (1968)	80	6,000	16	7	1.0
East Jordan	3,700 (1990)		370,000	440	7	22.0
Wayland	5,000 (1990)		500,000	850	5	31.0
Harbor Springs	7,000[d] (1970)		580,000[b] 460,000[c,e]	765[b] 425[c]	5	21.4
Leoni Twp.	9,000 (1975)	25,000	900,000	1,530	6	35.5
Roscommon Village	1,550 (1990)		155,000	264	6	16.0
Cassopolis	2,200 (1970)		220,000	374	5.5	18.5

a. Approximate average measured flow over a 5-year period.
b. Summer time—approximately 3 months.
c. Winter time—approximately 9 months.
d. 4,500 summer population; 2,500 winter population.
e. Includes 310,000 gpd infiltration.

Table 25-2. Spray irrigation application rates for several spray irrigation systems in Michigan

Project	Type of Spray Irrigation	Area of Spray Irrigation	Instant Application Rate	Application Rate	Yearly Application Rate (Period of time)
		acres	in./hr	in./hr	inches
Belding	solid set	15.6	0.12	2.0 3.0[a] 4.0	80[b]
Middleville	solid set, portable laterals	25.1 and 5.3	0.12 0.12	2.7[c]	(7 mo.) 80[b]
Ottawa Co. Infirmary	portable laterals	3.3	0.25	2	(3 mo.) 80
East Jordan	solid set, portable laterals	42.0	0.12	2.86	(7 mo.) 62
Wayland	traveling, center pivot	20.0 and 33.0	–	2.5	(7 mo.) 76

a. Different application rates on different crop areas; there are 5 different areas.
b. The length of the irrigation period is being determined by tests—the rest of the effluent will be disposed of into the nearby river.
c. Used for future expansion.

Table 25-2. (continued)

Project	Type of Spray Irrigation	Area of Spray Irrigation acres	Instant Application Rate in./hr	Application Rate in./hr	Yearly Application Rate (Period of time) inches
Harbor Springs	traveling, center pivot	30.0 and 21.3	—	4.0 4.3	(5 mo.) 88[d] (5 mo 95
Leoni Twp.	solid set	140	0.36	3.3	(6 mo.) 86.3
Roscommon Village	solid set	24.0	0.20	3.3	(6 mo.) 86
Cassopolis	solid set, fixed laterals	8.0	0.04	12.4	(2.5 mo.) 346

d. Approx. 2 months of storage has to be disposed by other means.

Table 25-3. Per capita costs for several spray irrigation systems in Michigan

Project	Acres of Land Purchased (Cost per Acre)	Cost of Ponds			Cost of Spray Irrigation			Total Treatment Cost	
		Total	Per Acre	Per Capita	Total	Per Acre	Per Capita	Total	Per Capita (not incl. Land)
Belding	—	$257,200	$ 5,000	$32.20	$ 91,980	$5,100	$10.50	$ 349,200	$ 42.70
Middleville	124.5 ($350)	159,600	7,250	72.50	62,800	2,060	28.50	260,650	118.35
Ottawa Co. Infirmary	already owned the land	a	—	—	a	—	—	32,800	520.00
East Jordan	used the airport property	110,000	5,000	44.00	82,500	1,960	32.00	380,000	151.00
Wayland	133 ($500)	165,000	5,325	33.00	100,000	1,890	20.00	365,000	73.00
Harbor Springs	—	198,000	9,300	39.80	75,900	1,480	15.15	849,700	170.00
Leoni Twp.	—	526,500	14,200	58.50	—	—	—	1,138,500	126.50
Roscommon Village	—	136,696	8,544	88.20	90,654	3,777	58.50	326,573	210.70
Cassopolis	40 ($395)	83,855	4,540	38.20	20,000	1,080	9.10	140,355	63.80

a. Package contract, no breakdown available.

spread" if only the amount of the initial local bond issue is taken into consideration. However, since all operating costs are also the responsibility of the local community, it is important to give them careful consideration in relation to the entire project. The following table indicates the range of operating costs for various facilities in Michigan. The activated sludge and trickling filter operating costs include an allowance for the cost of removing 80 percent of the phosphorus by chemical precipitation.

Community	Treatment provided	Population served	Operation & maintenance cost per year per customer
City of Grand Rapids	Activated sludge	More than 300,000	$9.00
City of Ironwood	Activated sludge	9,000	26.00
City of Otsego	Trickling filter	4,000	23.00
Village of L'Anse	Activated sludge	Less than 3,000	37.00
Leoni Township	Aerated lagoons followed by spray irrigation	9,000	11.00 (Est.)
City of Belding	Anaerobic-aerobic pond system followed by irrigation	5,000	17.00
Village of Cassopolis	Anaerobic-aerobic pond system with seepage lagoons	Less than 3,000	Less than $5.00 per year

Land disposal is not a panacea—it is merely another tool. During the same period of time our firm has been developing lagoon-irrigation projects, they have also been designing other types of treatment such as extended aeration systems, rotating bio-disc plants, aerated lagoons followed by chemical precipitation—and on occasion, septic tanks and tile fields. Today, many noble efforts are being expended toward the preservation of our environment, and our water resources in particular. The world is eagerly awaiting the discovery of the best method of treating and disposing of wastewater. It is not good judgment to regard any one method as the best. The dangerous implication in that label is that since "the best" has been found, there is no need to continue to seek better ways of doing the job. The search for better ways should be unending. If no way is considered the best, each wastewater project can be given individual consideration, the proper method can be selected on the basis of professional engineering judgment rather than emotion, and the search for a better way can continue.

Discussion

Francke: Mr. Williams, have you had an experience with plastic or rubber lined ponds?

Williams: No. They're much too expensive for our clients. We've used clay with varying success. With good workmanship and good clay material a good seal is possible. Bentonite and sand have not had good success. Sprayed-on asphalt has not been successful either. There have been a number of fascinating failures. It has been found that soda ash helps to seal a clay lined pond. The ponds that have leaked have ultimately sealed up rather well. The Michigan Department of Public Health does not encourage pond systems leaking unless they're planned to leak. Now there are some that are planned to leak. Hydrogeological surveys have been run and have determined the location of the groundwater table. In these situations there are no wells for domestic purposes down slope from the ponds.

Rhindress: I'm glad that last question was asked. In case anybody has any doubt, in Pennsylvania we do not like leaking lagoons, period.

26
Ecological and Physiological Implications of Greenbelt Irrigation with Reclaimed Wastewater

V. B. Youngner, W. D. Kesner,*
A. R. Berg, and L. R. Green**

Although Southern California is best known for its farmlands and urban communities, millions of acres are covered with chaparral, sage and woodlands. These wildlands are now largely confined to the foothills and mountains but still extend from the bluffs above the Pacific Ocean to the desert (Jaeger and Smith, 1966). To a great extent they remain in a primitive condition, but residential and recreational developments reach into them from every direction producing an intimate association between wilderness and human activity creating numerous problems new to the region.

Southern California has many local climates determined by elevation, proximity to the ocean and relationship to mountain ranges. Nearly all, however, are basically Mediterranean characterized by mild wet winters and long dry, generally warm, summers. Except for occasional brief thunderstorms, little rainfall occurs from April to November (Bailey, 1966).

The native vegetation is well adapted to this climate as many species become dormant or semidormant during the latter part of the dry season. As the long drought continues, the shrubs that make up the wildlands become increasingly dry and flammable. Hot dry "Santa Ana" winds often occur in autumn making the fire hazard extremely high.

Fires have been a part of the natural environment of the chaparral for thousands of years, rejuvenating the brush and maintaining a natural balance among shrubs, forbs, grasses and trees (Vogl, 1967; Sweeney, 1967). With the first winter rains following a fire many shrub and small tree species resprout from their bases. The new open spaces once covered by dense brush are quickly filled with shrub seedlings, grasses and other herbaceous plants.

However, today, because of the numerous settlements in these wildlands such fires cause great loss of property and often of human life and therefore are no longer acceptable. Fire control is now a general but costly practice through the region. Not unexpectedly fire

*Department of Plant Sciences, University of California
**Fire Research Laboratory, Forest Service, USDA

control by permitting excessive buildup of potential fuel has made fires that do occur many times more dangerous and difficult to contain. Many studies are underway to find new ways of handling the problem such as controlled burning, use of growth retardants and construction of fuel breaks.

Other problems are also created by the influx of people into the wildlands. Water consumption is excessive in many places causing a constant lowering of underground water reserves. To conserve more of the water from rain and snow improvement of watershed quality is imperative. Waste disposal facilities never really adequate, are falling further and further behind causing a serious pollution problem. Nevertheless the demand for recreational facilities such as campground and picnic areas by people from the urban centers is unabated. Although restriction on movement of people into the wildlands has been considered and even attempted, a strong legal basis for this does not at present exist and the destruction of a great scenic natural resource is everywhere evident.

Objectives and Design of Project

In 1970 a research project designed to find a partial solution to these problems was begun through a cooperative effort of the University of California, the U.S. Forest Service and the California Division of Forestry. Financing was obtained from the U.S. Department of Interior, Office of Water Resources Research through the University Water Resources Center and from other agencies, principally the San Bernardino County Flood Control District. The objective is to study the feasibility of using wastewater from the mountain communities to irrigate greenbelts of native and introduced plants. The concept is that such greenbelts strategically placed would reduce the wildfire hazard while disposing of wastewater, recharging groundwater reservoirs with purified water, and creating new manageable recreation areas.

Answers to numerous specific questions would determine the practical value of the project. Foremost among these are the following: 1) What rates of water application can be safely used on the rocky, often shallow mountain soils? 2) What degree of water purification can be achieved at the different rates of application? 3) Can the moisture content of chaparral plants be raised sufficiently to give them fire retardant qualities? 4) How will irrigation through the dry season affect the growth of chaparral species? 5) What exotic trees, shrubs and grasses will best meet the stated project objectives? 6) Will irrigation change the species composition of the chaparral community?

The study area is located on a gently sloping chaparral covered ridge in the Maloney Canyon of the San Bernardino National Forest (Goodin and Kesner, 1970). Although the elevation of the project site is 4600 to 4700 feet it is on the Mojave Desert side of the mountains so the mean annual rainfall is only about 25 inches and summer temperatures often reach 90°F. The soils are shallow sandy loams over a granite or decomposed granite parent material. Four distinct soil types have been mapped for the experimental area (Figure 26-1).

Soil A
Soil A has a dark grayish brown cobbly sandy loam textured surface soil which is slightly acid to neutral. The subsoil is a dark grayish brown loam. This soil ranges in depth from 10 to 18 inches. The parent material is a highly weathered granodiorite which can be augered to a depth of 50 inches or more. Five to 15 percent cobbles and stones are found on the surface of this soil. Along the south end of plots 8-8, 10-2 and 12-2, 15 to 20 percent boulders and stone are found on the surface. Permeability is moderate (2.50 to 5.0 in./hr.), maximum water holding capacity 5.5 to 7.5 inches and the erosion hazard is high on cleared areas and moderate on undisturbed vegetated areas.

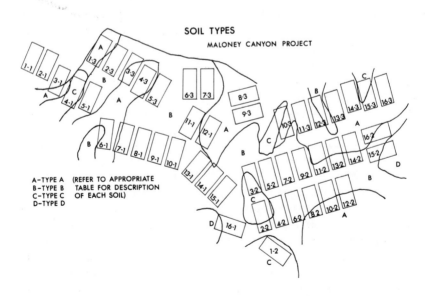

Figure 26-1. Soil map of the Maloney Canyon study area showing the relationship of soil type to the experimental blocks

Soil B

Soil B has a grayish brown to dark grayish brown heavy sandy loam slightly acid to neutral surface soil. The subsoil (in the B horizon) is a light to dark yellowish brown and brown medium to slightly acid sandy clay loam. Parent material is a granodiorite that begins at a depth of 24 to 45 inches which can be augered to a depth of five feet or more. Within the surface horizon cobbles will range from 0 to 15 percent while on the surface they will range from 15 to 25 percent with a few isolated areas having as many as 50 percent. Permeability is moderately slow (0.20 to 0.80 in./hr.), maximum water holding capacity is 15 to 25 inches and the erosion hazard is high on the cleared plots and moderate on the vegetative plots.

Soil C

Soil C has a grayish brown to dark grayish brown cobbly heavy sandy loam slightly acid to neutral surface soil. The subsoil (B horizon) is reddish yellow to brownish yellow medium acid to neutral sandy clay loam. Parent rock is a granodiorite that begins at a depth of 12 to 18 inches and is easily augered to a depth of five feet or more. Cobbles in the surface soil vary from 0 to 20 percent and from 0 to 25 on the surface with as much as 50 percent on isolated areas. Permeability is moderately slow (0.20 to 0.80 inches per hour), maximum water holding capacity is about 8 to 10 inches and the erosion hazard is high on the cleared plots and moderate on the vegetative plots.

Soil D

Soil D has a brown to dark brown loam neutral reaction surface soil. The subsoil (B horizon) is yellowish red, medium to slightly acid clay loam. The parent material is highly weathered granodiorite beginning at a depth of 25 to 35 inches which becomes hard fresh rock within a few inches. Cobble percentages on the surface and in the surface soil horizon range from 10 to 20 percent. Permeability is moderately slow (0.20 to 0.80 inches per hour). Maximum water holding capacity is 12 to 22 inches and erosion hazard is high on the cleared plots and moderate on the vegetative plots.

The vegetation is typical desert chaparral (Figure 26-2). Ceanothus (*Ceanothus greggii* Gray and *C. integerrimus* H. and A.), flannel bush (*Fremontia californica* Torr.) and bigberry manzanita (*Arctostaphylos glauca* Lindl.) are the principal shrub species. California black oak (*Quercus kelloggii* Newb.) and Coulter pine (*Pinus coulteri* Don.) are scattered throughout the area. The understory of various grasses and forbs is sparse under the heavy stands of brush but quite dense where the brush is light.

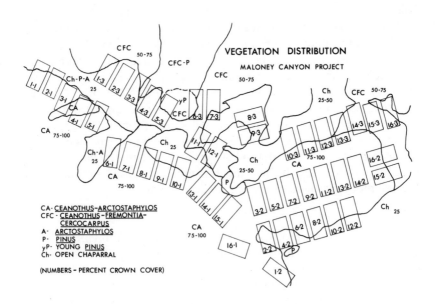

Figure 26-2. Vegetation map of the Maloney Canyon study area showing the relationship of shrubs and trees to the experimental blocks

The study area of 25 acres is divided into 48 plots, 100 by 200 feet.
Four irrigation treatments (0, 1, 2 and 3.5 inches per week) are
followed throughout the dry season. Within each irrigation treatment
there are blocks in which the native vegetation remains intact, others
in which the native vegetation has been cleared with subplots of
introduced trees, shrubs, grasses, and forbs. All treatment plots are
randomized and replicated three times (Figure 26-3). Species planted
on the cleared plots are shown in Table 26-1.

Water is applied through eight impact sprinkler heads on seven-foot
risers per plot. The entire system is automatically controlled. Wastewater is obtained from the Arrowhead Village sewage disposal system ponds located above the experimental area. The sewage treatment facility provides primary and secondary treatment and two ppm
chlorination prior to discharge of the water into the effluent ponds.
Present discharges from this plant average over 750,000 gpd of which
the experimental project uses only about 100,000 gpd. Since the
wastewater is derived almost entirely from domestic, nonindustry
sources, it is of relatively high quality (Table 26-2). The analyses may
be similar to those of most other mountain resort communities in
Southern California. Nitrates fluctuate from almost none to a high of
64 ppm. Testing procedures follow those of Standard Methods for the
Examination of Water and Wastewater and atomic absorption
spectrophotometric methods.

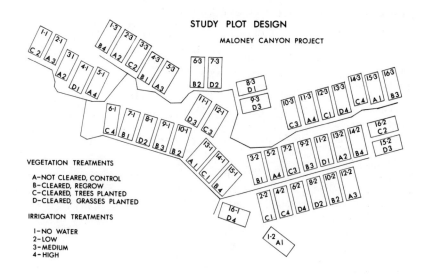

Figure 26-3. Plot plan showing vegetation and irrigation treatments

Table 26-1. Plant species introduced in clear study plots

Scientific Name	Common Name
Abies concolor	White fir
Pinus attenuata	Knobcone pine
Pinus jeffreyi	Jeffrey pine
Pinus sylvestris	Scotch pine
Pinus thunbergii	Japanese black pine
Pseudotsuga macrocarpa	Big-cone Douglas fir
Pseudotsuga menziesii	Douglas fir
Sequoia gigantea	Big tree
Libocedrus decurrens	Incense cedar
Pinus coulteri	Coulter pine
Pinus lambertiana	Sugar pine
Abies magnifica	Red fir
Pinus ponderosa	Ponderosa pine
Agrostis palustris	Pencross creeping bentgrass
Agrostis tenuis	Highland bentgrass
Festuca ovina	Sheeps fescue
Festuca rubra	Red fescue
Festuca rubra commutata	Chewings fescue,
Poa pratensis	Fylking Kentucky bluegrass
Trifolium repens	White clover
Festuca arundinacea	Tall fescue
Oryzopsis miliacea	Smilograss
Ehrharta calycina	Veldtgrass
Phalaris tuberosa var. stenoptera	Hardinggrass
Agropyron trichophorum	Pubescent wheatgrass
Agropyron intermedium	Intermediate wheatgrass

Table 26-2. Typical analyses of sewage effluent during 1971-72

	Sample					
	1	2	3	4	5	6
Ca (ppm)	19	20	–	24	24	24
Mg (ppm)	4	4	–	3	4	3
Na (ppm)	48	45	62	38	38	40
K (ppm)	8	13	12	16	16	14
NH_4N (ppm)	1	29	–	–	–	4
SO_4 (ppm)	20	20	–	–	–	12
Cl (ppm)	34	36	48	–	–	46
NO_3N (ppm)	15	6	4	1	1	2
PO_4 (ppm)	–	30	–	41.0	44	38
HCO_3 (ppm)	30	92	109	–	–	153
Conductivity ($EC \times 10^{-6}$)	350	364	410	505	545	390
pH	–	6.7	6.7	7.4	7.3	7.4
Hardness as $CaCO_3$	64	66	–	–	–	82
Total dissolved residue (180°C)	258	231	–	–	–	275
F (ppm)	0.4	0.3	–	–	–	0.5
B (ppm)	0.3	0.3	0.0	–	–	0.2

A complete weather station installed at the project site provides a continuous record of temperature, humidity, precipitation, wind velocity, wind direction, and evaporation. Soil moisture is measured by electrical resistance blocks placed one, two and four feet below the surface. Ground water is sampled at various depths by suction lysimeters (Youngner et al., 1971).

Specific vegetation studies as related to the irrigation treatments include the following: 1) Transpiration of native species as measured by a diffusion porometer (Van Bavel et al., 1965). 2) Photosynthesis of selected native species using the $^{14}CO_2$ method of Shimshi (1968). 3) Water potential of leaves of selected species measured by the pressure bomb (Scholander et al., 1964). 4) Increase in branch length of native species. 5) Fuel moisture levels (moisture content of twigs and branches of selected sizes). 6) Survival and growth (increase in height) of introduced trees. 7) Biomass, percent cover and frequency of various wild and introduced grasses and forbs.

Observations and Results

Results must be considered preliminary at this time since the study has been underway less than two years. Nevertheless a number of distinct trends are apparent.

Evaporation rates during the summer months in this area are extremely high often exceeding three inches per week. Consequently the low irrigation rate of one inch per week has had little effect on vegetation growth, establishment of new plantings and replenishment of fuel moisture. Apparently most of the water applied in this treatment is lost through evaporation before it can penetrate into the soil.

The two higher irrigation rates have clearly influenced tree establishment (Table 26-3). The highest application rate (3.5 inches per week) has been especially beneficial but the medium rate (two inches per week) has permitted satisfactory establishment of only certain species. Establishment in the nonirrigated treatment was limited to one block, with the exception of knobcone pine which has some survivors in all three replications. This block has the deeper finer textured soil with a higher water holding capacity (Soil B). Variability among replications is perhaps largely a result of difference in soil type.

Excellent stands of most introduced grass species have been obtained under a high irrigation rate. Under the two lower rates only the two wheatgrasses *Agropyron trichophorum* and *A. intermedium* and red fescue, *Festuca rubra*, have developed satisfactorily at this time.

On plots cleared of brush and irrigated but not planted to other vegetation, wild grasses are the most abundant species at the present. The density of grass stand increases directly with the irrigation rate. Yerba Santa, *Eriodictyon trichocalyx*, is also abundant and is especially noticeable on blocks receiving no water or only one inch per week. This is a small shrub, spreading by rhizomes, common to burned over or disturbed areas of the chaparral.

Moisture content determinations of the chaparral plants indicate that the two higher irrigation rates significantly increase fuel moisture

Table 26-3. Percent survival of coniferous trees one year after planting

Species	Control	Weekly irrigation in inches		
		1	2	3.5
	%	%	%	%
Scotch pine	13.0	20.8	65.2	95.8
Japanese black pine	22.2	20.8	69.5	63.0
Knobcone pine	50.0	30.7	33.3	33.3
White fir	6.3	0.0	0.0	15.3
Ponderosa pine	15.0	16.6	0.0	34.7
Incense cedar	10.7	6.6	16.6	25.9
Jeffrey pine	7.1	13.3	21.2	29.5
Sequoia	4.1	0.0	0.0	4.3
Coulter pine	14.8	8.7	0.0	10.0
Big-cone spruce	5.8	5.5	0.0	5.3
Douglas fir	0.0	11.7	8.7	18.2
Red fir	0.0	0.0	0.0	4.3
Sugar pine	0.0	15.1	3.3	17.2

(Table 26-4). The low irrigation rate appears to be insufficient to consistently maintain moisture levels above the control. Moisture content differences among plants from the four irrigation treatments are greatest in the smaller, generally younger, twigs of ⅛ inch or less in diameter which normally have a higher moisture content. Samples of this type from the nonirrigated plots range in moisture content from about 55 percent to about 122 percent of their dry weights at various seasons. Samples from the highest irrigation treatment range in moisture content from about 95 percent to about 143 percent of their dry weights at these same times. Thus a rather large elevation in fuel moisture content has been accomplished during the peak fire season when the brush is normally very dry. This may be particularly important to fire control as it occurs in fine twigs and leaves that may be most readily ignited. Chaparral growth is increased by the effluent water irrigation (Table 26-5). The increase in shoot length is to a great extent directly proportional to the amount of water provided. Increased chaparral growth, of course, may not be desirable relative to the fire hazard.

Soil moisture determinations in the irrigation treatments support the vegetation studies. In general, soils in the low irrigation treatment do not contain significantly more water at any depth than do those in the control treatment. Considerable variability in soil moisture has been observed in the 2- and 3.5-inch per week irrigation treatments. This is not unexpected considering the variation in depth, infiltration rate, and water holding capacity among the four soil types present in the site. Differences in the brush density and type would also influence soil moisture. At this time it seems that only the 3.5-inch per week application rate might be expected to significantly add to the underground water reserves under the conditions of this study.

As testing of subsoil moisture was started only in July 1972, data on water purification are still very meager. So far water has been sampled to a maximum depth no greater than four feet because of the rocky parent material encountered below that level. Nevertheless samples from a four-foot depth in the high irrigation plots show nearly 100 percent reduction of phosphates and perhaps as much as 50 percent reduction of nitrates below that of the effluent.

Our first tests for fecal coliform in the ground water show no colonies in 100 ml samples. Tests of the effluent water show as much as 1,228 colonies per 100 ml.

Conclusion and Summary

Although no conclusive results have been obtained during the short time this study has been underway observations to date are

Table 26-4. Moisture content (percent of dry weight) of *Ceanothus greggii* branches of three sizes as affected by irrigation treatments

	Twig Diameter in Inches											
	0.25 or less				0.25-0.50 inch				Over 0.50 inch			
	Inches of Water per Week				Inches of Water per Week				Inches of Water per Week			
Date	0	1	2	3.5	0	1	2	3.5	0	1	2	3.5
1971												
July	84.8	100.2	123.2	129.8	59.3	67.8	72.8	77.2	54.5	59.8	64.3	71.8
Aug.	62.7	75.3	98.8	106.7	54.0	57.0	64.2	64.2	47.0	45.5	58.2	61.8
Sept.	54.5	62.5	83.2	99.8	51.2	54.8	63.0	57.7	49.0	47.3	59.2	57.5
Nov.	61.5	79.0	87.3	94.0	54.5	55.5	55.2	55.7	—	—	—	—
1972												
June	122.0	122.3	136.2	142.9	71.7	71.1	76.9	76.0	57.4	57.8	62.3	63.2
July	85.2	77.2	99.0	97.9	62.7	64.1	66.8	82.9	51.7	56.8	54.5	61.4

Table 26-5. Mean growth of *Ceanothus greggii* branches as affected by irrigation treatments in 1972

Irrigation Treatment	Location of Branches		
	Top	North Side	South Side
	mm	mm	mm
Control	49	35	60
1 inch per week	92	61	51
2 inches per week	146	64	87
3.5 inches per week	152	118	143

sufficiently encouraging to make continued study highly worthwhile. Clearly, irrigation of chaparral during the dry season will increase the moisture content of the wood and leaves. The normal dormancy is apparently strictly drought induced and the brush will readily take up water when it is provided regardless of prevailing high temperature or species phenology. Future experimentation must try to relate these results to degree of fire retardation.

Conversion of chaparral brush lands to grasses and other plants presenting a lower fire hazard appears possible through wastewater irrigation. The most satisfactory species with particular reference to the use of the irrigated areas for recreation must still be determined.

Whether satisfactory water purification can be obtained through the shallow mountain soils is still uncertain but preliminary data are very encouraging.

Literature Cited

Bailey, H. P. 1966. *The climate of Southern California*. Univ. of Calif. Press, Berkeley.

Goodin, J. R. and W. D. Kesner. 1970. First Annual Report of the Maloney Canyon Project. Univ. of Calif. Water Resources Center. 33 pp.

Jaeger, E. C. and A. C. Smith. 1966. *Introduction to the natural history of Southern California*. Univ. of Calif. Press, Berkeley.

Scholander, P. E., H. T. Hammel, A. E. Hemmingsen, and E. D. Bradstreet. 1964. Hydrostatic pressure and osmotic potential in leaves of mangroves and some other plants. *Proc. Nat. Acad. Sci.* 52:118-125.

Shimshi, D. 1968. A rapid method for measuring photosynthesis with labeled carbon dioxide. *Jour. Expt. Bot.* 20:381-401.

Sweeney, J. R. 1967. Ecology of some "Fire Type" vegetation in Northern California. *Proc. Calif. Tall Timbers Fire Ecology Conf.* 7:111-125.

Van Bavel, C. H., F. S. Makayoma, and W. L. Ehrler. 1965. Measuring transpiration resistance of leaves. *Plant Physiology* 40:535-540.

Vogl, R. J. 1967. Fire adaptations of some Southern California plants. *Proc. Calif. Tall Timbers Fire Ecology Conf.* 7:79-109.

Youngner, V. B., W. D. Kesner, A. R. Berg and L. R. Green. 1971. Second Annual Report of the Maloney Canyon Greenbelt Project. Univ. of Calif. Water Resources Center Contribution No. 135. 22 pp.

Discussion

Dissmeyer: In Southern California there are some water repellent soils due to the combination of vegetation and fire. How has the spray application affected this problem?

Youngner: We have no information on the water repellent soils resulting from fire, because there has been no fire in recent years through this experimental area. The particular soil on this site is not water repellent. We have no difficulty in getting water into the soil, it's very permeable. There is some variation but, in general the permeability is high enough so that we have no problem with the rates we're using.

Unknown: What's happening to the dissolved solids?

Youngner: This is one of the things being looked at and anything I could say would be pure speculation at this point. Probably there will be a salt buildup. Even though the salt content of the effluent is not bad, in the two lower irrigation rates in which there is no deep penetration of the water whatsoever, there may be a salt buildup in time.

Unknown: What effect will the salt buildup have on the vegetation?

Youngner: Many of the species being used do accept a fair amount of salt tolerance. Once the root system gets down to a greater depth the salt problem probably is not going to bother the trees particularly. It will bother some of the other vegetation, such as the grass and so on, which are shallow rooted since the salt is going to be accumulating on the surface and in the surface layers. The shallow rooted plants are going to be the most drastically affected by the salt buildup.

27
Municipal Wastewater Disposal on the Land as an Alternate to Ocean Outfall

W. A. Cowlishaw and F. J. Roland*

This chapter attempts to take a look at land treatment as an alternative to ocean disposal of partially treated industrial and municipal wastes. The specific decision choice for Falmouth, Massachusetts, a community located on the western end of Cape Cod, will be used to highlight the political, engineering, and resource management factors of decisions that juxtapose land treatment against ocean disposal.

Present state plans, notably in California, are moving toward requiring a minimum of secondary treatment before ocean disposal and toward the prohibition of ocean disposal of municipal and industrial sludges. Selection of acceptable outfall locations is also becoming a more complex process which will result in the need for more costly transmission and outfall facilities. For example, the discharge into bays and harbor areas is becoming a thing of the past.

An example of the problem of obtaining public acceptability of an outfall location is the debate over the design of the new Melbourne, Australia treatment plant. The Melbourne metropolitan area (population 2.3 million) is located on the inner (west) side of Port Phillip Bay at a distance of 35 miles from the Pacific Ocean (Figure 27-1).

The original design for the 64 mgd treatment plant, located on the north side of the bay, included an outfall into the bay. Public pressure, however, has forced the development of a plan to pipe the effluent from the plant a distance of 35 miles to Bass Strait.

The problem of the treatment and final disposal of the accumulated sludge solids still must be dealt with. Indications are that land application of organic sludges for agricultural utilization will become a major management technique for this problem. The city of Philadelphia, for example, is presently advertising for bids to haul sewage sludge to land application sites in lieu of ocean dumping.

Factors Related to Ocean Disposal

The principal interrelated factors of concern which form the focus for the national debate on ocean disposal are summarized in the following principal items:

*Bauer Engineering, Inc.

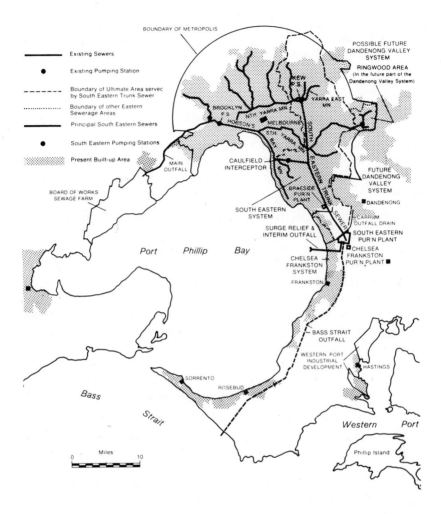

Figure 27-1. Melbourne wastewater outfall plan

1. Minimum level of waste treatment that will provide a reasonable factor of safety for the ocean environment.
2. Selection of an acceptable point of discharge for any regional area.
3. Disposition of accumulated separated solids produced in the treatment system.
4. Concern for potential long-term dynamic effects on local and general ocean environment and ability to develop cause and effect relationships.
5. Conservation and reuse of treated flows and constituent materials.
6. Selection of plant locations acceptable to residents of region.

7. Residual accumulation effects of periodic upsets in treatment and reduced treatment performance during periods of high stormwater flow.

Land Treatment as an Alternative

Land treatment provides a resources management choice to ocean disposal for public and technical consideration. Performance aspects of land treatment that offer attraction as a management choice include:

1. Achievement of the highest level of treatment which present technology can provide.
2. Return of renovated water to the immediately available water resource supply.
3. Recovery of nutrients and other materials to assist in agricultural production.
4. Opportunities for multipurpose site utilization (solid waste disposal, industrial and power utility cooling, recreational and open space uses).
5. Ability to control, monitor and take corrective action in impact areas of possible long-term deleterious effects (heavy metals buildup in soils and crops, nitrate buildup in groundwater).

As the level of required treatment increases no matter what the discharge point or dilution potential, as the point of acceptable discharge becomes more restricted and remote from metropolitan centers and when the sludge disposal problem is required to be dealt with in an environmentally acceptable manner, management at land treatment sites will become increasingly attractive.

Evaluation of Alternatives for Falmouth, Massachusetts

The evaluation of land treatment versus ocean disposal for Falmouth, Massachusetts constitutes a pilot study for the entire Cape Cod area (Figure 27-2). Great concern exists on the cape for the protection of the local water supplies (in terms of both quality and quantity) and the preservation of the recreational water environment. Projected population increases jeopardize both, as well as threatening offshore shellfish beds, interior pond levels, and natural assimilative capacities.

As a manifestation of the concern, the town of Falmouth has been the center of heated debate for the past few years concerning selec-

Figure 27-2. Map of Cape Cod, Massachusetts

tion of an acceptable management and facilities plan for waste treatment. A proposed ocean outfall plan to discharge wastes after receiving secondary treatment was rejected by the townspeople by a 2 to 1 vote. Evaluation of other alternatives was requested, specifically the cost and environmental consequences of a land treatment system. The opportunity to develop a land treatment plan was enhanced by the availability of a potential treatment site at the Otis Air Force Base, which is scheduled for deactivation.

System Service Area
The design capacity of the system will serve the 1990 requirements of the Falmouth region, which will have an estimated sewered area population of 25,000 during the three summer months and a population of 16,000 during the remainder of the year. The generated flow is 2.7 mgd during the three summer months and 1.6 mgd during the remaining nine months. This results in an average annual flow of 1.9 mgd.

The areas served by the system would include Falmouth Center and Woods Hole (Figure 27-3).

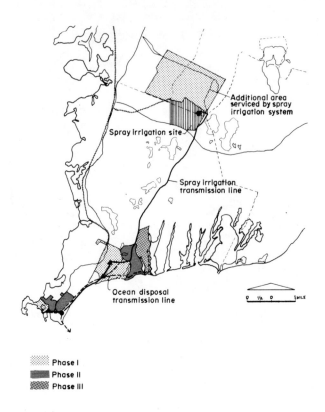

Figure 27-3. Spray irrigation system design for Falmouth, Massachusetts

Ocean Outfall Design

The ocean disposal system which has been designed for the Falmouth area was prepared in response to water quality standards established by the Massachusetts Water Resources Commission and the Federal Water Pollution Control Administration. It has been reviewed and analyzed by numerous engineering firms, and research and conservation groups, including members of the Woods Hole Oceanographic Institution.

The system consists of three basic components: (1) a collection and transport network, (2) biological treatment and (3) an outfall system.

Collection and Transport System. This consists of the network of sewers, force mains and pumping stations required to collect the wastewater from the service areas and transport it to the sewage treatment plant located at Woods Hole, 3,500 feet from Nobska Point.

Biological Treatment. The proposed activated sludge treatment plant would be located on an eight-acre site near Woods Hole. Here, the raw sewage would pass through a pretreatment structure, primary clarifiers, aeration tanks, secondary clarifiers and a chlorination contact tank before final effluent disposal.

Outfall System. The outfall system for Falmouth consists of a 30-inch diameter pipe extending 3,500 feet from the sewage treatment plant to Nobska Point and an additional 1,950 feet out into Vineyard Sound to a depth of 90 feet. At this location there would be a minimum return of the effluent to beaches and harbors; the tidal flow reaches maximum speeds; and the depth of the water provides for maximum immediate dilution.

The ocean disposal system designed for Falmouth is expected to meet all current secondary effluent standards of the federal government and the Commonwealth of Massachusetts.

The proposed outfall point has been the subject of considerable study by experts from the Woods Hole Oceanographic Institution, and the United States Geological Survey. It is regarded as the best location for an outfall on the cape if one is to be constructed. However, at many other locations on the cape it would be extremely difficult, if not impossible, to obtain an outfall that would approach the performance capability of the Nobska Point location. This is because most of the cape is surrounded by fairly shallow ocean waters whose tidal currents are slow and which travel close to bathing and shellfish areas.

Land Management System

The land treatment system developed for the Falmouth area entails the conveyance of wastes inland to a pretreatment and land irrigation site located within and adjacent to Otis Air Force Base. The design capacity of the system will serve the 1990 requirements of the Falmouth region and in addition a flow of 1.0 mgd generated by Otis Air Force Base during the summer months and 0.4 mgd during the remainder of the year. This results in an average total flow during the year of 2.4 mgd. The system consists of four basic components: (1) a collection and transport network, (2) biological treatment, (3) storage lagoons, (4) irrigation system.

Collection and Transport. The collection network consists of 72 miles of 4- to 24-inch laterals. The main transmission lines consist of approximately three miles of 8- to 16-inch pipe from the Woods Hole pumping station to the main Falmouth Center pumping station and approximately eight miles of 18-inch pipe from the latter pumping station to the Otis Air Force Base (AFB) sewage treatment plant.

Biological Treatment. The proposed wastewater irrigation system incorporates the existing treatment facilities of Otis Air Force Base. The base plant has been well maintained and can continue to function as a secondary treatment facility for both Falmouth and the Otis Air Force Base wastes.

The basic unit processes using the existing plant include: (1) a sewage comminutor for solids reduction, (2) a diffused air grease-skimming flocculation tank, (3) Imhoff tanks, which provide for primary sedimentation of solids and for solids digestion, (4) trickling filters, which provide biochemical oxidation of organic matter in the sewage, (5) final settling, and (6) sludge drying beds from which solids are returned to the land as a soil conditioner.

Storage Lagoons. Effluent from the final settling tank is discharged to the storage lagoon, where further sedimentation occurs and where the liquids are stored for irrigation. This component of the system provides the necessary flexibility for storing wastewater during periods of heavy rainfall or freezing temperatures.

The storage lagoon is sized to permit detention of four months of winter flow (267 mg). Its surface area is 54 acres, with a working water depth range of 13 to 33 feet. This variable depth results from a lagoon design which takes advantage of the natural topography, thereby minimizing excavation costs.

Irrigation System. The irrigation site area is located in Mashpee Outwash Plain consisting of glacial deposits of sand and gravel. These deposits are very permeable and previous well tests in the area indicate that the proposed wastewater site is geologically well suited for spray irrigation. Approximately 250 feet beneath the surface of the site lies the hard, dense basement rock.

The total required site including treatment facilities, storage lagoon, irrigation, and unused buffer areas is approximately 800 acres. The actual required irrigation area is 490 acres based on a two-inch per week application rate for an eight-month annual application period.

The method of water application would depend on the final areas selected for use. At present tracts of cleared flat land within the Otis Air Force Base site and a forested game conservation area are being considered for use.

In cultivated areas rotating irrigation rigs would distribute the wastewater on the land. In forested areas a fixed system would be used to minimize the disturbance of the natural setting.

Groundwater Flow

The water applied to the irrigation area will be allowed to percolate through the soil into the groundwater supply. The performance of the wastewater management system will be continuously monitored to assure protection of the groundwater supply near the irrigation site.

Due to the possibility of saltwater intrusion, the recharge of groundwater is considered of primary import. Several preliminary studies have been undertaken to estimate the change in groundwater flow due to the application of water at the irrigation site.

In general, it is calculated that approximately 775 million gallons of water annually will be returned to the ground at the spray irrigation site. This is equal to 84 percent of the total of 920 million gallons of wastewater treated.

Analyses indicate that the groundwater flow changes would be greatest in the vicinity of Coonamesset Pond, toward which some 70 percent of irrigation water will flow. The Ashumet Pond will receive 20 percent and the area between these two ponds would receive 10 percent. The present and predicted groundwater flow is shown in Figure 27-4. As is graphically shown, the estimated dilution of irrigation water to groundwater is in the order of magnitude of one to one.

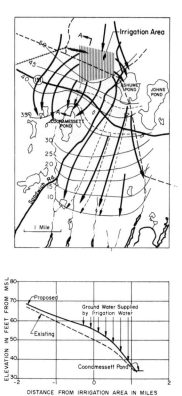

Figure 27-4. Groundwater flow patterns in the vicinity of the irrigation sites

Alternatives Comparison

Evaluation of ocean outfall versus land treatment for Falmouth must consider both cost and performance (impact) differences between the two systems.

Cost Comparison

Estimated facilities development and operating costs for the two alternatives are listed in Table 27-1. The land treatment system is shown to be least expensive on a unit capacity basis. This is due to the incorporation of the existing Otis Air Force Base facilities in the land system.

Impacts Assessment

The impacts of the alternative systems on the Cape Cod environment can be assessed in terms of the effects on the fresh groundwater table under the cape and in terms of the effects on shoreline water quality.

Ocean Disposal

This analysis is based on an ocean outfall which it is generally agreed, would offer acceptable levels of discharge and mixing and which would minimize the chances of any effluent returning to harbors, beaches or estuaries of the cape.

1. Probably the most serious implication of the ocean outfall sys-

Table 27-1. Comparison of total construction costs for Phase I of alternative systems

Cost of Facilities[a]	Land Treatment	Ocean Disposal
	Design capacity in mgd	
	2.4	1.9
Wastewater treatment facilities	$2,130,000	$3,390,000
Pumping station and force mains	2,440,000	1,460,000
Gravity sewers	3,890,000	3,890,000
Subtotal	$8,460,000	$8,740,000
Land acquisition	600,000	75,000
Engineering, legal and administration	846,000	874,000
Total	$9,906,000	$9,689,000
Capital cost per mgd capacity	4,127,000	5,099,000
Annual operating cost	83,000	85,000
Average annual total cost per mgd capacity	$ 336,000	$ 417,000

a. Utilization of existing Otis Air Force Base facilities is not entered as a cost item in land treatment system. Cost of land for land site is estimated equivalent value not actual price paid in any project. Annual costs based on 30-year bonding at six percent interest.

tem is that it diverts a substantial portion of the potential groundwater recharge, finally and irretrievably. After treatment, the entire amount is diverted to the coastal waters. Consequently, if pond lowering or intrusion occurs, remedies would be quite costly. It has been estimated that the amount which can be diverted without damage can not exceed ten to twenty-five percent of the total annual groundwater recharge of the area serviced. The estimated peak summer population of 1980 (497,000) would withdraw, although not necessarily divert, at a rate equal to approximately twenty-five percent of the annual recharge.

2. A major impact of the treated sewage effluent on the ocean is that of nutrients: carbon, phosphorus and nitrogen. Although a certain amount of these elements is required to maintain seafood productivity in coastal waters, excessive levels cause an overabundance of organic production with consequent undesirable effects on water quality.

3. In addition to the overall performance of the ocean outfall system (treatment and dilution levels), attention should be given to the reliability of the treatment plant itself. Shock loads, which occur quite frequently, could result in the dumping of untreated wastes for substantial periods of time, directly into the ocean.

4. Another consideration is the possible pathogenic bacterial or viral contamination of the receiving water. The effects of such contamination would largely relate to the shellfish areas which are an important economic sector of the cape.

5. Excessive amounts of organic carbons and toxic substances, such as heavy metals and nonbiodegradable hydrocarbons could cause long-term deleterious effects and should be excluded from any marine outfall system. These elements are rarely found in the cape wastewater because of the relative lack of industry.

6. A final point is that sludge resulting from the treatment process must be handled outside the system. Separate dumping or spreading areas must be acquired or secured for these wastes and procedures established to reduce odors and control leachate.

Land Treatment System

1. The spray irrigation system will return renovated water to the groundwater resource of quality suitable for reuse. If the water is returned at a point proximate to that of withdrawal, it can be considered to be replenishing the developed water supply

source. If not, it simply adds to the availability of fresh water on the cape. There is, therefore, the flexibility of withdrawing and transporting the treated water for use in injection wells or retention ponds to impede instances of intrusion or pond lowering.

2. The irrigation waters supply nutrients and organic matter to the land in sufficient quantities to enhance plant growth. This permits the conservation of commercial fertilizer which poses a special pollution problem in itself.

3. In contrast to the ocean disposal system, the spray irrigation system provides for disposal of both sludge and the septic tank pumpings. After adequate treatment, the activated sludge, including the treated septic tank solids, can initially be applied to the irrigated land as a soil conditioner; it can later be applied to those areas which are not routinely irrigated.

4. The spray irrigation system requires an extensive amount of land. Average requirements vary according to the design application rate, or length of irrigation period. For Cape Cod the land requirements are typically in the range of 200 acres per mgd, based on average annual application rates. Opportunities to alleviate some of the problems of site acquisition are discussed elsewhere in this chapter.

5. Irrigation areas can be an asset to the community, however, by providing useful open space. Other potential benefits include the control of urban sprawl and the preservation of agricultural use areas.

Critical Factors in Land Treatment Systems

The two major aspects of land treatment systems which are the focus of debate on general acceptance are: (1) the social and institutional problems of site acquisition and (2) the possible long-term effects of toxic substances on soils and crops.

Site Acquisition
Acquisition of large land site areas and the relocation of activities located thereon can create severe institutional, political, legal, and cost difficulties. In the Muskegon County, Michigan, project the decision was made to acquire and clear the irrigation site of private activities. This was dictated by regulatory requirements and characteristics of site ownership.

The Falmouth situation, on the other hand, documents the improved implementation potential achievable through joint federal, state, and local cooperation. Such opportunities would likely be available for many locations along the U.S. coastline and at interior locations. For example, the programmed closure of many military bases presents a special site development opportunity at many locations in addition to that of Falmouth.

In other situations the acquisition problem could be relaxed through the development of irrigation lease arrangements with local farmers. This has been practiced in California and other areas.

Toxic Effects

The problem of potential long-term accumulation of toxic substances in the soil and crops is an issue that is currently being given extensive attention. Experiences of a metals buildup in soils, increased crop intake, and reduced crop yield have been cited. There have also been experiences (notably Melbourne) of long-term operations with no apparent reduction in performance. In any assessment effort, it is important that information on metals buildup in soils and crop uptake with land treatment systems under study be related to naturally occurring variations to establish significance of change in any comparative analyses. Process dynamics in nature are subject to many variations.

The uncertainty factor for a long-term toxic effect on land appears to be less critical than that which ocean outfall poses for the marine environment. The relevant questions are: What is a potential toxic effect of sewage and what are the relative hazards of the impact areas for the various management choices — air, land, and water?

As indicated previously in this paper, the ability to control the effects of a land system to a specific site and the capability to continuously monitor this controlled environment, give land treatment a strong environmental safety margin.

Land application permits the development of a discrete control break in the food chain back to man and presents many opportunities for corrective action with the identification of a developing problem. Corrective action includes crop rotation, deep plowing, and liming. Such control is not feasible in the diffuse aquatic environment of the ocean with its complex overlapping food chain linkages.

Conclusions

The foregoing analysis indicates that the land disposal-spray irrigation alternatives for managing wastewater would better serve the needs of the Falmouth region — and those of the entire cape — for its effects in treating wastewater; the spray irrigation system is superior; its pollutant removal efficiency clearly exceeds the ocean outfall system in its effective removal of pollutants.

In addition to the efficiency and reliability of this system for purifying wastewater, it provides numerous related benefits applicable to the regional water resources:

1. The spray irrigation system returns a large percentage of the treated wastewater to the groundwater resources. There is no diversion of water. In addition, the returned water is of a quality suitable for public water supply.
2. The system offers flexibility for retrieving the treated water and transferring it to critical areas of local water table or pond level drop or saltwater intrusion.
3. The irrigation of marginal land for agricultural purposes will provide some usable crop—possibly grasses for fodder. The irrigation of forested land will increase production of the undergrowth for game food sources and permit additional monitoring of the site.
4. The utilization of wastewater for land irrigation will virtually assure that there will be no adverse effect on any marine life or on the recreational value of the cape waters.
5. An integration of the spray irrigation site with numerous other publicly funded projects can achieve such multiple purposes as curtailing urban sprawl or providing additional recreational open space areas.

All of the above advantages of the spray irrigation system are achievable at costs comparable to those for conventional secondary wastewater treatment.

Present Status of Project

At the March 6, 1972 Falmouth Town Meeting, the preparation of a definitive land treatment system engineering report was authorized. After State approval, a contract for this work between the Town and Bauer Engineering, Inc. was executed on August 31, 1972. Anderson-Nichols & Company, Inc. of Boston was authorized as a subcontractor to Bauer Engineering, Inc. to assist in the engineering of the local sewer systems.

This study was completed in January 1973, at which time a report titled "Wastewater Management Engineering Report, Town of Falmouth, Massachusetts" was published. The report was then presented to the Town and various State agencies for their review.

Preliminary approval of the report by the Massachusetts Division of Water Pollution Control has been received along with their comments and recommendations. The report is being revised to reflect these suggestions.

Upon final acceptance of the study by the Town and the State, it is anticipated that a Town Article will be presented to a future Town Meeting for authorization for the preparation of contract documents needed for construction of the project.

Discussion

Unknown: What is the status on this 1970 act that was passed by Congress concerning ocean dumping and how it will affect the ocean outfall?

Roland: I'm not familiar with the exact timetable on the federal act. There are also a number of state legislative activities which deal with sludge management and with the quality of water which must be achieved before discharge to the ocean.

Adams: What about the infiltration rates on the land? Is it pretty sandy soil?

Roland: It is a sandy outwash plain, but it consists of highly permeable sand and gravel material to a depth of about 50 feet where the water table is located.

Unknown: Is any conditioning to slow down the permeability proposed?

Roland: We are now proposing a rate of application of about two inches, which is similar to what's being done in many areas. We are not proposing any conditioning of the surface itself. It's the top two or three feet that can provide adequate renovation. A monitoring system will be installed to evaluate the water that percolates through to the groundwater reservoir.

28
The Role of Land Treatment of Wastewater in the Corps of Engineers Wastewater Management Program

James F. Johnson*

The continuing problems of environmental degradation, particularly that caused by the discharge of a broad spectrum of pollutants into our water courses, have prompted the Corps of Engineers to assist state, regional, and local governments in developing wastewater management plans toward their solution. As a part of its urban studies program, the corps will develop an array of plans in consonance with local planning agencies from which the people of the region could choose the specific plan which best meets their needs.

Wastewater management systems are comprised of structural and nonstructural components to collect, treat, transport, reuse, and dispose of all sources of waterborne wastes. These systems must be comprehensive in scope; they cannot ignore sources of pollutants, technologies, institutions, impacts, or public preferences. This chapter will address the role of land treatment in the Corps of Engineers Wastewater Management program, with particular emphasis upon its relationship to the planning process, the impacts associated with land disposal, and certain research needs related to land disposal of wastewater (Johnson, 1972).

The Department of the Army initiated a pilot Wastewater Management Program late in FY 1971 concentrating initially on municipal, industrial, and urban storm runoff wastes in four areas: Cleveland-Akron, Detroit-Southeastern Michigan, Chicago-Northwest Indiana, and San Francisco-Sacramento-Stockton. These studies are being conducted in cooperation with all appropriate state and local governmental units as well as the Environmental Protection Agency. In July, 1971, the corps prepared interim feasibility reports for the four areas in addition to the Merrimack Basin in New England (U.S. Army Corps of Engineers, 1971a,b,c,d,e). On a more local scale, the corps also is developing wastewater management plans for the people of Codorus Creek in Pennsylvania. Currently, a number of urban studies are being initiated which will meet a broader range of urban water needs, and wastewater management could provide benefits in the areas of flood protection, water supply, and recreation, to mention only a few.

*U.S. Army Corps of Engineers, Washington, D.C.

Program Objective

The wastewater program is directed toward improving the economic, social, and environmental welfare of the nation and, in particular, the regions under study. The effects of the wastewater management plans will be measured in accordance with the broad objectives proposed by the Water Resources Council (U.S. Congress, 1971).

In order to effectively plan and measure the performance of waste-water systems in contributing to the objectives, we must first identify specific planning objectives (or needs) which the system will address. The subsequent evaluation of wastewater management systems in terms of these planning objectives would provide the basis for comparison of alternatives. These planning objectives would address such issues as economic growth policies, resource use policies, and desired land use patterns. The planning objectives of the region will be specified in such detail as to preclude consideration of alternatives in direct conflict with higher priority objectives. For instance, elimination of an ecological resouree or isolation of a community or segment thereof by an alternative system would constitute a condition that is not acceptable.

Plan Formulation

The process of plan formulation is one involving a series of iterations whereby plans are developed, evaluated, screened, and redeveloped or refined. Specific technical goals direct the wastewater systems toward achieving these objectives.

These technical goals are: (1) to prevent the continued degradation of our water resources by waterborne wastes; and (2) to provide for the efficient reuse of treated or renovated wastewater and by-products. Achievement requires the application of the best technology for the collection, treatment, and management of wastewater (U.S. Army Corps of Engineers, 1972a). At successive screening stages, alternatives will be evaluated in conjunction with an active program of public involvement to assist the development of optimal plans. The refinement of the alternatives that remain through this screening process will reflect the desires expressed in public involvement.

Existing institutions that are related to the management of water and wastewaters will be identified but these will not constrain the development of optimal wastewater management systems. The impact of the plan on existing institutions will be analyzed, and a series of alternative implementation plans will be developed.

The selection of optimal wastewater plans will be made on the basis of the evaluation of beneficial and detrimental effects of the alternative, as well as a consideration of its associated opportunities and concerns. Information will be presented and displayed to illustrate the comparative differences among alternatives, their cost-effectiveness, and benefits and opportunities foregone by selecting one alternative vis à vis the others. In so doing, the presentation will clearly identify the detrimental effects of each alternative, and to what degree these could have been or could be eliminated. This information will be displayed in such a manner that responsible decision makers may observe the difference between systems as they relate to major issues and concerns in the study region.

Wastewater Treatment Systems

In order to meet the program technical goals, the wastewater systems will employ the most efficient biological, chemical, and physical waste treatment processes (including the soil-vegetative complex) or combinations of these. These processes will be employed in the land treatment systems as well as the more traditional treatment plant systems.

The land treatment facilities being designed generally would consist of biological treatment cells, storage basins, application facilities, and land treatment areas; as well as underdrains or other collective systems to provide for the reuse of treated wastewater. Three means are under study for the application of wastewater on the land:

1. *Spray irrigation* is defined as the controlled spraying of liquid onto the land, at a rate measured in inches per week, with the path being infiltration and percolation within the boundaries of the land disposal site.
2. *Overland runoff* is defined as the controlled discharge, by spraying or other means, of liquid onto the land, at a rate measured in inches per week, with the flow path being down-slope sheet flow.
3. *Rapid infiltration* is defined as the controlled discharge, by spreading or other means, of liquid onto the land, at a rate measured in feet per week, with the flow path being high rate infiltration and percolation (U.S. Army Corps of Engineers, 1972b).

Application of Wastewater to Land
The wastewater systems will be planned to promote the wise use of

wastewater resources in addition to meeting the water quality non-degradation goal. Significant benefits can be provided with proper planning and operation of the systems.

Because wastewater is a source of nutrient-rich irrigation water, it can be applied to improve the productivity of marginal agricultural lands or improve upon presently productive farmland. In particular, crops with high nitrogen requirements can be enhanced by the properly controlled application of wastewater. In addition, the nutrient-rich water can be applied to forest lands, recreation areas, and other open areas. Such use of wastewater throughout the United States is well documented (Law, 1968; Whetstone, 1967).

Wastewater also could be applied to degraded land such as strip mines and fallow lands to enhance them for future use. Certain lands also can be preserved for planned future use by creating "land banks" through interim use as land treatment sites.

Wastewater Reuse

The renovated wastewater cleansed by the soil-vegetative filter system will be available for reuse for a wide range of purposes. The water could be percolated to recharge the groundwater aquifer. In general, however, the systems call for collecting the cleansed effluent and returning it for specific uses. Reuse opportunities will be identified on the basis of the needs of the region for possible stream flow augmentation, recreational lakes, industrial cooling, industrial process water, industrial boiler feed, and municipal reuse.

Multiple Use of Land and Facilities

There also is an opportunity for multiple uses of the land and facilities required for wastewater systems. With regard to land treatment systems, we are studying such opportunities as the use of storage lagoons to accept and benefiicially use thermal discharges from power plants; the use of irrigation and treatment sites to provide habitat area that could be used for hunting and other recreation; and use of transmission rights-of-way for trails, bikeways, controlled access roads, and utility routes.

There also are significant opportunities in planning for the efficient multiple use of the required larger tracts of land. In many instances, land treatment may favor sites somewhat distant from population and congestion. The opportunities to locate facilities, such as airports, that seek these same characteristics should be identified within the framework of these regional plans. The desirability and potential for siting new towns and regional industrial parks also will be investigated.

Feasibility Studies

The feasibility studies were intended to identify the present and future wastewater management problems and to make a preliminary evaluation of the feasibility and consequences of alternative wastewater management plans in the five regions. In transmitting these feasibility reports to the secretary of the army and the Congress, the chief of engineers concluded that

> There are major improvements possible in the effectiveness of wastewater management systems to remove a broad spectrum of waste constituents be those systems water disposal, land disposal, or some combination thereof;
> There exist important opportunities and benefits associated with truly comprehensive wastewater management systems for water and waste constituent reuse, including the potential for new water supplies and recreation; and for a broad range of previously untapped opportunities related to social and environmental enhancement [U.S. Army, Secretary of the Army, 1971].

Of particular interest are his additional conclusions that

> Wastewater management systems requiring disposal to the land offer potentially new opportunities in selected areas including increased land production, management and reuse of wastes generated from other activities, and improvements to environmental quality and regional community values;
> Further investigations and studies are required with respect to technological concern for both water and land disposal alternatives. Such investigations must evaluate:
> (a) The effectiveness, reliability, and flexibility of large-scale advanced wastewater treatment facilities, both physical-chemical and biological processes;
> (b) The long-term viability and integrity of the land to serve as a natural processor of wastewater; and
> (c) The relative toxic effects of viruses, pathogenic bacteria, trace metals and other toxic materials upon the environment whether on land or in receiving waters;
> The institutional implications of the alternative wastewater management strategies will be most critical to any future decisions regarding implementation, and that future studies must fully address such consequences and suggest appropriate means to facilitate necessary institutional changes [U.S. Army, Secretary of the Army, 1971].

Survey-Scope Studies

The Congress acting upon the recommendations of the secretary of the army and the chief of engineers gave approval in late 1971 for the Army Corps of Engineers to proceed into the survey-scope stage in Cleveland, Chicago, Detroit, and San Francisco studies in FY 1972. The Merrimack study in Massachusetts will be resumed in FY 1973.

State-of-the-Art

Concurrently, the corps has undertaken state-of-the-art investigations to summarize the available knowledge relating to the feasibility of land application as a wastewater treatment process. The Army Corps of Engineers Cold Regions Research and Engineering Laboratory (CRREL) and a group of research consultants at the University of Washington agreed to prepare independent comprehensive technical assessments of the effectiveness and effects of land disposal of secondary treated wastewater (Reed, 1972; Driver *et al.,* 1972).

Each group studied spray irrigation, overland runoff, and rapid infiltration methods of application and treatment. Preparation of the reports included literature reviews, correspondence with experts involved in existing operations and current research, and personal observations at selected sites. The following were among the most significant conclusions:

1. The quality of cleansed effluent product derived from a properly designed and operated land disposal facility would approach drinking water-irrigation water standards.
2. The land disposal facility and the pretreatment steps must be carefully managed as a total system to provide optimum responses.
3. Any one of the three application modes can meet the quality standards if proper site conditions exist and proper operational criteria are employed.
4. Spray irrigation offers the highest degree of reliability and potential longevity of the three modes.
5. Heavy metals are largely removed from wastewater applied via spray irrigation, with the main mechanisms being ion exchange and fixation.

Both groups concluded that further investigation was needed, particularly in (a) overland runoff removal effectiveness; (b) transport of N and P to surface waters through erosion of overland runoff sites; (c) wind transport of pathogens by aerosols; (d) soil-chemical interactions, to include heavy metals; and (e) interaction of soils, climates, and loading rates to manipulate the carbon-nitrogen ratio.

Current Investigations

Accordingly, the Corps of Engineers is presently involved in exploratory efforts to (a) investigate the effectiveness of rapid infiltration basins at Fort Devons, Massachusetts, an Army installation; (b) analyze soil samples from Melbourne, Australia's sewage farm at Werribee; (c) develop and investigate performance of spray irrigation test cells (28 feet square, 5 feet deep) at CRREL; and (d) evaluate groundwater conditions in a joint effort with the U.S. Geological Survey and the city of Tallahassee, Florida, at the Tallahassee spray irrigation site.

Chicago Special Report

In proceeding through the survey-scope stage of the wastewater management pilot studies, the continued refinement of design costs has resulted in a position for land treatment systems more favorable than their position as presented in the feasibility reports.

In order to place the cost of alternative systems in perspective, the chief of engineers early in 1972 undertook a special study of the Chicago metropolitan area, with the assistance of Bauer Engineering for the purpose of (a) formulating least-cost wastewater management system alternatives; (b) detailing capital costs and operation, maintenance, and replacement costs of the alternative systems; and (c) analyzing the relative merits of alternative systems.

Although it is recognized that the special study was limited to providing a view of basic land, physical-chemical, and advanced biological treatment systems, the results underscore the comparative economic and technical feasibility of land treatment systems.

Specifically, the study concluded that (a) significant strides can be made toward achieving comparably high levels of treatment by all three alternatives studied. These levels appear to be compatible with the current corps program technical goal of minimizing water quality degradation from waterborne wastes; (b) costs of any one of the systems involve several billions of dollars; and (c) costs for land treatment may be lower both for capital and for operation and maintenance (U.S. Army Corps of Engineers, 1972b).

The current wastewater studies are now well underway through the survey-scope stage. The Corps of Engineers Districts are conducting these studies through a balanced use of in-house management and technical capabilities supported by the technical expertise of architectural and engineering consultants and scientific research firms.

Conclusion

The Corps of Engineers recognizes its responsibility to the nation and the regions under study to provide an array of comprehensive plans addressed to their overall needs. We seek to meet these needs through a planning process in which the full range of technologies is explored, the impacts associated with these technologies are addressed, and the resulting plans achieved within the framework of public involvement are set forth to the people of the regions to assist in their choice. The corps is not committed to specific technologies, but is convinced that all technologies, including both land application and treatment plant systems, must be investigated thoroughly in order to broaden the range of choice available to allow decision-makers to act in the best public interest.

Literature Cited

Driver, C. H., B. F. Hrutfiord, D. E. Spyridakis, E. B. Welch, D. D. Wooldridge and R. F. Christman. 1972. *Assessment of the effectiveness and effects of wastewater management.* U.S. Army Corps of Engineers Wastewater Management Report 72-1.

Johnson, James F. 1972. Regional wastewater management: a new perspective in environmental planning. *Water Resources Bulletin* 8(4):773-779.

Law, James P. 1968. *Agricultural utilization of sewage effluent and sludge, an annotated bibliography.* U.S. Federal Water Pollution Control Administration, Washington, D. C.

Reed, S. C. 1972. Wastewater management by disposal on the land. Special Report 171, Cold Regions Research and Engineers, Hanover, N. H. pp. 10-18.

U.S. Army Corps of Engineers, Buffalo District. 1971a. *Alternatives for managing wastewater for Cleveland-Akron Metropolitan and Three Rivers Watershed Areas.* Summary and three appendices.

U.S. Army Corps of Engineers, Chicago District. 1971b. *Alternatives for managing wastewater in Chicago-South End Lake Michigan Area.* Summary and appendices.

U.S. Army Corps of Engineers, Detroit District. 1971c. *Alternatives for managing wastewater for Southeastern Michigan.* Summary and ten appendices.

U.S. Army Corps of Engineers, San Francisco District. 1971d. *Alternatives for managing wastewater in the San Francisco Bay and Sacramento-San Joaquin Delta Area.* Summary and six appendices.

U.S. Army Corps of Engineers, North Atlantic Division. 1971e. *The Merrimack: designs for a clean river.* Summary and appendices.

U.S. Army Corps of Engineers, Office, Chief of Engineers. 1972a. *Wastewater Management Program: study procedure.*

U.S. Army Corps of Engineers, Office, Chief of Engineers. 1972b. *Regional wastewater management systems for the Chicago Metropolitan Area.* Summary and appendix.

U.S. Army, Secretary of the Army. 1971. *Interim report of the Secretary of the Army on the Pilot Wastewater Management Program.*

U.S. Congress. 1971. *Procedures for evaluation of Water and Related Land Resources Projects.* Committee print 92-20. Washington, D. C.

Whetstone, G. A. 1967. *Re-use of effluent in the future with an annotated bibliography.* Texas Water Development Board, Austin, Texas. 187 pp.

Discussion

Lyon: We've had considerable experience with land irrigation in Pennsylvania as you know, and also lagoon systems and we've found that many of them have failed because the work that led up to them was fine in the engineering area and fine in the economic area but very thin in the hydrogeological area. I have this same kind of concern about some of the papers and studies that are being made by the Corps of Engineers. For example, in Mr. Bauer's paper there's very little discussion of the hydrogeologic renovation capability. What specifically are the standards the corps is establishing for the hydrogeologic aspect of these studies?

Johnson: The corps' systems would be able to meet the standards set forth by the Environmental Protection Agency. In other words, they would meet the minimum requirements of any regulation that would be set forth by the EPA. Before we went into any advanced engineering designs today I think the corps' engineering division, which is beyond question as far as intense investigation requirements, would require some sort of an investigation. I'm not sure of the specific items since I'm not representing our engineering division.

IX / PRESENT STATUS OF GUIDELINES FOR LAND DISPOSAL OF WASTEWATER

29
Michigan's Experience with the Ten States Guidelines for Land Disposal of Wastewater

Donald M. Pierce*

Experience with land disposal systems in Michigan is very limited. Although nearly 50 communities have designed systems of this kind, only 2 of these have been in operation longer than one year. The widely publicized Muskegon County project may be in operation in 1973. At the end of 1972, 15 municipal spray irrigation projects, five using spreading or flooding basins, were completed and are now in operation. By the end of 1974 this number will have increased to about 50. Nearly all of these projects are in advanced planning stages. Thus there has been a rather extensive opportunity to use the guidelines adopted by the Great Lakes-Upper Mississippi River Board of State Sanitary Engineers—the so-called Ten States Standards (Ground Disposal of Wastewaters, 1971). They have been used with increasing respect and enthusiasm as experience has extended to an ever widening variety of field conditions. They are not, however, regarded as standards or rigid requirements any more than are other facilities, processes and practices for which standards or guidelines have been developed by this group.

Even in this early stage of operational experience some critical deficiencies in design have come to light. We are just beginning to recover from the shock of a series of misjudgments and oversights in technical areas new to us and not customarily within the experience of sanitary engineers—at least those in the east and midwest. The problems that have surfaced so early in the growth and development of an offspring heralded as the best hope of the ardent ecologist could probably have been avoided had the Ten States guidelines for ground disposal of wastewaters been put into practice. The real problem in

*Division of Wastewater, Michigan Department of Public Health

each case was some lack of understanding, both by the engineers designing the system and those evaluating and approving the design, of the natural forces which control the destiny of complex constituents of the waste particle when applied to the soil. It was not that they did not realize that they were dealing with matters a bit outside of their field. They knew this. It was not that they did not seek advice of other professionals more knowledgeable and experienced than they were in these matters. They did this. They conferred with hydrogeologists or geohydrologists, soil scientists, the crop specialists, the irrigation specialists and the drainage engineers and read pertinent publications. They even provided the specialists with some data and got some advice on how much more information and what kind was really needed to refine the design of the system. But here in their blissful ignorance they got off on the wrong foot. They made some value judgments of their own with too little information and just possibly too little real understanding and then they wrapped up the project for construction. Let me elaborate a little on where one project went astray.

A piece of land was chosen after a long search for spray irrigation of wastes from a community of about 2,000 with no adverse industrial waste constituents. Pretreatment was to be provided by primary sedimentation and aerated lagoons followed by disinfection. Wastes were to be spray-irrigated on some 75 acres roughly from April through October with provision for five months winter storage of the treated wastes. The treated wastes were to be sprayed at an average rate of two inches per week on a 16-hour-a-day basis. All wastes were to be contained within the property. Drainage systems traversing the property were to be abandoned or rerouted around the property. Soil borings on the spray area were interpreted to indicate a percolation capacity sufficient to accommodate the average two-inch application rate with rates during dry warm weather periods at least double this. This was the first big mistake. No underdrainage was proposed. This was the second big mistake.

The first indication of trouble obvious to the community and its engineers was much higher sewage flow than anticipated. This came to light the first year when the storage lagoon with projected capacity for five months storage overflowed in early January. During the ensuing eight months since then, soils have been demonstrated to be incapable of accepting rates of this magnitude without underdrainage and probably not even with good underdrainage. Runoff from the property to nearby drains continued throughout the summer months. Ponding in low areas has been severe and extensive. What are the consequences of this lack of predesign investigations and thorough analysis? 1) Gross nuisances from the ponding of wastes both on the property and on neighboring properties. 2) Discharge of inadequately treated wastes to the surface waters of the state exceeding stream standards. 3) Continuance of these conditions until a fully adequate program is devised and implemented.

Correction may require construction of an underdrainage system, acquisition of more land and installation of more irrigation equipment. It will also require considerations on vegetative cover, cropping regimens and other management aspects.

In somewhat similar circumstances, two small communities have developed land disposal systems, each utilizing spreading or flooding basins following raw waste stabilization lagoons. Both communities are quite small, using about 15 acres of land for irrigation to serve a population of less than 1,000. In both locations the basins were designed to accommodate an average application rate of about three inches per week for the six-month period with storage in the lagoons for the six months of winter. In each community, lagoons were placed in operation this spring with less than 75 percent of the properties connected to the sewer system. At our suggestion, one community directed its engineers and a geologist to confer with soil scientists and others to more fully evaluate the soil's capability. Preliminary analysis indicates application rates should be reduced to about one inch per week. Studies are continuing. At the other community soils are believed to have even less percolation capability. Obviously modifications, both in construction and management methods, must be made by each community to avoid serious pollution problems and gross nuisances.

These cases illustrate unsatisfactory performance attributable to tight soils with loading capabilities less than assumed in the design of the system, coupled with high groundwaters, inadequate drainage, and, in one case, topography conducive to sheet runoff. A quite different set of problems arise, of course, where soils have an extremely high percolation capability with groundwater moving from the disposal site to wells used for domestic water supply. In some respects, however, the designer and his special corps of technical consultants can identify and quantify the problems and their solutions for these conditions with greater precision and confidence than in other less obvious circumstances. Some soils obviously are more difficult to analyze than others as to their hydraulic capability and their ability to remove certain pollutants under a variety of weather conditions, application rates, cropping regimens, drainage systems and other effects. Perhaps most difficult of all are intermediate and long-range behavior patterns.

I must confess that as a state regulatory group, we have had less than a delightful experience with land disposal design and operation.

Our lack of experience has led to periods of uncertainty and apprehension. We have had to become familiar with technologies strange to us and have become more dependent on the judgment of technicians in a host of special, related disciplines. In some quarters we have been charged with unwarranted conservatism for our judgments in some aspects of design and operation. Quite paradoxically, these same judgments are sometimes viewed by those who oppose the land disposal concept as ridiculously generous in approving systems surely doomed to failure. There is room for both agitation and humor when you stand your ground in the middle.

Surely the most productive and rewarding experience we have had in administering this phase of our water pollution control program is working with the professionals who have had a great depth of knowledge in the many special fields involved. We find them in state departments of agriculture, health and natural resources, and in similar fields of work at universities and research institutions. It has been heartening to see how they can apply their knowledge to these problems in a truly team fashion and to witness their enthusiasm to delve into the more obscure aspects related to the peculiar and wide-ranging characteristics of wastewaters in an equally diverse environment.

Michigan has given the guidelines adopted by the Standards Committee of the Great Lakes-Upper Mississippi River Board of State Sanitary Engineers a good test this past year. With each project review and each field experience we are increasingly impressed that they are soundly conceived and fairly stated. They are gaining favor and acceptance with designing engineers and their consultants as a working guideline and basic reference.

Literature Cited

Ground Disposal of Wastewaters. 1971. Addendum no. 2 to recommended standards for sewage works, Great Lakes-Upper Mississippi River Board of State Sanitary Engineers.

30
Forest Service Policy Related to the Use of National Forestlands for Disposal of Wastewater and Sludge

Olaf C. Olson and Edward A. Johnson*

At this time the most accurate statement concerning the Forest Service's position to disposing of wastewaters and sludges on national forestland is that it's one of cautious optimism. It is cautious due to the dearth of proven results on the longer term effects of prolonged applications on the receiving lands. It is optimistic because of the scattered shorter term examples which have demonstrated that under carefully controlled and managed conditions, wastewaters and sludges can be recycled on selected sites without any apparent adverse effects. There are benefits to be gained. The wastewaters and sludges that are accepted for disposal have characteristics which can enhance the soil environment for plant growth, provided the soil-plant system is not overloaded beyond its capacity to assimilate the materials.

However, with some notable exceptions in the area of land reclamation and rehabilitation, it is generally true the primary concern of the Forest Service at this time is more one of aiding disposal with minimum detrimental impacts than it is one of looking to onsite benefits. This attitude supports the established policy that Forest Service programs, wherever possible, contribute to community development and to the improvement of the rural environment in general.

Federal Environmental Quality Requirements

All Forest Service policies concerning environmental quality must be consistent with policies determined at other levels. Planners must be aware, therefore, of applicable policies set by the president in his messages to Congress, executive orders and regulations issued in the Federal Register, the Council of Environmental Quality (CEQ), and the Environmental Protection Agency (EPA), as well as our own Department of Agriculture (USDA). They must also be aware of applicable state air, water, environmental quality, and public health standards.

*Division of Watershed Management, Forest Service, USDA

Executive Order 11514 of March 5, 1970, contains the following statements:

Federal agencies shall initiate measures needed to direct their policies, plans, and programs so as to meet environmental goals:
  a. Monitor, evaluate, and control on a continuing basis their agencies' activities so as to protect and enhance the quality of the environment.
  b. Develop procedures to ensure the fullest practicable provision of timely public information and understanding of Federal plans and programs with environmental impact in order to obtain the views of interested parties. . . .
  e. Review their agencies' statutory authority, administrative regulations . . . to identify any deficiencies or inconsistencies therein which prohibit or limit full compliance.
  f. Foster investigations, studies, surveys regarding ecosystems and environmental quality. . . .
  h. Promote development and use of indices and monitoring systems to assess environmental conditions and trends. . . .
  k. Issue guidelines.

Executive Order 11507 of February 4, 1970, concerns prevention, control, and abatement of air and water pollution at federal facilities. Among other things, it contains the following section 4(6)(b).

In those cases where there are no air or water quality standards as defined in section 2(d) of this order in force for a particular geographic area or in those cases where more stringent requirements are deemed advisable for Federal facilities, the respective Secretary, in consultation with appropriate Federal, State, inter-State, and local agencies, may issue regulations establishing air or water quality standards for the purpose of this order, including related schedules for implementation.

Another point of real significance is assigning heads of agencies primary responsibility for meeting operational and maintenance requirements in the standards section. This includes provisions for training of manpower. The Forest Service is working with EPA and other Federal agencies on training guidelines regarding qualifications and performance for individuals involved with environmental monitoring and surveillance and the continuing review to ensure that requirements are being met. Also, in time it is likely that planners might be faced with certification requirements in the states where monitoring is located.

The National Environmental Policy Act of 1969 (PL 91-190) requires environmental statements on each proposed major federal action affecting the human environment. The statements must be of sufficient detail to allow a responsible official to make determination of the environmental impacts to be expected from program implementation. Environmental values must be weighed objectively with economic development and social well-being goals over both the short and the long run. Also, taken into account are the comments of other agencies, individuals, and groups having interest in a project. This last item, consultation with others, is an essential consideration of the Act.

The Multiple Use-Sustained Yield Act of 1960 requires maintenance of the productivity of the land to assure perpetual optimum land output of the various renewable resources.

The Code of Federal Regulations, Title 40, Part 35, with interim regulations on pollution control that became effective July 1, 1972, sets forth requirements for basin control water quality management planning, adequacy of treatment, operation and maintenance of wastewater treatment works for prevention, control, and abatement of water pollution at federal facilities.

The general objective of the Department of Agriculture is to encourage land and water uses that will yield continuing maximum benefits to the people of the United States. Adjustments in land use to balance onsite and offsite needs should be made in ways that will make land and water available to an expanding population for living space, industry, commerce, and recreation. The systematic use of proven soil and water conservation techniques is encouraged to protect and develop land resources for future uses, to manage the soil resource for human needs, and protect and improve watersheds for both agricultural and urban uses.

The director of science and education in the secretary's office of the USDA has stated that in connection with the possible use of national forestlands for sewage disposal and nutrient recycling, any substance containing toxins in amounts specifically banned from agricultural use by federal law would not be permitted for land application. This means general and local standards and criteria for disposal of sewage on national forestlands must be developed to preclude environmental damages and undesirable ecological changes, and an effective monitoring system would be mandatory to ensure compliance with standards. Too, full coordination and cooperation will be maintained with EPA.

Land and Resource Use Requirements
on National Forestlands

As with other "special uses," wastewater and/or sludge disposal on national forestlands by an out-service group can only be done under a special use permit. Permit requirements include plans for application, surveillance, and followup management of the area. Sludges that have been stabilized by digestion or some equivalent process are acceptable. Acceptable wastewaters include those that have received primary and secondary treatment plus chlorination to reduce the health hazards. Chlorinated lagoon wastewater may be considered as equivalent to a secondary treatment. Permits require compliance with applicable federal, state, and local environmental, public health, and water quality laws and standards.

A land manager's decision to approve or disapprove an application for wastewater disposal is based on the possibilities of beneficial or adverse total environmental effects. Each application for a permit requires, therefore, a study and an analysis of the environmental factors involved in relation to the objectives and local land use demands of the area involved. The methods and techniques for applying wastewater on forest and range lands must be in accord with practices which can be publicly endorsed.

Status of Specific Policy Direction

Forest Service national policy direction is gradually being firmed and, naturally, at this stage is influenced by the experience and knowledge of many people and agencies.

It has been recognized that a combined effort within the Forest Service will be needed to formulate a uniform and specific policy direction to wastewater disposal. A strong supporting research program is obviously essential and initial state-of-the-art guidelines for sewage disposal on agricultural and forest lands have been prepared by James O. Evans of the Division of Forest Environment Research of the U.S. Forest Service, Washington, D.C. Certain land use and management plans for the area including required environmental quality surveillance will require periodic updating.

The Eastern Region of the U.S. Forest Service has recently issued a provisional guide entitled "Environmental Protection Criteria for Disposal of Treated Sewage on Forest Lands." The guide attempts to form a bridge between water quality standards and soil quality standards and includes suggested criteria levels that may ensure minimal hazard to environmental values. This guide was prepared by Hugh Cunningham, soil scientist, Monongahela National Forest, and has proved to be a valuable document.

As mentioned previously, regulation of the disposal system project must depend on a well-designed and implemented system of monitoring (data collection) and the interpretation of these data in terms of their meaning to total resource management on and adjacent to the specific site. Many of the recently passed laws and regulations pertaining to environmental values and the reflections of public attitudes make it essential that we document the effects of our management practices and activities on the soil resource as well as on the air and water resources. Physical, chemical, and biological characteristics and properties are all of concern.

Esthetics will also be provided for disposing of wastewater. The basic character of the landscape should be maintained with man-made alterations fitted to the immediate countryside. Special attention will be given to harmoniously joining size, shape, location, and dispersion of disposal sites so they respond directly to visual characteristics — form, line, color, and texture — of the surrounding landscape.

Future Outlook and Potential Impacts

Because the use of land for wastewater and sludge disposal places certain restrictions on other land uses, the selection of satisfactory disposal sites is in turn restricted. At the present time, the greatest opportunity for large-area disposal sites lies on those lands upon which activities and uses are already restricted — surface mined areas (land restoration), firebreaks, greenbelts, and the like. These may not be the best sites for this purpose, but widespread use of lands having greater potential or capacity for disposal will depend largely on public acceptance. This will come gradually with better understanding of ecosystem functioning and public involvement in the planning efforts at all stages. Small disposal sites can and are being located near the areas being serviced.

At the present time, there are 26 sites in national forests in 14 states involved in planning for land disposal of wastewater and/or sludges by sprinkler or flood irrigation. An increasing number of applications is expected for this type of use on national forest system land.

A word of prediction as to the future in the use and management of wastes and resources on national forestlands might be appropriate. The word is *balance;* balance between people's needs as reflected by demand and by the capabilities and opportunities at hand for waste disposal and utilization. The challenge of achieving balance is possible through careful planning and management. Progress is being accomplished toward this goal.

31
Spray Irrigation—The Regulatory Agency View

Richard C. Rhindress*

The Bureau of Water Quality Management of the Pennsylvania Department of Environmental Resources is the regulatory agency concerned with the protection from pollution of all the waters within the state. As such it has been aware of the growing interest in various techniques of land disposal for liquid wastes for quite some time. The increasingly stringent waste quality requirements for the discharge of wastewater to streams, coupled with the upgrading of requirements for wastewater treatment, plus the need for disposal in areas where streams are not readily accessible, have increased the importance of land disposal of liquid wastes. The point has been reached where it must be dealt with squarely as one of the alternatives for the treatment and ultimate disposal of wastewater.

A regulatory agency becomes aware of spray irrigation in two separate ways: first, when a new technique is promoted, and second, when enforcement officials view a number of existing problems. An environmental protection agency has an obligation to consider all techniques of waste disposal and to assess their applicability to various wastes and their impact upon the environment. The problems which we recognized from the earliest days of our experience with operating spray irrigation systems indicated that regulation was needed. The imposition of regulation, however, carries with it a responsibility to provide guidance in the construction and location of such facilities so that the potential user can develop a plan satisfactory to the regulatory agency. The experiences of the department with spray irrigation, the department's philosophy concerning the use of land disposal techniques, and some important concepts, which are included in the Spray Irrigation Manual will be discussed here.

Definitions

Under the general classification "land disposal of liquid wastes" there have been a number of confused interpretations of spray irrigation. The definition should be, "the application of wastewater to the land

*Ground Water Quality Management Unit, Pennsylvania Department of Environmental Resources

surface for treatment and/or ultimate disposal, using aerial dispersion (sprinklers) to distribute the effluent evenly over the land surface."

However, there are a number of other land application methods which have been confused with (and it might be said "passed off" as) spray irrigation. These methods are mentioned here because the regulatory agency found all of them must be considered as variations on a theme. For the most part they are significantly different; they usually require different technologies, and different site selection. One is the technique of spreading: driving a tank truck across a field, letting the effluent spew from the open valve, sometimes with the benefit of a spreading device. Another variation is simply open pipe discharge to a land area, often down a hillside. Third is the dumping of a sewage treatment plant sludges and septic tank sludges onto the land surface, with or without the benefit of spreading or burial. Several persons have chosen to call the application of even these nonsprayable wastes to the land surface a form of spray irrigation. Somewhat more akin to classic spray irrigation is ridge and furrow irrigation, where the effluent is spread through a series of shallow trenches. One other technique is the use of surface flow, much on the idea of a standard sand filter where the effluent is allowed to flood an area of ground and slowly sink into it. None of these techniques are equivalent to spray irrigation; however, to some extent they are each valid techniques of land disposal for liquid wastes *when properly executed.*

Classic spray irrigation, the aerial disposal of wastewater using a system of sprinklers, piping, and sprinkler nozzles will be delineated in this chapter.

Status and Regulation

Pennsylvania presently has 75 spray irrigation installations in operation, and another 10 to 15 in planning and design stages. The vast majority of these installations are relatively small, serving a single industry or small treatment plant. Most are industrial waste applications. The largest number of these are in southeastern Pennsylvania, primarily in the Great Valley or Piedmont. Most of those which are presently under permit from the state have their permits because they have had pollution problems in the past. Although regulation has always been possible under the Pennsylvania Clean Streams Law, a discharge to the land surface was not clearly recognized as a discharge to the waters of the commonwealth. It was considered similarly to septic-tank installations where the interpretation was that there was no direct discharge, therefore, no need for a permit. Spray irrigated water, of course, does discharge to groundwater by percolating down through the soils, overburden, and rocks to the water table. Thus it is definitely a discharge to the waters of the commonwealth as defined by the Clean Streams Law. A new program to bring all spray irrigation installations under permit will be implemented with the publication of the department's spray irrigation manual and new regulations.

Groundwater Discharges

At the same time that spray irrigation was becoming more prominent in Pennsylvania, officials as in many other states, were becoming increasingly aware of the need to protect the quality of groundwater. Many septic systems are not, in fact, doing their job of renovating waste completely before it reaches groundwater. Even the best sanitary landfills are recognized as sources of groundwater pollution. The spray irrigation project at The Pennsylvania State University recognized the potential danger of spray irrigation to groundwater. Spray irrigation presents itself as a new technique for the treatment and ultimate disposal of wastewater. It keeps wastewater out of the streams, but in doing so poses a very real threat to the quality of groundwater.

Unlike streams which can rebound from polluted conditions in a few years, groundwater does not experience the flushing action of stream flow. It does not experience the purifying effects of air, light, and biological organisms. Instead it flows very slowly, receives little dilution, has essentially no oxygen to degrade pollutants, and flows through a medium where surface tension tends to hold pollutants in contact with it.

The general public thinks that groundwater is clean, fresh and pure, and available in that state wherever they may choose to drill a well. Fortunately, for much of the state, groundwater has these properties.

Although both the law and the public attitude demand that groundwater remain drinkable, the conditions under which groundwater exists deny significant renovation. Therefore, the department's goal for groundwater quality is that it be usable for domestic purposes without treatment. It is imperative to preserve groundwater in its purest possible state. The technique of spray irrigation poses a very real threat of pollution.

Experience with the presently operating systems is generally poor. Two basic problem areas have been defined: (1) improper system design and (2) management errors.

Design Problems
Design problems can be traced to several sources. Waste treatment

plant designers have had little or no education or experience with this new technology. Attempts have been made to design systems without the understanding of the following basic tenets of spray irrigation design: First, spray irrigation is only an alternative method for disposal and treatment; second, spray irrigation must be integrated into the environment rather than imposed upon it; and third, as a dispersed operation, it will be far more difficult to control and manage.

Spray irrigation, and land disposal, have been advocated as the panacea for wastewater disposal problems. The literature has been attractive and promising. Unfortunately, very little of the literature speaks of potential problems and the limitations of such a technique. Thus, the consulting engineer has often been given a false sense of security. Any proposal to disperse wastes into the environment must consider the multiple constraints which the environment will place upon it. It is only after a thorough consideration of these constraints the decision can be made to use spray irrigation as an alternative to some other method of disposal, such as direct discharge to a stream or groundwater. For example, one agricultural waste was applied to a field for a number of years until eventually the soils were so altered that infiltration and percolation of the water was converted entirely to sheet runoff. The fields were entirely ruined and will be long in recovery. The loss of these agricultural lands and the degradation of groundwater in the area have forced the industry into acquiring both new lands and more expensive water source. In this case, it would have been far better to construct a direct pipeline to discharge to a creek over a mile away, or treat the waste so that the soil could accept it.

When using the "living filter" for waste renovation, it is extremely important that the whole wastewater treatment and disposal system be matched to the environmental capabilities rather than impressed upon it. The simple addition of the extra hydraulic load will be a major stress on the system. Further, the requirement that the soil system act as a treatment facility in decaying and renovating the waste is an added stress. Most natural areas are in a state of dynamic equilibrium. This dynamic equilibrium has the ability to respond to passing stresses.

However, when a stress is applied uniformly over long periods of time, equilibrium of the ecosystem is severely altered and may, in fact, be destroyed. For example, a soil with a fragipan layer will have a low permeability, and be capable only of accepting infiltrating water at normal precipitation rates. Dosages much above this result in waterlogged soils and runoff or swampiness. A second example: vegetative communities are adapted to a soil and its available moisture capacity. When spray irrigation applies a hydraulic stress, the vegetative system must adapt with the disappearance of some species and introduction of others. In addition, streams below the site will have to adapt to a different flow regimen with a different chemical quality. All this is not necessarily bad, although in all but one of the department's experiences, it has been. There are a few cases where environmental improvement may be realized through the stressing of the natural system. The assessment of the natural system, and the strains which it may show as the result of the new stresses are the prime subject matter of the department's Spray Irrigation Manual.

For several reasons, lack of control has been a major problem in the design of spray irrigation systems. Consultants have usually ignored the valuable assistance available from the agricultural irrigation industry and have pieced together a system of pipes and valves from a catalog. Agricultural irrigation systems are designed simply to get water to a field. There is little concern about loss and leakage until it becomes a major problem. Agricultural systems are designed for ease of mobility and minimum maintenance. They are also used primarily for a short season. Conversely, wastewater irrigation systems are generally to be used year-round, must be watertight, should rarely be moved or moved only in conjunction with a carefully designed plan, and should be considered part of a long-term investment and installation. Also, in the agricultural sense the irrigation system is part of the profit-making package. It is carried on the profit side of the ledger books, whereas a waste disposal system is usually considered as a liability—as something that must be done, but which is not important to the success of the operation. Thus it is rarely adequately funded. Further, it is usually located at a considerable distance from the plant and the base of company operations. Often, it is completely out of sight. Thus routine operations such as checking for blockages and turning valves to change irrigated sections of the field are often neglected or relegated to a minor priority in company operations. Thus the need for mechanical, electrical, or computerized control of the operations becomes very important to successful continued routine operations. Automation of the controls has been entirely neglected at the majority of sites.

With any new technique, there is the problem of education regarding its values and execution. Poor design of the spray irrigation systems presently in existence is due to the unfamiliarity of the design consultants with a new technique, and the technologies and equipment necessary to carry it out. Training courses and symposia are needed to fill this educational hiatus.

Management Problems
As has been mentioned, management and maintenance are a second major problem area for spray irrigation fields. Management views spray irrigation, or any waste discharge area, as a liability to oper-

ation and therefore consistently relegates its consideration to a very
low priority. Maintenance of a spray field is normally the responsibility of the bottom man on the maintenance staff. He, of course, is
usually the man called upon to fill in whenever there is another
important task to be done or when other employees may be absent.
Spray fields can go unattended for considerable periods of time without causing a problem. A well-operated spray field may, in fact, go for
many months without appreciable maintenance problems. However, a
single malfunction within the system can stress the ecosystem to its
irreversible limit. Thus, it is important to have maintenance over-
seeing the field on a routine basis. Unfortunately, the usual experience in Pennsylvania has been that when inspectors inspect the site,
they find evidence that no one has viewed the field or cared to make
necessary repairs for quite some time.

Some common problems are:

1. Broken pipe
2. Leaky joints
3. Vegetation blocking sprinklers
4. Valves and/or sprinklers corroded in position
5. Rutted areas from vehicular traffic in wet soils
6. Clogged sprayers
7. Unharvested vegetation
8. Swampy conditions with ponding, with even aquatic flora and
   fauna
9. Vector problems—flies, mosquitoes and rats
10. Anaerobic soil conditions producing swamp gases and other
    foul odors
11. Sheet runoff directly to adjacent streams
12. Waste material build-ups which inhibit plant growth—solids
    and greases.

In addition, we have found evidence of application of wastes which
are entirely nondegradable by the living filter system. These usually
are toxic and stress the field beyond recovery.

Solutions

The solutions to the problems with spray irrigation can come from
three levels: the designer, the management, and the regulatory
agency.

Design Solutions
The primary solution for the problem of securing adequate designs is

one of education. Engineering schools will have to recognize spray irrigation and other techniques of land disposal as valid waste management alternatives to be included in the curricula. For the continuing education of the graduate designer, the state regulatory agencies and professional societies will need to provide data and information on the new techniques. For the consultant, it is imperative at this time to go to those who have had experience both in the experimental development phases of land disposal and in the regulatory phases, and to learn from their experience. In addition, he should rely heavily upon the expertise available from the irrigation industry.

The following fifteen steps in the implementation of a spray irrigation installation were compiled by Lewis W. Barton, a spray irrigation consultant from Cherry Hill, New Jersey, and the author. They should serve as guidelines to anyone considering land disposal of liquid waste.

1. Before deciding on land disposal or spray irrigation, examine all the alternatives regardless of any apparent restrictions. Consider recycling of wastewater and direct discharge of treated wastes to a stream or to groundwater.

2. Weigh the motives for using land disposal. Is the desired result groundwater recharge? Agricultural irrigation? Green belt irrigation for fire protection? Or just plain final treatment and ultimate disposal? Or some combination of these?

3. Make a preliminary tour of the area (not just the site) with reference to suitable land, a route for the force main, sites for any pumping stations, field drainage, and lagoons for storage and flow equalization.

4. Study the effluent characteristics in detail. Assess their biodegradability by the living filter. Determine if any inorganics may be present which will not be removed by the soil system or which will poison the environment.

5. Select a site. Choose the best site available. Work with the local real estate man for an option or a lease. Work with a hydrogeologist and a soil scientist in making this preliminary site selection. If there is any doubt about the acceptability of the land for spray irrigation use, negotiate options or leases on double any amount of land you expect to use.

6. Map the selected site, showing contours, topography, soils, geologic structures, bedrock geology, streams, springs, wells, woodland areas, existing buildings, and present land use patterns for the designated acreage.

7. Choose sites for background and down-gradient groundwater quality monitoring.

8. Draft a preliminary proposal to the state regulatory agency which includes the above data and a preliminary design of the irrigation system. Secure their preliminary approval before proceeding with detailed design and further financial commitments.

9. Design the piping system, force main, and drainage; specify the hardware, field preparation, seeding, fertilizing, and agricultural maintenance.

10. Design and specify the automated programmers which will provide the central operating system, including pump signals and malfunction alarms.

11. Prepare and present the appropriate applications to regulatory agencies.

12. Bid the project and supervise construction. Establish and sample groundwater monitoring points before any other construction proceeds.

13. Prepare an operating manual that is simple and easy to follow. The operating manual is one of the most important pieces of the design engineer's task. It also is probably the most often neglected.

14. The design consultant should include in his contract monthly inspections of the operation for at least the first year. These inspections should involve the consultant, management, the operator, and the regulatory agency.

15. Conduct quarterly inspecting through at least the second year and even into the fourth and fifth year. These inspections will provide for continuing surveillance of system efficiency as well as for keeping the facility out of trouble with the regulatory agency.

Management Solutions

From the management point of view the main steps which can be taken are the following:

1. Responsibility for spray field maintenance should be a full-time position. Interviews with a number of maintenance personnel have indicated they consider their job a full-time project. Many have even suggested that we confer with management to help convince them of the amount of work necessary to keep a spray field functioning properly.

2. Put the effluent to some good use rather than just disposing of it; *i.e.,* use it for irrigation where it will be an integral part of company operations.

3. Maintain a schedule of routine inspections.

4. Wherever possible install a buried or permanently set system. Experience has shown that movable systems either do not get moved or suffer from severe wear and tear.
5. Do not try to overload the system as production increases. Redesign or add to the system.

Regulatory Solutions

Under present Pennsylvania law, the operator of a spray irrigation system which is disposing sewage is required to obtain a certificate for sewage treatment plant operation. As another step in solving problems with spray irrigation systems, the state may have to extend certification to all spray field operators. In fact, it may be desirable to make "Spray Irrigation Field Operation" one of the classes of certification. Certification of spray field operators would give the regulatory agencies a stronger lever for improved operations, as withdrawal of the certificate for improper operation of the facility could put the operator out of work and place his company in violation of the law for not having a certified operator. The present condition of many spray fields within the commonwealth suggests that this is a very likely path to follow. Again, the state has an obligation to provide information for training for spray field operator certification.

Other regulatory solutions include normal enforcement activity, design review and permitting, and the issuance of regulations and design standards.

Pennsylvania's Spray Irrigation Manual

The fast rising number of spray irrigation installations and applications indicates the Department of Environmental Resources should publish a manual or set of guidelines to site selection and system design. The manual would also include instructions for the preparation of plans and reports for securing a permit. The manual has been published as the Spray Irrigation Manual, Bureau of Water Quality Management Publication No. 31, and is available from the Bureau, located in the Fulton National Building, Third and Locust Streets, P. O. Box 2063, Harrisburg, Pennsylvania 17120.

Such a manual is necessarily written for a wide audience. It speaks to the consulting engineer and designer, the hydrogeologist and soil scientist. It also speaks to corporate management which may desire a spray irrigation system, and it often speaks to local officials and the land owner who knows very little of the technology or responsibilities involved. In speaking to a wide audience it is both an educational tool and somewhat of a design manual.

Writing a design manual is not entirely feasible since one of the main tenets of spray irrigation is that the system must be integrated into the environment rather than imposed upon it. And since the environment is extremely variable with respect to the groundwater, soils, geology, agriculture, and climate across the state, it is impossible to write a design book for all the possible variations in the environment. The manual assesses these variations in the natural environment. It speaks of concepts and their importance, and how each of them relates to the spray irrigation techniques of land disposal.

Basic criteria for spray irrigation have been set as a baseline from which judgment as to the acceptability of a site can be related. First, the entire waste handling package must be considered together: the pretreatment, the storage, flow regulation, and the irrigation system. It emphasizes that spray irrigation installations may be utilized only where the wastewater contains pollutants of such type and concentration as can be satisfactorily treated through distribution to the soil mantle. Generally, only biodegradable wastes are acceptable, and the equivalent of secondary treatment must precede spray irrigation. However, allowance is made for variability in earth materials, spray field use, and effluent constituents by stating that treatment requirements and performance criteria will have to be determined on a site-by-site basis. The prime consideration for site selection is the ability of the organic and earth materials to properly treat the waste.

One item which has caused considerable difficulty in drafting the spray irrigation manual has also proven to be a cause of much misunderstanding on the part of manual users. A large number of potential users for spray irrigation are industrial waste generators. These various firms will want to place a wide variety of biodegradable and nondegradable waste on their fields. Because of the wide latitude in constituents and concentrations it would be impossible to write a spray irrigation manual which tries to speak to each of these possible wastes. It is far more practical to write a manual which is oriented toward the spray irrigation of sewage. Considerations of industrial wastes must then be made as they compare to sewage. Flows and concentrations are calculated and adjusted as percentages of normal sewage effluent.

Manual Organization
Review of important points and concepts in the Pennsylvania Spray Irrigation Manual, with a discussion of the reasoning behind some of the more important ones follows.

Certain criteria have been stated for the pretreatment of waste, application rates, acceptability of soils, agricultural practices, etc.

These criteria have been set primarily as guidelines based upon spray irrigation of sewage effluent. However, throughout the manual there are numerous statements which demonstrate the department's intentions to be flexible and willing to consider special applications and experimental designs. Although a number of spray irrigation sites have been in existence throughout the country for many years, they have not benefited from a total environmental impact study before implementation and have usually ended in some form of pollution. The lessons learned from them have been mostly negative — what not to do. Thus, this technique is still in the developmental stage and justifiable experiments which vary from the basic criteria will be permitted.

For most water pollution control facilities, construction-ready plans are required with the permit application. But, because of the need for land purchasing and extensive testing and drilling programs to determine the subsurface geology and hydrology of the spray field, the department has instituted the preliminary review to determine the general acceptability of the proposed fields before capital investments or detailed designs are made. For a preliminary review the applicant submits:

1. A short statement of the nature of the project and wasteload characteristics; information on location, soils and climatology.
2. Preliminary spray field design and operation plans.

If the department grants preliminary approval of the spray fields, the applicant is notified and the complete permit application is then submitted. The preliminary approval does not approve the construction or operation, nor does it assure approval of the complete design report. Issuance of the Department of Environmental Resources permit must precede construction and operation.

A large section of the manual is devoted to some detailed explanations of factors that must be considered as they affect the renovation of the wastewater and its movement to groundwater. The department is very concerned that the best soils and geologic and hydrologic conditions are available for these processes, because once the wastewater reaches the water table only minimal renovation of the waste can be expected. Thus, extreme care must be exercised in assessing these environmental factors.

1. **Earth Materials.** The earth materials at a spray irrigation site may consist of soil, unconsolidated surficial deposits, weathered rock, and bedrock. Infiltrating wastewater will pass through these materials as it percolates to the water table. The earth materials near the land surface serve as a substrate for biological

activity, while the unconsolidated material, weathered rock, and bedrock may react chemically and physically with the wastewater. The texture of these materials must be such that a direct rapid movement (short circuit) of the irrigated water to the groundwater does not occur. Coarse sands and gravels, open fractures in bedrock, and shallow soils are all examples of conditions which may result in short circuits. The earth materials should be moderately permeable and of a uniform quality so they will provide slow but continuous downward movement of the infiltrating wastewater, yielding an adequate residence time for renovative reactions to take place. Detailed information on the geology, soils, and hydrology is necessary.

2. **Soils.** In addition to meeting the various textural criteria, the department urges that during the preparation of the field and installation of the equipment, particular attention be paid to avoiding disruption of the established soil profile as much as possible. Recommended application rates are based on the drainage and permeability of the soil, available moisture capacity, and the depth to the water table.

3. **Geology.** Once the irrigated wastewater leaves the soil zone and enters the zone of weathered and fresh bedrock, it is particularly important to know the structure of this rock. Are fractures present which will short-circuit the water directly to the water table or route it preferentially in directions which modify its assumed direct route to the water table? Will the waste react with the rock? The geology also affects the direction of movement within the water table as it flows through and away from the site.

4. **Hydrology.** Under most conditions in Pennsylvania, spray irrigated wastewater will recharge the local groundwater. With pretreatment, adequate dispersal of the waste, and properly chosen earth materials, the wastewater should be adequately treated during its passage through the zone of aeration to the water table. Thus, pollution of the receiving groundwater will be prevented. But once the wastewater reaches the water table only minimal renovation can be expected. Thus, to insure that the applicant has considered groundwater, its movement, and the potential result of its contamination, the department has required that monitoring facilities be placed beneath the site and in all directions of groundwater flow away from the site. In addition, a background water quality well must be established where the quality of water flowing into the area may be assessed for comparison. A secondary benefit to monitoring is that the data provide a valuable tool to the operator in limiting

potential legal action from nearby groundwater users. These
legal actions often are the result of fear and ignorance, thus the
acquisition and maintenance of background and discharge data
are imperative to the operator. These data also provide the
regulatory agency with data for evaluating the efficiency of the
operation. The submission of routine (generally, quarterly) reports of water quality data from both background and down-
gradient monitoring points is required. The exact chemicals
reported are dependent upon the waste. For sewage, routine
reports would include phosphate, ammonia-nitrogen, nitrate-
nitrogen and MBAS.

5. **Agricultural Practice.** Although the department has no specific
requirements as to agricultural practice, other than the maintenance of the vegetative cover on the field, it recommends that
the agricultural management coordinate closely with slopes of
the field and the excess hydrologic loads. Research projects
such as the one at Penn State University have demonstrated
that agricultural product yield can be significantly improved
using spray irrigation. Yet, relatively few farmers have been
willing to accept the long-term commitment to use the wastewater that is necessary to implement a system. Self-serving
industry systems apparently are working. But for municipal
sewage systems, this raises the questions of the applicability of
funding to the purchase or rental of spray fields, the desire of
the community to get into agricultural land management, and an
educational problem of convincing would-be lessees of the value of a long-term commitment.

6. **Research.** As stated previously, existing spray irrigation facilities have demonstrated that the technique has not been adequately planned or managed in the past. Certain research facilities and a few showplace operations have demonstrated the
value of spray irrigation both for wastewater treatment and
disposal, and as an agricultural benefit. However, these projects
have been limited in their scope and in the geographic diversity.
There is an immediate need to expand research and demonstration projects to soils and environments which are less ideal than
these research installations. New environmental constraints
must be tested, and engineering techniques of field preparation
and modification should be considered. Spray irrigation can be
integrated into a natural system and applied research will show
how this integration can take place, but spray irrigation cannot
be impressed upon natural systems.

Summary

Like all rapidly developing technologies, waste treatment and disposal by spray irrigation has suffered from misunderstanding, inadequate design, mismanagement, and misapplication. Conversely it shows great promise as a valuable alternative technique for wastewater management. New research and regulatory action will help, but a new attitude of environmental understanding is necessary by all potential users. The key to this understanding is the acceptance of the basic tenet that spray irrigation must be integrated into the environment rather than imposed upon it.

Discussion

Unknown: Is your experience on these spray irrigation systems any worse or better than the typical treatment plant?

Rhindress: Unfortunately I can't even discuss that because I have been strictly dealing with this as a geologist. I guess I'll have to turn it over to one of our other staff members, if they want to comment. These systems, however, are almost uniformly poor.

Reed: I would like to know where we are training these maintenance personnel.

Rhindress: We're not. It's something that we've got to get working on and get working on fast.

Hall: I notice in your manual the statement that under usual conditions the groundwater mound should be built up and should not reach within 10 feet of the ground surface. It seems from other discussions that this is a pretty difficult limitation. Do you find it that way or not?

Rhindress: It hasn't been. The manual was just published, so it hasn't been really a criterion for long. That criterion is based on some experiences, one of which is poor operation. We're being very conservative. Another thing is that we feel and have felt through experience and reading the results of research that we needed a large zone of aeration. We felt that 10 feet would be adequate. We're learning more about this all the time. We felt at the time of writing the manual that 10 feet would be a good level in terms of a safety zone and also that needed for the zone aeration.

Williams: I can't let that pass. Your rationale for a 10-foot zone escapes me completely. Why do we need 10 feet of aerated soil? What good does it do? Why not 20 feet or why not 2 inches? This is the groundwater mound when you are operating. This is not the normal groundwater table that you're talking about.

Rhindress: Right. One thing that I must point out and you've apparently not read the manual to this point, practically every value in there has a statement ahead of it or behind it or near it that says this is recommended. We can and will allow practically anything if we can be shown that there is reasonable evidence to believe that it will work. This is a guideline, not a set of criteria. As I said earlier, state specifications are not going to be written. They can't be written.

Kardos: But the trouble occurs when you put out a guideline like this and it gets into the hands of engineers. They look at the guidelines as state specifications because there are inferences that this is what you're thinking of, and if you put in a plan that deviates from these guidelines you're going to have trouble getting it approved.

Rhindress: All I can say is if I'm reviewing the plan, they won't have any trouble. I'll try my best to give the plan a fair review.

X / RESEARCH NEEDS

32
Research Needs—Land Disposal of Municipal Sewage Wastes

James O. Evans*

This stimulating symposium—probably the best and most informative of its kind ever conducted—has been the first comprehensive attempt to evaluate overall problems relating to the application of treated sewage effluent and sludge to forest, range, and agricultural land. It is certain this will not be the final such venture. It now seems appropriate to consider the direction of future research.

Assessment of the Situation

The need to determine the best methods of handling a residue problem which literally is man's own creation is of utmost importance. Most certainly the first man practiced land disposal, but gave no thought to pretreatment. As Adam's children multiplied and assembled in communities, often the disposal situation must have become a bit messy. Sometimes streams were used to flush away the problem—a practice that worked rather well as long as there was no overloading and other personal stream uses were limited either to upstream areas or to sites at sufficient distances downstream.

As the population continued to grow and congregate, through necessity man became wiser and eventually developed an impressive array of treatment-disposal facilities, some simple, others complex, and some highly advanced technically. But no treatment-disposal method has proven wholly adequate. Often one kind of pollution has been replaced by another, treatment-disposal costs are increasing, and sophisticated methods of disposal by discharge to and dilution in air or water have become commonplace. Regardless of the treatment method used, some residue always remains for ultimate disposal. Potential resources have either been destroyed, wasted, unused, or discharged to sites subjecting them to undesirable enrichment and environmental change.

*Forest Service, USDA, Washington, D. C.

Today the natural environment is under savage assault. Waste products of an accelerating technological development and expanding population are rapidly becoming man's most insidious and deadly enemies. A special report prepared several years ago for the Senate Committee on Interior and Insular Affairs states:

> The challenge is the rapid deterioration of the environmental base, natural and manmade, which is the indispensable foundation of American security, welfare, and prosperity. . . .
> It is becoming apparent that we cannot continue to enjoy the benefits of our productive economy unless we bring its harmful side effects under control.

Thoughtful Americans will agree there is but one answer: Quality of the environment must be restored and preserved. The cost will be high—both in money and in effort. But the costs of environmental pollution are even higher.

Each day in the United States about 100 billion liters (over 26 billion gallons) of sewage wastewater and roughly 10,000 metric tons (11,000 short tons) of dry sludge solids are produced (Evans and Sopper, 1972; Rosenkranz, 1972). Unfortunately all but a small percentage of the nutrient-rich sewage effluents are discharged into the nation's streams. Sludge is currently disposed as follows: 15 percent in the oceans; 25 percent by incineration; and a perhaps surprising 60 percent by land application (Rosenkranz, 1972). Included in this 60 percent portion are (a) liquid sludge applied as a fertilizer, (b) sludge solids applied as a combination soil conditioner-fertilizer, and (c) sludge buried in landfills.

This symposium has dealt with the problem of recycling municipal sewage wastes by land disposal. However, all questions have not yet been answered, and a few nagging new ones may have been uncovered. Sewage wastes should be considered not as refuse, but as useful resources (Evans, 1970). What research is needed to perfect the use of this so-called new resource? Fortunately, there is a good base upon which to build sound research programs. This fact has been amply demonstrated at this symposium, which has produced some excellent papers and provided much useful information about this rediscovered resource.

Needed—A Rational Research Program on Resource Recycling

The development of a rational recycling program in an integrated, comprehensive manner requires an almost infinite knowledge about the recycling process and ecosystem response. At the present time very little is known about either.

Research on basic ecosystem functions must be expanded. Stevens *et al.* (1972) have recommended using interdisciplinary teams of biological, physical, and social scientists to test and analyze large-scale, controlled, environmental manipulations. Land-disposal techniques and utilization of sewage effluents and sludges would be included in these manipulations.

Use of open-space land areas for sewage disposal invites consequent and perhaps undesirable ecological change. Studies must involve understanding the ecology of open-space lands and natural areas as well as emerging social patterns, viable economic units, transportation and mobility, innovative technological advancements, and physical and biological interactions among components of total communities.

All subjects, including those selected for research, must be visualized as occurring within one large area representing the ecosystem. Land disposal of municipal sewage wastes can be depicted as a small circle connected to other circles of similar dimensions and all located within the larger ecosystem circle (Figure 32-1).

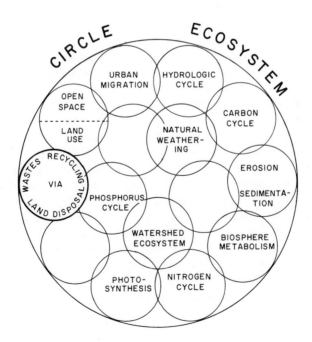

Figure 32-1. Sewage wastes recycling—a component of total ecosystem functions

Present finances and current knowledge will not allow implementation of grandiose schemes; practical and realistic plans must be made. Where should research begin?

Immediate Research Needs

1. The mechanics for efficient and effective handling of sewage wastes and their disposal on various land areas must be developed. Research is currently underway at Beltsville, Maryland, on the comparative merits of incorporating sludge into soils by burial in trenches at depths of two and four feet, by deep disking, by rotary tilling, and through other methods. Each of these methods should be compared with various types of aerial spray mechanisms, surface spreading techniques, and subsod or subsoil injection processes.
2. Economic factors relative to various or alternative handling and disposal methods require investigation and evaluation.
3. Although technical solutions to waste-management problems either already exist or can be found without undue effort, answers are also needed to many problems having their roots in the social, economic, legal, and political areas. Existing conditions and potential developments in the following areas urgently require investigation: (a) esthetics and public acceptance, (b) comparative costs, (c) competing needs and legal aspects, and (d) political implications and tradeoffs.
4. It has often been stated that major soil types or benchmark soils throughout the nation need study with respect to their ability to absorb, assimilate, degrade, adsorb, transmit, alter, and store various organic and inorganic substances present in sewage effluents and sludges. Hill (1972) has determined that several soils occurring extensively in Connecticut exhibit vast differences in permeability to, and capacity for removing ions from, a synthetic sewage effluent. Considerable research is needed on the interactions between various soil types and applied wastes so that major soil groups can be evaluated and rated according to their disposal capability.
5. Transport methods and costs, from sewage source to disposal site or nearby holding area, can play a decisive role in determining the feasibility of a sewage disposal program. They need thorough study and evaluation.
6. Determination of the role of microorganisms in the functioning of natural communities is needed. Also the ability of key soil

microorganisms to degrade, stabilize, and render sewage wastes innocuous, and conversely, the impact of the wastes or pollutants on the microorganisms must be determined.

7. Counteraction or reaction between applied wastes and soil insect and small macroanimal populations should be observed and evaluated.

8. Research should be geared to ascertain the degree of ultimate disposal achieved. Many current pollution-abatement technologies achieve little more than sophisticated dilution of sewage wastes.

9. Potential health hazards due to disposal practices require urgent, careful, and extensive investigation:

    (a) Unanswered questions have arisen concerning the potential of harm to humans from toxins or pathogens in aerosols produced by aerial spray application of sewage effluent.

    (b) Possible health hazards arising from sludge spreading must be evaluated and resolved. This means ascertaining the chance of pathogen transfer to susceptible hosts as a function of time since spreading and previous treatment of the sludge. It should also include assessment of possible toxic substances in plants grown on sludge-treated areas, such as nitrate in certain vegetables.

    (c) Improved alternatives or refined types of treatment for sludge which will eliminate health hazards posed by pathogens, nitrates, and other toxic substances must be developed. Pasteurization is one technique of likely feasibility for elimination of pathogens. Aerobic treatment followed by anaerobic treatment, or the oxidation-reduction process, is a very promising technique for reducing the nitrate hazard.

    (d) Alternative treatments in effluent disposal must be evolved to eliminate health hazards from nitrates and other toxic substances. Here again, the oxidation-reduction process has given promising results.

10. There is a need to devise superior techniques for irrigating effluent and spreading sludge beneficially on forested land. Such development should be particularly useful in the industrial East and to some extent in the Seattle-Portland belt of the Pacific Northwest, as well as in other Pacific coast forestland and brushland areas.

11. Long-term effects of various sludges on appropriate land areas should be determined. Sludges should include: (a) conventional digested sludge from domestic sources, (b) chemically stabilized sludge (lime to pH 11, etc.), and (c) sludges from industries (food, paper, textile, forest products, petroleum, etc.) which do

not contribute toxic quantities of heavy metals. Appropriate land areas include: (a) pasture, (b) plowed land, (c) orchards, (d) abandoned farmland, (e) forests, (f) deserts, (g) rangeland, (h) taiga and tundra, and (i) mine spoil and other disrupted soils. The effects include vegetation changes and runoff and groundwater quality as a function of dosage.

12. Assessment must be made of the tolerance of crops and forests to various heavy metals deposited with organic sewage sludges, that is, organic sludges which reduce the toxicity of these metals.

13. A thorough assessment of specific tree and agronomic crop growth responses to various effluent and sludge applications should be made.

14. The quantity and quality of groundwater recharge from effluent irrigation under various situations should be determined.

15. The methodology for, and efficiency of, effluent and sludge recycling in areas that remain frozen over extended periods of time need to be established.

16. Technically superior, better integrated, and more comprehensive environmental monitoring systems must be developed.

17. There is an urgent need for specific comprehensive research, including the research already listed, to establish adequate standards and guidelines for the use of sewage effluent as irrigation-fertilization and aquifer recharge water — and of sewage sludge as a fertilizer and soil conditioner.

18. Research is needed on the possibility of toxic conditions developing in certain plants resulting from excessive phosphate accumulations in soils.

19. And finally, odor problems must be considered. Wherever or whenever odor problems are apt to occur, they must either be prevented, eliminated, or effectively controlled.

Additional urgent research needs could be itemized but perhaps a halt to a listing of particular research needs should be made at this point. Whenever feasible, in research planning it is wise to make a habit of taking the broader, and more ecological, view. To illustrate this approach, an outline of elementary system analysis to the recycling and utilization of wastes in general by land application is illustrated. The illustration showing recycling and utilization of biodegradable wastes by land application (Figure 32-2) is an adaptation and extension of a schematic display devised by Besley and Reed (1972). The display is enlarged to include waste effluents and forest and rangeland disposal sites. The authors refer pointedly to the common practice in Europe and the Far East of recycling biode-

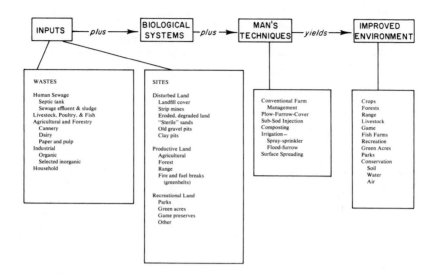

Figure 32-2. Recycling and utilization of biodegradable wastes by land application

gradable wastes to the land. They note the considerable amount of reluctance to use human sewage in this country and the more convenient and economical practice of using less bulky and plant-nutrient-balanced commercial fertilizers.

Through research we can determine whether it really is more economical on both a short-term and a long-term basis to use commercial fertilizers exclusively, rather than sewage wastes. The word "exclusively" is used because there just aren't enough sewage wastes produced in America to meet the farm fertilizer demands. Also, through research much more convenient methods of applying sewage nutrients than are currently known will be discovered.

Literature Cited

Besley, H. E. and C. H. Reed. 1972. Urban wastes management. *Jour. of Environmental Quality,* 1(1):78-81.

Evans, J. O. 1970. The soil as a resource renovator. *Environmental Science and Technology,* 4(9):732-735.

Evans, J. O. and W. E. Sopper. 1972. Forest areas for disposal of municipal, agricultural, and industrial wastes. Unpublished paper presented at the Seventh World Forestry Congress, Buenos Aires, Argentina, October 4-18.

Hill, D. E. 1972. Waste water renovation in Connecticut soils. *Jour. of Environmental Quality,* 1(2):163-167.

Rosenkranz, W. A. 1972. Unpublished data presented at OST Spring Review Meeting,

April 21. Data prepared by Municipal Technology Branch, Division of Research, Environmental Protection Agency, Washington, D.C.

Stevens, H. K., T. G. Bahr, and R. A. Cole. 1972. Recycling and ecosystem response. The Institute of Water Research, Michigan State University, East Lansing, Michigan, 124p.

List of Symposium Participants

Contributors to this volume are indicated by an asterisk.

Abel, George A.
Environmental Protection Agency
1200 Sixth Avenue
Seattle, Washington 98100

Adams, Lowell
Environmental Resources Association
P.O. Box 2259
Monterey, California 93940

Alaisa, Cornelio
Dept. of Water Resources Admin.
State of Md., State Office Bldg.
Annapolis, Maryland 21401

Amoroso, Edward
Pa. Dept. of Environmental Resources
P.O. Box 1467
Harrisburg, Pennsylvania 17120

Anderson, Donald F.
E.P.A., Tech. Division Office
1901 N. Fort Myer Drive
Arlington, Virginia 22209

Anderson, Robert
West Virginia University
Room 1132 Ag. Sciences Building
Morgantown, West Virginia 26330

Andreoli, Aldo
Suffolk County Health Department
County Center
Riverhead, New York 11901

Apgar, Mike
Roy F. Weston, Inc.
Lewis Lane
West Chester, Pennsylvania 19380

Ariail, J. David
Environmental Protection Agency
1421 Peachtree Street, N. E.
Atlanta, Georgia 30309

Askins, William
Pope, Evans, and Robbins
11 E. 36th Street
New York, New York 10016

Bagnulo, Aldo H.
N. Va. Planning District Commission
7309 Arlington Boulevard
Falls Church, Virginia 22042

Bahr, Thomas
Michigan State University
Institute of Water Research
334 Natural Resources Building
East Lansing, Michigan 48823

Ball, Robert C.
Michigan State University
Institute of Water Research
East Lansing, Michigan 48823

Barekman, Harlan C.
City of Monett
352 S. Belaire
Monett, Missouri 65708

Barnes, Norman
Skinner Irrigation Company
2530 Spring Grove Avenue
Cincinnati, Ohio 45214

*Bauer, W. J.
Bauer Engineering, Inc.
20 North Wacker Drive
Chicago, Illinois 60606

Baumgardner, Robert H.
Federal Highway Administration
400 7th Street SW
Washington, D. C. 20590

Bausum, Howard T.
Army Med., Environmental Engr. Res.
  Unit
Edgewood Arsenal, Maryland 21010

Beavin, Benjamin E., Jr.
Beavin Company
104 E. 25th Street
Baltimore, Maryland 21218

Beegle, Richard G.
Baker-Wibberley & Associates, Inc.
P.O. Box 1857
Hagerstown, Maryland 21740

Beemer, Edwin F.
7 Walton Drive
New Hope, Pennsylvania 18938

Behrens, John W.
Metcalf & Eddy
60 E. 42nd Street
New York, New York 10017

Benton, Raymond
U.S. Forest Service
6816 Market Street
Upper Darby, Pennsylvania 19082

Berry, Charles R.
U.S. Forest Service
Carlton Street
Athens, Georgia 30601

Berry, Wade
County of Los Angeles
301 North Baldwin Avenue
Arcadia, California 91006

Berzins, Agris
Dayton & Knight Ltd.
Box 247, 1865 Marine Drive
West Vancouver, B. C., Canada

Betts, Clifford A., Jr.
Betts Engineering Company, Inc.
518 Lookout Street
Chattanooga, Tennessee 37403

Boelter, Don H.
Northern Conifers Lab.
North Central Forest Experiment Station
P.O. Box 872
Grand Rapids, Minnesota 55744

Boggess, William R.
Dept. of Forestry
University of Illinois
Urbana, Illinois 61801

Bohley, Paul B.
The Gorman-Rupp Company
305 Bowman Street
Mansfield, Ohio 44902

Boke, Richard L.
Reynolds Metals Company
6601 West Broad Street
Richmond, Virginia 23200

Boswell, Fred C., Dr.
University of Georgia
Georgia Station
Experiment, Georgia 30212

Botts, Lee, Mrs.
Lake Michigan Federation
53 West Jackson Boulevard
Chicago, Illinois 60604

Bourgeois, W. W.
Forestry Service
202-130 Allard Street
Sault Ste. Marie, Ontario, Canada

*Bouwer, Herman
Water Conservation Lab.
Soil and Water Res. Div.
Agricultural Research Service
U.S. Dept. of Agric.
Phoenix, Arizona 85040

Bower, David A.
Muskingum Watershed Conservancy
    Dist.
1319 3rd Street, N.W.
New Philadelphia, Ohio 44663

Bradford, William W.
W. Va. State Department of Health
1800 Washington Street, E.
Charleston, West Virginia 25305

*Broadbent, F. E.
Dept. of Soils and Nutrition
University of California
Davis, California 95616

Brown, James L.
University of Minnesota
St. Paul, Minnesota 55100

Brown, Peter G.
Assn. for the Preservation of
    Cape Cod
Box 636
Orleans, Massachusetts 02653

Bull, Robert Keith
Harza Engineering Company
150 S. Wacker Drive
Chicago, Illinois 60606

Burge, Wylie D.
USDA, ARS
Beltsville, Maryland 20709

Buros, Krisen
Black, Crow & Eidness, Inc.
Queens Quarter # 673
Christiansted, U.S. Virgin Islands

Burrell, John
William T. Foster Associates
808 Bethlehem Pk.
Erdemheim, Philadelphia, Pa. 19118

Butler, Robert M.
Ag. Engineering Dept.
Pennsylvania State University
University Park, Pennsylvania 16802

Buzzell, Timothy
USA-CRREL
Hanover, New Hampshire 03755

Cadagan, Dan J.
Dan J. Cadagan Co.
P.O. Box 8011
Spokane, Washington 99203

Callahan, James E.
U.S. Army Engr. Div., N.E.
424 Trapelo Road
Waltham, Massachusetts 02154

Carlson, Charles
Waterways Experiment Station
OSAEC, U.S. Army Corps of Engineers
Vicksburg, Mississippi 39180

Carson, Burke, Jr.
Multrum Corp.
Skaneateles, New York 13152

Cartier, R. E., Jr.
Environmental Health Program
Southern West Virginia Regional
  Health Council
Route # 2, Box 382
Bluefield, West Virginia 24701

Celenza, Paschal
One Plymouth Meeting Hall
Betz Environmental Engineers
Plymouth Meeting, Pennsylvania 19462

Chaney, Rufus L.
USDA-ARS-Biol. Waste Mgmt. Lab.
Rm. 107, Bldg. 007, P.I. Sta.
Beltsville, Maryland 20705

Chapman, John
Valmont Industries
Valley, Nebraska 68064

Chase, F. E.
University of Guelph
Guelph, Ontario, Canada

Cherry, Rodney N.
U.S. Geological Survey
Rm. 410, 500 Zack Street
Tampa, Florida 33602

Christensen, Lee A.
Ag. Econ. Department
Michigan State University
Room 303, 1405 S. Harrison Road
East Lansing, Michigan 48823

Christman, Richard L.
Ohio Dept. of Natural Resources
1500 Dublin Road
Division of Lands & Soil
Columbus, Ohio 43221

Clapp, C. E.
USDA, ARS-University of Minnesota
Saint Paul, Minnesota 55101

Click, David M.
Army Corps of Engineers
Box 1159
Cincinnati, Ohio 45201

Conway, Charles R.
EPA-Region 1
Waltham Federal Center
424 Trapelo Road
Waltham, Mass. 02154

Conyers, Emery S.
Dow Chemical Company
2020 Building
Midland, Michigan 48640

Cooper, William J.
Army Med. Environmental Engr.
  Res. Unit
Edgewood Arsenal
Edgewood, Maryland 21010

Crane, John S.
Harza Engineering Company
150 S. Wacker Drive
Chicago, Illinois 60606

Crites, Ronald W.
Metcalf & Eddy Inc.
1029 Corporation Way
Palo Alto, California 94303

Cruess, Robert A.
N.H. Water Pollution Control Comm.
105 Loudon Road
Concord, New Hampshire 03301

Cunningham, Hugh
Monongahela National Forest
824 15th Avenue
Marlinton, West Virginia 24954

Curran, Stephen F.
Dept. of Environmental Resources
P.O. Box 2351
Harrisburg, Pennsylvania 17105

Curtis, Willie R.
USDA, FS, Northeast Forest Expt. Sta.
204 Center Street
Berea, Kentucky 40403

*Cutter, B. E.
School of Forest Resources
Pennsylvania State University
University Park, Pennsylvania 16802

Davis, David E.
North Carolina State University
Box 5577
Raleigh, North Carolina 27607

Davis, Ellen
Town of Brookhaven
205 South Ocean Avenue
Patchogue, New York 11772

Dawson, William R.
U.S. Army Corps of Engineers
502 8th Street
Huntington, West Virginia 25721

Delay, Edwin T.
U.S. Army Corps of Engineers
P.O. Box 919
Charleston, South Carolina 29402

Dennehy, Kenneth M.
Rain Machine, Inc.
P.O. Box 291
Windsor, Connecticut 06095

De Witt, Joseph W.
U.S. Army Corps of Engineers
P.O. Box 889
Savannah, Georgia 31402

Dillon, Donald L.
U.S. Army Corps of Engineers
1114 Commerce Street
Dallas, Texas 75202

Dissmeyer, George E.
U.S. Forest Service
1720 Peachtree Street NE
Atlanta, Georgia 30309

D'itri, Frank
Michigan State University
334 Natural Res. Building
East Lansing, Michigan 48823

Dotson, Kenneth
Environmental Protection Agency
Robert A. Taft Laboratory
Cincinnati, Ohio 45226

Dovak, John L.
Pa. Dept. of Environmental Resources
996 Main Street
Meadville, Pennsylvania 16335

Drawbaugh, Daniel B.
Division of Water
Pa. Dept. of Environmental Resources
Harrisburg, Pennsylvania 17105

Edwards, I. K.
Northern Forest Research Center
5320-122nd Street
Edmonton, Alberta, Canada

Ellingboe, James D.
Bureau of Reclamation U.S.D.A.
18th & C Streets
Washington, D. C. 20240

Elliott, William R.
Meyer Rohlin, Inc.
1111 Highway 25N
Buffalo, Minnesota 55313

*Ellis, Boyd G.
Dept. of Crop and Soil Science
Michigan State University
East Lansing, Michigan 48823

Elwood, John R.
Mass. Div. Water Pollution Control
100 Cambridge Street
Boston, Massachusetts 02202

Emerson, Richard
Mich. Water Resources Commission
Stevens T. Mason Building
Lansing, Michigan 48900

Enfield, Carl G.
Environmental Protection Agency
Washington, D.C. 20460

*Evans, James O.
U.S. Forest Service
14th & Independence Avenue
Washington, D.C. 20250

Ewell, Wesley J.
Cape May County Planning Board
Cape May Court House
Cape May, New Jersey 08210

Faucher, Francis D.
MDC Boston
20 Somerset Street
Boston, Massachusetts 02202

Fedler, Richard E.
Donohue & Associates, Inc.
4738 N. 40th Street
Sheboygan, Wisconsin 53081

Feinberg, Eli
State of Florida
Capitol Building
Tallahassee, Florida 32304

Ferullo, Alfred F.
Mass. Div. of Water Poll. Control
100 Cambridge Street
Boston, Massachusetts 02202

Fielding, H. Page
Delaware River Basin Commission
P.O. Box 360
Trenton, New Jersey 08603

Flanders, P. Howard
Vermont Dept. of Water Resources
Pavilion Office Building
Montpelier, Vermont 05602

Flett, Donald R.
N.J. State Water Poll. Control
Health, Ag. Building
Trenton, New Jersey 08625

Forester, Ted H.
Missouri Clean Water Commission
P.O. Box 154
Jefferson City, Missouri 65101

*Foster, D. H.
Dept. of Civil Engineering
University of Illinois
Urbana, Illinois 61801

Foster, William T.
William T. Foster Associates
808 Bethlehem Pike
Erdemheim, Philadelphia, Pa. 19118

Fox, Fred L.
Geonics
Box 101
North Branch, New Jersey 08876

Francke, Harry C.
Union Carbide Corp.-Nuclear Division
P.O. Box y
Oak Ridge, Tennessee 37830

Freeberg, Brian M.
Stewart & Walker, Inc.
15th Street & Bemidji Avenue, Box 634
Bemidji, Minnesota 56601

*Frost, Terrence P.
Water Pollution Control Commission
105 Loudon Road
Concord, New Hampshire 03301

Gansell, Stuart I.
Pa. Dept. of Environmental Resources
734 W. 4th Street
Williamsport, Pennsylvania 17701

Garner, Eugene F.
Metropolitan Sewer Board
350 Metro Square Bldg.
7th & Robert Street
Saint Paul, Minnesota 55101

Gentry, Claude E.
USDA, FS, Northeast Forest
    Experiment Station
204 Center Street
Berea, Kentucky 40403

Gerzetich, Robert M.
Consumers Power Company
212 W. Michigan Avenue
Jackson, Michigan 49201

Giddings, Todd
Todd Giddings & Assoc.
623 W. Foster Avenue
State College, Pennsylvania 16801

Gifford, Robert D.
Walla Walla Dist. Corps of Engr.
Bldg. 604, City-County Airport
Walla Walla, Washington 99362

Ginner, Gary F.
Minn. Poll. Control Agency
717 Dela. St., S. E.
Minneapolis, Minnesota 55440

Girgin, Joseph M.
Parsons, Brinckerhoff, Quade &
    Douglas
111 John Street
New York, New York 10038

*Goddard, Maurice K.
Dept. of Environmental Resources
Commonwealth of Pennsylvania
Harrisburg, Pennsylvania 17120

Goedde, Joe
Missouri State Park Board
P.O. Box 176
Jefferson City, Missouri

Goldfine, Neil A.
New Jersey Dept. of Env. Prot.
Box 1390
Trenton, New Jersey

Gottberg, Frank
Sprinkler Irrig. Supply Co.
1316 North Campbell Road
Royal Oak, Michigan 48067

Goydan, Paul A.
Koppers
440 College Park Drive
Monroeville, Pennsylvania 15146

Graves, Diane
N. J. Sierra Club
360 Nassau Street
Princeton, New Jersey 08540

Green, Therman W.
USDA-Forest Service
1720 Peachtree Road NW, Room 716
Atlanta, Georgia 30309

Griego, Alex R.
USDA-Forest Service
517 Gold Avenue SW
Albuquerque, New Mexico 87109

Guerrera, August
Suffolk County Water Authority
P.O. Box 37
Oakdale, New York 11769

Guldin, Lt. Richard W.
Wastewater Management Task Force
4H028 Forrestal Bldg.
Washington, D. C. 20314

Haines, Charles
Wright, McLaughlin Engineers
2059 Bryant Street
Denver, Colorado 80302

Hale, Daniel
Southern W. Va. Reg. Health Council
Route 2, Box 382
Bluefield, West Virginia 24701

Hall, Eric P.
Environmental Protection Agency
424 Trapelo Road
Waltham, Massachusetts 02154

Hall, George
Engineer-Operations
Teledyne Triple R
111 Service Road
Muskegon Co. Airport
Muskegon, Michigan 49441

Hall, Otis F.
Inst. of Natural & Environmental
    Resources
University of New Hampshire
Durham, New Hampshire 03824

Hanczar, William S.
Dept. Environmental Resources
734 W. 4th Street
Williamsport, Pennsylvania 17701

Handy, Eben N., Jr.
U.S. Army Corps of Engineers
P.O. Box 59
Louisville, Kentucky 40201

Hansen, William
University of Missouri-Forestry
1-31 Ag. Building
Columbia, Missouri 65201

Hanson, Lowell D.
Ag. Extension Service
University of Minnesota
Saint Paul, Minnesota 55101

Harlin, Curtis C.
Nat'l Water Quality Control Res.
    Program
Environmental Protection Agency
Ada, Oklahoma 74820

Harman, Edgar H.
Garrett County Health Department
Oakland, Maryland 21550

Harman, Oscar R.
Environmental Science
Garrett Community College
McHenry, Maryland 21520

Harris, W. F.
Environmental Sci. Div., Bldg. 3017
Oak Ridge National Laboratories
Oak Ridge, Tennessee 37830

Hart, William E.
Colorado State University
Ft. Collins, Colorado 80521

Hartmann, George Leonard
Environmental Protection Agency
Region VIII, 1860 Lincoln Street
Denver, Colorado 80203

Haskin, Millard
Bureau of State Parks
Dept. of Environmental Resources
301 Market Street
Harrisburg, Pennsylvania 17057

Hedlund, V. A., Jr.
Valmont Industries
Valley, Nebraska 68064

Heil, James
Suffolk County Health Dept.
County Center
Riverhead, New York 11901

Helfant, M. A.
Town of Brookhaven
205 South Ocean Avenue
Patchogue, New York 11772

Helmey, Edgar L.
Soil Conservation Service
P.O. Box 985
Federal Square Station
Harrisburg, Pennsylvania 17108

Hennessey, John J.
Brookhaven National Lab
Building 134C
Upton
Long Island, New York 11973

Higbee, Roger
Pa. Dept. of Environmental Resources
300 Liberty Avenue
505 State Off. Bldg.
Pittsburgh, Pennsylvania 15222

Higgins, George C.
The Dow Chemical Company
2020 Dow Center
Midland, Michigan 48640

Hill, L. W.
U.S.D.A. Forest Service
Institute Tropical Forestry
P.O. Box AQ
Rio Piedras, Puerto Rico 00928

*Hinesly, T. D.
Dept. of Agronomy
University of Illinois
Urbana, Illinois 61801

Hinkle, Richard L.
Pa. Dept. of Environmental Res.
1875 New Hope Street
Norristown, Pennsylvania 19401

Hoheneder, Joseph C.
York Co. Planning Comm.
220 S. Duke Street
York, Pennsylvania 17403

*Hook, J. E.
Dept. of Agronomy
Pennsylvania State University
University Park, Pennsylvania 16802

Hooper, Frank T.
School of Natural Resources
University of Michigan
Ann Arbor, Michigan 48104

Hortenstine, Charles C.
Soil Science Dept. (106 Newell)
University of Florida
Gainesville, Florida 32601

Hunt, Patrick G.
USA Engineer Waterways Expt. Station
P.O. Box 631
Vicksburg, Mississippi 39180

*Hunter, Joseph V.
Dept. of Environmental Science
Rutgers University
New Brunswick, New Jersey 08903

Huntington, Lee Ann
President's Council on
    Environmental Quality
722 Jackson Place
Washington, D.C. 20006

Ifft, Theodore H.
USDA Soil Conser. Service
4321 Hartwick Road
College Park, Maryland 20740

Inge, Andrew
Dept. of Environmental Resources
Bur. of State Parks, 301 Market St.
Harrisburg, Pennsylvania 17101

Irelan, Paul H.
Soil Conser. Service
Camden County
Berlin, New Jersey 08009

Jablonowski, Carl
U.S. Dept. of Agriculture
Forest Service, Allegh. Natl. Forest
P.O. Box 847
Warren, Pennsylvania 16365

Johns, J. M.
Johns Equipment Company
Route 2, Box 21
Farmville, Virginia 23901

*Johnson, James F.
Waste Water Management Task Force
Department of the Army
Corps of Engineers
Washington, D.C. 20314

Jones, Henry P.
J. Henry Jones, Inc.
3389 S. 8th E. Street
Salt Lake City, Utah 84106

*Jones, Robert Lewis
S. 410 Turner Hall
University of Illinois
Urbana, Illinois 61801

Jorgensen, Erik
Canadian Forestry Service
The Dept. of the Environment
4056 W. Memorial Building
344 Wellington Street
Ottawa, KIA OH3, Canada

Kam, William
U.S. Geological Survey
Trenton, New Jersey 08600
27 Canyon Road
Levittown, Pennsylvania 19057

Kappe, Stanley E.
American Academy Environmental Engr.
Box 1278
Rockville, Maryland 20850

*Kardos, Louis T.
Department of Agronomy
Pennsylvania State University
University Park, Pennsylvania 16802

Kasabach, Haig F.
N.J. Div. of Water Resources
P.O. Box 1390
Trenton, New Jersey 08625

Keller, James
Rist-Frost, Assoc.
21 Bay Street
Glenn Falls, New York 12801

Kelley, Harold A.
Jones & Henry Engrs. Ltd.
2000 W. Central Avenue
Toledo, Ohio 43606

Kelling, Keith A.
University of Wisconsin
Soil Department
Madison, Wisconsin 53706

*Kelly, George T.
Metropolitan Sanitary District of
   Greater Chicago
100 East Erie Street
Chicago, Illinois 60611

Kenyon, David D.
New England Division
U.S. Army Corps of Engineers
424 Trapel Road
Waltham, Massachusetts 02154

Kerfoot, William B.
Woods Hole Oceanographic Inst.
Woods Hole, Massachusetts 02540

Kerslake, Richard J.
Soil Conserv. Service
1608 Oak Hill Avenue
Hagerstown, Maryland 21740

Kestner, Joseph A., Jr.
One Kestner Lane
Troy, New York 12180

Kidder, Milady
Allegheny Health Department
40th & Penn Avenue
Arsenal Health Center
Pittsburgh, Pennsylvania 15224

Kittle, Benjamin L.
Dept. of the Army
S. Atlantic Division
510 Title Building
30 Pryor Street
Atlanta, Georgia 30300

Kline, John H.
Consumers Power Co.
212 W. Michigan Avenue
Jackson, Michigan 49201

Kolega, John J.
University of Connecticut
Storrs, Connecticut 06268

Kolzow, William C.
U.S. Forest Service
Building 46
Denver Federal Center
Lakewood, Colorado 80225

Konrad, John G.
Department of Natural Resources
Box 450
Madison, Wisconsin 53702

Koo, Robert C. J.
University of Florida
P.O. Box 1088
Lake Alfred, Florida 33850

Kotyk, Eugene
Environmental Protection Service
Dept. of Environment
106-501 Univ. Court
Winnipeg, P3T2N6 Man., Canada

Kraft, Daniel
26 Federal Plaza
New York, New York 10007

Kraybill, Richard
Bureau of Water Quality Management
401 Buttonwood Street
West Reading, Pennsylvania 19603

Krivak, Joseph A.
Planning Branch
Environmental Protection Agency
AFWP, Room 1007
Washington, D. C. 20784

Kronis, Henry
Ministry of the Environment
135 St. Clair Avenue, W
Toronto, Ontario, Canada

*Kudrna, Frank L.
Metropolitan Sanitary District of
    Greater Chicago
100 East Erie Street
Chicago, Illinois 60611

Kutzman, James S.
Environmental Protection Agency
Suite 204
1421 Peachtree Street, N.E.
Atlanta, Georgia 30309

Larson, Carl
Environmental Resources Association
P.O. Box 2259
Monterey, California 93940

Layman, John
The Stratton Corporation
Stratton Mountain
Stratton Mountain, Vermont 05340

Leischen, Nicholas
State of Florida
3399 Ponce De Leon
Coral Gables, Florida

*Lejcher, Terrence R.
Shawnee National Forest
U.S. Forest Service
Harrisburg, Illinois 62946

Lewis, Donald
Geography Department
University of Toledo
Toledo, Ohio 43606

Lindorff, David
Bureau of Water Quality Management
1875 New Hope Street
Norristown, Pennsylvania 19401

Little, Silas
Northeastern Forest Expt. Sta.
P.O. Box 115
Pennington, New Jersey 08534

Livingston, David
U.S. Silver & Mining Co.
1701 Lake Avenue
Glenview, Illinois 60025

Livingston, Robert
U.S. Silver & Mining Company
1701 Lake Avenue
Glenview, Illinois 60025

Lorenzen, Douglas
Department of Environmental Resources
Harrisburg, Pennsylvania 17109

Losche, Craig
U.S. Forest Service
c/o Forestry Sciences Lab.
Southern Illinois University
Carbondale, Illinois 62901

Ludington, David
Cornell University
Riley Robb Hall
Ithaca, New York 14850

Lunin, Jesse
U.S. Department of Agriculture
Ag. Research Service
Room 127 Admn. Bldg.
Beltsville, Maryland 20705

Lyon, Walter A.
Bureau of Water Quality Management
Dept. of Environmental Resources
Harrisburg, Pennsylvania 17109

Mace, Arnett
College of Forestry
University of Minnesota
St. Paul, Minnesota 55101

MacLauchlin, Robert
U.S. Army Corps of Engineers
536 South Clark Street
Chicago, Illinois 60605

Magnuson, Paula
Association for the Preservation
   of Cape Cod
Box 636
Orleans, Massachusetts 02653

Maneval, David
Appalachian Region Commission
1666 Connecticut Avenue, N.W.
Washington, D. C. 20235

Marino, James
Pennsylvania Department of
   Environmental Resources
996 Main Street
Meadville, Pennsylvania 16335

Markstrom, Donald
U.S. Forest Service
240 West Prospect Street
Fort Collins, Colorado 80521

Marsh, John
Engineering Enterprises
123 E. Tonhawa
P.O. Box E
Norman, Oklahoma 73069

McKernan, J. M.
York University
4700 Keele Street
Downsview 463, Ontario, Canada

McLaughlin, William
U.S. Forest Service
P.O. Box 3623
Portland, Oregon 97208

McMaster, Ronald
Milford Water Authority
Milford, Pennsylvania 18337

McNeill, Peggy
League of Women Voters
Bloomfield Avenue
Montclair, New Jersey 07042

McNenny, Darrell
USDA Forest Service
Missoula, Montana 59801

McWilliam, Peter
Christchurch Drainage Board
P.O. Box 13006 Armagh
Christchurch, New Zealand

Merritt, James
Department of the Army
So. Atlantic Div.
Corps of Engineers
510 Title Building
30 Pryor Street, S.W.
Atlanta, Georgia 30303

Metzger, Barbara
Environmental Protection Agency
26 Federal Plaza
New York City, New York 10007

Michael, Alan
Pope, Evans and Robbins
11 E. 36th Street
New York, New York 11803

Miller, Harold
Beavin Company
104 E. 25th Street
Baltimore, Maryland 21218

*Miller, Robert H.
Dept. of Agronomy
Ohio State University
Columbus, Ohio 43210

Minning, Robert
W. G. Keck & Associates, Inc.
4903 Dawn Avenue
East Lansing, Michigan 48823

Mizell, Roger
U.S. Forest Service
1720 Peachtree Street, N.W.
Atlanta, Georgia 30309

Montgomery, Wayne
Harland Bartholomew & Associates
165 North Meramec
Clayton, Missouri 63105

Moore, Harold
University of Delaware
College of Marine Studies
Newark, Delaware 19711

Moorshead, Frank
Roy F. Weston, Inc.
Lewis Lane
West Chester, Pennsylvania 19380

Morgan, Wayne
Kellogg's Supply Company
238 13 Cholame Drive
Diamond Bar, California 91765

Moser, John
Pennsylvania Department of
    Environmental Resources
300 Liberty Avenue
Pittsburgh, Pennsylvania 15222

Mudrak, Vincent
Pennsylvania Fish Commission
Box 200-C
Bellefonte, Pennsylvania 16823

*Myers, Earl A.
Dept. of Agricultural Engineering
Pennsylvania State University
University Park, Pennsylvania 16802

Near, C. R.
Hastings Irrig. Pipe Co.
P.O. Box 607
Hastings, Nebraska 68901

Neil, Forrest
The Metropolitan District of
    Greater Chicago
100 East Erie
Chicago, Illinois 60611

*Nesbitt, John B.
Dept. of Civil Engineering
Pennsylvania State University
University Park, Pennsylvania 16802

Newell, S. David
McDowell Manufacturing Company
P.O. Box 665
DuBois, Pennsylvania 15801

Newmann, Thomas
Environmental Engineer Service
State Department of Health
Lucas Building
Des Moines, Iowa 50320

Norris, Logan
U.S. Forest Service
Forestry Sciences Laboratory
3200 Jefferson Way
Corvallis, Oregon 97330

Norum, Edward
McDowell Manufacturing Company
P.O. Box 665
DuBois, Pennsylvania 15801

Nussbaumer, William
Tennessee Valley Authority
TVA Forestry Building
Norris, Tennessee 37918

O'Dell, John
U.S. Soil Conservation Service
R. 200 Fed. Courts Building
316 N. Robert Street
Saint Paul, Minnesota 55101

O'Leary, Phillip
Department of Natural Resources
Box 450
Madison, Wisconsin 53702

Oleson, Harry, Jr.
U.S. Geological Survey
500 Zack Street
Tampa, Florida 33602

Oleson, S. Melodie
SW Florida Water Management
    District
P.O. Box 457
Brooksville, Florida 33512

*Olson, Olaf C.
Environmental Management Section
Div. of Watershed Management
U.S. Forest Service
Washington, D.C. 20250

Otke, Ken
Missouri State Park Board
P.O. Box 176
Jefferson City, Missouri 65101

Overman, Allen
Agriculture Engineering
University of Florida
Gainesville, Florida 32601

Padgett, William
U.S. Forest Service
6816 Market Street
Upper Darby, Pennsylvania 19082

*Parizek, Richard R.
Dept. of Geology
Pennsylvania State University
University Park, Pennsylvania 16802

Parmelee, Donald
C. W. Thornthwaite Associates
Route 1, Centerton
Elmer, New Jersey 08318

Parrett, Neil
U.S. Army Corps of Engineers
HQDA (DAEN-CWE-S)
Washington, D.C. 20314

Parrott, Lawrence
McDowell Manufacturing Company
P.O. Box 665
DuBois, Pennsylvania 15801

Paschke, Robert
Rieke-Carrol-Muller Associates
Box 130
Hopkins, Minnesota 55343

Peffer, Jeffrey
Bureau of Water Quality Management
29 Chestnut Street
Lewistown, Pennsylvania 17044

Pepper, Leonard
Waterways Expt. Station
Box 631
Vicksburg, Mississippi 39180

*Peterson, James R.
Metropolitan Sanitary District of
    Greater Chicago
Research and Development Lab.
5901 W. Pershing Road
Cicero, Illinois 60650

Peterson, Mark
Extension of Agriculture
University of Missouri
Columbia, Missouri 65201

*Pierce, Donald M.
Division of Wastewater
Bur. of Environmental Health
Dept. of Public Health
Lansing, Michigan 48914

Pierce, James
Van Note-Harvey Associates
Box 623
Princeton, New Jersey 08540

Pierce, Robert
Water Resources Section
Lake Central Region
Bureau of Outdoor Recreation
Ann Arbor, Michigan 48104

Poloncsik, Stephen
Environmental Protection Agency
1 North Wacker Drive
Chicago, Illinois 60606

Poole, Allan
City of Naperville
305 Jackson Street
Naperville, Illinois 60540

Pound, Charles
Metcalf & Eddy, Inc.
1029 Corporation Way
Palo Alto, California 94303

Pounds, William
Pennsylvania Department of
    Environmental Resources
Box 2351
Harrisburg, Pennsylvania 17103

Pulsonetti, P. C.
Town of Brookhaven
205 South Ocean Avenue
Patchogue, New York 11772

Ragone, Stephen
U.S. Geological Survey
1505 Kellum Place
Mineola, New York 11501

Rasmussen, Dale
Hastings Irrig. Pipe Company
P.O. Box # 607
Hastings, Nebraska 68901

Ray, Griffith
U.S. Corps of Engineers
Ohio River Division
P.O. Box 1159
Cincinnati, Ohio 45201

Reed, Charles
Agricultural Engineering
Rutgers State University
New Brunswick, New Jersey 08903

Reid, Denyse
Princeton Conservation Commission
Township Hall
Princeton, New Jersey 08540

Reid, Michael
Ministry of the Environment
Plant Operations Branch
135 St. Clair Avenue
Toronto, Ontario, Canada

Reid, Robert
Town of Brookhaven
205 S. Ocean Avenue
Patchogue, New York 11772

Reid, William
Department of the Army
Corps of Engineers
Mobile District
P.O. Box 2288
Mobile, Alabama 36601

*Rhindress, Richard C.
Ground Water Quality Management Unit
Division of Water Quality
Dept. of Environmental Resources
Harrisburg, Pennsylvania 17701

Rhodes, John
John C. Reutter Associates
9th & Cooper Streets
Camden, New Jersey 08101

Riddle, William
Riddle Engineering
3847 State Line
Kansas City, Missouri 64111

Risley, Clifford
Environmental Protection Agency
1 North Wacker Drive
Chicago, Illinois 60606

Ritter, William
College of Ag. Science
University of Delaware
Newark, Delaware 19711

Rodrigue, Raymond
Co. Sanitation Dists. of Los Angeles
24501 S. Figueroa Street
Harbor City, California 90710

Rodriguez, José
Environmental Quality Board
P.O. Box 11488
Santurce, Puerto Rico 00910

*Roland, F. J.
Bauer Engineering, Inc.
20 North Wacker Drive
Chicago, Illinois 60606

Rome, Samuel
Pres's. Water Pollution Control
67 E. Madison (L. of W. Voters)
Chicago, Illinois 60603

Ruddo, Mike
W.S.S.C.
4017 Hamilton Street
Hyattsville, Maryland 20781

Russell, James
McDowell Manufacturing Company
P.O. Box 665
DuBois, Pennsylvania 15801

Ryan, James
Department of Soil Science
University of Wisconsin
Madison, Wisconsin 53700

Sabey, B. R.
Colorado State University
Fort Collins, Colorado 80521

Sargent, Benson
Environmental Engineering
Division of Protection
Pavilion Building
Montpelier, Vermont 05602

Sartz, Richard
North Central Forest Experiment Station
Forest Watershed Lab.
P.O. Box 872
LaCrosse, Wisconsin 54601

Schicht, Richard
Illinois State Water Survey
P.O. Box 232
Urbana, Illinois 61801

Schmidt, Joyce
State League of Women Voters
Environmental Quality Commission
Bloomfield Avenue
Montclair, New Jersey 07042

Schorr, Paul
N.J. Department of Environmental
    Protection
P.O. Box 1390
Trenton, New Jersey 08600

Schulze, K. L.
Department of Civil Engineers
Michigan State University
East Lansing, Michigan 48823

Schwert, Donald
Department of Forest Zoology
College of Forestry
University of Syracuse
Syracuse, New York 13210

Scilley, F. Maynard
USDA Soil Conservation Service
Room 200, Federal Center Bldg.
St. Paul, Minnesota 55101

Scott, Jon
Department of Atmospheric Science
State University at Albany
1400 Washington
Albany, New York 12222

*Seabrook, Belford L.
Div. of Municipal Waste Water Programs
Office of Water Programs
Environmental Protection Agency
Washington, D. C. 20460

Shafer, E. L., Jr.
Pinchot Institute
Northeastern Experiment Station
6816 Market Street
Upper Darby, Pennsylvania 19082

Shaffer, James
Department of Natural Resources
65 S. Front Street
Columbus, Ohio 43215

Shane, Richard
Argonne National Laboratory
9700 S. Gass Avenue, Bldg. 12
Center for Environmental Studies
Argonne, Illinois 60439

Shanklin, Don
USDA Soil Conservation Service
400 Midtown Plaza, 700 E. Water St.
Syracuse, New York 13031

Slack, Larry
U.S. Geological Survey
Rm. 414, 1309 Thomasville Rd.
Tallahassee, Florida 32303

Small, Maxwell
Brookhaven National Laboratory
Upton, New York 11973

Smith, Clyde
U.S. Army Corps of Engineers
P.O. Box 4970
Jacksonville, Florida 32201

Smith, Ivan
Mid-West Research Institute
425 Volker Blvd.
Prairie Village, Missouri 66208

Smith, James
Town of Amherst
Town Hall
Amherst, Massachusetts 01002

Smith, Milburn
U.S. Army Corps of Engineers
P.O. Box 17300
Fort Worth, Texas 76102

Smith, Thomas
City of Tallahassee
City Hall
Tallahassee, Florida 32303

Solomon, R. Charles
U.S. Army Corps of Engineers
P.O. Box 1715
Baltimore, Maryland 21203

*Sopper, William E.
School of Forest Resources
Pennsylvania State University
University Park, Pennsylvania 16802

Sowash, James
Pennsylvania State University
401 Old Main
University Park, Pennsylvania 16802

Speakman, James
Buffalo N.Y. Corps of Engineers
1776 Niagara Street
Buffalo, New York 14207

Stanley, Ronald
U.S. Forest Service
P.O. Box 1050
Tallahassee, Florida 32302

Stanlick, Harold
U.S. Forest Service
633 W. Wisconsin Avenue
Milwaukee,Wisconsin 53074

Stansbury, Jeffrey
5902 32nd Street, N.W.
Washington, D.C. 20015

Stephenson, Marvin
The Rockefeller Foundation
111 W. 50th Street
New York, New York 10020

Stetson, John
U.S. Army Corps of Engineers
2850 SE 82nd
Portland, Oregon 97266

Stevenson, Charles
Tech. Development
Curtice-Burns, Inc.
P.O. Box 670
Rochester, New York 14602

Steward, Kerry
USDA ARS PSR
3205 S.W. 70th Avenue
Fort Lauderdale, Florida 33314

Stewart, Gordon
University of Massachusetts
Amherst, Massachusetts 01002

Strand, Bruce
R. R. 1
Ava, Illinois

Strauser, Brad
U.S. Army Engineer District
210 N. 12th Street
St. Louis, Missouri 63101

Stucky, Glenn E.
Soil Conservation Service
7600 West Chester Pike
Upper Darby, Pennsylvania 19082

Sturm, William
430 W. Seymore Avenue
Cincinnati, Ohio 45216

Summers, Phillip
Forest Service
U.S. Department of Agriculture
Washington, D. C. 20250

Sutherland, Jeffrey
Williams & Works
250 Michigan, N.E.
Grand Rapids, Michigan 49503

Swafford, Benny
DAEN-CWE-Y
Forrestal Building
Washington, D. C. 20314

Sydnor, Bernard
Michaux Forest Garden Estates, Ltd.
Box 181
Fairfield, Pennsylvania 17320

Taber, James
Pennsylvania Department of
    Environmental Protection
Harrisburg, Pennsylvania 17101

Tabor, Lance
Southern W. Va. Reg. Health Council
Route 2, Box 382
Bluefield, West Virginia 24701

Tanner, Howard
Michigan State University
109 Natural Resources Building
East Lansing, Michigan 48840

Tarquin, Anthony
University of Texas-El Paso
Department of Civil Engineering
El Paso, Texas 79968

Tennant, Harold
R. M. Wade Company
Irrigation Division
1919 N.W. Therman Street
Portland, Oregon 97200

*Thomas, Richard E.
Nat'l. Water Quality Control Program
Robert S. Kerr Water Res. Center
Environmental Protection Agency
Ada, Oklahoma 74820

Thompson, D. R.
Pennsylvania Department of
    Environmental Resources
Rm. 513, S. Office Building
Harrisburg, Pennsylvania 17105

Thompson, Jack
U.S. Army Corps of Engineers
Room 5F-079 DAEN-CWE-M
Forrestal Building
Washington, D. C. 20314

Tofflemire, T. James
N.Y.S. Department of Environmental
    Conservation
50 Wolf Road
Albany, New York 12200

Turner, John
University of Missouri
1-31 Agriculture Building
Columbia, Missouri 65201

*Urie, Dean H.
North Central Forest Experiment Station
U.S. Forest Service
Cadillac, Michigan 49601

Vaccaro, Ralph
Woods Hole Oceanographic Inst.
Woods Hole, Massachusetts 02574

Van Aacken, Karen
McCombs-Knutson Assoc., Inc.
12805 Olson Memorial Highway
Minneapolis, Minnesota 55441

Vayansky, Thomas
Pennsylvania Department of
    Environmental Resources
300 Liberty Avenue
Pittsburgh, Pennsylvania 15222

Vermillion, Lois
Interstate Commission on Potomac
    River Basin
1025 Vermont Avenue, N.W.
Suite 407
Washington, D. C. 20005

Vhora, Mansukhlal
Yule Jordan & Assoc.
Box 337
Camp Hill, Pennsylvania 17011

Vodehnal, Dale
Environmental Protection Agency
Region VIII, Suite 900
1660 Lincoln Street
Denver, Colorado 80203

Voykin, Dale
Bureau of Water Quality Mgmt.
734 W. Fourth Street
Williamsport, Pennsylvania 16701

Wakat, Cynthia
U.S. Army Corps of Engineers,
    Regional Chicago District
2195 Dearborn
Chicago, Illinois 60604

Walker, Ian
Stony-Brook-Millstone Watersheds
    Associates
P.O. Box 171
Pennington, New Jersey 08534

Walker, John
USDA, ARS
Plant Industry Station
Beltsville, Maryland 20810

Waller, James
Wilmington District, U.S. Army
Corps of Engineers
Wilmington, North Carolina 28401

Ward, Richard
U.S. Department of Agriculture
P.O. Box 847
Warren, Pennsylvania 16365

Warner, John
USDA Soil Conservation Service
Room 40, Midtown Plaza
700 E. Water Street
Syracuse, New York 13210

Warther, Fred
Lake Contractors Inc.
7100 Lory Lane, Box 24
Lanham, Maryland 20801

Watt, J. Thomas
Van Reuth and Weidner, Inc.
5509 York Road
Baltimore, Maryland 21212

Webb, Jack
Environ. Control Corporation
153 E. Erie, Suite 404
Painesville, Ohio 44077

Weiss, Martin
Deer Island Th. Ph.
Metropolitan District Commission
P.O. Box 100
Winthrop, Maryland 02152

Welch, Allan
Bureau of Water Quality
996 S. Main Street
Meadville, Pennsylvania 16335

Wentzel, Eugene
Pennsylvania Department of
    Environmental Resources
401 Buttonwood Street
Reading, Pennsylvania 19602

Westlund, Carlyle
Groundwater Section
Bureau of Water Quality Mgmt.
P.O. Box 2351
Harrisburg, Pennsylvania 17120

Whaling, Patrick J.
Duke University
Beaufort, North Carolina 28516

Whitaker, James
Agricultural Engineering
University of Connecticut
Box U 15
Storrs, Connecticut 06268

White, Richard
Department of Agricultural Engineering
2073 Neil Avenue
Ohio State University
Columbus, Ohio 43210

Wikre, Dale
Minnesota Pollution Control Agency
717 Delaware, S.E.
Minneapolis, Minnesota 55440

Wiles, Carlton
Solid Waste Research Division
NERC-CIN EPA, 5555 Ridge Avenue
Cincinnati, Ohio 45242

Williams, Clarke
Marine Resources Council
Hauppague, New York

*Williams, T. C.
Williams and Works
250 Michigan Street, N.E.
Grand Rapids, Michigan 49503

Wilson, Charles
Louisiana Tech. University
Ruston, Louisiana 71270

Wilson, George
Geraghty & Miller, Inc.
44 Sintsink Drive East
Port Washington, New York 11050

Winnike, Richard
Corps of Engineers (MRD)
215 N. 17th Street
Room 7020
Omaha, Nebraska 68101

Wong, Walter
County of Monterey
Public Health Department
1270 Natividad Road
Salinas, California 93901

*Wood, Gene W.
School of Forest Resources
Pennsylvania State University
University Park, Pennsylvania 16802

Woodcock, Gene
Water Pollution Control Inc.
Box 337
Sumner, Iowa 50674

Wooding, Henry N.
203 Ag. Engr. Building
Pennsylvania State University
University Park, Pennsylvania 16802

Wright, Darwin
Office of Research and Monitoring
Environmental Protection Agency
Washington, D. C. 20460

Yesh, John
Department of Environmental Resources
383 Wyoming Avenue
Kingston, Pennsylvania

*Youngner, V. B.
Department of Plant Sciences
University of California
Riverside, California 92502

Zagar, Michael
Minn. Pollution Control Agency
717 Delaware Street, S. E.
Minneapolis, Minnesota 55440

Zagloul, Omar
Lindsay Manufacturing Company
Lindsay, Nebraska 68644

Zampogna, Ralph
Bureau of Water Quality Management
1875 New Hope Street
Norristown, Pennsylvania 19401

Zemaitis, William
Aerobic Systems, Inc.
4 West 58th Street
New York, New York 10019

Zimmerman, R.
Perma Engine
2010 Cogay Avenue
Winnipeg, Manitoba, Canada

Zoda, Arthur
N.J.D.E.P.
John Fitch Plaza
Trenton, New Jersey 08618

Zwalinski, John
Department of Environ. Resources
1875 New Hope Street
Norristown, Pennsylvania 19401

Zweig, Richard
U.S. Forest Service
Room 708, 1720 Peachtree Road
Atlanta, Georgia 30309